The Armed Forces and Democracy in Latin America

THE ARMED FORCES
AND DEMOCRACY
IN LATIN AMERICA

J. Samuel Fitch

THE JOHNS HOPKINS UNIVERSITY PRESS

BALTIMORE AND LONDON

© 1998 The Johns Hopkins University Press
All rights reserved. Published 1998
Printed in the United States of America on acid-free paper
9 8 7 6 5 4 3 2 1

The Johns Hopkins University Press
2715 North Charles Street, Baltimore, Maryland 21218-4319
www.press.jhu.edu

Library of Congress Cataloging-in-Publication Data will be found
at the end of this book.
A catalog record for this book is available from the British Library.

ISBN 0-8018-5917-4
ISBN 0-8018-5918-2 (pbk.)

TO LESLIE

With love, admiration, and thanks
for sharing this journey,
like all the others, with laughter
and understanding

Contents

Acknowledgments

This work is the culmination of a twelve-year study of civil-military relations in posttransition Latin American democracies. In such a long project, one incurs many personal and institutional debts. I gratefully acknowledge the support of the United States Institute of Peace, the American Philosophical Society, and the University of Colorado Committee on Research and Creative Work for their support of the fieldwork on which much of this analysis is based. The Inter-American Dialogue, the Ford Foundation, and the American University/USAID Democracy Projects provided additional opportunities to discuss these issues with Latin American scholars, military officers, and civilian leaders. Portions of chapter 1 are taken from an article that appeared in *Pacific Focus,* with the permission of the Center for International Relations of Inha University.

Over the years I have been aided by many colleagues who have been generous with their time, contacts, and criticism. Among these, Abraham Lowenthal, Andrés Fontana, Ernesto López, Felipe Aguero, Augusto Varas, Louis Goodman, Carina Perelli, Juan Rial, Johanna Mendelson, David Pion-Berlin, Brian Loveman, Enrique Obando, Deborah Norden, Fred Nunn, Wendy Hunter, Jennifer Schirmer, Berta García, Fernando Bustamante, and Leslie Anderson stand out, but any such listing invariably leaves out many other friends who have contributed their insights and encouragement along the way. In Ecuador, I received generous institutional support from the Corporación de Estudios de Desarrollo (CORDES) and from the Facultad Latinoamericano de Ciencias Sociales (FLACSO). In Argentina, the staffs of the Fundación Simón Rodríguez and the Centro de Estudios de Estado y Sociedad (CEDES) likewise provided valuable support. I am indebted to the Director of the Biblioteca Central de la

Acknowledgments

Armada Argentina, Capitán de Corbeta (retired) Luis Pons, and to the library staff of the Circulo Militar for their assistance with Argentina military journals. Luzie Mason, staff assistant at the University of Colorado Center for Public Policy Research, somehow managed to keep me in touch with the university during these various travels. Margarita Vallejo, Matthew Greene, Caroline Tolbert, and Karen Douglas provided invaluable research assistance. My deepest debt of gratitude is to the military officers of Argentina and Ecuador who generously shared their views with the inquisitive professor from Colorado. However, neither the individuals nor the institutions named above are responsible for the views expressed here, which are solely the responsibility of the author.

Introduction

As an armored personnel carrier battered down the front door of Venezuela's presidential palace, the president and his military chief of staff fled down a basement tunnel. The unexpected after-dark landing of the president's plane at the international airport instead of the downtown Air Force base forced the organizers of the coup into a desperate race to seize the chief executive while they still held the advantage of surprise. Emboldened by public opinion polls showing more than 80 percent professing little or no trust in the government, junior officers in the four biggest military bases mobilized their troops. While rebel paratroopers searched from office to office upstairs, Carlos Andrés Pérez hid under a raincoat and ducked out of a basement door into a waiting car, which raced through red lights to a nearby television station. Startled broadcasters quickly switched to the president, who began a series of predawn appeals calling on loyal officers to defend the Constitution against "a shameful action led by ambitious officers." Invoking the name of Venezuela's national hero, General Simón Bolívar, the rebels, led by Lieutenant Colonel Hugo Chávez, defended their action as necessary "to rescue the Venezuelan people from politicians, from demagoguery, and bureaucracy."[1]

West of Caracas, loyalist air force pilots strafed a rebel armored unit. As the defense minister and chief of staff hurriedly rallied senior officers against the threat of a coup led by their subordinates, the revolt began to falter. Messages of international support for the government poured in. When asked if he would negotiate with rebels who held the presidential residence, Pérez replied, "Give them bullets."[2] Surprised by the intensity of the intramilitary fighting and the lack of civilian mobilization against the government, captured rebel leaders called for their supporters to lay down their arms. At the end of the day, more than seventy people were dead and many more wounded. Over a hundred officers and a thousand soldiers were under arrest. After three decades as Latin America's leading example of democratic civil-military relations, Venezuela was in shock.

Nine months later, dissident officers tried again, this time bombing the presidential palace and nearby buildings. (Loyalists later claimed they had disarmed many of the bombs as they were being loaded.) Senior officers heading the coup and jailed members of the "Bolivarianos" blamed the violence on government corruption and its refusal to share the nation's oil wealth with the poor. Despite the rebels' success in capturing most of the capital's television stations and the endorsement of fringe left-wing groups, public support failed to materialize. More than two hundred people were killed.[3]

On Easter Sunday 1987, standing on the balcony where General Juan Perón used to address his supporters, President Raúl Alfonsín faced several hundred thousand anxious Argentines assembled in the plaza facing the Casa Rosada. For three days the government had struggled to overcome a tense stalemate with junior officers demanding an end to the trials for crimes committed in the military government's "dirty war" against leftist guerrillas. After weeks of rumors that a confrontation was imminent, in the industrial city of Córdoba Major Ernesto Barreiro refused a judicial order to appear in court. In a carefully planned act of solidarity, his regiment declared that it would resist any attempt to arrest him. Outside of Buenos Aires, the Infantry School joined the revolt; across the country, other units debated statements of solidarity with "Operation Dignity." Surrounded by officers in full combat gear and battle paint, a commando veteran of the Malvinas/Falklands war, Lieutenant Colonel Aldo Rico, called for an end to the trials, replacement of the army leadership, and a halt to government and media attacks on the military. With the backing of the High Command, the president gave orders to suppress the revolt, but those senior officers willing to comply found their authority undermined by a coordinated campaign of passive resistance to any attack on the rebel units.

Despite military statements that this was not an attempted coup d'état, civilian leaders rallied to defend the regime against the challenge to civilian authority. Putting aside decades of antagonism, Peronists and Radicals joined other parties in a pact to defend democracy. Multiparty commissions organized nationwide demonstrations against the military uprising. Before a joint session of Congress and civic leaders, Alfonsín pledged to seek a solution to the crisis but not to cede to military pressures. "Here there is nothing to negotiate;

Argentine democracy is not negotiable."[4] Attempts by political and religious leaders to find a mediated solution failed.

As the massive Easter rally grew restive, Alfonsín abruptly ended his speech with the announcement that he would personally go to the Campo de Mayo to seek the rebels' surrender. Arriving by helicopter, Alfonsín and a military aide met alone with *carapintada* leaders Rico and Venturino. Returning to the Casa Rosada, Alfonsín announced that the uprising had ended and that Rico was under house arrest. "Happy Easter," he proclaimed. "The house is in order." Although the government denied that any deals had been made, Rico claimed he and the president had come to an understanding. Shortly thereafter, the Army chief of staff resigned; two months later Congress approved a bill exonerating from prosecution lower-ranking military personnel "obeying orders" in the antisubversive campaign.

Three years later, Alfonsín's successor, Carlos Menem, ordered a quick end to the *carapintadas'* (from the Spanish word for camouflage-painted face) fourth revolt, this time on the eve of a state visit by U.S. President-elect George Bush. Angered by the loss of life in rebel attacks on a Buenos Aires barracks and the army command building, loyalist troops responded vigorously. For the first time, air force planes took part in the suppression of the revolt. With the rebels in jail facing stiff prison terms, Bush praised Peronist leader Menem for his success in controlling inflation and deregulating the Argentine economy and for Argentina's decision to send two warships to participate in the Gulf War against Iraq.[5] In 1992, Menem dispatched his foreign minister to Croatia to pay special tribute to the Argentine brigade participating in United Nations peacekeeping forces in the former Yugoslavia.

In late January 1981, President Jaime Roldós called to order the National Security Council. Shortly after his inauguration as Ecuador's first civilian president following seven years of military government, Roldós had approved military plans to expand the Ecuadorian presence in the Cordillera del Condor. Ever since the discovery of mapping errors in the Rio Protocol, which ended the brief but one-sided 1941 war with Peru, the unmarked border area on the eastern flank of the Andes at the headwaters of the Amazon had been a source of diplomatic and military conflict. The president, vice president, the president of Congress, the presidents of the Supreme Court and the Monetary Board, the chief of the Joint Staff, and various cabinet members listened intently as military commanders described the Peruvian helicopter attack on the Ecuadorian outpost at Paquisha, which left one dead and several wounded one day before the thirty-ninth anniversary of the Rio Protocol. Ecuadorian intelligence sources reported new troop movements into Peruvian forward posts and over-flights by Soviet-built planes and helicopters. Reports of a second attack and loss of contact with the army company defending the post heightened fears that this was the opening salvo in a larger Peruvian offensive to roll back Ecuadorian camps moving into the Cenepa River valley. The president declared a national state of emergency and ordered the mobilization of the armed forces. The border zone was placed under military control, though the decree did not include the economic mobilization favored by the Security Council staff.

With both countries on full alert, diplomats from the Rio Pact guarantor nations and the Organization of American States worked feverishly to prevent an escalation. A large demonstration in Quito protested the Peruvian attacks and defended Ecuadorian claims to be an Amazonian country. President Roldós flew to the border to meet with military commanders in the field and greet wounded soldiers evacuated from the combat zone. Despite hawkish voices on both sides, there was little enthusiasm for war in either country. Both eventually accepted a Brazilian proposal for a ceasefire; a military commission headed by senior naval officers worked out an accord for withdrawal of forces from the contested area.[6] Three months later, President Roldós and the minister of defense were killed in a plane crash. Despite personal affection for the young president, who eagerly accepted every invitation to fly or visit with the troops, Roldós is remembered by senior officers as having exceeded his authority as commander-in-chief in his desire to direct military operations, which the military refused.[7]

A decade after Paquisha, the interior province of Chimborazo was the focal point for Ecuadorian security concerns. Fearing the possible spread of Sendero Luminoso among the heavily Indian population of the sierra, Colonel Jorge Andrade Piedra instituted a comprehensive strategy of preventive counter-insurgency. Under his command, the Galapagos Armored Cavalry Brigade vastly expanded the scope and intensity of its civic action activities. At its headquarters in Riobamba, military and civilian instructors provide vocational training for truck drivers, health promoters, and artisan crafts. In the villages, military personnel gave literacy lessons and lectures on how to avoid cholera. Andrade has been pressuring the Ministry of Education for more funds. As a senior military officer in a province central to the politically sensitive "Indian problem," Andrade's request goes directly to the minister, but ministry officials advise delay. Leftist groups charge that the army is militarizing Indian education. Undaunted, Andrade calls for the Ministry of Agriculture to provide more agricultural credit and cheap fertilizer for Ecuador's most impoverished province. On market day, army trucks provide transportation for villagers and their goods. Working with village leaders to assess local needs, civic action teams help organize community projects for reforestation, road building, school construction, water and sanitation. Agrarian conscription units provide training in modern agricultural methods, using military-owned haciendas as demonstration projects and as in-house suppliers for local bases.[8] More than half of the fourteen hundred indigenous communities work with the military. Military officials acknowledge the intertwining of security concerns, development, and politics in these efforts:

The majority of the Catholic communities have accepted [the military's offers of assistance, but] the evangelicals are more open, more educated, and better prepared. . . . Liberation theology [mixing Catholicism] with foreign ideologies [promotes] subversion as the only hope of social transformation, a catastrophic confrontation, the class struggle.

The target is the minds of the citizenry, so psychological operations, integrated with civic action [and] community development, [are important] to neutralize opposition to the armed forces. Second, [the military] should pressure the government to devote more resources for development, [which is part of our] mission in the Constitution. . . . Through its influence, [the military has to] insure that [government] agencies act in a coordinated way to avoid conflict. Nobody wants internal war.[9]

These three fragments illustrate the complex tapestry of contemporary civil-military relations in Latin America. As recently as 1978, more than half of the region lived under military rule. Since then, beginning with Ecuador and Peru, civilian governments replaced military regimes in country after country. Today no military governments remain. Five countries — Mexico, Costa Rica, Colombia, Venezuela, and Cuba — have not had a military coup for more than thirty years. Among the more recent transitions, six countries have survived more than a decade without a new coup.[10] Yet the retreat from traditional patterns of military politics has been neither universal nor uniform.

Two attempted coups in Venezuela — long considered one of the most stable Latin democracies — remind us that longevity alone provides no guarantee against a return to traditional forms of military intervention in politics. Panama's General Manuel Noriega deposed two civilian presidents who disputed his control over the Defense Forces. In Haiti, the military overthrew that country's first two democratically elected governments, ending the de facto military dictatorship only under the threat of invasion by U.S. forces.

Near misses and frequent rumors of coups in other countries suggest that the classic questions of why coups occur are still relevant to the understanding of contemporary Latin American politics, but the more pressing challenge is to explain why military coups have so far been relatively rare events in the new democracies. Conversely, why are some countries still vulnerable to military actions that would be unthinkable in the rest of the region? If the traditional questions about the military in politics are still relevant, the answers to those questions may well have changed. Latin American militaries are often still viewed in terms of the stereotyped images of the 1960s (or Central America in the 1980s) as pro-American right-wingers. In the 1990s, the military threat to democracy has more often come from nationalist and populist movements of junior officers like the *Bolivarianos*. Which is the real Venezuelan military—the officers who sought to overthrow a corrupt and discredited president or those who ultimately defended the democratic regime? How do we account for the intense divisions within the Venezuelan and Argentine militaries?

Most observers see little threat of a return to direct military rule. In most countries, military power is exercised in other ways. The *carapintada* rebellions in Argentina are perhaps the most dramatic example of political action by the armed forces within the existing regime. In Peru, military support was crucial to President Fujimori's seizure of dictatorial powers in the 1992 *autogolpe* (a governmental coup). A year later, the Guatemalan armed forces first supported, then opposed, President Serrano's attempt to follow Fujimori's example. If democracy is more than just the absence of military coups, policymakers and students of Latin American politics must go beyond simpleminded dichotomies between civilian and military regimes. Contemporary civil-military relations in Latin America are characterized by complex patterns of direct and indirect military influence within nominally civilian regimes. To take one frequently cited example, in the first posttransition government in Brazil, active-duty military officers held six of the twenty-six cabinet positions.[11] Five years later, under President Collor, the number of military ministers was reduced to three. In Argentina, the military has had no representation in the cabinet since the return to democracy in 1983. Even in the National Defense Council, the military is consciously limited to an advisory role, in sharp contrast to the Chilean National Security Council inherited from General Pinochet. Effective military power thus varies significantly among the new democracies and over time.

There are likewise important variations in the extent of civilian control over military institutions. The 1980 Constitution denies the Chilean president his traditional role as commander-in-chief except in wartime. In other countries, the formal powers of the commander-in-chief are limited by the effective autonomy of the armed forces. Legislation inherited from the military regime often restricts presidential appointment of the defense minister and of military commanders. In countries facing active revolutionary insurgencies, civilian governments have been unable to control human rights abuses by military and paramilitary forces, with serious negative consequences for the legitimacy of those regimes. From the policy perspective, the difficulty is that contemporary civil-military relations in Latin America are, in fact, quite varied. Policies that make sense in Argentina could be counterproductive in Chile or suicidal in Guatemala.

The end of the cold war also poses new questions about the armed forces and democracy. In the 1970s, students of the Latin American military pointed to the rise of counterinsurgency missions and national security doctrines focusing on internal security as key factors in the emergence of long-term institutional military regimes in South America. With the return to democracy, to what extent are conflict scenarios different for the 1990s? Is the cold war really over in Latin America? Have the national security doctrines of the 1960s and 1970s changed, particularly in countries — Peru, Colombia, and until recently, El Salvador and Guatemala — still fighting revolutionary insurgencies? In the 1980s, U.S. policymakers tried very hard to enlist the armed forces of the Andean countries in the "war on drugs." In the 1990s, there are increasing civilian demands to deploy the military in the "war against crime." To what extent are the political consequences of military involvement in these police roles similar to or different from the antidemocratic effects of previous internal security missions? In part as a consequence of earlier "security and development" doctrines, over the last three decades many Latin American militaries have increased their socioeconomic development activities. The expansion of military industries and civic-action programs has gone largely unnoticed by academic analysts and policymakers, whose focus has typically been the interaction between military leaders and government officials. Meanwhile, new relationships between civil and military society have developed, including agrarian conscription brigades, military investment in multinational industries, and new fora for dialogue among academic experts, party leaders, and senior officers. The consequences of these new forms of (inter)penetration for democracy are still imperfectly understood.

Finally, as the Ecuadorian example suggests, the traditional mission of the armed forces as guardians of external security likewise raises questions about the proper relations between civilian and military authority in a democracy. Is war too important to be left to the generals? Is it too important not to be left to the generals? What are the implications of growing Latin American involvement in international peacekeeping missions? In an era of declining military budgets and sparse public interest in external threats, what is the role of Latin American legislatures in defense and military policy? What is the duty of military officers in a democracy if civilian policymakers fail to respond to internal security threats (as in the Ecuadorian example) or to external threats? Who defines the threats? Who decides what resources will be devoted to protecting the nation against them?

This book is a systematic attempt to update and expand our understanding of the armed forces and democracy in Latin America. The central normative question is what constitutes democratic civil-military relations. What are the minimal requirements for democratic consolidation? Is it enough that the military refrains from military coups and military governments? The central empirical question is what patterns of autonomy/subordination exist between the military and the civilian leadership in the new democracies. How have these relations evolved since the transition? To what extent is democratic control over the armed forces being subverted, consolidated, or institutionalized? The central theoretical challenge is to account for the variations between countries and over time. The central policy question is what can be done to promote effective democratic control in a structural and historical context conducive to autonomous and highly politicized armed forces. In addition to Argentina and Ecuador, which are discussed in detail, shorter case studies cover most of the other "new democracies." Given the limitations of the available research, this work makes no claim to cover every country in the region. It does, however, attempt to overcome the bias in the existing literature by analyzing two Andean countries (Peru and Ecuador) and two Central American countries (Guatemala and Honduras), in addition to Brazil and the Southern Cone (Argentina, Chile, and Uruguay). By design, the case selection emphasizes the diverse contexts for civil-military relations in the region.

Chapter 1 analyzes the institutional evolution of the Latin American armed forces. It rejects Huntington's thesis that professionalization leads to "objective" civilian control of the armed forces, arguing that the structural conditions and historical/cultural context in Latin America encourage politicized forms of military professionalism, which are the antithesis of civilian control. Nor has modernization solved the problem of military intervention in politics. Construction of a democratic system of civil-military relations will therefore require conscious attention to the special features of the Latin American context. Simply exporting U.S. or European models of civilian control is not enough.

Chapter 2 proposes a normative model of democratic civil-military relations and a typology of contemporary patterns of civil-military relations in Latin America derived from that model. It argues that civil-military relations are, in fact, more varied than generally acknowledged, but also that these patterns vary and evolve over time, rather than being fixed by either structural conditions or the nature of the democratic transition.

The future stability of both democratic and nondemocratic patterns of civil-military relations depends in part upon the extent to which traditional military attitudes have, in fact, changed since the transition to democracy. Chapter 3 reports the findings of more than a hundred and fifty interviews with military officers in Ecuador and Argentina regarding their beliefs about the role of the military in politics. It argues that democratic control is now widely accepted in the Argentine armed forces. In contrast, Ecuadorian attitudes toward the political role of the military are generally contradictory and ambiguous, reflecting the conflicting pressures of an unstable domestic political context in an international environment that discourages overt military intervention in politics. In both cases, I argue that military attitudes toward democracy cannot be understood without disaggregating the officer corps and taking seriously the internal debate among competing ideological factions over the military's role in the current regime.

The central question in Chapter 4 is the extent to which the national security doctrines of the 1960s and 1970s still persist, despite the transition to democratic regimes. Drawing again on the Ecuadorian and Argentine cases, I argue that there is strong evidence of both continuity and change in threat perceptions, theories of revolutionary war, and military views of national security policy. In Ecuador, the internal security threat legitimates an expanding military role in the economy and extensive civic action to build closer military ties to local communities. Both contribute to the trend toward a semitutelary regime, but compared to earlier decades, there is as yet no widely shared, coherent "national security" alternative to the current regime. In Argentina, there is greater doctrinal discontinuity, with significant changes in threat perceptions and military missions away from internal security toward international peacekeeping and regional military cooperation.

Chapter 5 is an appraisal of the policies of posttransition civilian governments in dealing with the armed forces. It argues that the successes and failures of military policy in the new democracies must be viewed in the context of the different patterns of civil-military relations that characterize posttransition regimes. Democratic leaders face different agendas and varying possibilities for reform. Looking at a decade or more of civilian rule, I argue that most civilian presidents have failed to exploit available opportunities for restructuring civil-military relations in more democratic directions. The costs of that failure include a continued threat of reversion to traditional patterns of military intervention, but also the more serious threat of tutelary or semitutelary military roles undermining democratic regimes from within.

Chapter 6 focuses on the policy implications of this research for Latin American and North American policymakers seeking to strengthen Latin American democracies through institutionalization of effective systems of democratic control. It argues for a "democratic professionalist" conception of the role of the armed forces within democratic regimes. Within that model, the missions assigned to the armed forces may be principally military, as in the European democracies, or may encompass more development and internal security functions, in keeping with the traditions of many Latin militaries. Because nonmilitary missions invariably enmesh the military in complex and politically charged issues, this "developmentalist" variant requires stronger policy controls by civilian authorities. Encouraging military acceptance of civilian control, in turn, requires institutional adaptation and reform to create a context in which democratic conceptions of civil-military relations become convincing and credible arguments in the debates within the Latin American armed forces.

In contrast to the pessimism that characterizes most academic writing about posttransition civil-military relations, I argue that political power of the armed forces has, in many cases, been significantly reduced. Current patterns are still mostly semidemocratic—in some instances, clearly nondemocratic. But other countries have achieved varying degrees of democratic control. Even in the best of cases, there is still much work to be done to institutionalize the role of the armed forces within the new democracies. In the worst cases, the struggle to create democratic civil-military relations may take a decade or longer. Nevertheless, the central message of this book is that such a struggle is possible, even under the difficult conditions facing contemporary Latin American societies. The outcome of that struggle will depend on the ability of Latin Americans to forge stronger institutions and shape a political context conducive to military acceptance of democratic control. The United States and other governments, international institutions, and nongovernmental organizations have an important, though secondary, role in reshaping the context of civil-military interaction. This book is dedicated to the proposition that scholars of civil-military relations also have something to contribute to the struggle for democracy in Latin America.

*The Armed Forces and Democracy
in Latin America*

CHAPTER ONE

The Military and Politics in Latin America

Institutional Development, Professionalism, and Political Context

The military has traditionally been a central force in Latin American politics. Nineteenth-century history is filled with generals who led the battles for independence from Spain and military leaders who ruled their countries for decades. In this century, military coups mark many key turning points. The armed forces were often the ultimate arbiter in crisis situations. Since World War II, only Mexico has had no military coup d'état. During the last fifty years, every country except Mexico and Costa Rica has had at least one significant period of military rule; most have had multiple military governments and military coups.

Faced with this long history of military participation in politics, analysts and scholars have conflicting views about civil-military relations in the new democracies. Those who stress cultural/historical explanations of Latin American politics have generally been skeptical about claims that traditional military attitudes have changed and sensitive to signs of continuing military power within nominally democratic regimes. On the other side, U.S. policymakers sometimes seem to assume that civilian government is the same thing as civilian control of the armed forces and that military intervention in politics is now a thing of the past. In part, this optimistic view reflects the assumption that, with modernization, Latin America will simply outgrow its traditional patterns of political behavior. In this view, as the Latin American militaries become more professionalized, they will put aside traditional attitudes and conform to the norms of civil-military relations practiced in the U.S. and European democracies.

Both these assumptions need to be examined critically. In this chapter, I argue that the optimistic view fails to account for the radically different context of civil-military relations in Latin America that makes civilian control of the military more difficult to achieve. The record of the last century clearly shows that neither modernization nor military professionalization have eliminated military intervention in politics. On the other hand, I argue that the culturalist view is unduly pessimistic. There are, in fact, substantial variations among Latin American countries in political context and past patterns of civil-military relations that offer greater or lesser opportunities for movement toward more democratic practices. The pessimistic view also underestimates the ability of Latin Americans, military and civilian, to learn from their own history.

Professionalization and Military Professionalism

The nature of the military profession is one of the long-standing debates in military sociology. Reflecting the U.S.-European focus of this literature, opposition to military intervention in politics is generally assumed to be an inherent attribute of military professionalism. Samuel Huntington's *The Soldier and the State* is still the most influential exposition of this thesis. Huntington argues that the increasingly complex technical requirements of warfare have led almost all modern countries to create militaries with professional officer corps characterized by extensive training and specialized norms of behavior. Like other professions, the military profession is a vocation combining expertise, societal responsibility, and corporateness. In contrast to its preprofessional counterparts, the professional military is distinguished by its specialized knowledge and its ethical code, which defines the military's societal responsibilities and its relationship with the rest of society. In Huntington's view, the essence of this code is its insistence on individual and collective subordination to higher authority and its opposition to intervention in matters outside its sphere of professional expertise. "The military ethic . . . holds that war is the instrument of politics, that the military are the instrument of the statesman, and that civilian control is essential to military professionalism."[1] Military professionalization thus naturally leads to adoption of professional norms conducive to civilian control of the armed forces.[2]

When applied outside of the European context for which it was originally formulated, Huntington's argument is conceptually and empirically deficient.[3] Conceptually it blurs the distinction between different levels of analysis, especially between the institutional attributes of a given military (for example, specialization and corporate coherence) and the attitudes and values held by the officers of that military (for example, definitions of professional behavior). By defining subordination to civilian authority as a characteristic of military professionalism, the empirical question of the relation between military professionalization and the political role of the military is reduced to a tautology. If the armed forces intervene in politics, by definition the military is acting unprofessionally.[4] In contrast, I will argue that, in the Latin American context, higher levels of military professionalization have historically resulted in more institutionalized military intervention in politics and high levels of military autonomy.

In the analysis that follows, professionalization is treated as an institutional **3** attribute and defined in terms of the technical development and complexity of the military career. Operationally the distinguishing characteristic of the professionalized military is the existence of a specialized military education and training system. Military professionalism is defined in terms of expertise, corporate identity, and norms of professional responsibility. At the collective level, professionalism is manifested in military expertise, impartial organizational norms, and corporate solidarity. At the individual level, professionalism is exemplified by specialized skills and adherence to professional norms. The political correlates of military professionalism are thus an empirical question open to investigation. Furthermore, I argue that the political content of military professionalism is not constant, but variable, depending on both military doctrine and the specific relationships between the military, the state, and the rest of society.

The Preprofessional Militaries

For most of the nineteenth century, Latin American militaries were, at best, minimally professionalized. The armies created to fight for independence from Spain were militias, similar to those who fought the U.S. Revolutionary War. Initially the officers were mostly from landed families, the creole elite of colonial society. But the twenty-year struggle for independence in Latin America allowed others from humble origins to rise through the ranks by virtue of their military skills or heroism. In Chile and Colombia, revolutionary heroes soon clashed with the landowning elite. In other countries, officers like Ecuador's first president, Juan José Flores, married into prominent families and entered freely into the political struggles of the day. Like George Washington, Andrew Jackson, and Alexander Hamilton, Latin America's early generals were frequently political and military leaders at the same time.[5]

After independence, Latin American politics was dominated by a series of military *caudillos* (military strongmen). With real power concentrated in the hands of large landowners, who controlled the local population, most nineteenth-century constitutions were statements of political ideals with little relationship to reality. In most countries, there was no real consensus on political models, national identity, or national boundaries.[6] Notwithstanding principled differences between centralists and federalists and liberals and conservatives, national politics was typically a fight between rival factions of the elite for control over the patronage and other meager resources of the state. In that fight, a personal military following was often the critical asset. Control of the government, in turn, allowed one to pay and expand one's military forces. Periodically new *caudillos*, often regionally based, arose to challenge the old regime and establish their own. Still, these were primitive military forces, in effect militias rather than regular armies. Civil wars between rival *caudillos* were usually small-scale affairs. Except in wartime, government troops rarely numbered more than a few thousand lightly armed, mostly untrained soldiers.[7] Not infrequently, government forces were defeated by the irregular armies of the opposition. Despite repeated attempts to create military academies, few officers received specialized military training. Battlefield or purely political promotions predominated. Officers and soldiers were only marginally differentiated from armed civilians.[8]

Classical Military Professionalism in Latin America

Between 1875 and 1925, in most South American countries increased primary product exports generated rising state revenues, which were used to finance the initial stages of military professionalization.[9] German and French military missions provided the technical expertise to train and equip armies that held a growing military advantage over irregular armies of civilians.[10] "Heavy artillery, repeating rifles and machine guns, rail transportation, steamships, telegraph, and improved roads slowly decimated regional *caciques* (bosses) and *caudillos*."[11] The European missions brought with them a classical European concept of military professionalism, embodying most of the central elements of Huntington's professionalist ethic. Professional norms stressed military hierarchy and discipline, subordination to the existing state authorities, and the development of military expertise.[12] In this view, military officers should be nonpartisan, apolitical experts in the arts and science of war, hence political involvements were by definition unprofessional. Professional codes of the day typically discouraged military involvements with political organizations, especially political parties, which also began to emerge during this period.

Particularly in the Southern Cone, military acceptance of the classical concept of military professionalism was facilitated by a favorable sociopolitical context and the prevailing doctrine of national security, aided by the prestige accorded to the European missions. According to the military doctrine of the era, the chief threat to national security was external aggression by neighboring countries employing conventional forms of military force. Although major wars have been rare in this century, the nineteenth-century War of the Pacific and the War of the Triple Alliance contributed to the perception that external threats were indeed real. Geopolitical doctrines stressed territorial defense to protect natural resources (essential for export-led development) and to preserve space for population expansion.[13] Given the external and conventional nature of the security threat, military expertise was defined in terms of mastery of military technology and the ability to lead military forces in combat. Thus the boundaries between military and nonmilitary expertise were relatively clear. The argument could be easily made that military involvements outside the purely military sphere necessarily detracted from the ability of the armed forces to improve their military capabilities. Military adoption of this definition of military professionalism was also enhanced by the social status of the new profession, which aspired to be an educated elite sharply differentiated from the uneducated and undisciplined armies of the *caudillo* period. Professionalization was seen by military and civilian leaders as part of a larger process of modernization and progress, thus lending the symbols of modernity and science to advocates of professionalism.[14]

Adoption of the classical conception of military professionalism was, however, also intimately linked to the emergence of political regimes dominated by the export oligarchy. The consolidation of an effective state predominance of armed force was essential in order to achieve the minimum level of political stability to attract infrastructure investments from foreign investors and sustain export-led development.[15] Classical professionalism's emphasis on loyalty and subordination to the state (*el orden constituido*) and its opposition to political involvements reinforced the power of the incumbent state authorities and inhibited political alliances between military officers and civilian groups opposed to the oligarchical regime.

The relationship of classical professionalism to the political context of the era is evident in two modifications of the pure version of the doctrine. First, in Latin America the military's mission included "internal order" as well as external defense. The army was used to suppress indigenous resistance to colonization, to overcome regionalist revolts, and to break strikes and repress demonstrations of nascent labor movements.[16] As a result of these internal-order functions, the pacifist tendencies of turn-of-the-century syndicalism, and the conservative ideological influence of the European military missions, the armed forces often acquired a strong antisocialist (later anticommunist) orientation early in their development.[17]

Second, where the export oligarchy was not able to establish a clear hegemony, civilian elites often opted for a model of civil-military relations that allowed *conditional* military allegiance to civilian authority, in contrast to the unquestioning obedience stressed in classical European professionalism. To overcome professional resistance to political involvements, civilian appeals were coached in terms of a higher loyalty—to the *patria* (fatherland) and to protection of "national interests"—superseding obedience to the president as commander-in-chief.[18] To varying degrees, the norms of classical professionalism were subverted. In the extreme case, especially in the less professionalized Central American and Caribbean militaries, the armed forces served as a political defense against challenges to elite interests in exchange for partial control of the government and opportunities for economic advancement through political patronage and corruption. Instead of apolitical professionals, the Central American militaries became a privileged politicized elite.[19]

Even in the larger, more professionalized South American militaries, the classic professionalist ideal was only partially realized. The Great Depression and the periodic economic crises inherent in primary-product export development and political challenges from rapidly growing urban groups undermined oligarchical control. Both elite groups and rising middle-class parties cultivated military alliances. The former appealed to conservative military values, to the identification of the military with the fatherland and the state, and to military fears of liberal democracy. Middle-class groups appealed to progressive sentiments (particularly among junior officers), to legalist opposition to electoral fraud, and to the symbolic association of constitutional democracy with modernity. Both sides appealed to military nationalism and to professional complaints about neglect of the military by incumbent governments.

Neither the old elites nor the new social forces were able to consolidate hegemonic regimes, where their "rules of the game" were accepted by the rest of society.[20] The resultant conflicts and political instability constituted a political environment in which unquestioning military obedience to state authorities was difficult, if not impossible, to achieve, despite professionalist efforts to limit military politicization. Political and economic crises undermined military confidence in civilian leadership. As a result, classic professionalist role beliefs lost their credibility.

At the same time, the military lessons of World War I, particularly the importance of national mobilization and industrial capacity, sparked military interest in state efforts to promote industrialization and national development.[21] Although the perceived threat was still external, military doctrine began to stress factors of national power other than military skill and existing forces,[22] anticipating a major theme in the redefinition of military professionalism after World War II. To the extent that those factors affected military security, they became a policy concern for the military, thus blurring the lines between military and civilian spheres of competence. Increasing military professionalization gave rise to a stronger corporate identification with institutional interests, which generated conflicts with civilian governments that failed to respect those interests. "Professionalization had the long-term effect of politicizing the armed forces to defend their corporate interests, which they identified as synonymous with those of the nation."[23] More extensive training also contributed to the belief that the military was better organized, better informed about national issues, more attuned to the needs of the population, and more patriotic than civilian leaders, especially politicians.[24] Thus, the political component of classical professionalism was increasingly perceived as obsolete — irrelevant to current political conditions and to the requirements of military security.

From 1930 until the 1950s, military professionalism continued to stress expertise and discipline. Particularly in the more developed countries, the armed forces asserted a growing de facto autonomy from governmental control, partly in an attempt to maintain nonpartisan norms for promotion and assignment in a politically unstable environment. Although the classical norm of subordination to state authority was not formally rejected, in practice the armed forces claimed a right to political autonomy in times of crisis. In the words of a Braziilian admiral, "Professionalism fortifies resistance to the temptation of excessive and precipitous involvement in the political and social life of the country, but does not impede the reasonable participation of the [military] force in exceptional situations."[25]

Divergent Cases

Within this general pattern, there were also important variations. In Chile, the landed elite acted quickly to limit the power of the military heroes of the War of Independence and to reestablish a strong state. Under the conservative leadership of Diego Portales, Chile forged an effective oligarchical republic. Military officers were recruited from the elite and, for good measure, counterbalanced by the large Civil Guard, controlled by local landowners.[26] Constitutional presidents wielded virtually unlimited executive power until the grow-ing complexity of Chilean elites led to introduction of a semiparliamentary system in the 1890s. "Early consolidation of state power, early elite prosperity, and relative elite homogeneity . . . all contributed to making Chile the first country in South America to establish a political system with highly institu-tionalized contestation and more than minimal inclusion."[27] Chile's success in two wars against Peru and Bolivia and its German training missions reinforced the self-perception of the armed forces as a military body rather than a politi-cal institution. Nevertheless, as the oligarchical regime came under increasing pressure from middle-class parties, the normative constraints of classical pro-fessionalism weakened. Reformist officers, many from nonelite origins, staged a coup in 1924, which allowed President Alessandri to overcome resistance from the elite-dominated Congress. Alessandri was, in turn, forced out by Lieuten-ant Colonel Carlos Ibañez, whose dictatorship was eventually brought down in the economic crisis sparked by the Great Depression. A spate of coups and countercoups, including a short-lived "socialist republic" led by an Air Force general, led to a reassertion of control by professionalist officers. This bitter ending to the Chilean military's first detour from its traditionally subordinate political role ushered in four decades of civilian constitutional rule.[28]

Colombia and Uruguay likewise differ from the general Latin American pat-tern, particularly in the development of strong traditional parties and a history of subordination of the military to civilian authority. In Colombia, initially the pro-independence forces were drawn from native-born officers and sergeants of the Spanish Army. The extended wars of independence decimated this gen-eration of officers. In its place arose a new military leadership, the product of the battlefield rather than the drawing room and gentlemen's clubs. Many were illiterate mestizos from the Venezuelan plains.[29] Following the collapse of Bolí-var's attempt to unite Colombia, Venezuela, and Ecuador in a single republic, the white elite forcibly expelled more than two hundred "foreign" officers. The army was cut to less than twenty-five hundred men, reduced to police duties on a pauper's budget, and deprived of their traditional right (*fuero*) to trial ex-clusively in military courts.[30]

Military force continued to play a central role in Colombian politics, but the key forces were partisan militias raised by Conservative and Liberal Party leaders of the agricultural and commercial elite. Numerous civil wars, includ-ing the turn-of-the-century War of a Thousand Days, in which an estimated hundred fifty thousand died, produced a complex sense of local and family identification with the traditional parties. Despite the efforts of several Chilean missions to professionalize the military, the Colombian army remained essentially subordinate to civilian political elites, a subordination based in part upon the government practice of only promoting officers loyal to their particular party. Not until Liberal-Conservative hatreds spiraled out of control in the late 1940s did the military step into the arbiter role common to other South American countries. After an estimated 100,000 deaths in *la violencia*, leaders of both parties supported General Rojas Pinilla's assumption of power in 1953, forming Colombia's first and only twentieth-century military government. When Rojas tried to move beyond his caretaker role and consolidate his own regime, party elites and other social groups united in opposition, forcing his resignation in 1957. Under the subsequent National Front government, civilian leaders moved to reestablish the military's traditional subordination, despite its growing role in internal security.[31]

The armed forces of nineteenth-century Uruguay were likewise closely linked to the traditional parties, in this case, the Colorados and the Blancos. After 1850, the army was dominated by the Colorados, but Blanco control of the national guard in Montevideo and the coast provided a counterweight.[32] As in Colombia, civil wars involving extensive mobilization of partisan armies helped spread party identifications beyond the small elite circles to which political participation was limited in other countries. Like Argentina, Uruguay developed a prosperous export agriculture—wool, mutton, and beef—which provided the economic basis for the political dominance of the Colorado Party. Intraelite divisions, nonlabor intensive agriculture, and an expanding economy facilitated the early emergence of a quasi-welfare state under the leadership of José Batlle (1903–07, 1911–15), who cemented a social pact with the middle class and the emerging working class, which helped avoid the constitutional breakdowns suffered by Argentina and Chile after World War I.[33] Despite the economic strains created by the Depression and political tensions resulting from the ninety-three year rule of the Colorado Party (1865–1958), Uruguay was an exception to the usual Latin American patterns of civil-military relations, with a small, moderately professionalized military, still tied informally to the Colorado Party but proud of its autonomy and constitutionalist heritage.[34]

As in Uruguay, the absence of easily exploitable resources or a large indigenous labor force made Costa Rica a relative backwater during the Spanish colonization. Unlike the conquistadors who settled the richer colonies, the settlers who came to Costa Rica tended to be smallholders, merchants, and artisans. Coffee exports provided an early agro-export expansion and the basis for a small but relatively open elite of plantation owners and merchants. After the "modernizing dictatorship" of Tomás Guardia, Costa Rica began to hold competitive elections in 1889, in sharp contrast to the electoral fraud practiced by the export oligarchy in most of the region. Expansion of public education reduced illiteracy to 40 percent by the turn of the century, which, in turn, permitted expansion of the franchise to the middle and lower classes. In 1917, an economic crisis precipitated Costa's Rica's last military government, which was ousted two years later.[35] The expansion of banana production along the Atlantic coast further stimulated the economy and strengthened the nascent labor movement, based in the mostly foreign-owned plantations. In 1948, the incumbent president, a reformist with ties to both the Catholic Church and the Communist Party, annulled the opposition victory in the presidential elections, claiming electoral irregularities. Opposition conservatives and the newly formed Social Democratic Party joined forces, with U.S. support, to defeat the army and oust the government.[36] In constitutional revisions a year later, the army was formally abolished and replaced with a small national guard without a permanent officer corps. In reality, the defeat of the army by a small group of irregulars and police officers was possible because the Costa Rican army was historically a small and only minimally professionalized force.[37] Nevertheless, the subsequent absence of an institutional military reinforced Costa Rican democracy. Despite growing social conflicts, economic troubles, and partisan divisions, the option of a military coup was definitively eliminated from Costa Rican politics.

Mexico followed a different path to an influential, but politically subordinate, military. The struggle for independence from Spain left Mexico economically devastated and politically savaged by a bewildering succession of military leaders. "From 1821–1860, Mexico had at least fifty separate presidencies, each lasting for an average of less than one year; thirty-five of these ill-starred regimes were led by army officers."[38] After the country lost half of its territory to the United States in the Mexican-American War, Benito Juárez imposed a brief peace, which ended in the modernizing dictatorship of General Porfirio Díaz. For more than three decades, Díaz encouraged foreign investment, promoted exports, and strengthened the Mexican state, including the national army and its paramilitary counterpart, the *rurales*. As the regime aged and became increasingly rigid, opposition emerged to the electoral fraud by which Díaz perpetuated his rule. Under pressure, Díaz fled to the United States and his regime crumbled. Fueled by deep social inequalities and falling real wages, the campaign for political reform escalated into a full-scale civil war with increasingly radical undertones. Although the new regime was eventually dominated by the moderates, the revolution of 1910–17 nevertheless transformed Mexican politics.

The military leaders of the revolution, most of them self-taught battlefield generals, formed the core of the new regime. Nevertheless, for their own survival, subsequent presidents began to separate the revolutionary veterans holding political office from those who remained on active duty. The Colegio Militar was reopened in 1924 to train a new generation of officers. The creation of a government party by President Calles began the process of institutionalizing the revolutionary coalition. During the 1930s, President Cárdenas accelerated the professionalization of the army, purging incompetent officers and retiring more of the old guard, but also incorporating the armed forces as one of the four sectors of the Party of the National Revolution (later the Party of the Institutional Revolution, the PRI), along with labor, peasants, and the popular sector.[39] Equally, if not more important, the progressive policies of the Cárdenas administration—including massive agrarian reform, labor legislation, and nationalization of natural resources—solidified the legitimacy of the PRI as a revolutionary regime, despite the conservative policies of subsequent governments.

In contrast to the initial dominance of the revolutionary generals—Obregón, Calles, Cárdenas, and Avila Camacho—since 1946, all of Mexico's presidents have been civilians. The percentage of military officers holding high political posts declined from 40 to 64 percent in the 1914–24 decade to 5 to 15 percent after 1946.[40] The armed forces have a respected and influential place within the regime, but the military sector of the party has been eliminated. The creation of a more professional military contributed to the development of civilian control in Mexico, but the post–World War II Mexican military was not, in fact, as highly professionalized as its counterparts in Argentina or Brazil. The military's close informal ties to the PRI suggest the importance of shared political values and interests, in addition to strong professional norms of discipline and subordination.[41] However, civilian control is also the result of a strong civilian party, a relatively cohesive and effective political elite, and the peculiar brand of inclusionary authoritarianism practiced by the PRI since its inception.

In addition to providing different starting points for cold war civil-military relations, these variations are important because they challenge the stereotyped image of Latin America as a universal, unbroken history of military domination from independence to the present. In fact, constitutional democracies in Chile and Uruguay functioned for decades with little or no military interference. In Costa Rica and pre–World War II Colombia, the military was generally a minor political force even when the civilian elite was divided. In Mexico, the military was tamed. In Costa Rica, it was eliminated. Although the armed forces have frequently been powerful political actors in Latin America,

11

the history of civil-military relations in the region contains significant variations, both between countries and over time, in the extent of military power and their relation to civilian governments.

The New Professionalism

The advent of the cold war in Latin America marked the beginning of another variation.[42] Changes in military doctrine and the political context combined to shape a new concept of military professionalism. Especially in the new war colleges established in the more professionalized militaries, World War II was seen as conclusive proof that the outcome of war depended only in part on purely military factors. In a cold war, with no clear boundaries between war and peace, the military's mission was not simply to defeat the enemy in the event of hostilities, but to protect the country's ability to achieve its national objectives, including—but not limited to—its territorial integrity. Thus the military's societal function was redefined as "national security" rather than war or national defense. Security depends on "national power," which is comprised of economic, psychosocial, international, and military factors.[43] The effect of this redefinition of the military's mission was to erase most of the boundary between civilian and military spheres of competence on which the anti-interventionist argument of the classic professionalism relied. In the new view, military expertise included not only military skills, but also training in other areas of national policy. National war colleges were created or expanded, with civilian and military students and a curriculum focused on national strategy. Since issues such as industrial development (or, for that matter, almost any major national policy) affected national power and hence national security, the military's security mission was interpreted as legitimating military participation (or consultation) in all such questions, thereby greatly expanding the area of professional involvement in political questions.

The second major change in military doctrine occurred in response to the Cuban Revolution. Cuba's realignment with the Soviet bloc and attempts to foment marxist revolutions elsewhere encouraged the perception that the most immediate security threat to Latin America was internal. The ultimate enemy was still external—the world communist movement led by the Soviet Union—but the agents of that enemy were now seen as operating internally in guerrilla movements seeking to overthrow the existing state. Given the gradations in revolutionary warfare—from political propaganda to regular military operations—and the belief that insurgents would seek popular support by exploiting socioeconomic grievances, the internal enemy was hard to separate from the

TABLE 1.1
Stepan's Old and New Conceptions of Military Professionalism

	Old Professionalism	New Professionalism
Function of military	External security	Internal security
Civilian attitudes toward the regime	Accept legitimacy of existing regime	Segments of society challenge legitimacy
Military skills required	Highly specialized, incompatible with political skills	Interrelated political and military skills
Scope of military's professional action	Restricted	Unrestricted

SOURCE: Adapted from Alfred Stepan, "The New Professionalism of Internal Warfare and Military Role Expansion," in Alfred Stepan (ed.), *Authoritarian Brazil: Origins, Policies, and Future* (New Haven: Yale University Press, 1973), 52.

civilian population.[44] In the eyes of many officers, the entire left wing of the political spectrum became suspect. Military opposition to communism was both ideological and a matter of institutional self-interest. After Castro dismantled the prerevolutionary armed forces, most officers equated a communist takeover with destruction of existing military institutions.

United States military aid and training programs contributed to this redefinition of security threats. The Rio Treaty and the postwar expansion of U.S. military missions and aid agreements throughout the region were predicated on a military alliance against a common enemy, Soviet communism. The rapid reorientation of U.S. military assistance programs after 1960 to focus on counterinsurgency confirmed the internal war hypothesis and provided material incentives and ideological support for redefining the mission of the Latin American militaries as protecting internal security against "indirect" communist aggression. Although often exaggerated, the internal threat was not merely imaginary nor a U.S. invention. After the Cuban Revolution, nearly every Latin American country experienced some attempt to emulate the Cuban experience. Until the 1979 Sandinista takeover in Nicaragua, none of these insurgencies succeeded, but they provided an important confirmation to military and civilian elites that the internal threat was real.

The political context was also changing as a result of postwar modernization. Urbanization and import-substitution industrialization produced a growing urban working class and an even larger urban subproletariat. The spread of education and mass communications increased levels of political participation. Working-class voters became a majority of the electorate. Populist leaders tended to dominate the new electoral politics, but radical parties and mass movements demanding structural changes also gained support. Moderate and conservative parties lost ground, although elite groups retained enough congressional seats and economic power to block major reforms. Despite increased industrialization — fueled in part by the spread of transnational corporations — export earnings were still heavily dependent on primary products, leading to recurrent balance of payments crises and periodic recessions. Weak civilian political institutions were unable to incorporate and channel the new political forces into constructive reforms or to manage the conflicts between working-class, elite, and middle-class interests. Constitutional democracies quickly lost their limited legitimacy. Eventually the political left and the right joined in denouncing constitutional regimes as ineffective, immoral, and incapable of change. Although the particulars of the regime crisis were different in each country, the common thread was the inability of existing institutions to cope with the new, higher levels of political and social conflict. Particularly when elites perceived their interests could not be protected within civilian regimes, calls for military intervention increased.[45]

At a time when civilian institutions appeared increasingly weak and fragmented, most Latin American militaries were culminating a period of increased professionalization. Financed in part by postwar economic growth and in part by U.S. military assistance programs, the armed forces increased in size and in their level of technical and organizational development. Entry requirements for officers were stiffened, professional norms were strengthened, and military education extended through a series of military schools, usually patterned on the American model.[46] Although the militaries of the smaller, poorer countries continued to lag behind their Brazilian, Argentine, and Peruvian counterparts, even the Central American militaries substantially improved their professional capabilities.[47] Individual officers' identifications with the military institution were strengthened, increasing the level of corporate solidarity and decreasing political penetration of the military by civilian groups. Particularly in the more advanced militaries, the senior ranks included graduates of the new war colleges and officers with considerable administrative and management experience. Higher professionalization thus enhanced the ability of the armed forces to formulate their own diagnoses of the crises confronting their societies.[48]

Even without higher professionalization, the changing sociopolitical context would have produced political instability and military coups. Together with the changes in military doctrine and military institutions, the social and political crisis produced a redefinition of military professionalism in terms of national security and the emergence of new military role beliefs. Given the perceived threat from externally inspired revolutionary insurgencies, all policies —

economic, social, and political (both domestic and international) — that could increase or decrease that threat were by definition matters of national security. Given the perceived inability of civilian leaders and civilian institutions to carry out the policies necessary to reduce that threat, military intervention to implement those policies became a professional duty. Given the perception that the armed forces possessed the unity, devotion to national interests, and the capacity for statesmanship that civilian politicians seemed to lack, direct military rule became a professional obligation to insure national security.

Differences in national context and in the ideological orientations of the officers involved produced different versions of this new conception of the role of the military.[49] Early versions of national security doctrine, particularly the writings of Brazilian General Golbery do Couto e Silva, emphasized the security and development linkage. Vulnerability to internal insurgencies was attributed to socioeconomic underdevelopment, which causes political instability and poverty, which revolutionary groups exploit to gain mass support. Hence the long-term solution to the new internal security threat was "development," that is, modernization and economic growth. The Alliance for Progress and the McNamara doctrine provided strong U.S. endorsement for the security-development linkage.[50] The obstacles to economic growth were typically defined in orthodox conservative terms, for example, excessive spending by weak governments unable to stand up to union demands and nationalist policies that discouraged foreign investment. In this view, the solution was a strong government to overcome the political barriers to "rational" economic policies by curtailing the power of the unions and their leftist allies. In the 1960s, the first Argentine and Brazilian military governments inspired by this doctrine were economically conservative and authoritarian, but not brutally repressive. Both were divided along predictable ideological lines over relations with the United States (nationalism versus internationalism) and the role of the state in economic development.

In Peru and Ecuador,[51] the security and development nexus was interpreted quite differently. Underdevelopment was viewed as the primary structural cause of revolutionary insurgencies, but the obstacles to development were defined as excessive foreign domination of the economy, unjust distribution of agricultural land, and elite-dominated political systems incapable of carrying out necessary reforms. In this view, "taking into account the close relationship between Well-being and Security, . . . the best way to combat [revolutionary war] is to eliminate the enormous social and economic contradictions that exist in the country by means of development."[52] Hence, overcoming the internal security threat required not the political exclusion of the masses, but a government capable of withstanding elite opposition to fundamental changes in socioeconomic structure. Thus the political role of the military was to act as a radical/reformist vanguard that would restructure a dependent and unjust economy, protect national and popular interests, and politically defeat the violent left through preemptive reforms.

A third variant emerged in the Southern Cone in the 1970s. Partly in response to new forms of urban guerrilla warfare, partly because of the failure of orthodox economic policies, the new variant was both more radically conservative and more repressive. In contrast to both of the earlier versions, revolutionary war was defined in ideological, rather than socioeconomic, terms. The threat to internal security was seen not as Castro-style insurgencies, but more broadly as "subversion." Thus, the enemy was not just revolutionary guerrillas, but all ideological forces rejecting the "Western Christian values" that the military held to be the essence of the national identity. The strategy of the international communist movement was perceived as a concerted campaign to undermine that identity and to create sympathy for revolutionary movements through infiltration of universities, cultural institutions, and the Catholic Church.[53] In this struggle, Latin America was the front line of an undeclared World War III, which was already under way.[54] According to two Argentine exponents,

The guerrilla is part of the problem, but not all [of it]. [The subversion] was much more global, [with] spiritual, cultural, economic, and psycho-social components; the military part was the guerrilla. [Subversion] was deeply rooted in the culture. Killing guerrillas was not the same as eradicating the subversion.

When the government of Isabel [Perón] self-destructed, very Gramscian revolutionary groups, the ERP and Montoneros, profited from the situation, with bombs, kidnappings, bank robberies, and assassinations . . . . Strikes became not the traditional strikes, but convulsion after convulsion . . . war became ideologized; [doctrine focused] on lifestyles, more than economic power. It was a subversion of ideas, [teaching] Marxist-Leninist dialectic, from private education to the universities. Everything was questioned. The proletarian struggle was taken to its purest Hegelian level.[55]

In Argentina and, indirectly, Uruguay, the French doctrine of counterrevolutionary war derived from Algeria and Vietnam influenced both the strategy and tactics of the antisubversive campaign.[56] The French focus on population control as the key to counterrevolutionary success and the emphasis on terror and counterterror as instruments for that control rationalized systemic repression of the ideological enemy.

The political consequences of the military's new beliefs about their role in politics quickly became evident. The military's tolerance level for civilian policy failures and political crises was significantly reduced. In some cases, the resultant coups occurred in the midst of sharp crises, but in others the triggering crisis was relatively minor. Unlike earlier interventions, the new wave of coups did not simply turn over power to an acceptable successor. Instead, the armed forces proclaimed their intention to govern for as long as necessary to insure national security and promote development. Although democracy was not formally rejected, military leaders made it clear that they did not accept the existing democratic systems and that an extended period of military rule would be necessary to create the political and economic conditions that would permit "true democracy." Although the organizational formula varied, these new military governments were to be institutional military regimes, not the personal rule of a particular officer, but rather the expression of the armed forces' collective responsibility for insuring national security and national well-being.

While the core values of military professionalism—hierarchy, discipline, and expertise—remained unchanged, the relationship between the state and the armed forces posited by classical professionalism was effectively inverted. Instead of an apolitical military under civilian control, the new professionalism led to a permanently politicized military using the state to control civil society.

Politicized Professionalism and Limited Democracy: Two Examples

At the conclusion of World War II, the Brazilian military ended the authoritarian regime headed by Getulio Vargas (1930–45) and announced a return to constitutional democracy. Assuming the role played by the monarchy in the nineteenth century, the armed forces reserved the right to act as the "moderating power" within the new regime. According to the 1946 constitution, the mission of the armed forces not only included external defense and maintenance of internal order, but also guaranteeing the orderly functioning of the executive, the legislature, and the judiciary. The military was to be obedient to the president, but only "within the limits of the law." The latter clause consciously conditioned the authority of the president as commander-in-chief upon a discretionary *military* judgment that the president was acting constitutionally.[57]

The first elections under the new regime were won by a retired general, whose term passed uneventfully. In 1950, however, Vargas returned to power with the backing of the centrist Social Democratic Party (PSD) and the Brazilian Labor Party (PTB). By 1954, the Vargas government faced growing economic difficulties, elite opposition to its prolabor policies, charges of corruption, and a scandal involving the killing of an air force officer by a member of the presidential guard. After an extended period of internal debate and wide-spread civilian appeals for military action, the armed forces demanded Vargas's resignation.[58] Vargas responded by committing suicide. A year later, the PSD candidate, Juscelino Kubitschek, defeated another retired general nominated by the opposition National Democratic Union (UDN). Conservatives mounted a major campaign to convince their military colleagues to cancel the election. Convinced that this campaign posed a threat to the constitutional order, the military intervened to install an interim president and reaffirm their pledge to respect the election results. Kubitchek's administration was marked by massive government spending for development projects and a surge of economic growth, despite corruption scandals and signs of economic distress at the end of his term.

In the 1960 elections, an expanded electorate and a charismatic personality resulted in a victory for Janio Quadros, the populist governor of São Paulo who had been adopted as a candidate by the UDN. Quadros's unexpected resignation in 1961 sparked an unsuccessful coup attempt by the military ministers seeking to block the accession of Vice President Joao Goulart, a controversial protégé of Vargas and head of the leftist PTB. Faced with strong opposition from Goulart's supporters, military leaders devised a compromise agreement to limit Goulart's presidential powers. A year later those powers were restored by a national plebiscite. Goulart proposed a number of major reforms — including land redistribution, enfranchisement of illiterates, and regulation of foreign investment — that antagonized domestic and foreign elites. Against the backdrop of the 1959 revolution in Cuba and widespread pro-Castro sentiments among the Brazilian left, many officers — and civilians — feared that Brazil was drifting toward communism. Goulart's refusal to punish leftist attempts to unionize noncommissioned military officers was the final straw. The 1964 coup marked the end of the military's moderator role and the beginning of twenty-one years of military rule.[59]

The instability of constitutional democracy in Brazil was primarily a result of the inability of its weak political institutions to manage the conflicts generated by rapid modernization, deep-seated social cleavages, rising participation, and a serious economic crisis. The military's arbiter role in civilian conflicts nevertheless made the armed forces a major arena for all of these conflicts. Progovernment and antigovernment civilians as well as antiregime groups logically sought to use the military's conditional allegiance to the government for their own political advantage.[60] Since the military performed the impeachment function, civilian institutions never developed alternative crisis-management mechanisms. Partly as a result of the growing sense of systemic crisis, but also as a result of the inherent instability of limited democracy, military officers increasingly lost confidence in the capacity of civilian leaders to govern, thus undermining a key assumption of the moderator model. With the emergence of the national security and development doctrine and the increasingly evident incapacity of the civilian regime, the belief that the military's political role should be limited to replacing one civilian with another civilian seemed increasingly outdated. Conditional democracy therefore gave way to direct military rule.

In Argentina, the military intervened in 1955 to oust President Juan Perón, following an intense opposition campaign by elite, middle-class, and Church leaders. After three years of interim military government, the armed forces fulfilled their promise to call new elections. The return to civilian rule was, however, conditional upon proscription of the Peronist Party and satisfactory civilian performance that did not, in the military's view, jeopardize vital national interests. As in Brazil, the military's guardian role reflected a basic distrust — shared by many civilians — of Argentina's weak political institutions, whose development had been stunted by earlier periods of military intervention and electoral fraud. Unlike Brazil, Argentina entered into this new "conditional democracy" already deeply polarized between Peronist and anti-Peronist sectors of society. That conflict was intensified by the adverse economic effects of the exhaustion of the early stages of import-substitution industrialization, including slow growth, chronic balance of payments problems, periodic recessions, and strong inflationary pressures.[61] In addition, Argentina under Perón had already achieved a high level of political mobilization of the urban working class. Although less threatening than the populist- and radical-led mass mobilization in Brazil in the early 1960s, the strong organizational base of Argentine unions made it more difficult for civilian governments to control inflation by imposing economic sacrifices on urban workers.

The military veto on electoral participation by the Peronist party followed logically from its identification of Peronism with the personal vices and policy failures that occasioned the 1955 coup. However, this exclusion created a perverse electoral logic that systematically undermined the legitimacy and stability of the new regime.[62] Peronists constituted roughly one-third of the national electorate, with the anti-Peronist vote divided between the Radical Party and a variety of smaller parties on the left and right. In an electoral system that impeded electoral alliances and required only a plurality to win, Peronist votes would provide a potential winning coalition to any party that could secure Perón's support, despite military opposition to any payoffs in return for that support. In the 1958 elections, the loser for the Radical Party's presidential nomination, Arturo Frondizi, split off to form a new party, the Intransigent Radicals, and bid for the Peronist vote. The Popular Radicals countered with a virulent campaign to attract the anti-Peronist vote, in effect deepening the polarization. Frondizi won easily but outraged his Peronist allies when military pressures and a balance of payments crisis forced him to adopt most of the economic policies he had promised to change. In the 1962 provincial elections, Frondizi gambled on allowing Peronist front parties to run independently, assessing it to be the only means of preventing a Peronist alliance with the opposition. Both Radical parties competed for the anti-Peronist vote, although the Intransigents were tainted by Frondizi's previous alliance with Perón. With the anti-Peronist vote split, Peronist candidates won in several key provinces, provoking the military to oust Frondizi and cancel the election results. In the 1963 presidential elections, both the Peronists and the Intransigent Radicals were vetoed by the military. A wild scramble of alliances ended in a Peronist decision to cast blank ballots, resulting in a victory by Arturo Illia, a little known leader of the Popular Radicals, with less than 25 percent of the votes cast. Given the initial polarization of the electorate and the military decision to ban the Peronists, rational behavior by party leaders led to collectively irrational election dynamics, which progressively destroyed any remaining civilian or military confidence in the country's political leaders.

Given the military's guardian role, the instability of the constitutional regime directly impacted the armed forces. The military factions that allied to oust Perón and ban the Peronist Party were nevertheless deeply divided about how to deal with Perón's legacy.[63] These intramilitary divisions reflected ideological differences within and between the services, as well as differences in the appeals that had been made by civilian groups to encourage Perón's overthrow. One line of opposition reasoning charged that Perón was an illegal and violent dictator, hence the military should intervene to defend the Constitution. Other opponents argued that Perón's prolabor policies, economic mismanagement, and corruption were undermining public morality and destroying the private sector. The hard-line liberal faction favored a period of military rule to eradicate all vestiges of Peronism, especially Peronist unions. Legalist officers hoped that working-class voters could be gradually attracted to less objectionable parties. After the Peronist victory in the 1962 elections, both sides agreed to oust Frondizi and then squared off over what to do next. During the next year, the internal conflict led to two serious clashes and a near civil war among opposing military factions. After the legalist victory in the military confrontation, the 1963 elections were won by the Popular Radicals, who had thrown their support to the military hard-liners. Fearing that the very survival of the military institution was endangered by its internal divisions, the Army commander, General Onganía, launched an all-out campaign to restore military discipline. Against very considerable odds he succeeded, but the elections scheduled for 1966 threatened to divide the military once more. The military's success in restoring its own internal order sharpened the contrast between the military's self-image as a professionalized, now unified elite and its negative view of the civilian leadership.[64] Although the leftist threat was less serious than in Brazil, the new security and development doctrine provided a rationale for an institutional seizure of power that would render moot the issue of elections. In a divided society, the military's guardian role politicized and divided the armed forces.[65]

21

Political Instability and Politicized Professionalism

The Argentine and Brazilian experiences suggest a number of important lessons about the politicized professionalism of the postwar era:

1. Politically, the military was not a neutral arbiter, intervening impartially on behalf of the national interest. Each crisis required the military to side with particular political and economic interests. In the process, they naturally alienated opposing interests. Purges of officers identified with the losing side in coup coalitions aggravated the ideological asymmetries between the armed forces and the rest of society, further limiting the military's ability to represent societal interests.

2. The military's conditional allegiance to civilian governments diminished the incentives to resolve policy conflicts within formal institutional channels by providing an alternative means of influencing government policy decisions. Groups with privileged access to the military and those with the ability to create situations which might provoke a coup (for example, strategically located unions) could effectively coerce government decisions through extralegal channels, whenever they disliked the results of the ordinary policy process. Over time, this *realpolitik* undermined the formal constitutional process. Even though the military's guardian role was a reflection of structural problems contributing to systemic instability, the inherent deficiencies of limited democracy insured that crises would erupt which would "require" the military to intervene.[66]

3. The military's veto power also undermined the legitimacy of civilian regimes, lending credence to radical critics who argued that constitutional rule was only a facade for elite and foreign interests using the military as their

instrument. The inability of weak civilian regimes to make meaningful reforms to incorporate the Peronists in Argentina or benefit the poor majority in Brazil deprived constitutional democracy of legitimacy in the eyes of the left, thus setting the stage for the emergence of revolutionary insurgencies. The military's conditional allegiance to democracy thus helped create the security threat which they blamed civilian governments for not controlling.

4. Each crisis increased military politicization and aggravated internal cleavages. Because the armed forces retained the ultimate power to decide the fate of the incumbent government, both the government and opposition groups were forced to seek political allies within the military. Efforts to professionalize and isolate the armed forces from societal influences were offset by increased civilian efforts to penetrate institutional boundaries. Because the political survival of the government depended in part on the factional balance within the upper ranks, political criteria inevitably competed with professional criteria in upper-level promotions and assignments.

5. As an institution designed to wage war, the armed forces lacked any regular structures for political deliberation to decide when and if intervention was warranted. In the absence of any formal mechanisms for consensus-building, political negotiation, or voting, political discussion proceeded via personal and political cliques, oblique conversations between superiors and subordinates, and ad hoc assemblies. Particularly in crisis situations, the deliberative process involved frequent violations of normal military hierarchies.

6. Given structural conditions conducive to instability, over time these weak democracies experienced repeated political crises, at the same time that they faced few immediate security threats. As a result, the military's guardian mission tended to take precedence over its purely military mission. Although normal military activities continued as usual during noncrisis periods, organizational innovation, technical proficiency, and preparedness were all lower than they would have been without the recurrent diversion of military attention to nonmilitary issues.

7. On both the military and civilian sides of the equation, the internal dynamics of limited democracies perpetuated political instability. Military beliefs that civilian leaders could not be trusted to govern wisely resulted in restrictions on democratic regimes which produced crises, which confirmed military doubts about civilian capabilities. Over time, more and more officers (and civilians) began to question the desirability of constitutional regimes. The original arguments in favor of a limited military role in politics were undermined and ultimately supplanted by arguments in favor

of direct military rule. The interaction of politicized professionalism and limited democracy produced a dynamic leading to military government, despite the best intentions of many professionalist officers. As a regime type, conditional democracies appear to be relatively short-lived, usually ending in more direct forms of military intervention.[67]

Institutional Military Rule: Left and Right

Historically most military governments in Latin America were personalist regimes, headed by a single officer ruling by decree. Although individual officers sometimes served in the cabinet—usually in the Interior Ministry to control the police—the armed forces had little or no institutional involvement in the government. In contrast, the military governments of the 1960s and 1970s were typically institutional military regimes dedicated to more or less indefinite military rule in order to correct what they viewed as serious economic and political obstacles to national security. Unlike most previous military regimes, these new military dictatorships pledged to make significant changes in the sociopolitical status quo. Conservative bureaucratic-authoritarian regimes[68] in Argentina, Brazil, Chile, and Uruguay came power in societies with relatively industrialized but faltering economies, high levels of political participation, and deep ideological divisions. Military and police forces were under attack by urban guerrillas; in Chile a marxist government was in power. Eliminating "the subversive threat" was thus the first priority, but stabilizing and restructuring the economy was seen as a necessary prerequisite for long-term "security and development." Imposing unpopular economic measures, in turn, "required" a strong authoritarian government willing to ignore societal protests. While there were varying degrees of commitment to the liberal economic model,[69] these regimes tried to open the economy to foreign competition, to deregulate foreign exchange markets, and to promote greater foreign and domestic investment, while simultaneously enforcing austerity and anti-inflation policies which reduced real wages and labor's share of Gross Domestic Product (GDP). Politically this required reducing the power of labor unions. Despite some "boom" periods under military rule, these were generally short-lived and far more beneficial to the elites and middle classes than to workers. In the "bust" years, the income of the poor plummeted, often dramatically. For industrial workers in particular, military dictatorship brought severe declines in employment, living standards, and political power. At the same time, all four conservative regimes were engaged in vigorous repression of leftist "subversion." The guerrilla threat was most severe in Argentina and Uruguay, but military fears

23

of marxist "infiltration" in education, the media, and labor unions led to disappearances, torture, and imprisonment of suspected subversives in all four countries.

In contrast, radical/reformist military regimes in Peru, Ecuador, and Panama sought to eliminate potential threats to internal security by reducing socioeconomic inequality and increasing state control over the economy, especially natural resources.[70] Peru's "Revolutionary Government of the Armed Forces" carried out a sweeping agrarian reform, nationalized the export sector, and promoted industrial profit sharing. The Ecuadorian military was less effective in overcoming elite resistance to land reform, but its nationalization of the petroleum sector dramatically increased central government revenues. Military efforts to redistribute income benefited only limited sectors of the working class, but the poor benefited from expanded government social policies and investments in infrastructure. The oil boom financed a huge expansion in state spending and expanded employment opportunities for workers and the middle classes. Although these reformist regimes were eventually pushed out in part by failing economies, civilian wages were seldom seriously hurt as an obvious result of government policy. Both regimes were ambivalent about political participation. In Julio Cotler's caustic phrase, "what the military and their experts understood by 'participation' was a military parade."[71] Traditional electoral and party politics was suspended, but within limits, opposition to the military government was tolerated. Unionization actually increased under military rule. Human rights violations were minor; torture and disappearances were virtually nonexistent.

Despite marked policy differences among these military regimes, all ultimately proved to be vulnerable to the same structural problems that plagued their civilian counterparts.[72] The economy remained dependent on international markets for primary products. Copper prices rose and fell under Pinochet; increases in oil prices benefited the Ecuadorian military, but deflated the Brazilians' "economic miracle." Rising interest rates and the post-1982 debt crisis hit both new civilian governments and military regimes in Chile, Brazil, and Uruguay. Urbanization, increased literacy, and the spread of television increased political awareness, despite varying degrees of media censorship and the absence of formal channels of political participation.

Politics: The Achilles Heel of Military Rule

Even the more enduring military regimes suffered from severe political difficulties inherent in institutional military rule.[73] Having abolished existing political structures and committed themselves to long-term military governments, each of these regimes was forced to develop an alternative structure of power. The most vexing problem was defining the relationship between the armed forces and the military government.[74] The officers who headed the military government had to be consistent with the general balance of military opinion at the time of the coup, but factors such as acceptability to civilian components of the coup coalition and accidents of seniority often produced military governments that were not necessarily representative of the armed forces as a whole. In practice, only a small fraction of the officer corps served in government posts. How could these officers—usually the highest ranking officials—be held accountable to the armed forces in whose name they governed? Conversely, how could those in power maintain the loyalty and support of those who held the key positions within the institution, especially troop commands?

25

A variety of arrangements were attempted. At one extreme, General Onganía in Argentina proclaimed that his was a government *of* the armed forces, but not *by* the armed forces. Hence the service commanders were in principle subordinate to Onganía as commander-in-chief. Neither they nor other officers were consulted on government policy. Inevitably Onganía's policy choices were opposed by groups within the military with different ideological orientations. When the government ran into a new economic crisis and renewed student and worker protests, Onganía was overthrown by officers who felt that he had saddled them with the responsibility for a government over which they had no control.[75] When the Argentine military returned to power in 1976, they tried the opposite formula, subordinating the military president to collective military rule through a junta composed of the service commanders, with cabinet and government positions divided among the three services. This "maximum participation" formula was equally unsuccessful in preventing service rivalries and avoiding policy conflicts.

Countries that started out with military juntas usually ended up with the senior army officer becoming increasingly autonomous from his navy and air force counterparts. To the extent that the government departed from the norm of collective military rule, it aggravated personal and interservice rivalries and raised divisive questions about whether the military president was subject to military regulations governing rotation and retirement. To the extent that the government abided by the junta principle, it suffered from the inefficiency and other vices of government by committee. Brazil managed to avoid some of these difficulties by devising a system in which the top generals selected a military president who governed for a fixed term of office. Like civilian presidents, he enjoyed substantial autonomy on most policy matters, but also understood the need for continuing military support to remain in office. The strict rotation of military presidents and intense negotiations in times of crises preserved the stability of the military regime, but not without serious intramilitary divisions and several near coups.[76] The only military president to "solve" the military/government problem was General Pinochet, who utilized Chile's unique military traditions to subordinate the armed forces to the military government rather than vice versa.[77] Officers served in the military government at the pleasure of Pinochet, who used his position as *generalissimo* of the armed forces and commander-in-chief of the army to manipulate promotions and retirements to insure military loyalty to his regime.

In a similar fashion, having closed Congress, the armed forces were forced to create new organizational mechanisms to perform the legislative function of defining policy alternatives and proposing new decrees to the junta or military president. The 1976–83 military regime in Argentina created the Legislative Advisory Council, consisting of three officers from each service. In Chile and Brazil, elements of the presidential staff were designated to perform this function, under the guidance of an officer with the personal confidence of the military president. In Peru, General Velasco created the Council of Presidential Advisors, largely staffed by young colonels who shared his radical views, thereby alienating more conservative officers who felt unrepresented in the military regime. In each case, abolishing constitutional mechanisms involved a cumbersome process of devising a military substitute, without benefit of any clear model or precedent for the organizational structure of a long-term military regime. Creating new structures involved uncertainty and confusion, contradictions between military hierarchy and political roles, and confounding of policy disagreements with disputes over structure and procedure for arriving at policy decisions.

Institutional military regimes also had difficulty constituting a new governing elite and building political linkages to civil society. By nature the military was suspicious of the existing political leadership and opposed to partisan alliances. In order to fill key government posts, particularly economic policy positions, the military turned to relatively unknown civilian technocrats whose ideological orientations were consistent with those of the military regime. Generally the civilian members of these governments were technically competent, but politically inexperienced in constructing political alliances, cultivating civilian support, and maintaining political legitimacy. Neither the military nor their civilian partners were particularly interested in constructing political linkages to other social groups to provide input on civilian demands or sustain civilian support over the long run.

This "apolitical" style of governing derives in part from the bureaucratic character of professionalized militaries, but also from the military's self-image as the embodiment of "national values" and guardian of "the national interests." The military sees itself as "above" society—above classes, above partisan interests, and above base economic motives. In this view—common to most bureaucratic institutions but exaggerated in the military—the policy preferences of representatives of civil and political society are suspect because they represent a *part* of the nation rather than the interests of the nation as a whole. Moreover, in the military's view, civilian groups are typically motivated by short-term, rather than permanent, interests. This preference for a government suspended above society deprived most Latin American military governments of organized civilian support, even from groups who were benefiting from government policies. Both the conservative military governments in Brazil and the radical military government in Peru were surprised by the lack of support for the military regime—and in some cases outright opposition—from the social groups they considered their natural allies. In part, this opposition was based on specific policies that ran counter to sectoral interests, but it also resulted from the lack of any structural linkages to the military regime and the absence of any regime commitment to be responsive to societal interests. The high degree of regime autonomy from civil society prized by the military was, in fact, a political liability.[78] In good economic times, sympathetic civilian groups acquiesced in military rule; in times that required sacrifice or acceptance of unpopular policies, the military found itself forced to rely on coercion to impose its policies and stifle dissent.

Even the more successful military regimes failed to find a formula for legitimizing permanent military rule. The crises that originally spurred the military takeover gradually lost their persuasive power as rationalizations for staying in power. After more than a decade, even sympathetic audiences were less moved by Pinochet's claim to have saved Chile from Allende. For the poor, especially youths who grew up under the dictatorship, the past was less relevant than current unemployment and real wages. Church leaders' criticism of the military's social policies and human rights violations added to the legitimacy problem.[79] Even for the military, democracy remained the ultimate ideal. Military presidents often envisioned themselves "elected" to preside over a new democracy, purged of subversive forces, unified in a common vision of the nation's future. However, on those rare occasions when they permitted relatively free elections, military governments were almost invariably surprised and disappointed by voter support for the opposition.

The structure of the military institution proved to be fundamentally maladapted to the political requirements of long-term military rule. Like other professionalized militaries, the Latin American armed forces are organized to facilitate the rational use of organized state violence in times of war. Although not always realized in practice, military organization is in principle vertical, centralized, and bureaucratic. In every case, there were serious disagreements within the armed forces on the key questions of policy on which any military government would have to define itself. These included foreign policy (especially relations with the United States), the economic model to be implemented, the degree of tolerance for civilian opposition, and the allocation of budgetary resources, including the military budget.[80] Whatever choices the government made, some factions of the military disagreed with those choices. Military governments, however, possessed no mechanisms for conducting policy debates, organizing factional divisions, or mediating and resolving internal conflicts.[81] Military structure provided no institutional means of taking a "vote of confidence" for/against the government or for linking internal factions to external constituencies.

In practice, the formal military hierarchy masked an informal and unstructured political arena. In the initial stages of the military government, the formal hierarchy usually prevailed. Officers not in the government accepted the policy decisions of the military cabinet despite their lack of direct influence over those decisions. Over time, as these policies failed to produce the desired results, policy conflicts within the military intensified. Power struggles within the military government spilled over into the rest of the military. Given the lack of any formal institutions for conflict management, these conflicts were typically amorphous and personalized, a subterranean struggle of shifting alliances and sotto voce criticism. Gradually opposition civilians found ways to penetrate the military's institutional boundaries to find disgruntled officers who shared their complaints about the military government. Behind the formal facade of military unity and hierarchy, the political process operated underground, rarely acknowledged until it exploded in an overt attempt to overthrow the existing military leadership. Some of these regimes were relatively long lasting, but the promised stability of military rule was often illusory. In fourteen years of military rule, Argentina had no less than seven different military presidents.

In the end, institutional military rule had serious negative consequences for military professionalism. Internal divisions over government policies and the distribution of power within the military regime undermined military discipline. Training and technical development suffered as senior officers were diverted to government functions. Surprisingly perhaps, military budgets did not always benefit from military rule.[82] Since promotions, assignments, and retirements affected the balance of power between supporters and opponents of the incumbent military leaders, political criteria inevitably entered into personnel decisions to the detriment of professional merit. Professional norms were subordinated to personal and political loyalties. The professional costs of long-term military rule were, in turn, a major factor in the decision to initiate a transition back to civilian government.[83]

Military Professionalism after the Transition

Based on extensive interviews with military officers in Argentina and Ecuador, there does not appear to be any clear consensus on the meaning of military professionalism after the return to constitutional rule. On the one hand, at the most intuitive, commonsense level of everyday language, "professional" and "political" are widely understood to be in tension with one another, if not antithetical. In that sense, the core of the professionalist argument is still relevant.[84]

I had no desire to govern. I wanted to live my professional life, live with my family, to live a tranquil life. For me it was a bother to have a public office. I was not prepared for this position, nor comfortable [with it].

I [am] a professional officer; [I've] never [been involved] in the political part.

[I have] always been in the professional part [of the military]. [I had] few contacts with politicians, except at meetings.[85]

This implicit understanding of military professionalism reflects the continuing importance of the basic assumptions of classical professionalism, according to which the military profession is defined by its specialized expertise. Advancing one's knowledge and skill within that specialization is thus the professional officer's exclusive dedication.

The exercise of the military profession is complex. If one wants to be a good professional, you can't be involved in politics, [and still keep up with] technological advances. Training never stops, like for doctors or psychologists.

With greater technification every day, [there was] no place, no time for politics . . . . I was in combat aviation, [which is] very specialized. You have to do exactly what you say; you can't be a fake, or morally insolvent, incapable of doing in practice what you say you are going to do. In the air force, there is no place for dissembling, which can put in danger equipment [worth millions] of dollars, your life, or [the lives] of others. It's the same for the pilot, the mechanic, or the specialized fireman. Politics has a lot of dissembling. The air force is very specific and very technical in that which you have to do. There is no place for other things.[86]

However, other interpretations of military professionalism also persist. As in earlier decades, some officers interpret military professionalism in purely military terms without drawing any particular political implications.

The member of the armed forces should be a special person, therefore the prerequisites to be an officer are tough. [He must be] intellectually, spiritually, emotionally, and physically [dedicated] to serving the *Patria*, [with a] love for national unity, for the dignity and integrity of the country. [He must] not have high economic aspirations or ambitions, [but rather] a total dedication to the service of the *Patria*.

[The professional officer] gives himself entirely to the institution. [He demonstrates] a high level of self-sacrifice, his honesty and morality, [his] gift of command, and [his] loyalty to the institution.[87]

Although such an officer might be primarily devoted to his military duties, this conception of military professionalism is not incompatible with a military role as guardians of national interests. Indeed, the emphasis on service to the fatherland and dedication to the military institution could be used to argue that the professional officer has a duty to support intervention in times of crisis, even if he does so reluctantly.

For most officers, democratic convictions or a duty to defend the democratic regime do not appear to have become part of the complex of personal qualities ordinarily associated with military professionalism. Nevertheless, there were exceptions.[88]

[I] don't agree with the old professionalism; the military professional without democratic conviction is nothing; it is acting without thinking.

[In] Argentina, [there] has been a distortion of the word "professional." A negative connotation has been attached to officers that were involved in politics. [The officer] that stayed with his troops was seen as more professional. [That's] false. You have to judge the knowledge, the personal qualities (loyalty, courage), the physical capacity, but also his adherence to democracy. Seineldín [is] a soldier, a fanatic [soldier], but he lacks adherence to democracy. Professionalism is a single whole — professional [knowledge], command, leadership, personal [virtues], democracy.[89]

Being "apolitical" could, in fact, mean *not* committed to a democratic regime and hence available to act as political guardians. These seemingly minor semantic differences reflect different conceptions of the relation of the military to the state. In Ecuador, for example, the constitutional ban on voting by military personnel has become increasingly controversial. Some supporters of the ban take the classic professionalist position that the military should not be involved in politics, especially partisan politics. Others stress the military's special role as guardians of the purity of the electoral process, and thus the need for the military to remain "above" politics. In contrast, the opponents argue that military officers are citizens, like other citizens, and hence should be entitled to vote, as they are in other democracies. In this view, denying the vote to the military is in fact an implicit reaffirmation of the military's role as political guardians.[90]

In Argentina, some officers endorsed General Juan Perón's concept of "integral professionalism," which stresses the military's participation in a wide range of missions in support of the government program for national development.

The army [should practice] an integrated professionalism at the service of the republic .... [The military should work on] its specific tasks, [and on] supporting petroleum [and] steel development. The army can support [development through] colonization zones, civic action, schools, irrigation, [and so forth], without abandoning its principal function. [The military cannot be] a force isolated [from society], waiting for the government to make a mistake.

[I reject] the vision of the army in the barracks, waiting for a political appeal .... [I want the armed forces] to work shoulder to shoulder, to be teachers, to build bridges, to build irrigation [dams], not to prepare for coups. The doctor [or] engineer [may be] dispensable [in other countries]; not in underdeveloped, poor Argentina, [not in] Latin America.[91]

Some non-Peronist officers agreed that the military has a development role in addition to its purely military functions.

I don't agree with the American idea of professional armed forces. . . . In every country, the military has a development role . . . . In the colonization of the far west, military forts created spaces for cities. There is still a colonization mission. The armed forces have other possibilities in development . . . . Railroads still have a role in opening up territory in Tierra del Fuego, where trains could be efficient. They could be constructed by the armed forces—Military Factories makes subway cars. The army built telephone lines and shortwave networks. Why not use people's abilities [and] skills—which are fundamental for isolated communities. I believe in [using the military for] development tasks, to use skills that could be useful in wartime, like building roads and bridges, like the U.S. Corps of Engineers.[92]

In Ecuador, the military's role in socioeconomic development is now part of its constitutional mission. The classical professionalist emphasis on a narrow definition of military expertise as war fighting contrasts sharply with the armed forces' expanded roles in a variety of nonmilitary tasks. Lack of expertise outside of the arts and sciences of war is no longer a very credible argument for military nonintervention in politics.

Recognizing that the classic professionalist model has long been anachronistic, especially for senior officers, the armed forces of Latin America—like their U.S. and European counterparts—have struggled to find a more "modern" definition of military professionalism, recognizing the multiple skills and qualities needed to succeed in an increasingly complex and technologically sophisticated world.

The old professional [was] a mercenary, ready to fight, a robot . . . . The profile of a professional [officer today is characterized] by a great capacity for adaptation . . . . [The concept] is not static, closed, [one model of professionalism] for all time, for all armed forces. I would say that, for Argentina, in today's world, [the attributes] of the professional [officer] vary—a professional of the most advanced technical [knowledge], [with] a humanist training that carries and places him in the role that military officers should have, [and] a capacity to manage . . . .[Preparing officers] only for war or technology [does not meet] the need for a professional culture. The old professionalism [is] not adequate. [Today professionalization] is not the same as the old professionalization.

If [the military man] is part of society, then he has to know the economic, social, and political reality of the country, to know how he can contribute, like other citizens, to the solution of the problems of the country . . . . Second, [it is] necessary to incorporate academic material on military [topics] and on the economic, social, and political [problems] of the country, so we have change [the officers'] study plans to give [military] leaders this capacity, to be able to diagnose the economic, social, diplomatic, [or] agricultural [problems], to know the reality to know what the armed forces could do to solve the vital problems, to support development . . . . The [military] professional knows all the parts of the country, [which] facilitates [his] understanding of national problems. [He needs] an appropriate channel through which to take problems to the government, to suggest solutions, to transmit his concerns. Therefore, the military should have an appropriate policy nexus with the government. [He should] not [make] demands or impositions, but rather counsel and recommendations of what the military believes is necessary for the solution of national problems.[93]

As the last quote suggests, there is a fundamental ambiguity in the expanded expertise and intellectual horizons of the modern officer. He may be a more understanding and broad-minded advisor on policy questions where defense policy interacts with other national objectives. But his advanced training in economic, social, and political problems facing the country may also promote the perception that military officers have a better understanding of those problems than civilian political leaders. That perception invites the continuation of politicized professionalism in posttransition regimes. As shown in the examples of Argentina and Brazil, military attempts to act as political guardians or tutelary powers undermine democratic regimes from within, with high costs for political stability and professional values.

Policy Implications

Over the last fifty years, Latin American countries have become increasingly modernized. Although still mostly poor, the population of Latin America is now predominately urban and literate. Access to the mass media, especially television, connects once distant provinces to burgeoning capital cities and the world beyond. Latin American economies remain dependent on exports, including traditional and nontraditional agricultural exports, but many are now more industrial than agricultural. Political participation has also risen. Partly because voting in national elections is usually mandatory, voting participation in presidential elections is frequently higher in Latin America than in the United States. Few Latin American societies today could be called traditional.

By itself, modernization has not resolved the problem of military intervention in politics. In a region with deep social divisions and weak political institutions, rapid social change and rising political participation have often led to increased political conflict and greater instability. In the postwar period, military coups and military governments have occurred in the most modern parts of Latin America — Argentina, Uruguay, Chile — as well as countries like Haiti and Bolivia. The region's richest country — Venezuela — has experienced more than three decades without a coup, despite a long history of military presidents; nevertheless, the threat of military intervention reappeared in the 1990s. The longevity of many of the new democracies is a cause for hope, but the long sweep of Latin American history offers little evidence for the theory that modernization will necessarily lead to democratic civil-military relations.

Likewise, the hopes that military professionalization would automatically lead to an apolitical military under civilian control have also been illusory. Largely as the result of the efforts of Latin American military leaders, backed in some cases by U.S. military assistance programs, the Latin American armed forces are today typically well-trained, well-organized forces, bearing little resemblance to the comic-opera images associated with dictators like Noriega or Somoza. Officers typically spend up to a third of their careers in specialized military training. Like modernization, professionalization has reshaped the military's relations to politics. Military *caudillos* and personalist regimes are things of the past. Military rule has become more institutional. The armed forces themselves are increasingly complex institutions, with multiple links to society and other state institutions. Pretransition Argentina and Brazil were among the most professionalized militaries in the region, with extensive training systems, meritocratic promotion, specialized career paths, and sophisticated technology, including supersonic jets, aircraft carriers, and embryonic nuclear weapons programs. Both were prototypes of "politicized professionalism."

Democratic systems of civil-military relations must therefore be consciously constructed in Latin America. This review of the evolution of the military's political role demonstrates the difficulties facing efforts to establish effective systems of democratic control of the armed forces. The long history of military participation in politics, dating back to the preprofessional armies of the post-independence era, predisposes many officers and civilians to tacit acceptance of the argument that the military is a natural part of Latin American politics.

The societal context is also less conducive to democratic civil-military relations. Latin American democracies are distinguished by their political and ideological pluralism. Although the elites remain economically and politically powerful, no class has successfully established its ideological hegemony over the rest of society. Conflicts over fundamental questions of economic policy and political structure are therefore deeper and more divisive than in the United States. Inequalities between the richest and poorest classes are also greater, creating a potential for polarization and political violence generally absent in developed democracies. The integration of Latin American economies into the global economy makes them subject to economic shocks and recessionary forces not subject to government control. Rapid social change and weak political institutions exacerbate the conflicts. As a result, political instability and internal security threats are to varying degrees inevitable.

These differences between Latin American democracies and European democracies are a matter of degree. The latter are also subject to international economic forces, class divisions, and ideological conflicts. Particularly in Mediterranean Europe—Spain, Portugal, Italy, and Greece—there are similar weaknesses in democratic traditions and in civilian institutions. Nevertheless, viewed cumulatively, the problems facing Latin American democracies are qualitatively greater. Latin American societies must deal with higher levels of political and social conflict. At the same time, they are more divided about the political principles, procedures, and institutions through which these conflicts should be resolved. Historically, the result has been a strong temptation for civilian groups to try to use the armed forces to influence the outcome. Yet, as seen above, military regimes have not provided solutions to these structural problems. Indeed, the inherent limitations of military organizations as political institutions makes them ill-equipped to manage the high levels of conflict characteristic of these societies. As systems of governance, military regimes ultimately failed, often with high costs to society and to the armed forces.

The challenge is therefore to devise professional norms and design institu-

34

tional mechanisms for civil-military relations that are consistent with democratic principles, but also adapted to the Latin American context. Neither modernization nor professionalization have resolved the problem of military intervention in politics. Still, this history teaches us that the political role of the armed forces is both varied and changing.

CHAPTER TWO

Contemporary Patterns of Civil-Military Relations

Origins and Evolution

The return to civilian government in Latin America has sparked heated de-bate about whether these are, in fact, democratic governments, dictatorships masquerading as democracies, or semidemocracies somewhere in between. In part, the debate hinges on what we mean by democracy. Here I follow Philippe Schmitter and Terry Karl in defining "political democracy [as] a sys-tem in which rulers are held accountable for their actions in the public realm by citizens, acting indirectly through the competition and cooperation of their elected representatives."[1] The essential procedural requirements for democ-racy include universal suffrage, honest elections, freedom of expression, and freedom of association. But democracy also requires democratic civil-military relations.

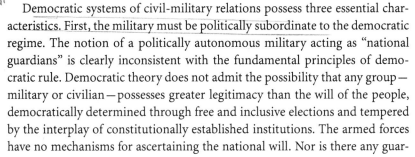 Democratic systems of civil-military relations possess three essential char-acteristics. First, the military must be politically subordinate to the democratic regime. The notion of a politically autonomous military acting as "national guardians" is clearly inconsistent with the fundamental principles of demo-cratic rule. Democratic theory does not admit the possibility that any group— military or civilian—possesses greater legitimacy than the will of the people, democratically determined through free and inclusive elections and tempered by the interplay of constitutionally established institutions. The armed forces have no mechanisms for ascertaining the national will. Nor is there any guar-

antee that military officers' conceptions of the national interest are superior to that of other citizens. Individuals and social groups have different visions of the "common good" and the policies necessary to serve that good. These conflicting views reflect different values and different perceptions of reality. But they are also in part rationalizations of private or sectoral interests in the name of the public good. Professionalization may give the armed forces greater autonomy from other social forces, but it does not make them a classless or objectively disinterested institution. The military has its own corporate and institutional interests to defend. Military officers are part of the existing social stratification; senior officers occupy a relatively privileged position within that social order. Military claims to represent "the national interest" must therefore be subject to the same skepticism as the claims of other elites. The Latin American military's traditional role as political arbiter or moderator is incompatible with democratic consolidation.

Lesser forms of military intervention *within* the civilian regime, including veto powers or political influence based on implicit threats of a military coup, are constraints on the free exercise of democratic authority, imposed by military actors who are outside the system of democratic accountability. In any of its varied forms, the subordination of constitutional authority to nondemocratic tutelary powers — civilian or military — is a fundamental contradiction of democratic principles.[2] Within limits, democratic consolidation is not incompatible with military influence. In established democracies, the armed forces have an important voice on defense and security issues because of their specialized expertise and vital mission. However, military influence is limited to their professional domain; even within that domain, civilian policies are not subject to a military veto. In a democracy, civilian officials must be able to act autonomously from the armed forces without fear of military disloyalty to the democratic regime.

Second, democratic consolidation requires policy control of the armed forces by the constitutionally designated civilian authorities to whom the military is professionally and institutionally subordinate. The existence of "reserved domains of authority and policymaking" not accountable to democratic control is a fundamental violation of democratic norms.[3] In consolidated democracies, the president and the congress define the threats against which the country must be protected and the missions to be assigned to the armed forces. Civilian officials determine the allocation of budgetary resources between defense and other competing priorities. Although the military, like other state institutions, may be granted a degree of autonomy in the normal exercise of its professional functions, the decision-making powers delegated to the military must be exercised within a democratically established legal framework and subject to oversight by the appropriate constitutional authorities.

Third, in consolidated democracies, military personnel are subject to the rule of law. Although subject to specialized legal norms that do not apply to civilians, members of the armed forces are neither denied ordinary constitutional rights nor granted special legal privileges by law or by actual practice. In particular, the armed forces respect the human rights of other members of the society. In violent confrontations or insurgencies, military force is employed in accordance with national and international laws governing treatment of combatants and noncombatants. Military personnel who violate those laws are subject to appropriate sanctions in a court of law.

In fully democratic regimes, the armed forces are neither policymakers nor political actors nor are they above the law.

Current Patterns of Civil-Military Relations

Measured against these criteria, posttransition governments in Latin America have been characterized by significant differences in the relationships between the armed forces, the state, and society. These different patterns of civil-military relations entail significant differences in the "rules of the game" for posttransition politics, in effect, different regimes.[4]

At one extreme, military-controlled regimes are characterized by the de facto political subordination of nominally civilian governments to effective military control. Despite the predominance of civilians in positions of formal authority, major policy decisions are made by the effective powerholder, normally the head of the army. In practice, civilian presidents are largely figureheads governing at the sufferance of the military commander. The clearest example of this pattern was Panama under General Noriega, who twice deposed civilian presidents when they challenged his personal control of the Panamanian Defense Forces. In Haiti, Presidents Manigat and Aristide were overthrown when they attempted to assert their independence from military control. Under international pressure, the Haitian military allowed a rump congress of anti-Aristide deputies, who "elected" a provisional prime minister and president, but real power remained in the hands of the military until the U.S. invasion.

In tutelary regimes, the armed forces participate in the policy process and exercise oversight over civilian authorities. The military's share of power within such regimes may vary, although their implicit veto power is usually respected when the issue involves intense and widespread military pressure. The further removed the issue from the military's "natural" concerns, the more likely the outcome will depend on whether the military's position is supported by important civilian groups. Military leaders speak publicly on a wide range of national policy issues relevant to national security. Civilian political actors, including the president, seek to influence policy decisions by mobilizing political allies within the military. The posttransition regime originally envisioned by General Pinochet was perhaps the archetype of a tutelary regime. Chile's 1980 Constitution provided for a National Security Council dominated by active-duty military officers, with a broad mandate to represent national security concerns before any government body.[5] Brazil under President Sarney was another prominent example of a tutelary regime. High-ranking officers participated actively in policy debates over constitutional revisions, agrarian reform, and labor legislation.[6] The difference between "military controlled" and "tutelary"

39

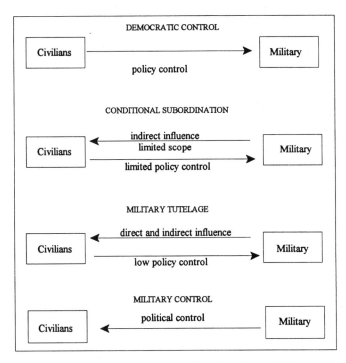

Uninstitutionalized   <-->   Institutionalized

FIG. 2.1   Posttransition Patterns of Civil-Military Relations

regimes is a matter of degree. In the former, the military effectively control a wider range of policy issues with little autonomous civilian involvement; in the latter, the armed forces participate in the policy process rather than simply imposing their preferences. Thus in Brazil, the armed forces have been an important political actor and active participant in national policy debates; in Haiti, the army was the dominant political actor, rather than one player sharing power with other political forces.

In regimes with conditional military subordination, under normal circumstances the armed forces abstain from overt intervention in political questions. Still, the military reserves its "right" to intervene to protect national interests and guarantee national security in times of crisis. For example, the Ecuadorian army debated whether to stage a coup canceling the 1988 presidential elections to prevent a possible victory by populist candidate Abdalá Bucarám.[7] In this model, senior officers rarely make openly political speeches or public pronouncements on policy matters outside the military sphere. One Ecuadorian officer describes the relationship as "a tacit pact. Civil society and the state respect the statutes of the armed forces, the Organic Law and the Personnel Law, [which permits] the self-determination of the armed forces . . . . The tacit agreement [is based on] mutual respect. The armed forces do not give their opinions about the politics of the country."[8]

Despite constitutional prohibitions, officers do deliberate when the political and economic failures of the government reach crisis levels. Both the government and opposition forces are aware that the military's loyalty to the civilian regime is conditional. Hence, civilian governments generally defer to military preferences on issues that might provoke military discontent. The armed forces thus exert an indirect political influence — though typically not a veto — on nonmilitary policies. In addition, the armed forces normally enjoy a high degree of institutional autonomy and a quasi-monopoly on security policy. The president and congress set the military budget, usually with only limited debate. "Institutional issues" are the exclusive preserve of the armed forces. The minister of defense is typically a military officer; service commanders are selected by the president within limits set by military regulations. In Honduras, for example, the military commander-in-chief is named by Congress from a list of three candidates presented by the Supreme Council of the Armed Forces; removing him requires a two-thirds vote of Congress. The military commander-in-chief is not subordinate to the president, but presidential orders to the armed forces must go through the commander-in-chief.[9] With some important differences, Peru, Ecuador, Bolivia, and Honduras have been marked by this characteristic combination of conditional political subordination and high institutional autonomy.

In regimes with consolidated democratic control, the armed forces are sub-ordinate in political and policy terms to the appropriate civilian authorities, including in most cases a civilian minister of defense. Civilian governments can prevail on issues where military officers disagree with civilian policy without threatening the stability of the democratic regime. Civilians exercise their responsibility to determine the military budget and set defense policy, with the appropriate consultation and advice from military experts. Civilian authorities also exercise their responsibility for oversight of military education and professional socialization and for military reforms necessary to insure democratic control.   **41**

Among the new democracies in Latin America, so far only Uruguay and Argentina approximate this pattern. In sharp contrast to Brazil, Argentina has had no military officers holding cabinet positions since 1983. Unlike Chile, military officers are advisors, not voting members, in the National Defense Council. Even in Argentina and Uruguay, however, subordination to democratic control did not include military accountability for human rights violations. In both countries, the military still has substantial autonomy in military organization, doctrine, and education. Hence, these cases are perhaps best categorized as partial democratic control. The armed forces no longer claim a politically autonomous "guardian" role. They accept the constitutional requirement that civilian authorities make the ultimate decisions about defense policy and the military budget. Nevertheless, democratic control does not effectively extend to the internal processes of the military, particularly those that involve socialization of the officer corps. As with the distinction between military dominance and military power sharing, the difference between full and partial democratic control is a question of the scope of effective control.

Within each of these types of civil-military relations, there are also important differences in the extent to which these patterns are institutionalized. Institutionalization has both legal-organizational and attitudinal components. In regimes with institutionalized democratic control, the armed forces voluntarily accept civilian control because they have internalized democratic norms. Military role beliefs stressing political and professional subordination are considered legitimate and binding; antidemocratic role beliefs are marginalized or nonexistent in the officer corps. Institutionalizing democratic control also requires creating a legal and organizational framework for the exercise of civilian control: organization and staffing of a civilian-led Ministry of Defense, the creation of the appropriate committees in the Congress to exercise legislative oversight, establishing the legal norms under which the armed forces will operate within the democratic regime, and providing institutional channels for managing conflicts between civilian and military authorities. The hallmark of an institutionalized system of democratic control is that in periods of crisis public attention is focused on constitutional mechanisms of conflict resolution rather than the possibility of a coup. Institutionalized democratic control of the armed forces is thus an essential component of the consolidation of democracy as "the only game in town."[10] In the 1970s, Venezuela was the leading Latin American example of institutionalized democratic control. The 1992 coup attempts are a vivid reminder that civilian control can also be deinstitutionalized through decay of the organizational mechanisms for that control or the return of role beliefs positing a suprapolitical status for the armed forces.

42 Nondemocratic patterns of civil-military relations also have varying degrees of institutionalization. In institutionalized tutelary regimes like Guatemala, the military's participation in national policy decisions is codified in national security laws and constitutional provisions; military autonomy from the rule of law is expressed in legal codes restricting civilian courts from exercising jurisdiction over military personnel. Formal and informal structures— for example, intelligence agencies, military industries, paramilitary organizations, and clientele networks—operationalize military penetration of other state institutions and civil society.[11] Military role beliefs legitimizing the military's tutelary role are reproduced and generationally transmitted through the military school system. Likewise, conditional military subordination may be institutionalized in special constitutional provisions legitimating the military's role as "guarantor of the institutional order," in statutes limiting presidential authority over military assignments and promotions, or through the absence of mechanisms through which civilian authorities could exercise oversight over military activities. On the other hand, except for a rump legislature and a paper presidency, the preinvasion regime in Haiti lacked any institutional mechanisms for exercising military dominance. The resulting reliance on brute force and intimidation aggravated its legitimacy problems, domestically and internationally. In principle, military tutelage or conditional subordination can be practiced without formal legal-institutional mechanisms or strong attitudinal backing for those practices, but such regimes should be more open to reform than those where such practices are built into the organizational structure and operating norms of civil-military relations.

The typology proposed here differs from the Stepan's analysis of the Southern Cone countries in terms of the contestation/acceptance of military prerogatives by distinguishing between those prerogatives through which the military exerts influence or control over civilian leaders—in Aguero's terms, "expansive entrenchment"—and those through which the military insulates itself from government control—"protective entrenchment."[12] While both dimensions are defining elements of democratic civil-military relations, the differences in the nature and direction of the subordination-autonomy relationship are significant in policy and political terms. Military autonomy from government policy direction may weaken democratic regimes; military control over elected governments calls into question the very nature of the regime. A military debate over whether to cancel the presidential election is obviously a more serious and immediate threat to democracy than the absence of a civilian minister of defense. In tutelary regimes, restricting the military's veto power to military/defense issues is a more important reform than restoring congressional approval of military promotions.

43

Second, despite the absence of sharp boundaries between differing types of civil-military relations, characteristic clusters of military and civilian behavior distinguish each of these patterns, as opposed to a simple continuum of political subordination/autonomy. This clustering derives in part from the logical implications of the political role assumed by the military. In regimes with conditional subordination, the armed forces must have a fair degree of institutional autonomy from the governments over whom they are supposed to act as guardians. Likewise, in relatively democratic regimes, the elimination of the military's political autonomy does not automatically entail the subordination of the military to civilian control of defense policy, but it would be unusual for congress not to have some interest in the military budget or for the president not to exercise at least formal control over defense policies.

Explaining Variations

The initial variations in patterns of civil-military relations were, in part, a product of the nature of the previous regime and of the transition from military rule. Except for Argentina, democratic transitions in Latin America were almost all gradual, negotiated transfers of power in which the military often imposed conditions on successor governments. In Ecuador and Uruguay, certain candidates were excluded from the first presidential elections. In Chile and Brazil, electoral systems devised during the military government overrepresented conservative, promilitary parties. Almost everywhere the military demanded and received a high degree of autonomy in its "internal affairs."

In virtually all of the Latin American cases, the outgoing military government was part of a hierarchical military regime ruling in the name of the armed forces, unlike the Spanish transition, where the authoritarian regime was staffed mostly by civilians and officers long since retired. In the latter case, Franco could be blamed for the excesses of the dictatorship, without attacking the armed forces directly. Even in Chile's highly personalized dictatorship, active-duty officers held a high percentage of government offices in the Pinochet regime, with which the army closely identified. Criticism of Pinochet was thus an affront to the military institution.[13] In every case, the negotiations governing the transition were conducted with the military itself. In setting conditions for the return to civilian government, the armed forces obviously had a vested interest in protecting themselves from retaliation for the actions of the military government(s) and in maintaining their institutional autonomy. Depending on whether the original military leaders had been overthrown, military negotiators sometimes tried to insure continuation of key programs of the military government.

On the other hand, by this point the armed forces also had an institutional interest in getting out of power. Faced with failing economies and a lack of civilian support, military officials needed civilian help to stabilize the economy and the cooperation of political leaders to carry out a managed transition.[14] Civilian leaders logically preferred to maximize their autonomy—that is, to reject military conditions for the transition—but they were usually as anxious to return to power as the military was to leave it. Selected civilian groups also benefited from the conditions the military sought to impose. Hence, opposition coalitions were subject to divide-and-rule tactics by the military. If opposition leaders refused to accept military conditions, the threat of a coup by military hardliners always lurked in the background. The debate over how far to compromise in order to avoid that threat further divided the opposition. As O'Donnell and Schmitter stress, democratic transitions in Latin America were prolonged, confused, and messy affairs, whose ultimate outcome was, at the time, quite uncertain.[15]

Thus far, this explanation only tells us that concessions and continued military prerogatives were more likely in Latin America than in civilian-controlled transitions like Spain, particularly where these were also transitions by collapse (Greece) involving minimal negotiation. It does not account for the variations within Latin America, for example, between Guatemala and Uruguay or Peru and Brazil. These differences derive in part from differing degrees of success or failure of military governments and differences in the policy programs of those regimes. Not surprisingly, in the most successful and long-lived military regimes, such as Brazil and Chile, there were stronger military pressures for a tutelary regime.[16] Tutelary powers would insure that the civilians maintained the core policies of the outgoing regime and that the mistakes that led to the formation of the military regime would not be repeated. Economic and political success were closely linked to the extent of unity/disunity within the armed forces. In contrast to Argentina's divided and disillusioned officers, the Brazilian and Chilean militaries' comparatively better performance in office helped keep moderate and "professionalist" officers allied with the government. Strong military support, in turn, enabled Brazilian military leaders to reject civilian demands for immediate direct presidential elections, and it allowed Pinochet to limit concessions to the opposition, despite his defeat in the 1988 plebiscite.[17] Economic success, civilian support, and military unity combined to strengthen the bargaining position of the armed forces and to enhance their ability to impose conditions on successor governments.

The nature of the military's program in the proceeding regime also had a significant impact on the initial posttransition regimes. The conservative military regimes of the 1970s—Pinochet in Chile, the *Proceso* in Argentina, and the de facto military dictatorship in Uruguay—all came to power in a climate of political polarization, deep economic crises, and varying degrees of urban insurgency. Austerity and anti-inflation programs produced sharp declines in real wages. Opening the economy led to the destruction of many local industries and sharp increases in unemployment. Military government meant real economic hardship for most of the civilian population. Unions were repressed; labor leaders and militants of leftist parties were prime targets for disappearances.[18] The intensity and extent of human rights abuses was accentuated in Argentina, but large-scale repression was a common feature of these regimes. These were also the most modernized Latin American societies with the most mobilized popular sectors and the most powerful unions in the region. Hence, high levels of coercion were necessary to demobilize civil society.

However, once the repression eased and political opposition reemerged, this also meant a high level of civilian resistance to extending military prerogatives and influence into the posttransition regime. This resistance was led by human rights groups and parties of the left—both relatively strong in the Southern Cone—but antimilitary sentiment was not limited to the left. In Argentina, severe repression and unequivocal military failure interacted to delegitimate traditional patterns of civil-military relations. Any pretense to military tutelage was intensely contested. In Chile, Brazil, and Uruguay, the attempts of exiting military regimes to assert tutelary powers reflected military alienation from civil society, distrust of successor governments, and the belief that the subversive threat was still present. Military prerogatives were also, however, highly contested by the civilian opposition. In Chile and Uruguay, strong civilian parties and military defeats in national plebiscites strengthened the bargaining position of the opposition. Thus, posttransition regimes reflected both military attempts to project conservative, antisubversive policies into the future

45

and strong civilian opposition resulting from the economic consequences and human rights abuses of the outgoing regimes.[19]

In contrast, the predecessor regimes in Peru, Ecuador, and, to a lesser extent, Panama were essentially reformist and relatively nonrepressive. To preempt demands for more radical social changes, reformist military governments promoted land reform and modernization of labor relations in agriculture. Attempts to redistribute income mostly proved ineffective, but sectors of the poor benefited from expanded government services and investments in infrastructure. Protesters and opposition leaders were sometimes imprisoned, usually for brief periods, but torture and disappearances were relatively rare.[20] In sharp contrast to the Southern Cone, unionization actually increased under military rule. Not surprisingly, economic elites and party leaders spearheaded the opposition to reformist military regimes. In every case, these were negotiated transitions. Particularly in Ecuador and Peru, factions of the outgoing government attempted to insure that the government went into the right hands in hopes that the next government would maintain progressive policies, but there was no real attempt to impose a tutelary presence in the successor regime, perhaps reflecting internal military divisions over reformist policies. In the absence of major internal security threats, the armed forces were content to rely on existing national security legislation to cope with future problems. Reflecting the lower degree of civil-military polarization, civilian leaders felt no great need to repeal those potentially repressive laws. In this context, it was easier for the military to revert to its traditional arbiter role, reserving its right to intervene again "if necessary" and preserving a high level of institutional autonomy, than it was to construct a military consensus on a tutelary alternative. It was likewise easier in this context for civilian politicians to accept the military's role as an implicit power within the constitutional regime. The conditional subordination model was thus not seriously contested on either side.

Guatemala and El Salvador could be considered a third cluster of cases, characterized by major internal wars begun initially in opposition to traditional military regimes. In both countries, the creation of a democratic regime was closely linked to the counterinsurgency effort. Salvadoran junior officers initiated the transition in the reform coup of 1979, fearing that indiscriminate repression and the military's traditional alliance with the elite were generating rising popular support for leftist guerrillas. Despite resistance from the more hardline elements of the military, free elections (without the left) and a de facto military alliance with the Christian Democratic party were necessary to secure approval from the U.S. Congress for military and economic assistance programs essential to sustaining the war effort. The result was a curious "condominium" regime, in which the government exercised almost no real control of the military's conduct of the war but maintained a limited sphere of autonomous policy action through the support of the United States. In both Guatemala and El Salvador, a controlled transition to a limited democracy was part of the military's counterinsurgency strategy. Tutelary control over policies related to security and development was justified in the name of national security because, unlike the Southern Cone cases, these posttransition regimes were still engaged in "hot" civil wars. Civil society was weakened by a long history of harsh repression of organizations suspected of subversive sympathies. Intense and prolonged human rights abuses and the associated societal polarization decimated the political center, leaving few civilian organizations capable of contesting military power in the new regimes.

47

Finally, in many cases, posttransition patterns of civil-military relations represent a return to the practices of earlier civilian regimes. Since there is no clear regional model to emulate nor any undisputed basis in current doctrine for any particular model of civil-military relations, historical experience provides a key reference point for civilian and military definitions of the "normal" and "legitimate" relationships between civil and military authority. As chapter 1 has shown, there are important differences in those historical models. In Uruguay and Chile, the point of reference is a long history of formal military subordination to constitutional authority, which legitimates civilian opposition to a tutelary regime.[21] In Brazil and Peru, the military was traditionally a major political actor and the ultimate arbiter in times of political crisis; in Ecuador and Honduras, the military has traditionally been a less dominant political force.

The initial posttransition regimes were thus neither a simple continuation of military domination under civilian guise nor did they automatically conform to democratic norms of civil-military relations. Even in Argentina, democratic control was still partial and highly contested. On the positive side, military attempts to create tutelary regimes were also contested. Military dominant regimes were a distinct minority. In regimes that adopted the conditional subordination model, the military retained an important political role without, however, greatly impinging on the everyday operations of elected governments. Reflecting the different legacies of military rule and prior history, the interaction of civilian and military elites produced varied starting points for the subsequent evolution of civil-military relations.

Posttransition Dynamics

Not only have posttransition patterns of civil-military relations been quite varied, they have also proven to be variable over time. Early analyses tended to assume that the initial relations of dominance or subordination between the military and successor governments would be relatively enduring.[22] Once cast in a particular mold as a result of the nature of the democratic transition, those patterns would be difficult to change. Once again, reality has proven more complex than expected. At least four different dynamics can be identified. On the negative side, the huge burden of foreign debt inherited from military regimes left the new democracies heavily dependent on the good will of the International Monetary Fund (IMF), the World Bank, and foreign creditors. The diversion of public funds and export earnings to pay the debt reduced other expenditures, especially social programs, and starved local capital markets. During the mid-1980s, Latin America suffered a net outflow of roughly $25 billion a year to the developed countries. Local economies stagnated; real wages declined sharply.[23] The economic crisis weakened democratic governments and eroded the legitimacy of civilian institutions, reinforcing military resistance to democratic control. Likewise, internal wars have encouraged tutelary regimes as military officers exerted political pressure for more resources and for policies deemed necessary to undercut popular support for the guerrillas. Counterinsurgency wars were generally run by the military rather than the government. Human rights violations were often massive and rarely punished. On the positive side, civilian leaders have been surprisingly resistant to military tutelage; political competition from elected officials has successfully challenged military intromission into many nonmilitary policy arenas. Finally, comprehensive peace settlements in Guatemala and El Salvador have increased civilian contestation of military aspirations for a permanent tutelary role. In the sections that follow, these dynamics are illustrated in the Honduran, Brazilian, and Guatemalan cases. These countries are arguably among Latin America's worst cases in terms of initial conditions and imbalances between civilian and military institutions. But even here, military tutelage has been resisted and reduced, though not eliminated. The resulting regimes are still less than democratic, but more malleable and less military dominated than expected.

Historically civil-military relations in Honduras lacked the tradition of brutality and violence that characterized El Salvador and Guatemala. As the poorest country in the subregion, Honduras had relatively low levels of modernization and political mobilization. Low population densities and abundant land allowed Honduras to avoid El Salvador's intense conflicts over agricultural land. Its relatively homogeneous mestizo population spared it Guatemala's deep ethnic divisions between *ladinos* and *indios*. The elite—mostly landowners and merchants—was smaller, more permeable, and less entrenched. Historically, the largest landowner was the United Fruit Company, which gave Honduras its reputation as a "banana republic," but also lent a certain nationalist legitimacy to unionization and land reform efforts viewed as "communist" elsewhere in the region. Politics was historically dominated by two traditional parties, the National Party and the Liberal Party, and by civilian rather than military *caudillos*. The army achieved minimum levels of professionalization much later than the rest of the region.[24] Not surprisingly, the new generation of more professional officers emerging in the 1950s took a more active role in politics, first as an arbiter of disputes between the traditional parties, later in a series of military governments. In the 1970s, the government of General López Arellano combined the personalism and corruption typical of Central American dictatorships, with a modest agrarian reform and tolerance of labor and peasant groups.[25]

The 1979 revolution in neighboring Nicaragua led to strong U.S. pressure for a regime with more respectability, domestically and internationally. Elections were held for Constituent Assembly in 1980 and for president in 1981. However, as provisional president, General Policarpo Paz ensured a military veto over cabinet appointments, military control over internal and external security, and impunity for past military transgressions.[26] Like his Guatemalan counterpart, Honduras' first civilian president, Roberto Suazo was content to cogovern in a regime in which the armed forces were the dominant partner. Honduras quickly became a key U.S. base in Reagan's war against the Central American left. During the mid-1980s, the armed forces received nearly $50 million a year in U.S. military aid to overlook illegal bases for *contra* forces trying to overthrow the Sandinistas in Nicaragua.[27] Paz's successor as commander-in-chief of the Armed Forces, General Gustavo Alvarez, quickly organized his portion of the Central American wars, creating special counterinsurgency units and demanding tougher antiterrorist legislation. In short order, he decimated nascent guerrilla groups, infiltrated peasant and labor organizations, and repressed the student movement. Human rights groups denounced the use of torture and the growing number of disappearances to no avail.[28] Alvarez was eventually removed from his command by the Supreme Council of the Armed Forces, which accused him of cronyism in promotions and failure to consult on policy matters. Recalling the brief but bitter 1969 war with El Salvador, nationalist officers were especially angered by an agreement with the United States permitting Salvadoran officers to be trained at bases in Honduras.[29]

Like the rest of Latin America, Honduras was hit hard by the growing debt crisis. Rising interest rates and declining primary product prices forced debtor countries to use higher proportions of their export earnings for debt service. Despite the influx of U.S. military and economic aid, per capita income declined from 1979 to 1983. Unemployment was estimated at 20 to 25 percent of the Honduran work force. "By the end of 1984, massive street demonstrations, protesting unemployment, new taxes and repression, were practically a weekly event in the capital."[30]

Under pressure from the armed forces, President Suazo gave up his attempt to illegally extend his term, but the 1985 elections ended in a complex stalemate, with the ruling Liberals winning the presidency in spite of the fact that their candidate received fewer individual votes than the National Party front-runner. The military vetoed the president's choice for foreign minister and continued its monopoly of security policy, negotiating its military aid package directly with the U.S. embassy. During the 1980s, Honduras was thus a classic example of a military-dominant regime. Weak civilian governments exercised almost no real authority over the armed forces. The "war against communism" provided a convenient rationale for military control over major areas of national policy, with little or no oversight by congress or the president. Military prerogatives in security policy and institutional autonomy were among the highest in the region.[31]

Yet, in a remarkably brief span, the political power of the Honduran military was substantially reduced. The election of Rafael Callejas and the return to power of the National Party produced no immediate changes, as both the government and the military seemed more interested in enriching themselves than in signs of growing civilian criticism of the armed forces. However, after the electoral ouster of the Sandinistas and the signing of the Central American peace accords, the United States dramatically reduced its military aid program.[32] The military's once unconditional supporter suddenly became a high-profile critic of military corruption and of impunity for its abuses of the civilian population. As the climate of fear receded, civil society and the mass media became more vocal. The newly appointed human rights commissioner uncovered a series of corruption and human rights cases, further embarrassing the military. A presidential commission headed by the Archbishop of Tegucigalpa recommended replacement of the military-controlled police with a civilian criminal investigation unit. Despite some saber rattling by officers unhappy with all the negative publicity, military leaders tried to deflect the criticism with minor concessions and pledges of internal reforms.[33]

These events provided a propitious context for the Liberal candidate, Carlos

Roberto Reina, the former president of the Inter-American Court of Human Rights, who won the 1994 elections promising to curb the power of the military. Reina was careful to reassure military leaders that the institution would be respected, but insisted on the need for reform. The military *fuero* (the right to trial by one's military peers) was restricted to military crimes by officers on active duty.[34] Five officers were charged with death squad activities in the 1980s and reports of human rights abuses dropped sharply. Despite persistent military opposition, President Reina pushed through a gradual abolition of obligatory military service, ending the forced impressment of lower-class youth. Under pressure from private sector elites, the lucrative state telephone company was removed from military control.[35] The military budget was cut by 10 percent, despite military protests that an all-volunteer force would cost more rather than less. By 1994, military personnel had been reduced more than 40 percent.[36] Under Reina, the military no longer participates in nonmilitary policy debates. The government has also demanded submission of a detailed line-item budget for the armed forces, rather than a lump-sum request. Accusations of widespread military involvement in the drug trade added to the negative public image of the armed forces. A veiled threat to overthrow the government at a tense meeting of the president and the military's Supreme Council only led to more criticism.[37]

By the mid-1990s, the end of the cold war, the dramatic change in U.S. policies, the reactivation of civil society, and societal condemnation of military corruption and human rights abuses radically changed the balance of political forces, putting the armed forces on the defensive. So far, the military has resisted attempts to eliminate the position of commander-in-chief of the Armed Forces. The national police, though now mostly demilitarized, are still under military control. Distrust between the Liberal and National Parties still leads to occasional civilian invitations for the military to play an arbiter role. Nonetheless, civil-military relations have evolved from a military-dominant regime to a variant of "conditional subordination" not unlike that of Ecuador and Peru.

The evolution of Brazilian civil-military relations is also surprising since the initial years of posttransition government are often cited as the prototypical example of a tutelary regime.[38] The commanders of the three services were automatically members of the cabinet. In addition, the head of the Armed Forces General Staff, the head of the Military Cabinet (who also served as the secretary-general of the National Security Council), and the military head of the National Intelligence Service (SNI) held ministerial rank, giving active-duty military officers nearly one-fourth of the cabinet seats.[39] High-ranking officers routinely made policy statements on nonmilitary matters. In contrast

51

to the multiple forms of military presence in the civilian regime, military accountability to civilian authority was minimal. The president was nominally the commander-in-chief of the armed forces, but Sarney treated the military as an independent power. In his campaign against Constituent Assembly proposals to create a parliamentary system and to reduce his term of office, the military was a powerful ally. In other areas, such as agrarian reform, military and civilian opposition ultimately forced the government to abandon major policy initiatives.

Even before the end of Sarney's term, however, the balance of power began to shift. As Wendy Hunter argues in her seminal analysis of the dynamics of the posttransition regime, civilian political leaders had strong incentives to decrease the sphere of military tutelage. Notwithstanding heavy pressure from a well-organized military lobby, the 1988 Constituent Assembly modified the traditional constitutional language authorizing the military's moderator role, making military action to uphold the institutional order dependent on authorization by one of the three branches of government rather than an autonomous military decision. The military successfully beat back a proposal to create a single Ministry of Defense, which would have reduced the military presence in the Cabinet, but the Assembly abolished the National Security Council over strong military objections. (Sarney then created the National Defense Council and transferred the old NSC staff to the new body.) Despite military complaints that strikes could disrupt the economy and paralyze strategic industries, the Constituent Assembly approved a constitutional guarantee of an unconditional right to strike. Subsequent efforts by the army and the government to reimpose strike restrictions by decree were rejected by Congress. Even conservative politicians were reluctant to support a measure seen as highly unpopular with working-class constituents.[40] Absent any credible threat of a coup, legislators gave higher priority to electoral considerations than to placating the military.

Electoral politics also led to increasingly serious raids on the military budget. According to the new constitution, Congress can modify the budget presented by the executive, but cannot increase the total amount of government spending. Budgetary politics is thus a true zero-sum game. In a political system with very weakly institutionalized parties and low levels of party identification, Brazilian politicians typically attract voters by pork-barrel projects that boost services and employment in their district and provide clientelistic payoffs for their supporters. Unlike the United States, military expenditures have relatively little constituency appeal. In contrast, public works, transportation, and health spending produce tangible political benefits. Every year since 1988, the military budget has been raided to finance other, more politically salient projects. De-

spite vocal military complaints about declining salaries and aging equipment—
and supplemental appropriations from weak presidents—the military share of
the federal government budget declined from 20 percent to 15 percent in seven
years of civilian government. Military personnel dropped 40 percent. As a percentage of GDP, military spending dropped from 0.76 percent to 0.20 percent.[41]

While Sarney saw the military as a like-minded political ally, his successor Fernando Collor saw them as a competitor and a potential check on his
own freedom of action. He named a civilian to head the SNI, thus reducing
the number of military officers in the cabinet. Subsequently, he downgraded
the vast internal and external security agency to an advisory body, the Secretariat for Strategic Affairs.[42] Given the history of repression during the military regime, like President Alfonsín in Argentina, Collor found that asserting
greater control of the military—curbing the SNI and ending the military's
nuclear weapons program—was politically quite popular. Once his public support evaporated in the corruption scandal that ultimately led to his impeachment, Collor was forced to be more accommodating to the military, but previous military prerogatives were only partially restored. The Brazilian military's
declining political power over the first decade of civilian rule is all the more
impressive, given the weakness of civilian institutions and the absence of any
sustained civilian effort to consolidate a system of democratic control of the
armed forces.

Nevertheless, the competition between elected politicians and would-be
military politicians resulted in a cumulative process of pushing the military
out of civilian policy areas where they had once wielded substantial power. A
favorable international context and a strong professionalist/constititutionalist
faction within the Brazilian army and navy also limited the ability of military
hardliners to fight their loss of influence more aggressively. Like Honduras,
Brazil has not achieved a democratic system of civil-military relations. Nevertheless, the original tutelary regime has been restricted and transformed in less
than a decade into a fluid, weakly institutionalized variant of conditional subordination.

Finally, Guatemala illustrates the unexpected but important role that the
Central American peace accords have played in challenging the traditionally military-dominated politics of that region. While the ultimate outcomes
are still in doubt, the peace process has spurred a major debate over current patterns of civil-military relations.[43] In Guatemala, the military has long
been the dominant political force. From 1954 to 1985, eight of the nine presidents were military officers, installed either by coup or electoral fraud.[44] The
tutelary regime in Guatemala was a deliberate effort by the "professional-

ist" faction of the military to forge a new pattern of civil-military relations to replace the military-elite alliance, which had ruled the country since the CIA-sponsored coup in 1954.[45] Faced with a growing challenge from marxist guerrillas—and alarmed by the Sandinista revolution in Nicaragua—younger officers became increasingly concerned that the flagrant corruption and illegitimacy of the old military-civilian regime were contributing to popular support for the guerrillas. Constructing a new regime to combat the internal security threat thus became an integral part of the military's counterinsurgency strategy.[46] Reflecting the increased professionalization of the Guatemalan military during the 1970s, the Center for Military Studies elaborated and disseminated a national security doctrine, which formed the basis of a series of annual plans designed to crush the guerrilla forces and allow a gradual transition to a new institutional structure. Although the 1985 constitution declares that the army is "apolitical, obedient, and nondeliberative,"[47] military writings make it clear that military participation in policy decisions affecting national security is not considered political, but rather a professional duty.

Security and development are defined as the essential prerequisites for national stability, "understood as the equilibrium between the four factors of national power: political, economic, psychosocial, and military." In addition to its primary responsibility for the latter, the military also participates institutionally in the other three areas and in the integration of national strategies and policies to insure the survival of the state and the welfare of the nation.[48] The Army was the prime force behind the "Poles of Development" program and the Inter-Agency Coordinating Committees overseeing social and economic projects in areas affected by the guerrilla insurgency. The military's social security institute and the Army Bank manage a broad portfolio of private sector investments, which finance retirement, housing, and other benefits for the armed forces.[49] At all levels of command, the army Directorate of Civil Affairs is a regular staff department responsible for psychological operations and "counterterrorist" propaganda, local development projects, civic action, model villages, social intelligence, and training and indoctrination of reserve forces and "self-defense" committees. At the national level, the State Security Council is headed by the Army Secretariat of Intelligence (G-2). Military and civilian ministries are represented in the Security Council, which has broad responsibility for all matters affecting national security.[50]

Within this tutelary regime, there were initially few countervailing forces to offset the power of the armed forces.[51] The Christian Democratic government of Vinicio Cerezo, elected in 1985, came to power as the partner—in some respects the junior partner—of the military faction led by General Héctor Gramajo, who became minister of defense. Speaking to a group of senior officers in 1987, Gramajo urged his colleagues to forget the old notion of the military as arbiter and to respect "the institutional order, *sharing with the government, the responsibility to provide the common good.*"[52] Cerezo publicly acknowledged that there were limits on his powers as president, including issues, like accountability for human rights violations, that could not be raised and areas that were reserved to the armed forces, for example, the conduct of the internal war.[53] At the same time, there were serious divisions within the military regarding socioeconomic reforms, the limits of civilian authority, and counterinsurgency strategy. In 1988, these conflicts resulted in two unsuccessful coup attempts, backed by business groups opposed to the Cerezo government.[54] The continuing economic crisis, declining real wages, and the lack of socioeconomic reforms quickly eroded Cerezo's initial support from labor and progressive groups. Without popular support, the government became even more dependent on its military allies to overcome the conservative opposition. As a result, the government was unable to curb continuing human rights abuses by the security forces. The official human rights agency reported 599 "extrajudicial" killings and 140 disappearances in 1990 alone.[55]

The sacrifice of the Christian Democratic reform program and the party's consequent loss of public support led to a conservative victory in the 1991 presidential elections.[56] With the backing of a former military ruler who was barred from the presidential race, Jorge Serrano was elected by a substantial margin in a runoff between two conservative candidates. Serrano's victory was cheered by the business sector and by officers opposed to General Gramajo, but the president tried to avoid a break with the "reform" faction of the military. Relations with the armed forces were complicated by international pressures to reduce human rights violations and Serrano's promise to pursue negotiations with the Unidad Revolucionaria Nacional Guatemalteco (URNG) guerrillas. The military reluctantly agreed to negotiations as part of the Central American peace process, but publicly opposed any concessions to those they considered to be "defeated militarily".[57] With the government making only vague statements about its terms for ending the conflict, the negotiations stalled. Despite the delays, the parties did agree to a United Nations mission to monitor human rights. The U.N. human rights expert was outspoken in denouncing violations by the army and police forces and forcefully condemned the effective impunity of the violators from any legal sanction. She also attacked forced conscription and abuses by peasant "self-defense" patrols in the "model villages." Over time, the U.N. presence highlighted the human rights issue and simultaneously shifted attention away from individual abuses to the whole pattern of military power in the posttransition regime.[58]

Faced with a wave of unexplained bombings, public disorders, and a bitter battle with Congress over the activities of the presidential security unit, Serrano suddenly decided to emulate President Fujimori of Peru. After consulting with military commanders, the president announced that he was assuming "emergency powers" to rule by decree. Top officers first endorsed the *autogolpe*, but then backtracked under heavy international pressure from the United States and the Organization of American States (OAS). "The United States and several European governments sent an unequivocal message: Return to constitutional rule or face the immediate suspension of trade privileges, economic aid, and access to international credit. This stand immediately convinced wavering Guatemalan business leaders to abandon Serrano."[59] A loose coalition of civilian organizations mobilized to defend the democratic regime. As antigovernment protesters took to the streets, the Constitutional Court declared Serrano's actions unconstitutional. Despite orders and pleas from the president, the army refused to send troops to close Congress. Faced with strong domestic and international opposition, Serrano was forced to resign.

Congress appointed former human rights procurator, Ramiro de León Carpio, as Serrano's replacement. Despite hopes that the new government would craft a breakthrough in the peace process and reshape the Guatemalan regime, de León turned out to be largely a caretaker president. The brief resurgence of public support for Congress evaporated in a corruption scandal implicating over a hundred members of parliament. The subsequent impasse in relations between the executive and the legislature, headed by former dictator Rios Montt, led to rumors of a coup and a shake-up in the military high command, but eventually ended with the passage of a referendum moving forward elections for Congress and the presidency.[60] With Rios Montt again legally excluded, center-right candidate Alvaro Arzú won the 1995 elections.

In his first year, Arzú retired a substantial number of senior officers implicated in human rights and/or corruption charges.[61] As the peace negotiations neared a conclusion, the final and most difficult item was the role of the army. The presence of U.N. observers and the mobilization of grass-roots organizations in the Assembly of Civil Society raised hopes that the peace process would lead to demilitarization of the Guatemalan regime. The Assembly proposed that "the Minister of Defense and all members of the cabinet should be civilians; all counterinsurgency related ideology, policies, structures, mechanisms, and units should be eliminated; the army's composition and intelligence capacity should be downsized to the minimum possible level, allowing only for capacity to meet external threats; mandatory conscription should end . . . ; all the army's economic capacity should be transferred to other state agencies; . . . [and] military courts should be abrogated.[62] Not surprisingly, the final agreement was less sweeping, calling for a one-third reduction in the size and budget of the armed forces, reorganization of the police and the state intelligence agency under the control of the Ministry of the Interior, and restrictions on the jurisdiction of military courts. The government also preemptively disbanded military-controlled "self-defense" patrols.[63] Despite protests by human rights groups, the URNG and the armed forces backed a 1996 law granting an amnesty to both guerrillas and the military for criminal actions committed during the thirty-six-year civil war. The amnesty does not cover "genocide, torture, or forced disappearance."[64] But, if military courts retain jurisdiction over military personnel accused under this exclusion, it is doubtful that those responsible will be sanctioned.

Nevertheless, as in El Salvador, the legal incorporation of the URNG into the democratic process may alter the dynamic of Guatemalan politics by giving a significant voice to those who actively contest the military's political prerogatives. Over time, this new correlation of political forces is more likely to provide a favorable context for constructing a real system of democratic control of the armed forces. Still, it remains to be seen whether the incorporation of the left as a legal party will, in fact, be more than the final stage in the modernization of old forms of military intervention in politics. The military strength and political influence of the URNG appear to be significantly less than that of the FMLN in El Salvador, resulting in fewer concessions in the peace accords and the likelihood of a more difficult battle over implementation of the agreements regarding the police and the armed forces.[65]

Policy Implications

In these three "difficult cases," posttransition patterns of civil-military relations have changed significantly from the initial civilian governments. In Honduras, fears of contagion from the Nicaraguan revolution of 1979 first led to a military-dominant regime in which the military brutally repressed suspected subversive groups and blatantly defied civilian authority over the armed forces. After a decade of military dominance, the 1990s brought a series of changes—the Central American peace accords, changes in U.S. policy, and a more active civil society—that created a political context conducive to reducing the power and autonomy of the armed forces. Human rights abuses and corruption scandals seriously damaged the public image of the armed forces. In Brazil, competition from elected politicians has eroded the military budget and marginalized military influence in areas where it initially exercised important tutelary powers. In Guatemala, the peace process has led to greater contestation of military pre-

57

rogatives, even though the ultimate outcome is still in doubt. In all three cases, the political power of the armed forces has been challenged; in Honduras and Brazil, the military's tutelary role has been substantially reduced. The military remains an important political actor, but the general tendency seems to be that the military is becoming relatively less important, in effect, one actor among many. Although the evidence is mixed, the trend seems to be toward conditional subordination as the modal pattern of civil-military relations in the new democracies, rather than military tutelage.

In addition to the dynamics cited above, two other factors contribute to this tendency. First, a tutelary regime presupposes a certain degree of military consensus around a particular "political project," which serves as the reference point for military attempts to steer civilian policies "in the right direction." To the extent that the military is, in fact, divided over key policy issues, it cannot exercise a coherent tutelage over civilian governments. More so than most of their Latin American counterparts, the Brazilian and Guatemalan militaries did have articulated national security doctrines and their own military projects.[66] Yet, in each case there were also factions within the military opposed to those projects. Particularly in Brazil, traditional conceptions of military professionalism persisted within portions of the officer corps, so attempts to exercise military tutelage were not universally accepted, even within the military. Instead of confronting united and coherent military pressure for particular policies, civilian governments could usually find ideologically compatible and/or professionalist officers for high-command positions, placing would-be tutors in the awkward position of publicly contradicting their superiors. Whereas defense of the military budget or military autonomy typically unites the armed forces around shared institutional interests, military tutelage aggravates the ideological divisions within the armed forces. Internal divisions within the armed forces, in turn, allow civilians opposed to the military tutelage to push for alternative models of civil-military relations.

Second, although the international environment was initially not as favorable as the NATO/European Union pressures for democratization of civil-military relations in Southern Europe,[67] over time the international context in Latin America has become increasingly less tolerant of major departures from democratic norms. The end of the cold war removed the major source of cross-pressure constraining U.S. support for more democratic civil-military relations, making it more difficult for U.S. or Latin American military leaders to defend semidemocratic regimes or human rights abuses as necessary to fight the spread of communism. In the 1990s, U.S. support for democracy has been far more unequivocal than it was under Ronald Reagan. In Honduras, the shift in U.S. policy played a major role in undermining the military-dominant regime.

Latin American leaders have also become more aggressive in promoting the collective defense of democracy as a fundamental norm of inter-American relations. The 1991 Santiago Resolution on Representative Democracy provides for immediate convocation of the Permanent Council of the Organization of American States in the event of any interruption of "the legitimate exercise of power by [a] democratically elected government" in any member state. The 1997 Washington Protocol amended the OAS Charter to allow suspension of any member country where the democratically elected government is overthrown by force.[68] The OAS actively intervened to push for restoration of a constitutional government in the Peruvian and Guatemalan *autogolpes*. In both cases, diplomatic actions were backed by threats of economic sanctions. European countries and the United States cut off economic and military aid to Guatemala; the United States threatened to withdraw trade benefits. "It was this threat that apparently got business leaders to join other groups in civil society to press for Serrano's removal."[69] When unconstitutional actions by the military or the executive are actively contested by civil society, the threat of international sanctions provides an important advantage to the opposition.[70]

Military attempts to impose tutelary regimes thus face a fundamental constraint — without a credible coup threat, military leaders have relatively little recourse when the government refuses to accede to the policy preferences of the military. Military rebellions like the *carapintada* revolts in Argentina offer an alternative to the traditional coup, but involve high risks of accentuating internal divisions within the military and exacerbating tensions with civil society. The institutional costs of rebellions thus generally outweigh the prospective benefits, unless there is a severe threat to institutional interests.[71] Over time, civilian leaders in Brazil, Honduras, and Guatemala have learned that they can take actions opposed by the armed forces without jeopardizing the survival of their government as long as they maintain a modicum of political support and political legitimacy.[72] Weak governments that have lost their public support will be logically less inclined to antagonize the armed forces by challenging military prerogatives or refusing to listen to military "advice." But the military's power in such situations rests perhaps less on the threat of a coup than the threat that military leaders will publicly condemn government policies, thereby increasing the odds that the government will be impeached or held hostage by the civilian opposition. As long as civilian actors are willing to abide by the constitutional rules, civilian defiance of military tutelage is usually

59

not that costly. The military threat to democratic regimes is increasingly a bluff that lacks credibility.

In sum, posttransition civil-military relations have been both varied and variable. The interplay of the central dynamics — external debt and political decay, internal warfare and peace negotiations, and political competition between the military and elected leaders, in a context of internally divided militaries and strong international support for democracy — has produced conflicting tendencies with no determinate outcome. Still, even in these worst cases, tutelary regimes have proven difficult to implement, much less institutionalize.

Notwithstanding that positive outcome, current patterns of civil-military relations are still undemocratic. Serious human rights violations continue in Guatemala. Honduras has been plagued by terrorist bombings apparently aimed at forcing the government to halt prosecution of corruption and human rights cases.[73] Civilian governments have only recently, and intermittently, begun to assume responsibility for defense and security policy. In all three countries, the armed forces still enjoy a high degree of institutional autonomy. Traditional notions of the military as the ultimate guardian of national interests and national security persist in much of the officer corps. Repressive national security legislation remains on the books. As Felipe Aguero observes, "The armed forces are in truth a constant presence, as a permanent institution of the state, even if democratization pushes them out of the foreground of events and they cease to be a daily source of instability and uncertainty."[74]

Still, the variability in outcomes — between countries and over time — suggests that opportunities exist for active policy intervention to promote more democratic civil-military relations. If military dominance or military tutelage is not preordained, maybe not even likely under current conditions, civilian efforts to construct and institutionalize democratic control of the armed forces may be more feasible than previously anticipated. Even in difficult situations, skilled civilian leadership, with public support and international backing, can reduce the political power of the armed forces.

60

CHAPTER THREE

Military Role Beliefs in New Democracies

Ideology and Context
in Argentina and Ecuador

Following World War II and again in the late 1950s, Latin America experienced the fall of military dictatorships and establishment of democratic governments. In both instances, these turned out to be only brief interludes before the next wave of military intervention. Not surprisingly, many scholars questioned whether the democratic transitions of the 1980s would be a permanent change or just another swing in the pendulum, a new democratic era or a superficial change in the presidential palace. The answers depend significantly on how military officers define their political role in the new democracies.[1]

In the narrow sense, "role beliefs" refer to military conceptions of their role in politics.[2] What forms of political action are considered legitimate? Under what circumstances? What is the military role in different policymaking processes? In a broader sense, role beliefs include the entire complex of attitudes that define officers' normative models of civil-military relations. Role beliefs thus include explicit and implicit notions of the proper relationships between civilian authorities, the armed forces, and society. To the extent that military officers reject civilian control in principle, even regimes that have temporarily reduced the military's political power are likely to face strong military resentment and continuing efforts to reestablish the military's traditional prerogatives. To the extent that military beliefs legitimize a suprapolitical role as national guardians, authoritarian constitutional norms and repressive national security legislation can be used to legalize regimes that are democratic in name only.[3] Military beliefs about their political role are thus central to the conflict over alternative models of civil-military relations. Changes in military role beliefs are a necessary, though not sufficient, condition for institutionalizing effective democracy in Latin America. The failure to transform role beliefs is likely to lead to hollow democracies, democratic in form, but not in substance.[4]

Research Design

The analysis that follows compares military role beliefs in Argentina and Ecuador, two countries with dissimilar militaries and distinct sociopolitical contexts. As shown in Table 3.1, Argentina is a larger, more modernized country, with a semi-industrial economy and capital-intensive agriculture; since the turn of the century, it has had a literate, predominantly urban, and racially homogeneous population and probably the largest middle class in Latin America. Under the leadership of Juan Perón, Argentina developed a highly mobilized working class in the 1940s, with near-universal political participation. Since the 1950s, Argentines have suffered from recurrent balance of payments deficits, cyclical stagflation, and chronic political instability, including two periods of extended military dictatorship, 1966–73 and 1976–83. The latter epitomized the conservative military regimes of the 1970s, combining neoliberal free-market economic policies with intense repression of leftists and other "subversive" forces. Compared to its Brazilian and Southern Cone counterparts, it was unquestionably the least successful of these regimes.

Ecuador is smaller and poorer than Argentina, in some respects a more typical Latin American country. Like its Andean neighbors, it has significant Indian and mestizo populations in a highly stratified society. Until the 1970s, the economy was based largely on agricultural exports—bananas and other coastal products—with substantial persistence of precapitalist forms of land tenure well into the postwar period. In 1972, oil exports ushered in a decade of relatively rapid growth, light industrialization, and rising revenues for what had been one of the poorest governments in Latin America. Historically, Ecuadorian politics was elitist but relatively nonviolent.[5] The diffusion of mass literacy in the 1950s and 1960s was accompanied by the rise of populist and reformist movements and a gradual rise in mass participation, culminating in the introduction of universal suffrage in the 1978 Constitution. Still, Ecuadorian politics remains largely centered on personalities and clientelism, rather than parties or platforms.[6] Reflecting its history of segmental incorporation of nonelite groups, Ecuadorian political culture is intensely moralistic and sectarian,

TABLE 3.1
Socioeconomic and Political Comparisons: Argentina and Ecuador

	Argentina	Ecuador
Population	34 million	11 million
1960–93 growth rate	1.5% per year	2.8% per year
Urban population	88%	57%
Human development		
Human development index (rank)	0.885 (30th)	0.764 (64th)
Life expectancy at birth	72 yrs.	69 yrs.
Adult literacy	96%	89%
Access to safe water*	71%	71%
Economic development		
Adjusted real GDP per capita	$5,814	$4,400
Calorie supply/minimum	130%	106%
Per capita GDP growth 1965–80	1.7%/year	5.4%/year
GDP growth 1980–93	0.5%/year	2.6%/year
Labor force in agriculture	12%	33%
Labor force in industry	32%	19%
Communications		
Newspapers per 100 inhabitants**	14	6
Televisions per 100 inhabitants**	22	9
Elections and parties		
% of population voting 1962/60 [a]	43%	17%
% of population voting 1983/84 [a]	51%	31%
Electoral volatility, posttransition [b]	20%	38%
Congress seats held by pre-1950 parties [b]	82% ***	16% **
Index of party institutionalization (rank) [b]	9 (6th of 12)	5 (10th lowest of 12)
Effective number of parties [b]	2.7	5.8

SOURCES: Socioeconomic data: United Nations Development Programme, *Human Development Report 1996* (New York: Oxford University Press, 1996). Unless otherwise noted, figures refer to 1993 estimates.
 [a] Ronald McDonald and J. Mark Ruhl, *Party Politics and Elections in Latin America* (Boulder, Colo.: Westview Press, 1989), 160, 315.
 [b] Scott Mainwaring and Timothy Scully, "Introduction: Party Systems in Latin America," in Mainwaring and Scully (eds.), *Building Democratic Institutions: Party Systems in Latin America* (Stanford, Calif.: Stanford University Press, 1995), 8, 13, 17, 30.
 *1990–95   **1992   ***1993

63

but not particularly ideological. Like Argentina, Ecuador has had two recent periods of military rule, 1963–66 and 1972–78. Both military regimes were mildly reformist and politically ineffective, but free of the widespread human rights abuses that marked military governments in Central America and the Southern Cone.

Ecuador could therefore be considered a "worst case" for democratic civil-military relations, though it lacks the additional burden of guerrilla wars faced by Peru and Guatemala.[7] Ecuador returned to democracy through a negotiated transition that guaranteed substantial autonomy for the armed forces. In the absence of any traumatic experience with the previous military regime or

TABLE 3.2
Interview Samples

Status		Rank		Service	
Ecuador 1991					
Active Duty	6	Generals*	41	Army	30
Retired	38	Colonels	2	Navy	12
		Majors	1	Air force	2
Argentina 1985					
Active Duty	5	Generals	27	Army	41
Retired	44	Colonels	10	Navy	5
		Lt. Colonels	3	Air force	3
		Majors	2		
		Capts./Lts.	7		
Argentina 1992					
Active Duty	33	Generals	23	Army	45
Retired	37	Colonels	25	Navy	19
		Lt. Colonels	9	Air force	6
		Majors	6		
		Capts./Lts.	7		

* Includes the equivalent ranks of the other services.

major changes in structural conditions, Ecuador should be a likely case for the persistence of traditional attitudes toward military intervention in politics. Still, the posttransition regime has survived seventeen years and seven different governments. Argentina, on the other hand, is typically characterized as a "most favorable case" for changing traditional patterns of civil-military relations because of the glaring failures of the military regime and its defeat in the Malvinas/Falklands war. Even here, however, there are skeptics.[8] So, there is controversy in both cases about the degree of continuity and change in military thinking about their role in politics.

The analysis that follows is based on in-depth interviews with military officers in Ecuador (1991) and Argentina (1985 and 1992). The Ecuadorian sample consists of mostly retired officers, although enough active-duty officers were included to insure that the attitudes encountered among the retirees were not atypical of those still on active duty. Over 90 percent were general rank officers, including members of the High Command from the first four posttransition governments. The sample includes many, if not most, of the key leaders in civil-military crises since 1979. The preponderance of army officers reflects the size and political importance of the army relative to the other forces. The 1985 Argentine sample has a similar structure, with the army, retired officers, and the senior ranks predominant. Given the difficulties of interviewing military officers in the midst of the human rights trials, the 1985 interviews focused on sampling different military viewpoints. The second set of Argentine interviews seven years later includes twenty reinterviews within a substantially larger and more representative sample. Given the clashes between junior and senior officers in the late 1980s, the second Argentine sample includes middle- and lower-ranking officers on active duty, as well as officers forced into retirement as a result of the *carapintada* revolts.

The interviews followed a semistructured, open-ended format and lasted anywhere from one to seven hours, although two hours was typical. The questions probed officers' perceptions and interpretations of the previous military regime, their conception of the role of the military in the new regime, and military relations with civilian governments. In each case, specific crises were discussed, in order to analyze the relation between general norms and behavior in concrete situations, and to elicit the rationales for alternative military responses to those crises. The interview material is rich and multilayered, so insofar as possible, I have tried to let the diverse voices of these officers speak directly to the questions addressed here. The analysis has three key objectives:

To describe the role beliefs of Ecuadorian and Argentine officers in terms of a typology that includes the military's role *within,* as well as *against,* civilian regimes;

To construct a dynamic model of how military role beliefs change over time in response to (1) learning from past experience, (2) the domestic context, and (3) the international context; and

To move beyond the conception of the military as a unitary actor to show how the internal divisions within the armed forces affect the debate over alternative definitions of the military's role in politics.

The final section of the chapter addresses the policy implications of this analysis for both U.S. and Latin American governments seeking to institutionalize more democratic forms of civil-military relations.

Military Role Beliefs

At first glance, the interviews suggest striking changes in military attitudes. In response to a direct question about the role of the armed forces in politics, the overwhelming majority of Argentine officers said the military should be subordinated to the constitutional authorities (55 percent), stick to its constitutional missions (22 percent), and not intervene in politics (7 percent). Another 10 percent argued the military should be an active participant in a national project under civilian leadership. Among Ecuadorian officers, less than 20 percent defended traditional views of the armed forces as the guardians of the national interest or guardians of national security. A majority favored the constitutional definition of the military's role: external defense, internal order, and contributing to socioeconomic development.

Yet this is not an accurate or reliable reading of military beliefs about their political role in either country. Ecuadorian officers in particular varied significantly in their view of the political roles necessary to carry out the constitutional missions of the armed forces. Depending on one's interpretation, the constitutional mandate can be read as anything from strict subordination to broad guardian or tutelary powers. A more comprehensive description of role beliefs requires viewing the responses in the context of the whole set of attitudes in each interview, rather than individual statements in isolation.[9] If we treat role beliefs as belief systems, we can identify several qualitatively distinct positions on what the military's role in the new regime should be. The first model corresponds quite closely to the North American conception of an apolitical military under civilian control. This *democratic professionalism* is exemplified in statements by Argentine and Ecuadorian officers:

[The military's duty is] to comply with their role as armed forces, to support the democratic system, and [the policies] established by the government of the day, without transforming themselves into censors or guardians of government efficacy. The voters are the judges of governments.

[Today the armed forces believe in] the democratic way, respecting democracy. The problems of democracy should be solved democratically.

The armed forces [should stick to] an ascetic, integrated professionalism, [to] their professional tasks. . . . [We] have to strengthen democracy and discourage civilians from promoting military coups. The armed forces should not govern; . . . [they] don't know how to govern . . . . As many times as they have tried, the military always ends up losing the most. When [the armed forces] dedicate themselves to their professional tasks, [they] don't have time for other things.[10]

In terms of Huntington's distinction between "objective" and "subjective" civilian control, the democratic professionalist model combines a subjective commitment to democracy as the preferred political system, with a belief in a professional ethic that differentiates and separates military and political affairs.[11] Proponents of this model constitute roughly one-third of the sample in both countries.

The second model, *classical professionalism*, argues for the subordination of the military, in both political and policy terms, to the constitutionally designated civilian authorities. Statements by proponents of this perspective stress the separate functions of the military and the government and the subordination of the armed forces to higher authority.

[I] believe that the military is not the solution for the political and social problems of the country. [Military] intervention [in the government] will split apart the armed institution itself. Even in a crisis, the political leaders are the ones [who should be] called upon to solve them. . . . The [military] command should have a very clear understanding of [their] subordination to civilian power, that is, to the executive, [acknowledging] the principle of [civilian] authority and [military] subordination, without restricting [the military's right] to express its opinion. The military is one more advisor [to the government], like the [other] fronts. The decisions [are] taken by the executive. [That] is what we see in the military institution. The general staff advises the commander, but once the decision is made, we obey.

After the military expresses its opinion, you have to respect the [government's] decision. If the government (*poder político*) decides, who says the policy adopted is contrary to the national interest? I can't interpret what the national interest is. That's up to society and to the government, not to one man, [even though] I know what I think it is.

Each of the powers of the State has its proper function. The function of the armed forces is defense. The function of the Economics Ministry is economics. The political function belongs to the politicians. I believed and I believe [now] that the mission of the armed forces is to prepare themselves to defend the sovereignty of the country. The military is not responsible for education, the economy, or public health, but for external defense. When the armed forces get involved in everything—safeguarding education, public health, morals, culture, and above all the politics [of the country]—they forget to prepare for their military mission.[12]

While the classic professionalist model rejects military intervention in politics and accepts civilian control, it lacks the affirmative commitment to a democratic regime characteristic of democratic professionalism.

A third variant envisions the armed forces as an active participant in the national project defined by the constitutional authorities. In this view, the military should have some degree of influence in deference to its vital societal role. Thus, the military's role is to be a *power factor* within the constitutional regime.

The role of the armed forces should be the same as it is in the United States. [The military] is a factor of power. It has interests; it has to be in the system. [The military] is the armed fist of any serious state. [Look at] the Gulf [or] Grenada. One shouldn't exclude the military power from national policy. The armed forces should never again participate in a [military] administration. [They] always lose professionalization and hierarchy. Stepping into the administration is not the same as stepping into power; except in marxist systems, the [economic] power is on the other side. Presidents change; the powers remain.

The army has to be a power factor within the lines set by the Constitution and the institutions. [We] older generals say that the colonial army ended in 1983, including [intervention to] change the government. [Now we] are hoping to be a factor within the system of constitutional limits.[13]

As both these quotes suggest, this role belief is ambiguous about the limits of the military's political influence and silent about the military's role when governments do not concede to the armed forces their "rightful place" within the regime.

In contrast, some officers in both countries advocate *conditional subordination* to civilian authorities, arguing that in normal circumstances the military should stick to its military affairs, but that in crisis situations the armed forces are obligated to safeguard the highest national interests of the Nation, even if that entails overthrowing the incumbent government and assuming power temporarily. As a former Army commander in Ecuador explained,

the military is immersed in national problems like everyone else. They see the same problems and [experience] the same frustrations. The political factors [that lead to coups] are not created by the military, but by the politicians. The absence of [dedication] to the objectives of the country and [to providing] benefits for the country, when [there is] nothing but [conflicts] of interests, including partisan [interests], creates a political space — anarchy, lack of security, instability, loss of productivity and investment — creates conditions [for which there is] no political solution, [which] therefore motivates the armed forces to attempt to salvage the chaotic situation of the country. Political instability [and] internecine political struggles [have a] decisive [impact] on the economy, education, and investment, so [there is] instability. The country is neutralized, blocked; it tends to lose its ethical principles. [There are] strikes, stoppages, demonstrations. [The situation becomes] unsustainable. The moment arrives when someone [has to] impose order. But [military intervention] should be only temporary, not long term. [The government should] make the maximum use [of its time in power] to put [the country] in order, [which requires] immediate measures — political, economic, and social. As soon as possible, [the military should] return to normal democratic politics, for example, changing the party law, [convening] Congress, rectifying [the problem] and [then] leaving power.

Military regulations traditionally defined the Argentine army's role as "safeguarding the highest national interests of the Nation . . . to defend its honor, its territory, the Constitution of the Argentine Nation and its law, guaranteeing the maintenance of internal peace and insuring the normal operation of its institutions."[14] In theory and in practice, this traditional conception of the military's mission as political guardian and arbiter involves substantial military autonomy from civilian authority.

A small number of Ecuadorian officers endorsed a *tutelary* model, grant-

68

ing the military a high degree of autonomy and an institutional voice in policy matters related to national security broadly defined.

The [armed forces] have the right to deliberate. [That] can contribute to strengthen the democratic system. [The armed forces] are deliberating when we use force. [They] need to express [their viewpoint], to give [their] opinion. Yes, [the armed forces] should be a brake [on the government]. . . . The Constitution provides for the participation of the armed forces in policy [matters]. If we are the guarantors of the juridical order of the state, we are obliged to suggest to the government — to the Executive or Congress — measures that we believe are desirable in order to prevent a breakdown of this juridical order.

If the armed forces are able to detect that these threats exist, one of their important roles is to make it known, to make people see, and get the necessary corrective actions taken, or avoid the problem while there is still time. The National Security Law says there should be National Security Council liaisons in all public organizations.[15]

Noticeably absent in these interviews were any proponents of the belief that the armed forces should, under certain circumstances, take power for a more or less indefinite period in order to create the conditions necessary to national security and development. In both countries, a majority of those interviewed espoused role beliefs accepting the principle of civilian control within a constitutional system. However, roughly a third of the Ecuadorian sample rejected the principle of the subordination of the armed forces, arguing for a traditional arbiter role or for a tutelary role as an active policy voice on matters of national security and development. Even so, this represents a substantial reduction, perhaps one half or more, of the proportion of officers subscribing to an arbiter/guardian role in the mid-1960s.[16]

Looking at the interviews again as belief systems, there are major differences in the degree of ambiguity and contradiction in the beliefs of individual officers. Ambiguity includes vague descriptions of the influence the military should have as a "power factor," intimations that the principle of military subordination may not apply under certain circumstances, or statements that leave unspecified the conditions under which the military might take over.[17] Contradictions include affirmations of the principle of nonintervention in politics coupled with support for intervention in a specific crisis or advocating the unconditional subordination of the military and simultaneously criticizing the government for not treating the armed forces as an important political force.[18] But the concept of contradictions, as used here, also includes more complex situations where the logical implication of one belief component is contradictory to another belief. For example, many officers argued that the military should be subordinate to civilian control, but described civilian governments as incompetent, ineffective, petty, and corrupt. At a minimum, these two ideas are in tension with each other.

Some degree of ambiguity and contradiction is normal in the belief systems of all human beings, military or civilian.[19] Nevertheless, for both descriptive and theoretical purposes, it is important to distinguish between those officers whose support for civilian control is clear, unambiguous, and coherent with their other beliefs, and those whose views of the military's role are characterized by high degrees of ambiguity and contradiction. While it might be tempting to simply disregard formal statements of belief in democracy as masking the military's "true" sentiments, doing so would misrepresent the real complexity of military thinking about their role in the current regimes. Accurately mapping military role beliefs requires resisting the urge to force complex belief systems into simplistic prodemocratic or antidemocratic boxes.

Seen from this perspective, there are important differences in role beliefs in the two countries. Although the samples are not equivalent, Table 3.3 shows that the Ecuadorian respondents had a substantially higher degree of contradiction and ambiguity among officers who argued for the subordination of the military to constitutional authority. Allowing for minor ambiguities and contradictions, only 30 to 35 percent of the 1991 sample could be classified as clear and consistent defenders of democratic role beliefs. (There were also ambiguities and contradictions among those who favored more interventionist military roles.) In contrast, the Argentine sample is characterized by a solid core of officers consistently articulating democratic role beliefs; contradictions and ambiguities exist, but these tend to be minor. Opposing viewpoints have only limited representation. Particularly among active-duty officers, the notion of the military as political guardians is overwhelmingly rejected. Longitudinal comparisons are tricky, given nonrandom samples. The Argentine data suggest a shift over time toward more consistent and unambiguous support for democratic role beliefs. The twenty officers interviewed in both years show significant declines in contradictions and ambiguities. The interview data are consistent with the conclusions of Argentine analysts that the "military issue" is dead in Argentina.[20] In a 1996 interview, a retired officer associated with the most hard-line military faction disclaimed any interest in the existing military. "For us, these are no longer the armed forces." If one equates the armed forces with their traditional political role, the interview data suggest he is correct.[21]

On the other hand, the political role of the military in Ecuador is still very much a matter of debate. Compared to the 1960s, there appear to be more professionalists and fewer officers who view the military as the guardians of national interests. Still, despite the apparent shift toward more democratic role

70

TABLE 3.3
Military Role Beliefs in Ecuador and Argentina

	Ecuador (%)			
	1991 (N = 37)			1991 (N = 37)
Democratic professionalist				
Coherent	5		Unambiguous	11
Minor contradictions	19		Minor ambiguities	11
Major contradictions	14		Major ambiguities	16
Subordination to constitutional authorities				
Coherent	3		Unambiguous	0
Minor contradictions	8		Minor ambiguities	8
Major contradictions	5		Major ambiguities	8
Guardian of national interest/ Conditional subordination				
Coherent	11		Unambiguous	0
Minor contradictions	14		Minor ambiguities	21
Major contradictions	11		Major ambiguities	16
Guardian of national security/ Tutelary model				
Coherent	3		Unambiguous	0
Minor contradictions	3		Minor ambiguities	3
Major contradictions	5		Major ambiguities	8

	Argentina (%)				
	1992 (N = 67)	1985 (N = 43)		1992 (N = 67)	1985 (N = 43)
Democratic professionalist					
Coherent	34	26	Unambiguous	33	16
Minor contradictions	0	5	Minor ambiguities	3	16
Major contradictions	1	5	Major ambiguities	0	2
Subordination to constitutional authorities					
Coherent	22	2	Unambiguous	18	2
Minor contradictions	18	14	Minor ambiguities	18	7
Major contradictions	8	14	Major ambiguities	12	21
Participant in national project/ Power factor					
Coherent	5	12	Unambiguous	0	2
Minor contradictions	2	2	Minor ambiguities	2	9
Major contradictions	0	5	Major ambiguities	5	7
Guardian of national interest/ Conditional subordination					
Coherent	1	0	Unambiguous	0	0
Minor contradictions	0	5	Minor ambiguities	3	2
Major contradictions	4	12	Major ambiguities	3	14
Guardian of national security/ Tutelary model					
Coherent	0	0	Unambiguous	0	0
Minor contradictions	3	0	Minor ambiguities	3	0
Major contradictions	2	0	Major ambiguities	2	0

beliefs, Ecuadorian officers are divided and uncertain regarding their political role, with no single dominant perspective. In Ecuador, the political context is such that even officers with clearly democratic predispositions often have ambiguous and contradictory beliefs about the role of the military within the current regime. Conversely, in Argentina, the historical and political context constrains all but the most authoritarian officers to at least formal acceptance of democratic norms of civil-military relations.

72 Toward a Dynamic Model of Military Role Beliefs: Learning from Experience

These differences in role beliefs stem, first and most directly, from the radically different experiences of the Argentine and Ecuadorian armed forces with the last military regime. The 1976–82 *Proceso de Reorganización Nacional* (*Proceso*) in Argentina ended in economic crisis and near universal civilian repudiation. The widespread use of torture and disappearances in the "dirty war" against leftist guerrillas and other "subversives" resulted in domestic and international condemnation. But the crowning blow was the military's swift defeat in the ill-planned attempt to retake the Malvinas/Falklands Islands from Great Britain. Despite competent performance by some units, particularly the Air Force, the Argentine military was not prepared to confront a highly trained and technologically superior enemy.[22] The unconditional surrender of Argentine forces quickly led to the overthrow of the Galtieri government and a hasty transition to civilian rule.[23] In contrast, the military governments of General Rodríguez Lara (1972–76) and the Triumvirate (1976–79) that succeeded him in Ecuador were inexperienced but mild-mannered *dictablandas*. The progressive reforms promised by Rodríguez Lara evaporated in the face of elite opposition and intramilitary divisions, but human rights abuses were virtually nonexistent. The economy boomed as the newly opened oil pipeline dramatically increased export income and government revenue. Despite its internal divisions, the military regime ended in an extended, negotiated transition, including a plebiscite on a new constitution containing expanded voting rights and other political reforms.[24]

The differences are readily apparent in military perceptions of the previous regime. In Ecuador, over half those interviewed considered the military government a success; one in four deemed it a mixed record with pluses and minuses. In contrast, Argentina officers overwhelmingly condemned the *Proceso* as a failure. "The military [government] was a political disaster and a military disaster." "In addition to a political, economic, and social failure, you have a military failure."[25] Roughly half the Argentine sample mentioned the military victory in the antisubversive campaign as the *Proceso*'s only accomplishment; the other half cited no positive achievements. Nearly everyone cited multiple failures: the Malvinas war, the economy, civilian opposition, and the political reaction against human rights abuses in the dirty war. In contrast, Ecuadorian officers praised the accomplishments of the preceding military governments — the investments in public infrastructure, the long-range planning and vision, honest and effective public administration, economic growth, new legislation, and modernization of military equipment — although some were critical of Rodríguez Lara's personalism and of the loss of professional development resulting from the preoccupation with government, rather than military, issues.   **73**

Failed military regimes are not a sufficient cause for changing interventionist role beliefs. History is always subject to multiple interpretations. Hence the critical question is how these militaries view the lessons of history. In Argentina, the experience of the *Proceso* and its traumatic aftermath resulted in the widespread conclusion that the armed forces "are incapable of making good governments." "I have witnessed every coup since the first revolt against Perón in 1951. [They] always started with enthusiasm, with idealism, and they always ended badly."[26] Most officers drew direct implications for the political role of the military.

First, the armed forces do not have the capacity, nor the training, nor the knowledge to govern the country. They are not [an adequate] political solution for the country. They will not be an alternative [to the government] ever again. Second, the armed forces, the army, has suffered, especially in its professional preparation, as a result of having dedicated [its] people to tasks outside of the institution.

[The lessons are] never again to return to take power, even if the country disintegrates internally. If [there are] external threats, the armed forces [will act within] their specific function. . . . If [there is] a bad government, let the citizens go to the Plaza de Mayo. Let them settle it. Let the armed forces never [again do so].

In the time of Frondizi and Illia, [we] believed in the active protagonism of the armed forces when the politicians didn't run the country [properly]. We believed in the armed forces to safeguard the highest interests of the nation. After 1982, neither the civilians nor the military believed in that.

The armed forces have learned that the worst civilian government is better than the best military government.[27]

One Ecuadorian officer drew exactly the opposite conclusion, arguing that the Ecuadorian experience proved that it was *not true* that the worst civilian government is better than any military government.[28]

These "lessons" are critical because they constrain—or fail to constrain—the political roles that one might plausibly postulate for the armed forces. In Ecuador, not only were the officers less likely to perceive failures in the previous regime, but they were also far less likely to offer explanations for those failures. Those that did tended to blame Rodríguez Lara's personalism or weak leadership. By implication, then, a different military leader might generate better results. Although Argentine officers offered no single explanation for the failures of the *Proceso*, their collective responses stress the inherent limitations of the regime—the military's lack of preparation for the task of governing and lack of consensus regarding government policies and, secondarily, the regime's lack of political legitimacy and the inapplicability of military methods for running the country. Relatively few mentioned reasons that could be easily changed by a subsequent military regime, for example, the economic policies of Martínez de Hoz, the division of the government between the three forces, or just staying in power too long. Less than 10 percent blamed the failures on General Videla or the juntas' leadership. If we take all of the statements regarding the lessons of the previous regime that constitute arguments against military government in general, rather than arguments against a particular military government (for example, that the leaders followed the wrong policies), we can construct a rough index of the depth of argument against a return to military rule in each case. Multiple reasons for a conclusion are an indication of strongly held attitudes, which are more likely to endure.[29] In Argentina, the median response was three arguments against military rule. Even if some of the arguments are subsequently invalidated, it seems unlikely that most or all could be unlearned, barring a catastrophic collapse of the civilian regime. Not only are these arguments interlinked and mutually supportive, they are also salient issues that have been extensively debated in internal military discussions and civil-military dialogues for more than a decade.[30] Equally important, nearly 20 percent of the Argentine officers offered five or more reasons. In the internal debates within the military, the latter are almost certain *not* to be persuaded by the available counterarguments. In the most unfavorable political scenarios, this core of militant anti-interventionists would be the anchor for a blocking coalition opposed to any overt return to military rule. In the current climate, in Argentina such a return would simply be unthinkable. Given the multiple traumas of the *Proceso,* opposition to traditional patterns of military intervention in politics has become a near-hegemonic belief.[31]

In Ecuador, the lessons of the previous military regime provide a relatively "thin" argument against a return to military rule. The most common reading of the Ecuadorian experience is that military governments brought important

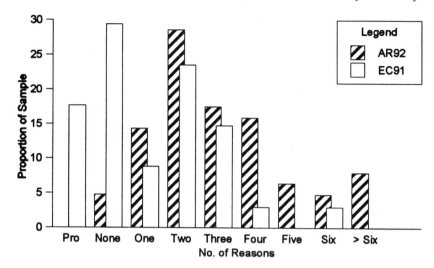

FIG. 3.1 Depth of Argument against Military Intervention

benefits for the country at the expense of significant professional costs, hence direct military rule should be avoided if possible. Still, some officers drew prointerventionist conclusions from their previous experience; nearly 30 percent mentioned no anti-interventionist lessons. Over 80 percent said military governments have been better than civilian governments.[32] The unspoken conclusion is that the military could return to power if necessary, although most would prefer to work within the current regime. An overt return to military rule would have to overcome significant minority resistance, expressed primarily in professionalist arguments, hence much will depend on the context in which that debate occurs.

The National Context

The performance of civilian institutions has long been recognized as a key element in Latin American civil-military relations.[33] To the extent that civilian governments can avoid the kinds of crises that led to military intervention in the past, they obviate any need for the armed forces to depart from their normal military roles. Conversely, to the extent that posttransition governments repeat the failures of the past, attempts to encourage less interventionist role beliefs are likely to fail.

The unfortunate government of Isabel Perón in Argentina provides a template for the kind of situations civilian governments need to avoid. Regardless of its historical veracity, the Argentine military's recall of the 1976 context is significant because it reconstructs the conditions perceived as justifying the military overthrow of an arguably democratic regime. In its principal elements, the crisis combined all of the classic ingredients for a Latin American coup: a threat to national security that directly threatened the armed forces, an economy spiraling out of control, a government incapable of resolving the problems, civilian institutions unable to remove the government by constitutional means, and strong civilian support for military intervention to resolve the crisis and restore order. The logic favoring military intervention as the preferred solution was strengthened by negative perceptions of the civilian leadership, in contrast to the positive image of the armed forces as the only disciplined institution capable of rescuing the country from chaos.[34]

76

Controlling Security Threats

From this perspective, the first critical element in the military's assessment of the domestic context after the transition is the level of perceived threat of "subversion" under subsequent civilian governments. In marked contrast to the 1960s and 1970s, the posttransition period in Argentina and Ecuador has been relatively free of the intense anxiety about internal security threats that marked earlier decades. In Argentina, the military was brutally effective in wiping out rural and urban guerrillas and their supporting networks. Sobered by the human and political costs of the revolutionary adventures of the 1970s, most of the Argentine left has renounced violent methods and embraced some form of democratic socialism. But the trauma of the *Proceso* also discredited the left, weakening its voter support, in contrast to Brazil, where the democratic left has emerged as a significant electoral force. Despite the dramatic terrorist attack on the La Tablada barracks in 1989 and continued military concern with "subversive" ideas, the "communist threat" was mostly a nonissue during the Alfonsín and Menem administrations. Most officers opposed the revisions to the National Defense Law, which gave primary responsibility for internal security to paramilitary security forces, but that debate was not tied to any immediate internal threat.

In Ecuador, the radical left has historically been much weaker; electoral politics has mostly been dominated by various forms of populism. Despite a brief surge of Castro-inspired activity in the 1960s, terrorist and guerrilla actions were rare until the mid-1980s. During the conservative administration of Febres Cordero, a new leftist group *Alfaro Vive ¡ Carajo!* conducted small-scale operations, but was quickly stamped out in a dirty, but brief, campaign waged by mostly nonmilitary forces.

In recent years, however, concern has grown over the possibility of a Sendero Luminoso-style movement in Ecuador. Although still subject to severe poverty and social discrimination, the indigenous population of the Andean provinces has become increasingly mobilized. Groups representing indigenous peoples of the oil-rich Amazonian region joined with highlands Indians in a nationwide strike in 1990, which immobilized many towns and highways. To date, the indigenous movement has been consciously nonviolent, but the leftist rhetoric of the Confederación de Nacionalidades Indígenas del Ecuador (CONAIE) fuels military concern. CONAIE is pushing for radical land reform, nullification of rural debts, and constitutional recognition of Ecuador as a multicultural, multinational society. But its most troubling demand from the military perspective is for recognition of large territories as indigenous homelands with semisovereign rights, including control over natural resources.[35] The mobilization of indigenous communities and the presence of Sendero Luminoso in neighboring Peru combined to spark fears of a possible insurgency. Still, thus far, this is only a potential threat, far short of the active guerrilla warfare that scarred Argentina in the mid-1970s. The absence of an active security rationale for interventionist role beliefs was a major change in the 1980s. However, the reemergence of a perceived internal threat in Ecuador in the 1990s has again fueled military debates over how to respond when civilian governments do not adopt the kinds of policies the armed forces view as necessary for avoiding the kind of endemic civil war that has engulfed Peru.

Protecting Institutional Interests

A second critical element in the military's evaluation of civilian government is its treatment of the military's institutional interests. Here the two cases diverge markedly. Responding to widespread civilian condemnation of the military regime, in Argentina President Alfonsín curtailed military prerogatives and insisted on the subordination of the armed forces to civilian control. Early in his term, he strengthened the powers of the civilian Ministry of Defense and reduced the authority of the military commanders. In a series of highly publicized confrontations, senior officers were summarily dismissed for making what the government considered political statements in public; within two years, more than fifty generals were forced into retirement.

Military spending was slashed dramatically. According to the most detailed accounting, total military expenditures (including pensions) fell 40 percent

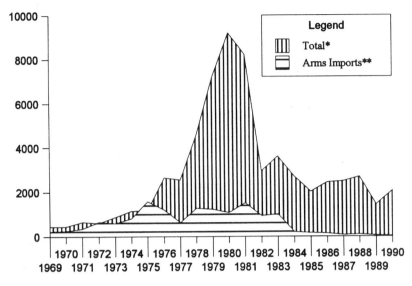

* millions of current US $ (from Scheetz 1994)   ** millions of 1982 US $ (from Scheetz)

FIG. 3.2   Military Spending: Argentina

from 1983 to 1987.[36] Excluding pensions, the army budget decreased by nearly 70 percent during the Alfonsín administration; the navy and air force budgets fell by 38 and 55 percent, respectively.[37] Arms imports dropped sharply; the military share of central government expenditures was cut in half.[38] In a inflationary economy, real military salaries fell an estimated 50 percent.[39]

By far the most controversial measure was the repeal of the military's self-amnesty and the subsequent trials of military leaders in civilian courts for criminal actions committed during the "antisubversive campaign." Five of the nine members of the three military juntas were convicted and sentenced to prison terms ranging from four years to life. The administration's antimilitary policies, coupled with its disinterest in substantive issues of defense policy and military reform, convinced many officers that the government's real agenda was to destroy the armed forces. Despite a belated government attempt to limit the scope of the prosecutions, human rights groups and sympathetic judges filed charges against several hundred officers. In April of 1987, junior officers led by camouflaged Special Forces veterans of the Malvinas war—the *cara-pintadas*[40]—staged a military revolt demanding an end to the trials and the removal of the Army chief of staff. Presidential orders to suppress the revolt were nullified by military refusal to attack the rebel units. After the dramatic

TABLE 3.4
Military Rating of Government Policies Affecting Their Institutional Interests

	Argentina: Alfonsín (%)	Argentina: Menem (%)	Ecuador: Combined (%)
Favorable	0	46	30
Mixed	7	37	9
Negative	88	4	8
No Mention	5	13	53
Responses	$N = 58$	$N = 46$	$N = 53$

meeting between Alfonsín and rebel leader Lieutenant Colonel Aldo Rico, the revolt came to a confused ending, with Rico agreeing to be placed under house arrest. The government claimed to have made no concessions to the rebels, but quickly presented to Congress the Law of Due Obedience, which effectively protected junior officers against prosecution. For the rest of his administration, Alfonsín pursued a zig-zag course of concessions and toughness, punctuated by two more *carapintada* revolts.

The Peronist government elected in 1989 came to power in the midst of a serious economic crisis. Conscious of the need to focus on economic issues and to create an image of stability, President Menem pledged to end "the military problem," pushing through an amnesty, which ended the trials, and later issuing a pardon for the convicted members of the juntas. Military salaries fell again and then recovered, but military spending dropped from 3.5 percent of GDP in 1989 to 1.9 percent in 1991.[41] Nevertheless, when challenged by another *carapintada* uprising in 1990, Menem demanded and got swift military action to smash the revolt. Although the military's budget problems have worsened, Menem seldom misses an opportunity to socialize with the military or to praise their patriotism and professionalism. The contrast with Alfonsín in symbolic terms could scarcely be greater. As a result, Menem gets generally favorable or mixed ratings for his treatment of the military, despite the lack of budgetary payoffs, compared to the overwhelmingly negative evaluation of Alfonsín's military policies.

Since the democratic transition in Ecuador, civilian governments have generally pursued a policy of cautious accommodation with the armed forces. In contrast to Alfonsín's attempts to subordinate the military, Ecuadorian presidents have respected the expanded autonomy gained by the armed forces during the previous regime. Although the president is the titular commander-in-chief, he or she must appoint the commanders of each force from among the three most senior officers. The armed forces maintain a formal military

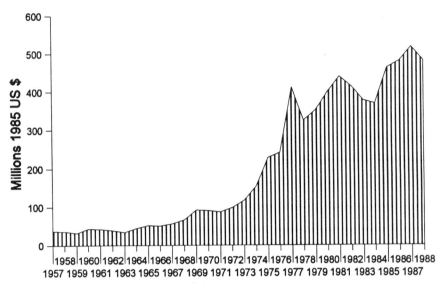

FIG. 3.3 Military Spending: Ecuador, 1957–1988

subordination to the president and, until recently, senior officers rarely spoke in public on political matters, unlike the more active policy voice of the military in tutelary regimes. The president is, however, a slender reed of civilian authority since he or she has no independent staff of civilian experts in defense policy or civil-military relations. Congress has virtually no role in budgetary control or oversight of the armed forces.[42] Until the mid-1990s, the legislature did not have a standing committee on national defense. The tacit bargain — characteristic of regimes with conditional military subordination — divides the policy table into military and nonmilitary components. Subject only to the approval of the president, the armed forces are free to run their half of the table and to formulate defense policy; on the other hand, except for the military's development activities, the armed forces generally do not interfere in policy matters outside the military realm. By tradition, the minister of defense is a retired military officer rather than a civilian. The minister is the crucial intermediary between the president and the armed forces, representing the views of the military in the cabinet, but also representing the president's policies to the military High Command and the General Staff.

Although salaries began to erode in real terms in the 1990s, military budgets — which grew explosively during the years of the oil boom, based in part upon earmarked revenues from oil — expanded in response to the 1981 clash with Peruvian forces in Paquisha and grew another 30 percent under Febres Cordero. As a result, government treatment of the armed forces has generally been a nonissue in Ecuador, with the exception of Febres Cordero, who was praised for his material and symbolic support of the armed forces and criticized for his questionable compliance with military personnel laws. On balance, Ecuadorian presidents have avoided one potentially destabilizing factor that has in the past contributed to interventionist role beliefs. The cost of that accommodation strategy has been a high degree of military autonomy from effective civilian control.

81

Managing the Economy

Beyond these two policy areas, which are directly salient to the armed forces, military evaluations of civilian performance tend to focus on the overall state of the economy and the general success or failure of civilian institutions in running the government, particularly in crisis management. Economic development has always loomed large as a fundamental task for Latin American governments. Faced with the debt crisis of the 1980s, managing the economy — more specifically, avoiding economic collapse — was perhaps the single most pressing government responsibility. As such, the economy provided the acid test of the ability of civilian leaders to govern. The economic performance of civilian governments in both countries has been mixed, but on the whole not the disaster that many analysts feared. In Ecuador, oil revenues provided a cushion against the worst effects of the debt crisis, even though falling prices and rising interest rates put an end to the economic boom of the 1970s. In 1983, and again in 1987 when a major earthquake ruptured the oil pipeline, GDP declined, but overall per capita income remained fairly steady for the decade. Civilian governments faced a tighter budgetary climate, but, in fact, government spending increased in real terms. Inflation was persistent throughout the 1980s, but well below the hyperinflationary rates experienced elsewhere.[43]

In Argentina, the Alfonsín government was immediately hit by a backlog of economic demands in reaction to the conservative antilabor policies of the *Proceso*. In its first year, the economy recovered somewhat, but inflation hit 1,000 percent, twice the rate that preceded the 1976 coup. The government devised a heterodox stabilization policy that controlled inflation, at the cost of a sharp recession in 1985. Positive growth rates returned for the next two years; however, balance of payments problems also returned. From 1982 to 1989, interest payments on the external debt averaged 50 percent of export earnings. The last year and a half of Alfonsín's term were marked by a severe economic crisis, with a cumulative decline of nearly 10 percent in GDP and 4,000 percent inflation in 1989.[44] Coupled with the loss of political support resulting from the concessions to the military on human rights issues, the economic collapse left the government in shambles. Alfonsín's personal popularity plummeted from 82 percent favorable ratings in 1984 to 36 percent in 1989; the government's approval rating dropped from a high of 48 percent to less than 10 percent,[45] forcing the government to move up the presidential transition by six months after the Radical Party's humiliating defeat in the 1989 elections.

Newly elected President Carlos Menem astonished virtually everyone by his stunning reversal of traditional Peronist economic policies. Nevertheless, his steadfast embrace of free trade and free market policies stabilized the economy and reduced inflation to previously unheard of rates. The social costs of those policies have also been high, particularly for pensioners and public sector employees. Still, most Argentines credit Menem and former Economy Minister Domingo Cavallo with having rescued the country from economic chaos. In summary, despite its political fragility, Ecuador has not confronted the kind of severe posttransition economic crises that have shaken civilian regimes in Argentina, Peru, and Brazil. In Argentina, both the poor and the middle class have been hit hard by the rising cost of living and declining real salaries. Politically, the blow was cushioned by the fact that the worst crisis came at the end of the Alfonsín administration and by the general determination to defend the democratic regime at all costs rather than suffer another round of military intervention. Menem's ability to stabilize the situation and restore positive economic growth rates has so far prevented the loss of regime legitimacy that seemed imminent in the late 1980s.

Managing Political Crises

Military officers also judge civilian leaders in terms of their political management — their ability to maintain public support, to keep the government stable — and their ability to handle crises when they occur — to avoid the perception of a power vacuum, a chaos in which no one is in control. In Argentina, civilian leaders of virtually all ideological persuasions, but especially the two major parties, emerged from the *Proceso* with a deep commitment not to repeat the errors of the past, particularly the habitual disloyalty to democratic rules of the game. When the *carapintada* revolts erupted, leaders of the Peronist and Radical Parties joined with moderates on the right and left to defend the constitutional regime. The mass media also played an important role in exposing the abuses of the "dirty war" and denouncing any hint of military wavering from the principle of civilian control. Although the Alfonsín government was hit by frequent strikes in its later years, union leaders were careful to avoid the violent, indefinite duration general strikes that destabilized non-Peronist governments in the 1960s.[46] The existence of two major parties, despite various fragments on the right and left, helped facilitate cooperation in moments of crisis. The centrist reaction against the excesses of the 1970s reinforced the mainstream parties and the more moderate wings of the right and left.

In contrast, the political fragmentation and petty partisanship of the civilian leadership in Ecuador have largely discredited the democratic regime, despite its milder economic problems. The 1978 Constitution and the new Political Parties Law introduced a number of reforms intended to strengthen Ecuador's historically weak political institutions.[47] Partly as a result of the subsequent congressional repeal of the minimum vote requirement for national parties, the reforms had little or no effect. Term limits barring most representatives from reelection to the unicameral legislature guarantee a high proportion of inexperienced, single-term legislators. With ten or more parties represented in Congress, none holding more than a minority of the seats, incentives for responsible behavior are minimal. Although the 1978 Constitution created the Tribunal of Constitutional Guarantees to arbitrate constitutional conflicts, Congress, the president, the Supreme Court, and the Tribunal itself have engaged in a seemingly endless series of disputes over their respective powers, with frequent mutual accusations of unconstitutional behavior. The presidency of Febres Cordero was notorious for its semipermanent constitutional crises, but intransigent and intractable executive-legislative disputes have been a constant feature of posttransition politics.[48] Three incidents symbolize the decay of democratic politics in Ecuador:

In 1991, a nation-wide television audience waited from mid-afternoon till well past midnight as President Borja was unable to deliver the traditional Independence Day address to Congress because repeated walkouts and refusal to compromise prevented that body from reaching the minimum number of votes necessary to elect a presiding officer. Four years later, President Durán Ballén returned the favor by walking out and refusing to deliver the annual address, because two-thirds of Congress was absent.

After failing to win the presidential nomination of the Social Christian Movement, veteran politician Sixto Durán Ballén simply formed his own party, Ecuador's nineteenth, and won the 1992 elections. Not surprisingly, his coalition won only 15 of the 77 seats in the legislature. Once in office, his popularity dropped from 60% approval to 10% in the first year.

According to one count, more than one-fourth of the members of the 1992–1993 legislature abandoned, or were expelled from, the parties which elected them.[49]

The cumulative effect has been to severely erode civilian and military confidence in the current regime. Sixty percent of the Ecuadorian officers interviewed gave negative or mostly negative ratings to posttransition civilian governments, compared to less than 30 percent of the Argentine sample.

Societal Support

Studies of coups and military governments have repeatedly stressed the importance of civilian support and political alliances as key factors in military intervention in politics. Rarely have the armed forces of any Latin American country acted alone; no military government has ever been a purely military regime. The political relations between the armed forces and civil society are equally crucial to the construction of posttransition systems of civil-military relations.

In Argentina, the traumatic experience of the *Proceso* and the painful postwar coming to terms with the "dirty war" and the Malvinas defeat radically delegitimized the armed forces in the eyes of virtually all segments of civil society, including most of the military's traditional political allies.[50] Free market policies helped some sectors of capital, but adversely affected others, particularly import-substitution industries. The antisubversive campaign sometimes snared the offspring of elite families, and the two-year public accounting of the "dirty war" by CONADEP and the trial of the juntas also impacted elite views of the military. In a 1985 interview, an Argentine businessman recounted his hatred of Peronism and his intense dislike for Alfonsín's "socialist" policies. Nevertheless, he said, "We should never go back to military governments .... They are not competent to govern .... They are still defending those who committed murder, torture, robbery. They say it was necessary, the only way to fight communism, but now we know that they killed many innocent people, who had nothing to do with terrorism. If we compare [Argentina] to the Nazi experience, the Germans—all my family, uncles, cousins, friends—nobody justified the Nazi regime; nobody said the Jews deserved it." When asked how the private sector would respond to a Peronist-leftist government, he blanched visibly and responded, "It would be a disaster. The few private enterprises that remain would give up, go home, give up the business, but they would not go back to calling for the armed forces. Among my friends, the people I know, nobody wants another military government."[51] From the elite perspective, the Malvinas/Falklands war with Great Britain was the final proof that the military was neither a reliable nor entirely rational ally. Public opinion polls in the mid-1980s showed near unanimous support for the prosecution of military officers for human rights violations; the armed forces ranked near the bottom in questions about public confidence in national institutions.[52]

The effect on military role beliefs was direct and powerful. Officers who supported civilian control of the military received strong civilian backing; those who dared to speak on political matters were publicly condemned; attempts to defend the antisubversive campaign were met with moral outrage. Even for officers with less than democratic beliefs, there was no publicly acceptable alternative discourse. In this climate, it was easy for professionalist officers to argue that relegitimating the armed forces as an institution required strict subordination of the military to civilian authority, despite the negative reaction to Alfonsín's military policies. Any return to military intervention in politics would fail, given the internal divisions within the military. Any failed intervention might trigger "the Costa Rican option," a national decision to abolish the armed forces. Despite intense military opposition to the human rights trials of junior officers, the organizers of the *carapintada* movement recognized from the beginning that any attempt to overthrow Alfonsín, even without a military takeover, would be opposed by force within the military and categorically rejected by the rest of society. As a result, the Semana Santa revolt was carefully constructed as a revolt against the Army chief of staff. Rebel leaders took great pains to disavow any intent to act against the government, even though the refusal to carry out Alfonsín's order to suppress the revolt was a blatant defiance of his constitutional authority as commander-in-chief. Public opinion in opposition to traditional patterns of military intervention in politics thus severely constrains the range of alternative role beliefs that can be plausibly argued in Argentina.

In contrast, public opinion in Ecuador shares the military's positive perceptions of previous military regimes and its negative views of civilian performance. In a 1991 survey conducted in the two largest cities, nearly 80 percent of the respondents rated the armed forces and the Church as the nation's two most trusted institutions. Large majorities expressed their distrust of the legislature, the executive, and the judiciary. Almost 85 percent said they lacked confidence in the political parties. These perceptions, in turn, result in a high level of civilian support for an active military role in politics.

Sixty-five percent said they would prefer a coup if populist candidate Abdalá Bucarám won the 1992 presidential elections.

Seventy-six percent agreed that "if the national interests are in danger in times of crisis, the armed forces should intervene to change the government."

Seventy-seven percent agreed that "if national security is threatened, the armed forces should take over the government."

Eighty-five percent agreed that "the armed forces should avoid coups, but should pressure the government when they see that things are not going well," in effect, the tutelary option.[53]

86

While most Ecuadorians still prefer democracy over dictatorship in principle, in practice the Ecuadorian people are deeply disillusioned with the current democratic regime. In a 1996 survey, 80 percent said that they would defend democracy if it were threatened, but half said they would accept an authoritarian regime in extraordinary circumstances.[54] Not surprisingly, many Ecuadorians endorse the military's role as a tutelary guardian of the national interests and an alternative government if necessary to defend "national security."

The International Context

The impact of the international context on military role beliefs is less visible. In Argentina, the shift in formal role beliefs toward subordination to civilian authority was overdetermined by the confluence of domestic factors. The military's disastrous experience in the *Proceso*—especially the military defeat in the Malvinas—was probably sufficient in itself to discredit traditional notions of the military as a guardian of the national interests. The intense antimilitary reaction to the horrors of the antisubversive campaign and widespread condemnation of ideas associated with that period combined to produce a powerful pressure for fundamental changes in civil-military relations that a discredited and divided military could not resist. Thus, Argentine officers rarely mentioned external factors in either set of interviews; those that did generally stressed their secondary impact. Even so, in the uncertainties of the moment, strong support from the United States and the rest of the international community was undoubtedly important for Alfonsín in the Semana Santa revolt. President Bush's endorsement of Menem in the face of the Seineldín uprising in 1990 likewise bolstered the government's position, regardless of whether it changed military behavior.

Military statements indicate their awareness that the international climate had changed. One of the leaders of the Semana Santa revolt recalled, "We started from the assumption that everything was against us—the international context, [and] the national context."[55] A critic of the *carapintadas* agreed, "The world is different [now]; the international context includes democracy in all countries of the world . . . . To break the rules of the world game that is consolidating itself, was an act of desperation. . . . Swimming against the current of the world is irrational." [56]

While U.S. opposition to military governments and the possibility of international sanctions received some attention, military references to the international context tended to focus more on the general climate of opinion and on the need for Argentina to regain international respectability. One officer recalled working in an international organization during the *Proceso:* "People looked at me like a criminal. In Europe, the military government was considered a mafia of delinquents in uniform who opposed human beings." [57] Acceptance in the international community meant changes in the role of the military:

> The problem of Argentina is that we have always been estranged from the world. We believed that there is no international order, that there are no actors with the power to police that order. We found out differently in the Malvinas.

> To progress ahead, to have relations with the First World, Argentina will have to be democratic. Before, the U.S. promoted military governments. That's not possible today. You can't do that in today's world. The concept of the world is different now. There have to be civil-military relations that are legal and normal.[58]

Even if the international context merely reinforces the domestic reasons for redefinition of civil-military relations in Argentina, the existence of that reinforcement — as another supportive layer of causation, another line of argument — is not inconsequential.

In Ecuador, the constraints imposed by the international environment are more apparent, though not always consciously acknowledged. One army officer argued that in the 1986 revolt by Air Force commandos that briefly held President Febres Cordero hostage,

> [i]nternational policy and the United States played an important role. Officers who might think about a coup had to consider what might happen. . . . International opposition was important because of economic pressure. If the U.S. imposes economic sanctions on a small state like Ecuador, it could cut traditional exports like bananas and coffee and oil. The government would not be able to pay the salaries of the armed forces or the public administration, which imposes limits on military idealism. The cure could be worse than the disease.[59]

Another officer noted, "There is a constant fear that if Ecuador has a coup the country will be isolated." [60] For a small, economically vulnerable country, the threat of economic sanctions has to be taken seriously. Other officers stressed the change in U.S. policy in particular: "Latin American military dictatorships have been eliminated by the international context, . . . by U.S. pressure for democracy. As long as there is U.S. support . . . there will be continuity in the system of formal democracy." "The government of the United States will not permit military governments anywhere. If we are dependent countries, [the ability of] the armed forces to take power [is] limited."[61]

For officers predisposed to democratic or professionalist norms of civil-military relations, the international context provides an additional argument against direct military intervention in politics. For others, the conflicting impulses generated by the domestic environment and the international context are a primary source of contradictory role beliefs. Asked about the relative merits of civilian and military governments, an Ecuadorian officer expressed the general view: "Military governments do 30 to 40 percent more. Civilian governments are looting the country, selling democracy to the highest bidder. The degeneration of Congress is a scandal. That could push the people to call for a government of order. The military are the only ones who could do it, but it is not a good time for that." An army officer pointed to the likely direction for resolution of that contradiction: "The military are more aware [of the country's problems] and better trained than the civilians. If the context is not right for military government, the military has to put itself behind the civilian [leaders] to make sure they are marching in the right [direction]."[62] If the external environment demands formal democracy, but the civilian leaders are incapable of effectively managing a democratic regime, then the military must act politically within that regime. Historically the Ecuadorian military has had neither the self-confidence nor the aggressive political posture of their Guatemalan or Peruvian colleagues. Hence, Ecuadorian proponents of a tutelary military role tend to favor a softer, semitutelary system, with active military "advice" on matters related to national security but not military imposition of policies, especially on nonmilitary matters. Nevertheless, in a regime where many officers are still only conditionally loyal, military "advice" is a subtle but powerful form of pressure. In 1982, opposition from the Army Council of Generals led to the resignation of the minister of defense, a retired admiral, following a speech in which he endorsed President Hurtado's call for a national debate to set conditions for an end to hostilities with Peru along the ill-defined frontier established after their 1941 war. Shortly thereafter, Hurtado dropped the proposal.

Although the proportion of officers advocating the tutelary model in 1992 was fairly small, those numbers are likely to increase as long as civilian institutions remain weak and fragmented, and international conditions are perceived as unfavorable to direct military intervention. A tutelary or semitutelary "solution" resolves the contradiction between the domestic and international context, in a manner consistent with the military's view of the civilian leadership as fundamentally irresponsible, without risking confrontation with the United States or isolation from the world community.

In return visits to Ecuador in 1995 and 1996, I found ample evidence of increasing military participation in politically charged policy debates.

• The armed forces actively opposed both bids submitted for construction of a second oil pipeline, charging that national security concerns had been sacrificed in the rush for lucrative contracts and payoffs. Under pressure, the government asked the two consortia involved to submit new proposals. Military opposition was also a key factor in the Durán government's decision not to push for privatization of the national electricity company.

89

• The Army Council of Generals appears to have played a critical role in resolving the 1995 impasse between Congress and the president over the appointment of a new vice president.

• In a two-day conference of military officers and various civilians, top army officials were outspokenly critical of the neoliberal economic model espoused by the Durán government. They were emphatic in condemning systemic corruption and the absence of civilian political leadership. The chief of the Army General Staff argued that Ecuadorian "democracy" had brought neither justice nor development nor security. "If the hegemonic power groups are constantly increasing their power at the expense of society's ability to choose its own destiny, . . . the question we must ask is, 'Are we really living in democracy?' "[63]

Although the regime remains nominally democratic, the armed forces have assumed an increasingly active policy voice on matters of concern to senior officers, including the future of the current system. In contrast to Argentina and the cases discussed in chapter 2, the trend in Ecuador has been toward an increasing military role in politics.

While the underlying dynamics — economic crisis and political decay — are similar to other cases, three events accelerated the movement toward what is now arguably a tutelary regime. First, the military's solid performance in the 1995 border war with Peru in the Alto Cenepa further bolstered the prestige and popularity of the armed forces. For the first time in the long history of that border dispute, Ecuadorian forces held their own against Peru, inflicting substantially higher casualties and aircraft losses against their larger and usually better equipped rival.[64] Public opinion polls now show the armed forces rank ahead of the Catholic Church in terms of public trust in institutions; government institutions, especially political parties, are overwhelmingly distrusted. In meetings with senior officers, these surveys were almost always mentioned.

Second, after three years of only moderately successful efforts to bring down inflation, the government of Sixto Durán Ballen virtually collapsed in a corruption scandal involving the misuse of secret funds by Vice President Dahik, who fled to Costa Rica, requesting political asylum on the grounds that he could not receive a fair trial in Ecuadorian courts. Partly as a result of stiff U.S. opposition, the armed forces resisted civilian entreaties to take over, but the scandal further discredited the civilian political leadership. Instead of acting energetically on the corruption issue, President Durán engaged in a prolonged battle with the head of the Supreme Court over who would control the microfilm records of the vice president's secret bank account. To add insult to injury, voters rejected every item in a multi-item referendum on the government's long-awaited constititional reforms, which managed to confuse even the lawyers without addressing any of the fundamental flaws of the current system.

Finally, faced again with a bewildering array of candidates in the 1996 elections, Ecuadorian voters ended up with a runoff choice between Jaime Nebot, a conservative protégé of Febres Cordero, and fiery Guayaquil populist, Abdalá Bucarám. Despite military grumbling about Bucarám's history of antimilitary statements, Army Commander Paco Moncayo — hero of the 1995 war and leader of the nationalist-reformist sector of the military — pledged publicly that the armed forces would respect the election results. From the perspective of the nationalist wing of the army, Bucarám was the lesser of two evils since his opponent had pledged to deepen Durán's free-market policies and to include military industries among possible privatizations. Given his unstable support, Bucarám would also be less likely than Nebot to challenge military prerogatives.

Playing on voters' fears of more austerity programs, Bucarám won handily, but his promises of government giveaways to the poor soon foundered on the hard realities of an empty treasury and accumulated foreign debt. Bucarám's erratic personal behavior and authoritarian responses to any opposition provided a field day for the media and political critics. Government officials starred in repeated corruption scandals, while the public awaited the government's oft-postponed economic plan. In the end, the economic package was not that different from the previous government's policies, except for an Argentine-inspired proposal to tie Ecuador's exchange rate to the dollar. The government's economic program was denounced by economic elites and the opposition majority in Congress before it was even fully announced. Union leaders and opposition parties mobilized a massive protest, putting an estimated two million demonstrators in the streets. The crisis culminated with a congressional decision to declare the presidency vacant, on the grounds that the president was "mentally incompetent," rather than go through the impeachment process. That decision, however, left both the vice president and the president of Congress claiming to be president, while Bucarám barricaded himself in the presidential palace. Subsequent negotiations brokered by General Moncayo resulted in an agreement permitting the vice president to assume the presidency temporarily until Congress could elect an interim president.[65] Bucarám quickly flew into exile to avoid corruption charges. Resolution of the crisis without a coup further enhanced the military's image as "the guarantors of democracy."

Disaggregating the Armed Forces

With some notable exceptions, academic analyses of the Latin American military tend to treat the armed forces as a unitary actor. Although individual officers play a somewhat larger role in journalistic accounts, in the social science literature references to "the military" are commonplace. "The military" takes actions (for example, "retreats to the barracks"), expresses emotions (such as, "resentment of government policies"), and possesses attitudes (for example, "distrust of civilian politicians"). Compared to civilian institutions, the armed forces may be relatively cohesive and disciplined, particularly when threatened. But the internal divisions within the armed forces are also critical to understanding military behavior. The collapse of military regimes is inexplicable without the fissures between the officers in the government and those who remained in military posts.[66] In the literature on democratic transitions, O'Donnell and Schmitter stress the complex interplay between the *"blandos"* (soft-liners) favoring a negotiated return to a civilian regime and the *"duros"* (hard-liners) trying to derail the transition process.[67] Yet, these simple distinctions are not very satisfactory. The O'Donnell-Schmitter analysis does not adequately account for the origins of the factional divisions between hard- and soft-liners nor what happens to those factions after the transition is completed. The *carapintada* revolts in Argentina, the failed coup attempts in Venezuela, and Serrano's unsuccessful *autogolpe* in Guatemala all point to the central importance of divisions within the military. The unresolved question is how to conceptualize and analyze these internal differences.

Drawing on the three sets of interviews in this study, I argue that the key differences are ideological. Although military officers are distinguished by their high degree of institutional socialization and their strong identification with the military institution, they obviously do not all think alike. Both by social origin and in their daily lives, military officers are part of the larger society. Hence, it should not be surprising that the political divisions of society are reproduced within the military. More than twenty-five years ago, Martin Needler suggested that "on top of the primary set of conditioning factors such as those which the American voting studies indicate are the significant ones in terms of determining party preferences (family tradition, social and economic level, and ethnic or other particularistic identification) is imposed a second set of factors peculiar to the military profession: rank, branch of service, occupational specialty, and career pattern."[68] In Argentina, virtually the entire political spectrum has had some presence in the military. Although the human rights abuses of the *Proceso* reinforced the military's public image as a monolithically right-wing caste, in fact, leftist junior officers participated in clandestine dialogues with the Montoneros in the early 1970s.[69] Peronist officers are underrepresented, especially at the highest ranks, but constitute an important fraction of the officer corps. While most officers would be considered conservative in U.S. terms, in practice there are important distinctions within the military "right," including liberal internationalists, the nationalist right, traditional conservatives, and the Catholic ultraright.[70] Ecuadorian politics has traditionally been less ideological and more personalized; hence, ideological divisions within the officer corps are less sharply drawn than in Argentina. Nevertheless, there are obvious differences between the more hard-line conservatives, traditional liberals, and various moderates and reformers, and between pro-U.S. and nationalist officers.[71] In both countries, these ideological positions include differing definitions of the preferred economic model, conflicting conceptions of the relation between the state and society, alternative international alignments, and divergent interpretations of "democracy." In both militaries, these ideological factions generally exist without any formal organization, behind the facade of institutional unity and nonpartisanship.

The relationship between ideology and military role beliefs is mostly indirect. There is no necessary relation between political beliefs and alternative models of civil-military relations. In Argentina, the disastrous experience of the *Proceso* and a hostile domestic and international context combine to constrain the range of plausible role beliefs to some version of civilian control, regardless of one's ideological position. In Ecuador, the poor performance of civilian institutions and the relative success of the previous military regime encourage the persistence of traditional role beliefs and ambiguous or contradictory beliefs about civilian control, despite international opposition to any return to military rule.

Nevertheless, within the limits imposed by the domestic and international context, there are significant ideological differences. In the 1985 Argentine interviews, liberals and conservative officers were more ambiguous and contradictory in their beliefs about the political role of the military and somewhat more likely to stress subordination to constitutional authority than a positive loyalty to the democratic regime. Conversely, officers identified with the reform wing of the Peronist Party, the Radical Party, or the left were more likely to be coherent and unambiguous in their role beliefs and somewhat more likely to espouse democratic professionalist views rather than just subordination to civilian authority. In the 1992 interviews, officers identifying with the principal liberal[72] party, the UCD, were more likely to espouse the political subordination of the military and nonintervention in politics, in essence, classic professionalism; those associated with the Radical Party or Frondizi's MID were more likely to argue for a democratic professionalism. Reflecting Peronism's transformation from a movement to a mainstream party, by 1992 its followers were more united in favor of a democratic professionalist position. On the other hand, supporters of MODIN, founded by former *carapintada* leader Aldo Rico, maintained the traditional Peronist conception of the armed forces as a partner in a national project, a notion with roots in Peron's conception of a nationalist trade union–military alliance.[73] Officers who defined the military's role as a *factor de poder* were prominent in the leadership of the *carapintada* movement. Six of the eight officers espousing guardian or tutelary roles said that no party represented their political views. Given the smaller sample size and greater dispersion across categories, the Ecuadorian results are more ambiguous, but self-identified conservatives and liberal internationalists were more likely to espouse conditional subordination; reformists and the moderate left were more likely to support democratic professionalist role beliefs.

The principal effect of ideology is to form the prism through which civilian (and military) performance in office is evaluated. For military officers as well as ordinary citizens, what you "see" depends on where you stand. Government policies and programs applauded by one ideological viewpoint will be condemned as contrary to the national interest, or a threat to national security, from a different vantage point.

In Argentina, the liberal internationalists, for example, were scornful of Alfonsín's decision to join the Non-Aligned Movement and skeptical about his imposition of wage and price controls. Even as he defended the "profoundly democratic traditions" of the Argentine military, one high-ranking liberal officer from the *Proceso* argued that Alfonsín needed "to cut spending, bureaucracy, [and] speed up privatization" and seek better relations with Washington. Like many Ecuadorian officers, he seemed to believe in democracy in principle, but not to have much confidence in this democracy, in contrast to the "good relations" between the armed forces and constitutional governments from 1853 to 1930! Seven years later, he said,

I voted for Alfonsín and not for Menem. As a government leader, I believe Menem is much more perceptive of Argentine needs, much more imaginative and active in his solutions, even when there is a large dose of corruption. Faced with the needs of Argentina, Alfonsín believed that the solution was in [being] the prime minister, not in [dealing with] the economy, social problems, and politics. I give Menem a 7, [and] Alfonsín a 4. [Menem] has done things that make people continue believing in democracy. Menem could make changes happen in the country, [especially] the economy, and [make] his party, [which has] always been authoritarian, more democratic. [That has been] his great merit, without having changed his policy toward the armed forces. But he has [also] made the military feel useful — [sending] the frigates to the Gulf and [army troops] to Croatia.[74]

A liberal navy officer concurred:

Menem has been an infinitely better government than the Radical administration. [He has] an integrated national policy. The armed forces never had the courage or never knew how to convert to a liberal state, whether for lack of ability or because of the resistance. With the Radicals in power, it should have been a government of liberty and liberalism, [but Alfonsín] followed the old statist concepts. . . . [Today] the conditions for destabilization don't exist. The armed forces have changed their perspective. They are an element of the government; [but] they are not the political power. The government could get into a crisis or tough times, but not the system. The armed forces support the policies of Menem and Cavallo for the economy.[75]

On the other side, a retired army officer with political views closer to those of the Peronist left was relatively sympathetic toward Alfonsín in 1985 and cautiously optimistic about the future. Seven years later, at the midpoint of the Menem administration, he was bitterly critical of the government's economic policies and its close relations with the United States.

[There is] no real mission for Latin American militaries, except those assigned to them in the New World Order — the fight against drugs [and] participation in international forces such as the Persian Gulf and Yugoslavia. They will also have to have an internal security mission. The IMF [International Monetary Fund] economic model creates increasing resistance from the populace — the same as in the U.S. In Argentina, over 50 percent of the population is below the poverty line. Cholera is spreading; tuberculosis has returned. But there is no prospect for any way out. Under the Brady plan, it will take us twenty years to pay back the new loans, and that's only one-half of the debt. What are we going to do with the people left out by that model — retirees getting $150 a month, workers making $250 per month. With a minimum wage, you can't live — pay the rent, eat — it's one-quarter to one-third of the basic family budget. Without repression, this model wouldn't work. You have to convince the people to suffer through it with billy sticks and rifles. . . . With the new world order, the best thing to do would be to dissolve the armed forces. If by some magic, criminals disappeared, we would get rid of the police. If there are no conflicts, we shouldn't invent missions. In the new world order, the armed forces have no role. . . . There isn't any political alternative today in Argentina. The Peronists and the Radical Party are exactly the same; the same domestic power groups are in control. The international powers — the United States [and] Western Europe would prefer the Radicals — the same liberal model, but the UCR is cleaner, less corrupt, maybe more thoughtful and more gradual, but the same result. Menem will leave three-quarters of the population impoverished in two years; the Radicals will do the same in ten years.[76]

A conservative nationalist echoed the criticism of Menem's foreign policy:

[Menem's] foreign policy is excessively subordinated to the U.S. [There is] a race to be the most loyal to the U.S., handing over things in negotiations with no return. Perhaps [it has produced] some economic gains, [but I don't like] genuflecting [before the U.S.]. [Argentina's] participation in the Gulf was ably played; the benefits outweighed the costs. It was a symbol of the change from the tradition of non-alignment. The Condor and nuclear policy [were] ceded without negotiation, without benefits [in return], giving up a long-term effort. In fields where Argentina had advanced technology, [they] gave it up, giving up [our] limited margin for negotiation [in exchange] for supermarkets.[77]

These differing views of government policies are clearly rooted in different ideological vantage points. Not surprisingly, a significant part of the shift toward more coherent and unambiguous military support for civilian control in Argentina comes from the large contingent of liberal internationalist officers who are now much more likely to see the democratic system as capable of embodying their views than in 1985. While conservative nationalists dislike Menem's foreign policy, their criticism is muted by the success to date of his economic policies, by Argentina's new international respectability, and by the professional and political benefits of active military participation in international peacekeeping forces. Leftist officers are more alienated from the democratic system under Menem, but constitute only a minuscule fraction of the officer corps.

In Ecuador, the ideological divisions are more muted and often overlain with personal loyalties. Yet despite restrictive military personnel laws, each civilian government was, in fact, able to construct a military high command that was in general terms ideologically sympathetic to its views. Roldós and Hurtado drew support from the more reformist and nationalist elements of the military. Conservative and liberal officers applauded Febres Cordero's economic policies, his support for Reagan's policy in Central America, and his strong anticommunism. The ability of each new civilian government, with the partial exception of Rodrigo Borja, to find support within a sector of the armed forces was (and is) an important impediment to military intervention in a system institutionally predisposed to poor government performance. The fact that control of the government has alternated between conservative and reformist parties has likewise helped prevent even greater alienation from that system.

The impact of ideology should not be overstated. Officers combining elements of different ideological positions are probably as common as those representing the pure ideal types. One air force officer, for example, stressed that he was a liberal, but also a nationalist. Another candidly acknowledged, "I have my own amorphous beliefs."[78] Among career-minded officers with little political vocation, most hold only vaguely articulated political positions. Precisely because of these variations within the officer corps, the strong institutional identification with the armed forces plays a critical role in intramilitary politics. Appealing to shared institutional interests is the key strategy for communicating across ideological differences. Threats to the "armed institution" contribute to the construction of cross-factional alliances. In the internal politics of the military, ideologically discrete factions normally represent a minority of the officer corps, so each faction must seek alliances and try to win support from the ideologically less committed. Without alliances, no consensus on military action is possible.

Thus the Semana Santa revolt against Alfonsín won widespread military support, even among Navy and Air Force officers and factions ideologically opposed to Rico's populist nationalism, because the movement was carefully constructed to focus on the defense of the institution and the protection of junior officers against prosecution for human rights abuses. In an atmosphere where many officers, especially conservatives, believed that Alfonsín was trying to destroy the armed forces, Operation Dignity succeeded because it was perceived as a moral defense of the institution. Rico's subsequent revolt failed in large measure because it was perceived by many officers as defending his own personal interests, in defiance of institutional rules and disciplinary norms.[79] The Villa Martelli revolt ended in stalemate, with Colonel Seineldín appealing to conservative and nationalist officers for revindication of the military's fight against subversion and attacking Army Chief of Staff Caridi for having violated institutional rules in his persecution of Rico's supporters. Although Caridi alienated some of his initial supporters, he could nevertheless claim to have won concessions from Alfonsín on the trials and media attacks. Privately he could also appeal to liberal officers distrustful of Seineldín's nationalist and fundamentalist views.

After Semana Santa, the *carapintada* movement was increasingly divided by ideological tensions between Rico's nationalist, populist wing and Seineldín's ultra-Catholicism. The Catholic right was historically anti-Peronist. Most of Rico's military associates in his new party are former Peronists, and the party's program draws heavily from the conservative nationalist variant of Peronist ideology. Differences in personal style accentuated the ideological differences, which fellow officers readily identified:

> Rico is Western and Christian, [but he] separates religion from politics. Seineldín [is] a converted Muslim, who believes that [divine] law supports politics. [He is] more fanatic than a nonconvert, a Muslim, therefore a fundamentalist. Personally, [he is] a very good person; he gives [his] example to his men. Rico is more direct, less friendly than Seineldín, who tries to please everybody. From an ideological perspective, Rico is a popular nationalist. Seineldín is an elitist nationalist.
>
> On the military side, Seineldín is the prototype of military discipline and subordination, a military man through and through, [someone who is] naturally disciplined. Rico has been undisciplined and rebellious since the Colegio Militar. . . . Seineldín [is] nationalist and very Catholic, not populist. Rico is more populist and nationalist.[80]

97

By December 1990, having ended the trials and promised a pardon for the juntas, Menem could blame Seineldín's supporters for sacrificing the military institution's hierarchical character on the altar of a personal crusade. Once the human rights issue was removed from the agenda, the right-wing argument looked more and more partisan, rather than institutional, and the professionalist argument for military discipline became more compelling. Reduced to his own narrow ideological base, Seineldín was no longer the powerful figure of Villa Martelli.

The Internal Debate Model

The *carapintada* revolts were a dramatic instance of what is usually a much less visible process of political debate within the armed forces. Typically these discussions focus on alternative courses of action—the merits and demerits, advantages and risks, of acting or not acting—in a crisis situation. But action alternatives cannot be divorced from the larger debate about the political role of the armed forces. Should the armed forces intervene? What kind of intervention? What the military should do in a particular crisis depends in part on the norms that are postulated for military conduct in general. The interview evidence suggests that these norms were actively debated after the transition to civilian government.

For many years, the armed forces have studied the question "What is the role of the armed forces in the country?" It is a question [that is] under permanent evaluation.

At the level of colonels and generals, the Council [of Generals] discusses internal problems and [problems] of the country. The generals talked to the colonels.

The military talks about the military dictatorship, [about] how to counter political criticism of the armed forces, [about] military participation in the politics of the country.[81]

Although the reality is undoubtedly more confused and unstructured, the underlying process can be conceptualized as ideologically distinct factions offering alternative conceptions of the role of the military in politics, seeking support from other factions and from ideologically less committed officers in an internal debate about what should be done, given the context as they perceive it.[82] The rules that govern this internal debate and determine its outcome are, at best, poorly understood since these discussions normally take place in private with no public records. Nevertheless, based on the interview data and theoretical analogy, I hypothesize that to be persuasive in this debate arguments must be credible, relevant, and attractive to outside constituencies.[83]

Arguments must be credible, which requires that they be viewed as fitting or consistent with the perceived context. Thus when confronted with a description of a Brazilian-style tutelary role, Argentine officers repeatedly responded that such a role would not be feasible in Argentina.

This is not the role of the armed forces, not in Argentina. [These are] different situations, different levels of culture, different transitions, and different political classes. The Argentine military has been burned; they want nothing to do with politics.

The Brazilian, Chilean, and Argentine models [are] all different. In Brazil, in 1985, [there was] a transition negotiated with Tancredo Neves, which closed the circle on the past, [keeping] seven ministers for insurance . . . . In Chile, Pinochet is the guarantee . . . . [In Uruguay,] the Naval Club Pact [dealt with] human rights. . . . In Argentina, we know that we are not the solution to the country's problems. We had two tries and we failed.

In Brazil, [the military is] still strong. [It's] a different concept, [coming after] a military government with a different structure, incorporating many civilians, with no fight against subversion, no Malvinas, not ending with the trauma of Argentina. [The armed forces] coparticipated in the military government with the civilians, who continue to respect the armed forces. No politicians came to discredit the military.[84]

Negative; absolutely not. . . . Never again. We have to learn from history. Tutelary regimes are traditional in some countries — Paraguay, Bolivia — but things are changing. . . . We are infinitely further away than before from that kind of situation in Argentina.[85]

In contrast, many Ecuadorian officers clearly felt that it was not only feasible for the military to play a tutelary or guardian role, but that the failures of the civilian political leadership made it necessary for the military to play a more interventionist role.

Democracy [in Ecuador is] shaky, embryonic; it has other faults that have to be corrected. The political structures are inappropriate for democratic life, especially the party structure and the incongruence between the philosophies and actual conduct of the parties. The parties are controlled by personal groups, which impedes democracy. The political ignorance of the people [is such that many] members do not know the name of the party.

[There is] political immaturity and democracy, a lack of policy objectives, of [clearly defined] paths [that] lead to definition of the objectives of the nation. [There] is inconsistency, a lack of continuity from one government to the next. What should be the behavior of the military to guarantee democratic development and the well-being of the people? [The armed forces] can't be supporting all [the civilian governments], excusing them, [because that just] perpetuates the immorality and inefficiency.

[Latin American] sociopolitical structure makes it necessary . . . that the armed forces become a regulating element, not an arbiter, so that the presence of the armed forces acts as a brake on the excesses of [government] powers and permanent deficiencies of [our] leaders. Except for Mexico, the [political systems] of the rest of Latin America are weak, [with] a total absence of leaders. The regime of parties has not functioned; [the parties] are prostituted and discredited. The people have lost faith. According to the surveys, 96 percent of the public is opposed to the current government; 50 percent prefer a dictatorship. . . . The politicians fear the armed forces because they don't behave ethically as they should and they run [the government like] a political cause, not in the technical sense, but [in the sense of] serving [their own] economic and political groups. They are always afraid that the armed forces can throw them out. I see this as positive, [for] the military to be a brake.

[The military] is the guarantor of the constituted order. Therefore it cannot be subject to the power that it has to guarantee. [The armed forces] are guarantors of the electoral process. [Therefore] their link is not to a political party, but only to the president who is the commander-in-chief. The intermediary is the minister of defense. [One of our] achievements [is to have] a military [Ministry of Defense]. [That's] not like the U.S. . . . [The Ecuadorian legislature] is not like the U.S. Congress.[86]

Note the explicit link in these statements to the perceived capabilities of civilian and military leaders. Ecuadorian officers frequently argued that military officers are more competent than civilian leaders because (1) they understand and value national objectives; (2) having served in frontier garrisons, they know the entire country; (3) they are better educated in military schools than in civilian universities; and (4) they study and analyze the problems facing the country.[87] In contrast, the image of the armed forces as the moral reserve of society, the guardians of the national interest, is hardly credible in Argentina.

In addition to credibility, to carry weight in the internal debate, arguments

99

must be relevant to the concerns facing the armed forces. Ecuador faces a potentially significant internal security threat, hence reformist versions of the 1960's security and development doctrines are still perceived as relevant. One of the weaknesses of professionalist arguments in Ecuador is that they do not really offer any rationale that connects support for the democratic regime to avoidance of a Sendero-style conflagration. Tutelary arguments, on the other hand, can be rationalized as necessary for national security, given a political class that seems unwilling or unable to mobilize resources for the kind of pre-emptive civic action programs many army officers feel are necessary to forestall a full-scale insurgency.

In Argentina, except for sporadic terrorism, the "communist threat" is virtually nonexistent. In the aftermath of the societal reaction against the dirty war, anything associated with "national security doctrine" is *verboten*. Given the absence of a visible internal threat and efforts by both Alfonsín and Menem to resolve border issues with traditional rivals Chile and Brazil, the Argentine armed forces face serious questions about whether the country really needs a military. In the context of the military's search for both a professional rationale and a means of relegitimating itself in the eyes of civil society, Menem's endorsement of Argentine participation in the Gulf War and support for active involvement in peacekeeping forces in the former Yugoslavia found strong support, even among nationalist sectors of the military who are critical of Menem's close ties to the United States. The military's growing overseas role has, in turn, begun to foster what might become a new "international security doctrine," according to which the armed forces are integrated into the democratic regime as an instrument of foreign policy, largely in peacekeeping roles. In order for the military to undertake such a mission, it must respect international norms supporting democracy and an apolitical military professionalism. Hence, international missions and apolitical roles have become implicitly linked, much as internal security and interventionist role beliefs were linked in the 1960s.

Finally, in order to succeed in the internal debate, competing conceptions of the military's role in politics must be able to attract outside support, to be considered legitimate by other social actors. Thus, one of the limiting factors for Seineldín's fundamentalist faction has been the sharp societal condemnation of its views by all but the most conservative Catholic groups. Professionalist arguments, on the other hand, have enjoyed strong support from the U.S. and Western European countries and their military representatives. As noted previously, the Argentine military's traditional social alliances were effectively shattered by the *Proceso*. In less dramatic fashion, the experience of a second military regime with reformist intentions did not endear the armed forces to

Ecuador's elites, who pointedly refused to support the regime, even after it watered down or dropped most of its initial reforms.[88]

On the other hand, Ecuadorian officers favoring guardian or tutelary roles are obviously emboldened by public opinion polls showing widespread civilian disillusionment with the democratic regime and strong support for military intervention under certain circumstances. While a public claim to a tutelary role might draw international criticism and/or negative reactions from leaders opposed to an expanding military policy voice in areas traditionally reserved to political and economic elites, the de facto expansion of the military voice enjoys support from civilian groups worried about the lack of predictability in government policies. After some initial resistance, the private sector supported the creation of a military bank during the "antistatist" administration of Febres Cordero on the argument that its existence would deter irresponsible future governments who might be tempted to nationalize the banking system as Alán García had done in Peru.[89] The investment guaranty logic is at least part of the rationale for the army's part ownership of several automobile assembly plants and a variety of other businesses with no direct military function.[90] Thus far, the role expansion of the Ecuadorian military has been relatively low-key, a slow movement toward a semitutelary regime relying largely on indirect influence, as opposed to the more aggressive tutelage exercised by their Guatemalan or Brazilian counterparts. Yet it remains to be seen, given this softer approach, how other social actors will respond to the expansion of military influence beyond its usual spheres of operation, particularly if military tutelage focuses on growing socioeconomic inequalities.

Policy Implications

The first policy conclusion to be drawn from this research is perhaps the most obvious. If role beliefs are determined most directly by the domestic context of the internal debate about the military's role in politics, then civilian leaders must seek to do what they can to reshape that context and improve government performance. Their ability to change the history of the previous military regime or to reshape the international system is obviously very limited. Hence, the attention of political leaders seeking to consolidate and institutionalize democratic civil-military relations must be directed to concrete actions to create a political climate where military subordination to civilian authority will be perceived as reasonable and logical. Arguments for democratic control of the armed forces are not credible when civilian leaders are viewed as corrupt, self-serving, narrowly partisan, or irresponsible. While military notions of what constitutes proper leadership are sometimes exaggerated, most officers — like most civilians — expect only a honest effort to solve complex problems, a willingness to cooperate with others, and a commitment to play by the constitutional rules.[91] Political leaders who do not attempt to meet those minimum expectations directly contribute to the disillusionment of both the public and the armed forces. Delegitimation of the democratic regime in turn supports arguments for military autonomy from civilian control and for interventionist political roles. Given an international context that is hostile to the traditional notion of the military as a guardian and arbiter in times of crisis, irresponsible civilian behavior favors arguments for indirect forms of military influence and tutelary or semitutelary regimes.

Empowering democratic institutions thus remains the first step in any program to consolidate and institutionalize more democratic civil-military relations.[92] In some countries, this may require reconstructing constitutions or reforming basic institutions, particularly the party structure. Unless civilian leaders develop and exercise their capacity for institutional reform, the poor performance of civilian institutions will remain a powerful argument against civilian control.

The second policy implication is that a long-term strategy for promoting democratic role beliefs will in most countries require a concerted effort to reinforce the core of professionalist officers and enhance their resistance to appeals from their more ideologically oriented comrades. As one officer put it, "[Educational reforms should] target the 'middle' [of the officer corps]. [The idea is] not to change the sausage, but [to fix] the machine that manufactures faulty sausages. The Military College trains the professional middle, [but it is] a weak middle, [like] a liquid cargo, [that] sloshes [first] to one side, then to the other; [that is] used by [both sides], that wrecks the truck of the armed forces."[93] Arguments in favor of democracy are important to promoting democratic professionalist role beliefs, but these arguments are most likely to be persuasive to officers already identified with the majority parties. In most countries, substantial numbers of officers are not likely to hold mainstream political viewpoints or to be identified with any party. For these officers in particular, and for the average officer with only vaguely defined political views, the critical arguments will have to be professional and institutional reasons for resisting interventionist appeals. The experience of military defeat — Ecuador's 1941 war with Peru and Argentina's war with Great Britain in the Malvinas — has been the most powerful argument against traditional patterns of civil-military relations. In military forces that have already achieved a moderate level of professionalization, professionalist arguments have a strong basis in military socialization and institutional norms, plus historical reinforcement from recent experience. Even Ecuadorian officers are widely conscious of the professional costs of the last military regime.

Professionalist arguments are, however, likely to be undermined unless there are real opportunities to practice the military profession. Simply put, if there is no professional military role to play or no resources with which to play that role, the professionalist rationale for staying out of politics lacks credibility. Military officers may still choose to subordinate themselves to civilian authority, but they will have to have other reasons for doing so. Without entering here into all the complexities of the debate over military missions, suffice it to say that professionalist arguments for the subordination of the military to civilian control are less compelling if the military's primary missions are, in fact, nonmilitary, that is, anything other than the deterrence of potential military aggression and the capacity to respond militarily to that aggression if deterrence fails. Even the peacekeeping mission, which may provide a different rationale for democratic professionalism, does not entail the same penalties for short-term political intervention or lapses in professional capabilities as the classic military responsibility for territorial defense.

Independent of the question of missions, the armed forces have to have the minimum resources necessary to function in their professional role. In Argentina, the severe budgetary cutbacks in the mid-1980s and again in the early 1990s have sharply curtailed the military's ability to maintain normal training and readiness procedures. Flying time for pilots, sea time for ships, and rounds fired by artillery and infantry units have all been severely constricted. All three services, but especially the army, have been hurt by cuts in military personnel, particularly conscripts. As a result, the three armed forces had 11,000 officers in 1991, but only 12,000 conscripts; 23,000 noncommissioned officers provided the basic cadre of soldiers and sailors.[94] Despite recent salary increases, pay levels for junior officers are still low relative to the European/U.S.-level cost of living in the capital, so second jobs outside the military are now commonplace, especially among noncommissioned officers. For segments of the armed forces, the military has become a part-time profession. While the military itself must bear an important part of the blame for its failure to reduce the officer corps to a size consistent with the budgetary resources available, civilian disinterest in defense policy has also contributed to the lack of basic operating resources. In Argentina, anti-interventionist beliefs are probably sufficiently strong among both military and civilian leaders to withstand military complaints about inadequate funding and the loss of the professionalist rationale if the part-time military becomes permanent. However, the budgetary crisis has also affected militaries like Brazil with radically different political histories and others like Peru facing serious security threats. In those contexts, the lack of a military budget consistent with the professional missions assigned to the military may undercut professionalist arguments for subordination to civilian authority, particularly when budget cuts are disconnected from any analysis of defense policy and the resources needed to sustain that policy.[95] The size of the military budget and the missions assigned to the armed forces are legitimate topics for democratic debate. If, however, the only countries with generous military budgets and adequate military salaries are those with politically autonomous or tutelary militaries, that fact will not pass unnoticed in debates about alternative role beliefs.[96]

Finally, the internal debate model suggests the need for policymakers in Latin America and the United States to work together in a conscious effort to shape the terms of that debate. The first critical issue is who participates in this discussion. In Argentina, the rest of the Southern Cone, and to a lesser extent Brazil and Peru, there is now a small but active community of civilian policy specialists and academic experts who are engaged in ongoing dialogues with the military about defense policy and civil-military relations. In Ecuador, outside of those civilians trained by the military itself, there are still relatively few civilians with the expertise to participate as effective interlocutors. Effective civilian participation requires a basic understanding of military concepts and terminology, a willingness to listen as well as speak, and a commitment to taking seriously the military profession. In Latin America, military officers have always been engaged in conversations with civilians; the question is which civilians participate in these conversations on what terms and what issues. An open and honest debate with autonomous civilians who share a commitment to democratic values and the requisite expertise is obviously quite different from military conversations with provincial elites or civilian students in war colleges run by the military. In Argentina and Ecuador, I was struck by the difference in the tone of the interviews, particularly the tenor of military criticism of civilian leaders, in the major cities versus provincial bases, where the primary interaction is with other officers or like-minded local elites. Although the number of observations is limited, I am quite convinced that regular interaction of military officers with civilians capable of debating politics and civil-military relations on an equal footing has a significant impact on military discourse. In this sense, the efforts of various Latin American institutes, the Ford Foundation, and the U.S. Agency for International Development to create multiple fora for encounters between political leaders, academics, and military officers have contributed to a new climate for civil-military relations, especially in the Southern Cone.

The second step toward reshaping the debate is the effort to make the case for democratic professionalism. Military leaders complain, with some justification, that civilian leaders are much clearer about what they don't want than about what they do want. At a minimum, civilian leaders and scholars need to specify the norms of military and civilian behavior appropriate to democratic regimes and to abide by those norms. Designing those norms in an institutional-historical context that is radically different from the United States or Western Europe is no trivial task. Copying U.S. rules for civil-military relations is no more likely to succeed than simply copying U.S. battle manuals. Civilians and military officers who support democracy must work together to make a positive case, an affirmative rationale, for military acceptance of democratic control, even in a context much less favorable to that argument.

In sum, military role beliefs in Latin America are still in flux. Based upon this research, there appears to be more change in traditional military views than most scholars expected at the beginning of the democratic transition. Particularly in Argentina, there is strong evidence of real progress toward institutionalization of role beliefs supporting a democratic model of civil-military relations. On the other hand, the interview data suggest that Ecuadorian military attitudes toward civil-military relations are uneven, ambiguous, and contradictory. The risk of a reversion to a traditional guardian/arbiter role is still present, although the hostile international environment has so far discouraged overt intervention. However, weak civilian institutions and civilian and military disillusionment have led to less visible forms of intervention in a semitutelary regime. The challenge for the future is to restructure the context and to reshape the debate to maximize the chances that democratic beliefs will prevail.

CHAPTER FOUR

National Security

Ideology, Doctrine, Threats, and Missions

In the academic literature on the rise of institutional military regimes in Latin America during the 1960s and 1970s, many scholars stressed the emergence of new military doctrines emphasizing internal security and guerrilla warfare.[1] According to Joseph Comblin,

> The permanence of Latin American military regimes implies the existence of an ideology that transcends national peculiarities and maintains the structure and coherence of them all. The ideology is called "the Doctrine of National Security." . . . [According to this doctrine], the presence of international communism is everywhere; there are potential guerrillas everywhere. . . . Social conflicts, political oppositions, discussion of ideas, ideological or cultural non-conformism are vivid manifestations of the omnipresent revolutionary war, . . . total, generalized, and absolute war.[2]

In Comblin's view, national security doctrine obliterates the distinctions between violent and nonviolent politics, between internal security and external defense, between dissent and subversion. In the name of national security, military rule is justified to stamp out subversion and impose rational policies for the pursuit of national objectives. Human rights violations become acts of war.[3]

To the extent that military doctrine contributed to interventionist role beliefs, it is important to assess whether these doctrines have changed since the transition to democracy. Although it would be unrealistic to expect immediate changes in military thinking as a result of ending military rule, if these ideas persist, they are likely to encourage military resistance to more democratic role beliefs and to legitimate arguments for military prerogatives incompatible with democratic consolidation.[4]

Any serious analysis of doctrinal continuity and change must, however, begin by attacking the conceptual morass surrounding the discussion of national security doctrine in Latin America. The term "doctrine" implies a set of teachings, often a set of principles or a creed. In military parlance, doctrine is typically used in a narrower sense to refer to particular strategic or tactical principles, such as the doctrine of massive retaliation. Ideology, on the other hand, is usually defined as a generalized set of political ideas, a political world-view, such as liberalism or communism.[5] To treat doctrine, especially military doctrine, and ideology as more or less interchangeable terms obfuscates the question of the relationship between the two. As shown below, the interaction between doctrine and political ideology in the Latin American militaries is both important and complex. Second, most analyses of national security doctrine exaggerate the uniformity of Latin American military thinking about internal security and politics.[6] While Comblin's synthesis may represent the thinking of General Pinochet or General Camps, it is nevertheless an abstraction drawn from many different threads, a composite many Latin American officers would reject as unrepresentative of their views. Finally, reifying the doctrine of national security lumps together a number of disparate elements that vary temporally and geographically. Comblin's conception of the doctrine of national security combines:

1. A conceptual framework linking national security, strategy, national objectives, and national policy;

2. A conflict hypothesis stressing internal security, specifically the threat of revolutionary insurgencies sponsored by the international communist movement, rather than conventional external threats;

3. A theory of revolutionary war defining the nature of the internal security threat and the appropriate military and policy responses to that threat;

4. A rationale justifying human rights violations (torture, disappearances) as necessary means to eliminate the revolutionary threat;

5. The thesis of security and development, causally linking the internal security threat to socioeconomic underdevelopment; and

6. The belief that direct military rule is justified when the policy failures of civilian governments endanger national security.[7]

Considering each of these elements separately provides a more accurate understanding of the past as well as a better starting point for assessing posttransition changes in military doctrine.

Although the concept of total war can be traced back to the Napoleonic "nation-in-arms," World War II provided persuasive evidence of the impor-

107

tance of factors other than military forces in being. Industrial mobilization, natural resources, science and technology, national unity, and statesmanship all played a critical role in the Allied victory. Nonmilitary factors were thus increasingly seen as vital to a nation's ability to defend itself. The concept of national defense was thus replaced by "national security," defined as the ability of the nation state to achieve its national objectives/interests in the face of the actions of other nation states. National strategy integrates the military, political, economic, and psychosocial elements of national power to formulate comprehensive policies for the achievement of permanent and current national objectives.[8]

From the beginning, this new conceptual apparatus was closely tied to a cold war hypothesis of bipolar conflict between the "free world" and "international communism," with Latin America aligned on the side of "Western Christian civilization." Although Argentine and Brazilian writings on internal security and revolutionary war predate the Cuban revolution, Castro's victory and subsequent alignment with the Soviet Union dramatically increased military concern with the "communist threat."[9] Leftist attempts to emulate the Cuban experience and massive U.S. military aid programs reinforced military

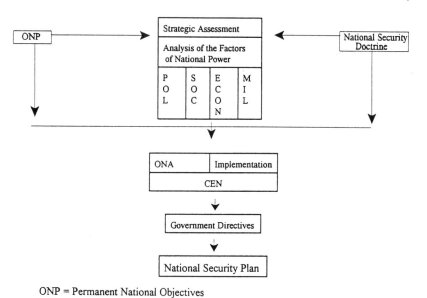

ONP = Permanent National Objectives
ONA = Current National Objectives
CEN = National Strategic Concept

FIG. 4.1   National Security View of Policymaking. *Source:* Crnl. Alfonso Littuma Arízaga, *Doctrina de Seguridad Nacional* (Caracas: Ministerio de Defensa, 1967), 143.

fears that guerrilla warfare was the immediate and urgent threat to national security. Castro's decision to abolish the existing armed forces — like the Sandinistas' decision twenty years later to replace the Guardia Nacional with a new revolutionary army — made it clear that the armed forces would be the first victims if the revolutionaries prevailed. By the early 1960s, both the language of national security and the new vision of revolutionary insurgency as the primary security threat were nearly universal within the upper ranks of the Latin American militaries.

From the beginning, however, there were competing interpretations, reflecting the ideological position of their proponents. Doctrine was adapted to ideology. Relatively vacuous concepts of security, insurgency, and development were given specific content according to the ideological predispositions of different military authors. In the 1960s, moderate conservative versions stressed the linkage between insecurity and underdevelopment. In a climate of increasingly radical populism and economic recession, the armed forces were called upon to restore political order and create conditions for renewed economic growth in order to avoid a Castro-style insurgency. In Peru and Ecuador, nationalist officers forged a radical/reformist variant, arguing that poverty and discontent were the result of social inequalities, foreign domination of the economy, and U.S. policies designed to keep Latin America underdeveloped. Hence, security could only be achieved through military-directed efforts to reform socioeconomic structures and promote development. In the 1970s, a new emphasis on the ideological nature of the revolutionary threat gained adherents among the Southern Cone militaries. In this view, the armed forces were the defenders of Western Christian values against a worldwide communist conspiracy to subvert the free world from within.

Although it is tempting to identify these variants of national security doctrine with the countries in which they achieved notoriety, even within those countries these interpretations of national security doctrine were hotly debated since each implied different policies to achieve "security" and "development." In the 1970s, there were "peruvianist" factions in both the Argentine and Uruguayan armies;[10] in Peru and Ecuador, the second stage of the radical/reformist military regime was closer to the "Brazilian" model than to their original programs. In Brazil, the early years of military rule were marked by repeated clashes between the liberal internationalist faction headed by Castelo Branco and the nationalist developmentalist faction headed by Albuquerque Lima.[11] Differences in national and international context selectively aided or restricted the diffusion of these variations by making them more/less credible, relevant, or attractive to different military audiences, but ideological affinity was arguably the more important factor, at least for those officers with relatively well-defined world views.

Despite these variations, the national security doctrines of the 1960s and 1970s provided a common intellectual foundation for a new military role belief stressing the professional duty of the armed forces to assume control of the government when civilian leaders proved incapable of providing the necessary conditions for internal security or development. Although this role belief drew on earlier conceptions of the military as the "guardian of vital national interests," it clearly expanded the legitimate duration of military rule as well as the military's collective responsibility for those regimes. National security thus became a justification for institutional military rule.

If we define doctrine as officially taught ideas, one can make a good case based on Argentine and Ecuadorian military journals that national security concepts and the conflict hypothesis of the "internal enemy" did become official military doctrine in the 1960s and 1970s. On the other hand, there were different interpretations of the security-development linkage and different theories of revolutionary war. Thus, some elements of military thinking about national security did become "doctrine"; others did not.

The *Boletín de Educación del Ejército,* which began publication in 1960, was the Argentine army's official journal for military education and, hence, provides the most direct evidence regarding doctrine. Articles on communism and revolutionary war appear sporadically in the early 1960s, but the overwhelming focus is conventional warfare until the military takeover in 1966, when an entire issue is devoted to a revised program for "Internal Leadership." This mandatory instruction for officers and soldiers included sessions on "Communism confronts Christian Civilization," "Communism and the Concepts of Person, Family, State, and Liberty," "The Spiritual Needs of the Combatant," and "Beyond Military Life," all devoted to the conflict between marxism and the Western way of life. Revised programs were published in 1972, 1976, 1979, and 1981. In the *Boletín,* there is little evidence of a "national security doctrine" in Comblin's sense. As seen in the following passages, the official indoctrination is more accurately and simply characterized as virulent anticommunism.

The Marxist (Pedro Rojo): has ideologies that enslave and hatreds that destroy, . . . foments rebellion until the seizure of power in order to impose the worst slavery later[,] . . . is deprived of all rights and "obligated to the Party[,]" . . . is prohibited from any political dissent. If he does, he is confined to inhuman concentration camps or psychiatric hospitals. Lives under an imposed atheism, denies the transcendence of man.[12]

We are in a clash of two systems. The red forces seek the gradual implantation of communism around the world . . . . He who thinks his own country is an island, with no more threat than comes from the subversion within its borders, is mistaken . . . . The local subversion, as small as it may be, is always the appendage of a global homogeneous whole centrally directed by the leading Marxist-Leninist states, who have made ideology the principal means of domination . . . . *Subversion is all covert or overt action, insidious or violent, that seeks the alteration or the destruction of the moral principles and style of life of a people.*[13]

How does marxism operate? It infiltrates unions, political parties, the Church, clubs, schools. . . . It does not respect human life, it kills innocent people for political ends. It hinders the development of the Nation: strikes, speculation, robbery, unwarranted increases in prices. Its only objective is to destroy peace and provoke chaos. It promotes moral corruption through the distribution of drugs, the creation of entertainment centers, [and] gambling places, with the objective of destroying people from within. It foments hate and disunity in society, accentuating the class struggle, confrontation between fathers and sons, employers and workers, young and old.[14]

The official dehumanization of the internal enemy and the portrayal of marxists as the agents of external aggression seeking to destroy Argentina's identity as a Western Christian nation undoubtedly contributed to a climate legitimating widespread human rights violations as acts of war, although attributing exclusive causation for human rights abuses to military "ideas" about communism seems as simplistic as attributing such violations exclusively to military dictatorships.[15]

The diffusion of this Manichean vision of the internal enemy was the result of a complex interplay of structural and situational factors, particularly the deep political schisms of Argentine society and the increasingly violent confrontation of right and left beginning in the late 1960s. Despite extensive military preparation for rural insurgencies, urban terrorism and guerrilla warfare caught the Argentine Army off guard. In terms of everyday life, 1975–76 was a war for the military and police. Officers lived in constant fear of bombings, assassination, and kidnapping of family members.[16] Every officer knew someone who had been killed. By my unofficial count, roughly equal numbers of military officers died in the antisubversive campaign as in the Malvinas/Falklands war with Great Britain. When the military assumed power in 1976, the "campaign against subversion" became more systematic and centrally organized. A nationwide network of clandestine detention centers was created to round up and interrogate suspected subversives. Particularly in the beginning, tactics were mostly improvised on the spot by the police-military teams that ran the centers.[17] Torture was justified, not in terms of doctrine, but rather by the need to extract intelligence information quickly before guerrilla cells disbanded or moved to a new location.[18] Execution of suspected subversives was defended as no different from shooting the enemy in wartime. The deaths of innocent victims were excused as unavoidable casualties of war, no different from Hiroshima or Vietnam. In this atmosphere of fear and intense threat, perhaps the most important idea was the argument that, in war, victory is all that counts. Saving Argentina from communism justified any means. Hard-line officers argued that antisubversive war required fighting fire with fire, terror with terror, clandestinity with clandestinity, assassination with assassination. In a war with no rules, no moral limits, torture became an interrogation technique; stealing from victims became "war booty"; taking their children became a way to prevent kids from growing up to be subversives. In the name of Western Christian civilization, the armed forces descended into a moral abyss. Disappearances multiplied into the thousands.

National Security Doctrines After the Transition

The critical question is "How have these different components of national security changed (or not changed) since the transition to democracy?" To what extent do antidemocratic doctrines of national security persist, despite nominal military acceptance of civilian rule? In the analysis that follows, I argue that significant changes have occurred in some areas of security doctrine, despite substantial continuities in other areas. The remainder of this chapter considers the conceptual framework, threat perceptions and military missions, theories of revolutionary war, and military role beliefs. Although the evidence from the interviews and from Argentine and Ecuadorian military journals is incomplete, I conclude that there has been a substantial degree of *disarticulation* in these various components of national security thinking, especially in Argentina. The absence of a coherent "doctrine of national security" is not the same as a positive commitment to a democratic theory of civil-military relations. Nevertheless, the lack of a clear antidemocratic alternative is a step forward relative to the 1960s and 1970s.

At the most elemental level, the conceptual framework of national security remains an important element of military thinking in both Ecuador and Argentina. In the latter, the public reaction against the dirty war and its association with the doctrine of national security led to some substitution of the term "national defense" for "national security." The emphasis on external security in posttransition defense policy reinforced that trend, but the change in vocabulary was undoubtedly greater than the change in military thinking. References to "the four fronts of National Power" — military, political, economic, and psychosocial — and to the need for a comprehensive national strategy are still commonplace.

In itself, the vocabulary of national security is of little significance. In the United States, the same vocabulary and a whole set of national security institutions coexist with a reasonably stable and open democratic system. In Latin America, however, the conceptual language of national security and strategy is typically infused with an organic, corporatist view of society and politics that implicitly denigrates democratic politics and civilian politicians.

What Alfred Stepan calls the organic statist view of politics has a long history in Latin American political culture, particularly in the military. In this view, political elites should coordinate the harmonious functioning of the component parts of society to achieve the common good, including the restructuring of civil society when necessary to achieve that goal.[19] Hence, politics is defined as "the art of achieving the common good."[20] In military writing, national security becomes synonymous with this collective good. Policies to serve that good come from the harmonization of the military, diplomatic, economic, and psychosocial "fronts" in a concerted, integrated national effort to achieve national objectives.

> The power of the state should be a balanced power, with the diverse sectors that make up the power of the state not acting as separate components, but working in a totally interrelated manner. . . . In healthy countries, where the state functions adequately . . . it works as a whole because these are not problems of governments, but of states.

> [Civilian governments have suffered from] a lack of integration, of leadership, and of understanding among the three powers. Politics has not been taken as a serious business, but rather as a personal [conflict] or [competing] interests. The permanent national objectives have been neglected, not consolidated. . . . [Civilian governments] always criticize the past; [there is] no continuity; [they do] not take the best parts of the previous government. The national objectives should have support from whatever government [exists]. You can't be changing your objectives all the time. The permanent struggle among the parties is the worst aspect.

> The National Security Council is . . . the highest mechanism of the State for setting permanent national objectives [and] current national objectives, [and] policies and strategies appropriate for the times in which the country is living. The national objectives should not change with every change of government.[21]

National objectives and national interests are seen as permanent and general, transcending individual governments or regimes. Other interests are denigrated as partisan, narrow, or selfish.

As Brian Loveman and Thomas Davies have emphasized, in both its traditional and more contemporary forms, this military view is profoundly antipolitical.[22] When combined with an organic statist perspective, the national security framework privileges a unitary vision of the Nation, a State that is not accountable to civil society, and a top down understanding of policymaking as an exercise in technobureaucratic rationality. In this view, democracy is implicitly defined as a regime in which the Nation elects a leader who reflects its values and then lets that leader govern in accordance with the common good.[23] In the interviews, officers from both countries complained that their political systems did not live up to that ideal.

[In 1975], the country was living in a pseudodemocracy, like now. It had the formal institutions of a democracy — it had an elected government — but it was not a true democracy because there were not solid, clear, distinct parties where the citizen could elect a party that represents his ideas.

The political system has to be democratic.... The party monopoly has to be done away with.... Deputies [in Congress should be] representatives of the Nation, not of [special] interests.

The population — and the armed forces are part of the population — sees this struggle of interests, where the common interest always comes in last.

[Ecuador] needs a strong democracy [with] civilian and military [participation], with the total support of the armed forces, [with] more power. [The power] of Congress should be limited. The executive, with military support, a good cabinet, good ideas [is what we need].[24]

This approach to governance systematically undervalues and misunderstands the normal play of conflicting social interests, the importance of institutional mechanisms for political participation and accountability, and the inevitability of ideological conflicts over both the objectives and instruments of state policy, in short, all the vital elements of democratic pluralism. Military antipathy to pluralistic politics is reflected in the idealization of "the statesman" as a modern-day philosopher-king and the consequent denigration of "politicians." Citing Plato, Aristotle, and Saint Thomas, one Argentine officer defines the statesman as "one who seeks truth, acts for justice and the common good, and elevates his thinking (and therefore his ideas) above the purely material plane."[25] Others echoed this vision:

A Nation has to be an integrated thing and it should be the statesmen who use the instruments [of power] to pursue the objectives that the country needs.

The Argentine politician is not prepared for the leadership of the state. There have to be statesmen, a person [identified] by his qualities, first, of comprehension of the internal consensus of the Nation [and] clear objectives for his people and, second, of [the country's] position within the world [and] a realistic view of the strengths and weaknesses of [that] position. Alfonsín is a politician, [seeking] to increase support for his government.

[At the Instituto de Altos Estudios Nacionales, we held] seminars for the presidential candidates on national objectives and their role in the government. How can you have a government when the political leaders don't know what the permanent national objectives are![26]

The failure of civilian leaders to live up to this ideal is frequently attributed to the "political immaturity" of Latin American societies. As Ecuadorian officers explained:

[The problems of] civilian government are due to Ecuador's [level of] maturity. Congress is a demonstration of [our] immaturity. [They deserve] a grade of 10 out of a 100. Our political immaturity is truly a punishment . . . . The solution is that the politicians have to be better trained—in the political sciences—to be trained as statesmen. [We] need a national consensus; [we] need governments [that are] tough and strong.

The immaturity of [Ecuadorian] politics is disgraceful. [Politicians] are not interested in the welfare of the country. Politics [is] improvisation, monetary gain, [serving] economic interests, not an interest in service [to the country]. The training of politicians lacks a mystique, [lacks] inspired people.

[If] the political parties . . . don't understand that the country comes before partisan or even ideological interests, [then] there is no political maturity, because the first value for the citizen in the scale of human values is the *Patria*.[27]

The failure of civilian regimes to function like "mature democracies" in turn provides a rationale for an autonomous role for the armed forces as guardians or checks on irresponsible politicians. The institutionalization of an organic statist view of politics in the language and bureaucratic structures of the national security apparatus thus contributes to disillusionment of military officers with democratic politics.

Changes in Threat Perceptions

The second common component of national security doctrines in Latin America has been the focus on indirect aggression by the international communism movement working through local marxists, leftist fronts, and guerrilla groups. The threat to national security was thus both external (in origin) and internal (in its specific agents and principal battlegrounds). However, even at the height of the cold war concern with revolutionary wars, internal security was never the exclusive military preoccupation. In Ecuador, the border conflict with Peru was always a prominent concern, despite the new threat of guerrilla warfare.[28] In Argentina, only last-minute mediation by the pope averted war with Chile in 1978 over the Beagle Channel. Throughout the 1970s, the annual

TABLE 4.1
Threat Perceptions

	Yes (%)	No (%)	No Mention (%)	Number
Ecuador 1991				
External: Peru	64	14	21	39
Other external	12	15	73	33
Insurgency/Subversion	73	7	20	41
Drugs/Narco-terrorism	46	9	46	35
United States	2	5	90	30
Argentina 1985 (1992)				
External: Chile	70 (54)	21 (25)	9 (10)	33 (48)
External: Brazil	38 (15)	16 (45)	47 (40)	32 (47)
External: Great Britain	44 (10)	6 (15)	50 (75)	32 (48)
Insurgency/Subversion	56 (6)	24 (29)	21 (65)	34 (48)
Sendero spillover	3 (25)	3 (2)	94 (74)	31 (49)
Drugs/Narco-terrorism	0 (37)	0 (16)	100 (47)	30 (51)
United States	10 (2)	3 (0)	87 (98)	30 (45)

NOTE: Tabulation of responses to the question, "If you were the Minister of Defense, what would be your hypotheses of conflict for the year 2000?" In the 1985 interviews, the question was phrased in terms of threats to national security. Multiple responses permitted.

exercises for students at Argentina's War Academy were mostly conventional war campaigns or problems like seizing a bridge or attacking an enemy-held town that could apply to either conventional or nonconventional warfare.[29] Hence, the question is not whether there has been a "return" to conventional war hypotheses, but rather the relative importance attributed to external versus internal security.

As indicated in Table 4.1, a substantial majority of Ecuadorian officers interviewed in 1991 stressed both internal and external threats, particularly the border conflict with Peru and the threat of a Sendero-type insurgency among the indigenous population of the sierra. Just under half also cited the threat of drug trafficking and "narco-terrorism." Although no comparable data are available for the pretransition period, the available evidence suggests that the conflict hypotheses for the Ecuadorian military have not changed substantially, despite the end of the cold war.

In contrast, the Argentine data show more evidence of discontinuity and change in threat perceptions. In 1985, prior to the fall of the Berlin Wall, over half of those interviewed still listed internal insurgency/subversion as a threat, despite the official government position that there were no hypotheses for internal conflict.

The struggle against subversion [has] ended its military side; the political aspect continues. The East-West conflict is still present.

My purely personal opinion is that there is subversion in the world, in Lebanon, in Colombia, in Central America. It is not a leaderless, spontaneous thing; there are schools training terrorists in Libya, in Cuba, in Russia. It is an organized business. I believe that the subversion in Argentina was defeated in the fight against subversion, but now it seeks to avenge itself by other means and is attacking the armed forces. The subversion always attacks the strongest institutions of society, above all the armed forces because they are the most indispensable to destroy in order to take power. [The subversion] is using the mass media, is using the judiciary, to discredit the armed forces as if we were all assassins.[30]

However, even in 1985, most Argentine officers stressed external conflicts, particularly the traditional military rivalry with Chile and, to a lesser extent, Brazil. Over 40 percent cited the conflict with Great Britain in the Malvinas/Falklands. 117

Seven years later, a number of changes were evident.[31] First, despite the terrorist attack on the La Tablada barracks in 1989, the hypothesis of a return to 1970s-style subversion or guerrilla war virtually disappears, particularly among officers on active duty. In its place, there is increasing concern with drug-financed terrorism and the possibility that Peru's Sendero Luminoso might extend its guerrilla operations into the Andean provinces of the Argentine northwest. Still, only a third of the Argentine officers interviewed saw narco-terrorism as a threat; nearly that many specifically denied that internal insurgency or subversion would return as a security issue.

Perceptions of potential external threats also changed. The establishment of the Mercosur and accompanying efforts to promote diplomatic and military integration with Brazil, Uruguay, and Paraguay are reflected in the significant decline in the number of officers listing potential conflicts with Brazil; nearly half said that traditional conflict hypothesis is no longer relevant.[32] Expectations of conflict with Chile also decreased somewhat, reflecting diplomatic success in settling a number of long-standing border issues and efforts to engage Chile in the Mercosur common market. The Menem government's commitment to seek a diplomatic resolution to the Malvinas/Falklands conflict and its policy of alignment with the United States likewise contributed to a sharp drop in expectations of conflict with Great Britain. As one retired general candidly acknowledged, there are few immediate threats to Argentine security.

External threats in reality are very limited. From here to 2000, I don't see any conflicts that couldn't be resolved through diplomacy, negotiation, or regional mediation. Subversion is potentially a threat, but politically the left has really declined. It could still happen in Latin America; the odds could increase if the world economy crashes. There could be outbreaks in Brazil like Peru, but [it's] not a problem here . . . . Drugs [are] not a big problem in Argentina; [there are] no producers or big traffickers.[33]

In sum, the traditional hypotheses of external and internal conflict remain strong in Ecuador. Nearly three-fourths of the Ecuadorian sample see insurgency and subversion as significant threats. In contrast, only a third of the Argentine sample list narco-terrorism as a threat; a quarter are concerned about spillover from Peru's guerrilla war. Numerous comments in the interviews suggest that even these are viewed as relatively remote or secondary threats, compared to the guerrillas of the 1970s or the threat of a Sendero-type movement in Ecuador.

118

Military Roles and Missions

Conflict hypotheses are significant because of the military roles and missions that can be justified in terms of those threats. The fear of internal insurgency is important because it creates a security rationale for an expanded military role in economic development and for military intelligence activities targeting the political left. Still, the correlation between internal security threats and expanded military roles is not perfect or automatic. As Crahan notes, the security and development thesis antedates military concern with counterinsurgency. Military efforts to support industrialization, infrastructure improvements, and technological capacity can also be justified in terms of total war concepts for external security.[34] Hence, the important question is to what extent have military perceptions of the appropriate missions of the armed forces changed relative to previous decades.

In Argentina, both the official missions and military attitudes changed significantly. With the collapse of the *Proceso*, public outrage against the antisubversive campaign led to strong political pressures to limit the military's role in internal security. After three years of debate and delay, Congress approved the new National Defense Law in 1988, which defined the role of the armed forces as external security. Although the military was not prohibited from participating in internal security, planning hypotheses for internal conflict were banned, as was any domestic use of military intelligence.[35] Subsequent legislation, again delayed by controversies over the doctrine of national security and the dirty war, reaffirmed that internal security is the primary responsibility of the security forces: the police, the Gendarmería, and the Prefectura Naval (Coast Guard). In accordance with this redefinition of responsibilities, the Gendarmería has expanded and modernized.[36] If, however, the security forces are overwhelmed, the president can order the use of the regular armed forces by declaring a state of siege. In keeping with this view of the use of the armed forces for internal security only in exceptional circumstances, the law forbids the development of doctrine, equipment, or training of the military for internal security missions; these functions are assigned to the new Subsecretariat for Internal Security in the Ministry of the Interior. Despite the organizational dependency of the Gendarmería and Prefectura on the Ministry of Defense, control over the police and security forces is to be exercised by the Internal Security Council and ad hoc crisis committees based in the Interior Ministry. A joint Senate-House committee was also established to provide oversight for internal security operations, including observance of international human rights accords.[37]

In the 1985 interviews, the National Defense Law's proposed changes in the traditional responsibilities of the military for external and internal security were highly controversial. Seventy percent of those interviewed listed internal security as a mission of the armed forces, in most cases second only to external defense, despite government policy restricting the use of the military in internal conflicts. By 1992, this controversy was largely limited to retired officers, 60 percent of whom defended the military's role in internal security. In contrast, only a third of the respondents on active-duty listed internal security as a military mission. Particularly among active-duty officers, there appears to be widespread acceptance of the official position that regular military forces are the last resort in cases of insurgency or internal disorder. The current Army chief of staff, Martín Balza, has insisted that a deterrent role in external defense is the military's primary mission; subsidiary missions include participation in international peacekeeping, logistical and technical support for antidrug programs, providing assistance in natural disasters, and assistance to local communities.[38] As noted in Table 4.2, the peacekeeping role is now widely accepted. In contrast, only a fourth of the active-duty officers listed development or civic action as a mission, compared to half of the retired officers. Although the dismantling of the army's industrial complex (*Fabricaciones Militares*) is still controversial among military engineers and nationalist factions of the military, most officers appear to have accepted the fiscal necessity of reducing the losses charged against the rest of the military budget. Participation of the military in counternarcotics operations is still debated, but the debate is mostly hypothetical since Argentina is a transit and consumer country, rather than a drug producer. To a substantial degree then, civilian and military authorities in Argentina have succeeded in defining the military's principal mission as external defense, with international peacekeeping playing an important secondary role. Other missions, including internal security, are now distinctly secondary.

In Ecuador, on the other hand, there is virtual unanimity that the missions of the armed forces include external and internal security, as well as contributing to socioeconomic development, which the 1978 Constitution elevated to

TABLE 4.2
Missions of the Armed Forces

	Yes (%)	No (%)	No Mention (%)	Number
Ecuador 1991				
External defense	90	2	8	40
Internal security	85	2	12	41
Economic development/Civic action	97	0	3	38
Drug control	47	18	34	38
International peacekeeping	0	0	100	34
Argentina 1985 (1992)				
External defense	97 (93)	0 (2)	3 (5)	32 (56)
Internal security	71 (51)	13 (20)	16 (29)	31 (51)
Economic development/Civic action	42 (44)	0 (6)	58 (50)	31 (50)
Drug control	0 (48)	0 (32)	100 (20)	29 (54)
International peacekeeping	3 (81)	0 (5)	97 (14)	29 (58)

a constitutional duty. Faced with the possibility that the indigenous movement could turn into a Sendero-style civil war, the army has instituted a far-reaching program of preventive counterinsurgency, including assistance to local communities with development projects, transportation, and education. The socioeconomic mission of the armed forces has also resulted in a growing complex of military-owned industries.[39] Originally funded from oil revenues earmarked for the Junta Nacional de Defensa, the Army's Industrial Directorate (DINE) owns its own munitions factory and produces uniforms and other supplies for the armed forces. DINE is also a partner in eighteen mixed enterprises employing more than 25,000 people in steel, metalworking, chemicals, cement, and ceramics. Although initially oriented toward "basic industries" that supply the armed forces or other state agencies, DINE later expanded its investments in companies supplying inputs for the construction and metalworking sectors. The most dramatic indicator of its expanded portfolio is its minority participation in several automobile assembly plants jointly owned by major car manufacturers and local capital. In the late 1980s, DINE entered the mining sector in joint enterprises with local and multinational corporations. The army's agrarian conscription program, begun by the 1963–66 military government, trains recruits in farming technology and provides a cheap source of labor for a dozen haciendas owned by the army, which supply nearby military bases and sell their excess production on the open market. Several banana plantations and a shrimp farm produce goods for the export market. Shrimp exports and investments in the automotive sector have been particularly profitable, generating funds for further expansion. Planned projects include a five-star hotel, a fertilizer plant, paper mill, and pharmaceuticals. The Navy operates a merchant marine fleet (TRANSNAVE), an oil tanker fleet (FLOPEC), and a shipyard serving military and civilian clients. By law a certain percentage of oil and other exports must be carried in Ecuadorian bottoms, guaranteeing TRANSNAVE and FLOPEC a share of the shipping market. The Air Force runs the Civil Aviation agency, its own cargo and passenger line (TAME), and an aircraft maintenance facility. The Corps of Engineers constructs public works for state and semiautonomous agencies and provides security and maintenance services for oil and gas pipelines.

The military's role in development and in coordinating the mobilization of national power in times of national emergency—internal or external—pro- **121** vides a rationale for a growing military presence in education and civil defense. The military academy, now the Escuela Superior del Ejército, is fed by ten military high schools, which draw from an expanding network of military-style elementary schools. The Escuela Superior Politécnica del Ejército (ESPE) has become arguably the country's premier scientific-technical university, serving a student body that is 95 percent civilian. The Institute of Higher National Studies, the Ecuadorian national war college, trains civilians—principally upper-middle-level government employees—and a limited number of senior officers in national security planning and strategy. The 1979 National Security Law, decreed just before the political transition, provides for an extensive military role in national mobilization, which has in turn led to the formation of various paramilitary auxiliaries, especially youth groups, who participate in civil defense and civic action activities.[40]

Neither civic action nor military industries are in themselves objectionable. Many of the military's services to the poorest sectors of Ecuadorian society are laudable. Despite certain state subsidies, the military's economic enterprises seem to be efficiently run and collectively profitable. Nevertheless, the expanded military role in civic action, in the economy, and in education involves serious tensions with the ideal of democratic civil-military relations.

First, all of these activities are to a very large degree initiated and controlled by the military. Both the goals and the specific activities of the armed forces in civic action and social services are established by the armed forces. While these are in principle subject to the authority of the president acting through the minister of defense, there is no evidence of active civilian policy direction or oversight of these activities. Military commanders often lobby other government agencies for personnel and budgetary resources to support various development activities; typically the initiative comes from the military seeking civilian participation in military projects, rather than vice versa. Given current patterns of civil-military relations, the expanded missions of the armed forces effectively enlarge their already considerable scope of autonomous action. To the extent that military enterprises are indeed profitable, military autonomy is further increased by the ability of the armed forces to self-finance their activities outside of the already modest mechanisms of budgetary control. In 1991, it was estimated that FLOPEC and TRANSNAVE provided roughly 8 percent of the Navy's expenditures through off-budget revenues.[41]

Second, these expanded missions invariably involve the armed forces in politically controversial policy questions. Expanded civic action programs in the sierra have drawn the armed forces into a complex alliance with evangelical groups against grass-roots organizations allied with progressive sectors of the Catholic Church. Given its internal security role, the military has a decidedly partisan view of left-wing organizations representing the indigenous peoples of the Amazon and the sierra.[42] Socioeconomic roles also create vested institutional interests that each military force must defend. Given its network of industries, the army is, for example, an interested party in policy debates over the reform of labor laws. Military investments in automobile assembly plants may be affected by the tariff reductions in the Andean Pact, which will expose the industry to greater foreign competition. Not surprisingly, the Association of Retired Generals and Admirals took an active role in opposition to the Durán administration's 1994 privatization proposals, arguing that they threatened vital national (and institutional) interests. A year later, the Joint Command opposed a government-union proposal for privatization of the state electric company because it failed to recognize hydroelectricity as a strategic resource, requiring prior consultation with the armed forces before issuance of contracts or permits.[43] In other cases, notably the automotive sector and the military-owned Banco Ruminahui, the military presence serves—implicitly or explicitly—as an investment guarantee against government nationalization of that sector of the economy. In contrast to the military's vision of itself as the embodiment of national interests, as a result of its development activities, the military's concrete interests are increasingly that of an industrialist, employer, investor, and property owner.[44]

Third, the expanded role of the armed forces in providing social services and entrepreneurship inevitably entails opportunity costs in terms of the failure to develop civilian institutions capable of fulfilling those social functions.

By converting the armed forces into the instrument through which certain social groups resolve their concrete needs, the possibility is diminished that those groups will constitute [their own] horizontal organizational networks or increase their political participation ... [to] demand that the State fulfill its responsibility to civil society. In this way, the social service activities of the armed forces become a mechanism of social control similar to that of political clientelism.[45]

Financed in large part by the infusion of oil revenues, over the last two decades the scope and intensity of military penetration of civil society has increased without a corresponding growth in governmental control of the armed forces or mechanisms for military accountability to the larger society.

Theories of Revolutionary War

The final and most complex question of doctrinal continuity concerns theories of revolutionary war.[46] Military involvement in internal security missions need not automatically result in human rights violations or other risks to democracy. Given a perceived threat to internal security, there are multiple ways of defining that threat and the appropriate military and nonmilitary responses. Italy, Spain, and Great Britain have all confronted violent revolutionary movements without the systematic use of torture or disappearances. Enforcing the rule of law during internal wars is perhaps the most difficult task facing policymakers trying to promote democratic control of armed forces in Latin America. The success or failure of that effort will depend in part on the intensity of the threat, but also on the doctrines that inform the interpretation and responses to the threat. Hence, it is important to ask whether doctrines of revolutionary war have, in fact, changed.

Initially, there was substantial continuity in the Argentine doctrine of ideological warfare. More than three years *after* the return to democracy, the army officers' association published *La ideología y la nueva guerra* in its recommended reading series. Citing Gramsci, the military author claims that the struggle between Christianity and marxism is centered not on the battlefield, but in religion, philosophy, culture, and politics.[47] The fundamental field of battle is civil society. Its chief protagonists are the intellectuals because of their crucial role in maintaining or undermining the ideological basis for legitimation of the current social order.

> In revolutionary war, ideology is the fundamental means to achieve the objective so highly prized: the mind, not only of the adversary, but also that of [those who are] indifferent and the confused. . . . Revolutionary conflicts are initiated "imperceptibly," and when its [overt] manifestations appear, it is perhaps too late . . . . In revolutionary war, there is no front or rear, due to its very nature, hence it is impossible to establish limits. . . . Revolutionary conflicts are essentially cultural, political, and social processes, rather than military [conflicts].[48]

In this view, guerrilla warfare is only the culmination of a long, prior war of infiltration, propaganda, political organization, and ideological penetration

in order to undermine the existing order and destroy the enemy's will to resist. For the armed forces, therefore, the enemy is not simply the guerrilla, but
rather "the subversion [that] seeks to capture the population to the detriment
of the spiritual and material authority of the government."[49]

Consistent with this ideological definition of the threat, some Argentine officers emphasized the continuing problem of subversion in the 1985 interviews.

I can't believe that . . . the guerrilla [problem] will never return. [It] will return because
[that] is still a part of marxism. . . . [We] have to react to this cancer that the country
has. [There are] rumors of [leftists] training popular militias. There have to be strong
intelligence services. [You can] see the subversion in the television, radio, movies, films,
[and] political dialogues that are subtly putting [their] ideas in or discrediting ideas that
[are] the basis of democracy. The University Council is infiltrated by subversives. [You
can] see [it] in the schools, in my daughter's high school, in the student center in the
high schools. The press comes out with stories of the Mothers of the Plaza, which is a
destructive act in plain view.

When subversion occurs in education, culture, the communications media, who will
preserve the democratic system?[50]

From this perspective, any political views not based in a conservative Catholic conception of Argentine values are by definition subversive. In its extreme
form, even moderate elements of the political left become part of the internal
enemy. Consistent with this view, clandestine documents circulated by retired
officers and army intelligence units depicted the Alfonsín government as thor-
oughly infiltrated by communists and fellow travelers.[51] Nevertheless, even in
1985, this perspective seemed to be limited to the more conservative sectors of
the military. Even as they defended the military's actions in the antisubversive
campaign, most officers talked about the armed conflict with rural and urban
guerrillas rather than the ideological threat.

In contrast, a 1990 volume, *La Violencia Antidemocrática en el tiempo, en
el mundo, y en la Argentina,* utilized in the Navy Intelligence School, defines
the internal security problem as violence by antidemocratic groups.[52] In this
view, the armed forces exist to defend democracy rather than a "national identity." Democracy is interpreted as the existing democratic regime, rather than
a Western Christian life-style.[53] Although terrorism and subversion are given
extensive treatment as methods of revolutionary struggle, the author (a retired
officer) distinguishes between youthful rebellion and revolutionary action and
between the legal and violent left. Revolutionary violence in Argentina is attributed to a complex amalgam of sociological and ideological conditions,
including social modernization, a faltering economy, the decline of traditional
social norms, rising anomie, and "a subculture of violence" within certain sec-

tors of the Peronist left. Unlike most military accounts, this work specifically points to the origins of marxist and Peronist guerrilla organizations in the political polarization that occurred in the latter stages of the Onganía regime[54] rather than in the chaos of Isabel Perón's presidency. Although it devotes most of its pages to the revolutionary left, the analysis includes right-wing terrorist groups, such as the Triple-A (Argentine Anti-Communist Alliance), and makes at least brief references to human rights and state terror.[55] Though hardly a complete break with the theory of ideological war, *La Violencia Antidemocrática* nevertheless represents an alternative account of the problem of internal security.

125

Because internal security is now legally the responsibility of the national police, the Gendarmería, and the Prefectura Naval, most civilian efforts at doctrinal reform have focused not on the military, but rather the security forces. Congressional advisor José Manuel Ugarte and the Fundación Arturo Illia have worked closely with the Gendarmería to develop a legal and institutional framework for responding to future threats. Ugarte's book, *Seguridad Interior,* analyzes various Latin American cases, but places particular emphasis on European models—Spain, Italy, and West Germany.[56] Ugarte criticizes the confounding of national defense and internal security, arguing that each has its own distinct strategy and methods. He defines internal security as the "full operation of the constitutional, legal, and regulatory norms of the Republic." The objective of internal security is the effective operation of the state of law within the national boundaries and the defense "of the democratic and constitutional system of the Argentine Nation, [and] the life, liberty, and personal integrity of its inhabitants." Hence the only justification for employing the security forces is the breaking of the law. Internal security does not exist to "impose ideologies nor [to insure] unconditional subordination to the state."[57]

These books are at most a starting point for more detailed analysis, but they demonstrate clearly the existence of a debate within the armed forces and the larger society over the nature of the internal enemy and the appropriate responses to that threat. More than a decade after the trial of the juntas there is also, belatedly, a military debate about human rights abuses in the antisubversive campaign. In 1985, criticism of torture and disappearances was limited to a small fraction of retired officers; among active duty officers, defense of the dirty war was nearly universal.

[In wars, there are always] excesses. [Look at] Hiroshima, Nagasaki. Truman was not tried because Truman won. [The bombings violated] the rules of conventional war, when the war was already won. [There were] probably political objectives. [Sometimes you have to choose] one person's life over another. . . . [It was] the same as Great Britain in Northern Ireland [or] the French bombings [in Algeria]. Who was tried for the war in Algeria? I am not applauding sadism, but posing [these questions]. . . . If the armed forces had not triumphed over the subversion, [Argentina would be ruled today by] Firmenich [and] Santucho. Wars are won when you can. [Wars involve] two wills, yours and the enemy's. [It's not a question of] means and ends. War imposes [its own] ethic [, which] is not like times of peace.

[You fight] the wars that circumstances impose. Terrorism [is] irrational; antiterrorism should not be [irrational] also. I don't accept robbery [or the use of antisubversive operations to settle] personal feuds, [but you have to] annihilate the enemy. [You have to] break [the enemy's] will. [The rule of war] is surrender or die. You have to break [his] will. We won the war.

If the Montoneros were the enemy and the armed forces . . . received the mission to annihilate the subversion, the actions resulting [from that order] were acts of war. Thus, here there was a war, which we suffered, and war is a political phenomenon, not a juridical [act]. As a result, to judge the winners of that war and to pretend to justify or vindicate the motives, proposals, and conduct of those [who are] exclusively responsible for unleashing [the war] and its development is an irrational and aberrant act. . . . It is the equivalent of condemning the surgeon who removed a malignant tumor because of the scars left by his scalpel.[58]

By 1992, the antisubversive campaign was an open topic for criticism in military schools and private discussions, though rarely in public. Despite the general consensus that the antisubversive campaign saved Argentina from marxism, General Videla's decision to fight a clandestine war, secretly executing prisoners without trial, was widely criticized.[59]

Faced with the guerrilla threat, the military was totally subordinated to the *Proceso*, a government that did not comply with any of its objectives, that seriously compromised the future of the armed forces and caused a serious conflict with the society. The struggle against subversion was a military success, but a total political defeat, which suggests that the means utilized [in that struggle] were not appropriate for internal security. The *Proceso* opened up Pandora's box and ended up with violence for violence's sake.

It should have been done openly, formally, in uniform. If we had the truth, [if we were] right, we have to fight with our arms, not with the methods of terrorism.[60]

Public acknowledgment by military commanders that human rights abuses were committed during the military regime—and junta member Massera's angry denial—are the outward signs of a discussion that has been quietly taking place for some time.[61] In that debate, Massera no doubt speaks for some active duty officers, but the bulk of his military support comes from retired officers. Representing the opposing perspective, one army major said simply, "In 1976, with democracy, with the law, we could have ended the struggle against subversion in six months."[62] Congratulating the graduates of various army schools in 1992, Army Chief of Staff Balza pointedly underlined the subordination of the armed forces to the political system and the obligation of all officers to obey legitimate orders, but only legitimate orders.[63] Three years later, Balza admitted that the Army had used "illegitimate methods" in the fight against subversion and that the armed forces must assume their share of responsibility for the past. Again, he reiterated that no one is obliged to carry out an immoral or illegal order: "He who violates the Constitution is breaking the law. He who gives immoral orders is breaking the law. He who carries out those orders is breaking the law. He who employs unjust, immoral means to achieve an end he believes just is committing a crime."

127

Neither the current balance of military opinion nor the ultimate outcome of this debate can be predicted with any certainty. Nevertheless, three factors have changed significantly since 1985. First, the passage of time and Menem's amnesty have progressively delinked the issue of the methods used by the anti-subversive campaign from the defense of the institution against the multiple attacks of the Alfonsín years. Criticism of the dirty war is no longer disloyalty to the institution. Second, with the collapse of communist regimes in the Soviet Union and Eastern Europe and the evident weakness of the Argentine left, the doctrine of ideological war lacks credibility. Today Massera's outbursts or the writings of retired General Benjamín Menéndez sound like echoes of "the dinosaurs." Third, as a result of the purging of rebel officers after each of the four *carapintada* revolts, the officers most sympathetic to the hard-line position are now mostly outside of the military institution.

Analysis of the Ecuadorian case is complicated by the lesser number of military writings on the subject, but the interview evidence suggests a parallel debate over the nature of the internal threat and the appropriate policy response. A few officers expressed what appears to be the Ecuadorian equivalent of the doctrine of ideological war.

[Despite] the failures of the communists, the ideas persist, [now] trying to disguise themselves under the guise of indigenous [peoples'] reforms. [There are] increasing conspiracies against the armed forces because the military are a brake that avoids the collapse [of the state].... The [Borja] government is part of the marxist, terrorist subversion. [There are] serious questions about its involvement in drugs. In Colombia, Peru, and Ecuador, narco-terrorism [is] increasing. [It's] absolutely, positively integrated. The result is the intervention of the government in the indigenous uprising. What is happening is the complicity of the government in provoking conflict.... Underneath all this is the desire to keep pushing the class struggle, [and] the conception that the lower strata [ought to] seize power, without education, without culture, [so that] others [can] capitalize on that power. The extreme left, that now doesn't have a floor to stand on, is using the issue of the indigenous people. The Democratic Left and Popular Democracy disown the concept of the Western Christian world in favor of a Cuban-type doctrine.[64] Still, the predominant view emphasizes the socioeconomic roots of revolutionary violence.

I have studied the problems of internal security in Eastern Europe and the U.S.S.R. Not one [of these revolutions occurred] for ideological reasons. The essence is the sociological reality.

Subversion is the result of the lack of satisfaction of basic needs. The solution is sociopolitical, socioeconomic. . . . The changes in the world, in Eastern Europe, in the Soviet Union, the dismantling of communism have decreased local branch operations, but [there are] still people that don't want to accept the fate of socialism. . . . CONAIE [is] not subversive, [but it is] class-based. [It] is only part of the indigenous movement. The majority are independents.

In this view, Ecuador's ethnic and social conditions are exploited by the extreme left, spreading subversive ideas that could lead to violent confrontations, therefore the armed forces and the government must attack the causes, the social conditions giving rise to the discontent.[65] Note the potential here for overlapping the ideological and sociological perspectives.

The problem is sociopolitical. All [governments] have neglected the Indian. . . . But [the problem] is also manipulated by the politicians [and] groups that have lost [at the level of] global strategy, the extreme left, [who] are looking for Indian votes. [Given their lack of education, the Indians] are easy to fool. . . . The Catholic Church that [once] controlled the countryside [is now] getting into the political area [under the influence of] "liberation theology," [which is nothing but] a marxist sonata. The Socialists, the Social Democrats, which are part of the Fourth International, ¡Alfaro Vive Carajo!, [are] the extreme left. The Indian is not proletarian; [the problem is] based on the social problem. The Constitution [gives the military responsibility for] external and internal security [and] contributing to development. The National Security Law [spells out these] intrinsic obligations. [The armed forces] have to watch out for and support development, [so we created military] industries, agrarian conscription, and civic action. Taking this thinking [seriously], the joint staff is disposed to put [our best] efforts into [solving] the social problems [of the country]. It is necessary [to address internal security problems] not with bullets, but with social and political [measures]. [The military] wants [to do] good for good's sake. We are not being political. . . . The common question [for Ecuador and Peru] is how to confront [this type of threat]. . . . [We] can't wait until it explodes [like Peru], [so we are] fighting [it] before it explodes.[66]

Despite the perception that these actions are "not political," this vision of the security problem legitimates a tutelary role to pressure the government for development programs that would reduce the threat of insurgency. Frustration with government responses to those pressures contributes, in turn, to the dis-

128

illusionment with the civilian regime, reinforcing the argument for military tutelage.

Finally, as detailed in chapter 3, the interview data from Ecuador and Argentina show no evidence of a "national security" role belief legitimating institutional military rule. Officers who endorsed a "guardian role" for the armed forces regarded any return to military government as a short-term transitory measure. While this result is heartening, it represents less of a change than it might appear. Even in the Ecuadorian military government of 1963–66, only a third of the senior officers were "developmentalists"; nearly half advocated a more traditional role as "guardians" in times of national crisis.[67] Evidence of **129** splits over the duration of military rule in other military governments suggests that doctrinal justifications for indefinite military rule in the name of national security were never universally accepted in most Latin American militaries. Even in the 1960s and 1970s, justifications for military rule tended to be largely situational, stated in terms of the concrete circumstances that "required" the armed forces to take over.[68] Explicit defense of military rule as a general model was relatively rare. Military rulers regularly promised an eventual return to democracy, even when they tried to institutionalize long-term regimes. Hence, for many officers, the transition to democracy does not represent a radical change in role beliefs, but rather a return to "normalcy."

Context, Continuity, and Change

In conclusion, there are elements of both continuity and change in military doctrines of national security. As in previous decades, there are also important variations — between individual officers and factions, across countries, and over time — which defy any simple generalization. The Ecuadorian military's thinking about questions of internal security and development, institutionalized in the Instituto de Altos Estudios Nacionales, still draws heavily from the Alliance for Progress and the U.N. Economic Commission for Latin America. As such, current military teachings have more in common with the Junta Militar of the 1960s than with the doctrine of national security applied in the Southern Cone in the 1970s. In contrast to the brutal abuses of the dirty war, the Ecuadorian response to the twin pressures of the indigenous movement and the international context includes a cautious but ongoing dialogue with local human rights groups. In Argentina, traditional threat perceptions and military missions have been substantially modified. Despite some criticism, the traditional colonizing mission and development role have been replaced by a far more modest role in disaster relief and community assistance and by active participation in international peacekeeping forces. The military's role in internal security has been reduced to a reserve force to be utilized only if other forces are overwhelmed. That change is still bitterly opposed by some officers, but the new definition of military missions—in particular, the primacy of external defense—is widely accepted within the active ranks. The concept of revolution as ideological war persists, but that view of the internal security problem appears to be a minority perspective in both countries. The Argentine military's increasingly marginal and specialized role in the larger society contrasts sharply with the Ecuadorian military's expanded penetration of civil society in education, civic action, and the economy. The lack of effective civilian policy control over the Ecuadorian armed forces and the increasingly active military lobby for policies consistent with its vision of "security and development" involve serious tensions with democratic norms of civil-military relations.

In both countries, the military's technocratic view of national security policy encourages disrespect for civilian leadership. The structural deficiencies of civilian institutions make that problem far more severe in Ecuador than Argentina. Other elements of national security doctrine, including theories of revolutionary war and the security-development linkage, are now actively contested not only in the larger society, but within the military itself. In the 1960s and 1970s, the national and international context combined to produce temporary military convergence around specific versions of national security doctrine in Brazil, Peru, Argentina, and Chile. An Argentine officer recalled the 1976 crisis as a moment when "the armed forces [were] perfectly coherent, [with] a single doctrine. [They were] the only instrument to save the fatherland."[69] Except perhaps for Chile, doctrinal consensus was transitory. Ideological divisions over the substance of government policy quickly reemerged once the immediate threats to military security were suppressed. Following the return to democracy, there is no evidence of marked doctrinal discontinuity, but the internal disagreements also persist. The fall of the Berlin Wall, the collapse of communist regimes, and the global triumph of democracy all contribute to an international context that is markedly different from the 1970s and radically incongruent with the hard-line view of Latin America as the ideological battleground for "World War III." In Argentina, the experience of the *Proceso* discredited the previous national security doctrine, even within the military. In Ecuador, the sociopolitical view of internal security, which commands a substantial degree of consensus, could become a coherent rationale for a tutelary military role within the current regime if the threat intensifies and the current weaknesses of civilian institutions continue. Still, so far there is no agreement on the political implications of that interpretation of the security problem. For officers who focus on external defense, the conflict with Peru still provides a credible professionalist argument for limiting the military's role in politics. For others, the international context provides strong incentives to find solutions to the internal security problem within some form of constitutional democracy. At least in these two countries, democratic governments in the 1990s do not confront a coherent doctrinal justification for nondemocratic role beliefs. Relative to prior decades, there is now a substantial degree of disarticulation between the various components of military thinking about national security.

Policy Implications

The internal debate within the Latin American armed forces regarding national security in the new international environment provides an opening for a wider debate on the linkages between democracy and internal and international security. Consolidating and institutionalizing democratic patterns of civil-military relations will require significant changes in current doctrines of national security. The concept of national security is not in itself inconsistent with democratic control of the armed forces. Military doctrine in the Western democracies acknowledges that national security is affected by many factors other than military power. In democratic regimes, this premise is the basis for institutional mechanisms for coordination of foreign policy, defense policy, and economic policy. It is not used as an argument for extending military control into nonmilitary policy issues or subordinating other national objectives to national security. The difference is reflected in national security councils, which bring together *civilian* ministers, who are *advised* by mixed staffs of military officers and civilian experts, rather than security councils, like that of Chile, in which military officers are de jure voting members. National security is, as many officers reminded me, also the duty of civilian leaders. That duty cannot, however, bind political leaders to a military vision of national security or subordinate democracy to security.

The second necessary step toward reshaping national security doctrines is an effort to develop within the Latin American armed forces a more sophisticated understanding of politics and government. Military officers often speak of political leadership as a process of defining the country's long-term national objectives, designing strategies to overcome obstacles to the realization of those objectives, and efficient execution of those strategies. Ecuadorian officers, complaining about various policy problems, argued "all this is a product of a lack of leadership and credibility of political officials, of the absence of national objectives clearly expressed by the government."[70] This view of governing as an exercise in synoptic rationality is common to bureaucratic elites, but seemingly exaggerated among military officers. In the extreme case, national policy-making is reduced to a deductive, top-down process of coordinating the economic, military, diplomatic, and domestic "fronts." There appears to be little or no questioning of the assumption that one could derive an objectively defined specification of "the national interests" or "the common good." Modern notions of "bounded rationality," complex systems, or organizational behavior[71] do not appear to be part of military curricula, even at the higher levels of the military training system. As long as synoptic rationality remains the normative standard, civilian leaders will be denigrated as politicians, rather than "statesmen." Although the organic statist concept of politics long predates the national security framework, the language of national security legitimizes the teaching of a particularly narrow view of policy and politics. The inability of even military regimes to measure up to the requirements of the synoptic model provides an opening for reconsideration of the appropriateness of that model for societies characterized by their social and ideological diversity. In the short run, political leaders and political scientists need to engage their military colleagues in a dialogue about basic assumptions of politics and government. In the long term, more sophisticated understandings of politics need to be incorporated into both basic and advanced military education.

Third, Latin American countries need to develop appropriate doctrines for the defense of democracy against revolutionary violence and terrorism. In established democracies, national security doctrine is rarely applied to internal security. Control over terrorism and domestic disorders are basically police functions, rather than missions assigned to the armed forces. Latin American countries face a substantially greater potential for political violence and organized attempts to overthrow democratic regimes by force. Military doctrines stressing the threat of ideological subversion from within are hostile to democracy and prone to human rights violations that undermine the legitimacy of the democratic state. Counterinsurgency doctrines stressing the socioeconomic roots of revolution are more benign in terms of policy impacts and human rights. Nevertheless, they encourage greater military penetration of civil society and a military lobby pushing for policies the military deems necessary to counter the insurgency threat. Democratic regimes cannot deny the existence of internal security problems. They cannot, however, solve those problems by applying current military doctrines without jeopardizing the democratic character of the regime. At a minimum, democratic governments must clearly delineate the lines between police and military roles in internal security. Insofar as possible, the armed forces should be removed from primary responsibility for internal security, without denying the need for trained counterinsurgency forces to intervene when antidemocratic forces attempt to establish a territorial base. Ultimately democratic regimes will need to develop an alternative counterinsurgency doctrine that acknowledges the *political* character of the internal security problem and takes advantage of the legitimacy and inclusiveness of democratic regimes to isolate and politically defeat violent antiregime forces.

Reshaping the doctrinal trends of the last four decades will be a lengthy and complex process. Evidence that such changes are possible can be seen in the emergence of new doctrines focusing on regional security. Argentine, Brazilian, and Chilean officers and civilian experts have conducted an extensive dialogue focusing on subregional security, confidence-building measures, and military integration, particularly within the context of the Mercosur. Although not yet accepted as official doctrine in any of the countries in question, these efforts have produced a growing literature on regional security and such unconventional topics as arms limitation agreements, peacekeeping, and international conflict management.[72] From the perspective of civil-military relations, the importance of these efforts is that they begin — implicitly or explicitly — with the premise that these arrangements are possible because these are democratic regimes and, hence, worthy of cooperation and trust, even among countries that have historically been military rivals.[73] The Argentine interviews demonstrate clearly the possibilities for change in traditional threat perceptions dating back to the nineteenth century. These efforts have also contributed to democratic civil-military relations by making these aspects of military doctrine a matter of public debate and dialogue, rather than a reserved arena limited to the armed forces.

133

CHAPTER FIVE

Military Policy and Democratic Consolidation in Latin America

Civilian leaders in unconsolidated democracies are confronted with a basic policy dilemma. To the extent that they attempt to reduce the political power of the military or increase civilian control of the armed forces, their actions are likely to increase civil-military conflict and undermine military confidence in the new regime, thereby increasing the short-term risk of a coup. On the other hand, civilian failure to push for changes in nondemocratic patterns of civil-military relations increases the long-term risk that posttransition regimes will be neither democratic nor stable. In Guillermo O'Donnell's rather pessimistic view, Latin America risks "backsliding into authoritarianism, either through the 'quick death' of a conventional military coup or through the 'slow death' of a gradual erosion of democratic practice."[1] This chapter analyzes civilian policies toward the armed forces in a variety of Latin American contexts. Based on those cases, I propose a framework for explaining the success or failure of those policies. The chapter concludes with suggested strategies for promoting more democratic forms of civil-military relations, taking into account the diverse starting points of the posttransition regimes.

Military Policy and Democratic Civil-Military Relations

Military policy is defined here as the entire set of government policies that deal with civil-military relations, that is to say, the relationships between the armed forces, the state, and the rest of society.[2] Military policy is therefore distinct from defense policy, whose objective is to provide for the defense of the country against current and future threats to its security. On the constitutive level, military policy aims at constructing and maintaining a particular model of civil-military relations. On the operational level, military policy involves the day-to-day operation of that system, particularly the execution of responsibilities assigned to civilian authorities in that model. In established democracies, policy debates tend to center on the military budget and substantive issues of defense policy; military policy is mostly operational, routine, and highly institutionalized. In new democracies, operational considerations are important, but logically secondary to the more fundamental question of defining the power and authority relations between civilian and military institutions.

A military policy for democratic consolidation takes as its ultimate objective the creation of a system of civil-military relations insuring democratic control of the armed forces. Over time, such a policy entails reducing the political power of the military over the government, extending civilian authority to include control over defense policy, and incorporating the armed forces within the rule of law. In all three areas, military policy involves the creation of an institutional framework through which democratic control is exercised and maintained.

135

Although civilian governments in Latin America operate under different systems of civil-military relations, the common challenge is to move toward more democratic relationships with the armed forces. In most countries, changes in current patterns of civil-military interaction are essential to the long-term survival of democratic regimes. However, attempts to restrict the political influence of the armed forces are likely to be viewed as unwarranted civilian interference with the military's ability to carry out its responsibilities for national security. Civilian attempts to reduce the military's institutional autonomy may be viewed as threatening the institutional interests of the armed forces. In the short-term, then, the task of military policy is to reduce the military's power and extend government control over the military, while managing the situational calculus facing the armed forces so that the "costs of democracy" are less than the costs of a military coup.

Over the longer term, however, civilian policies that antagonize the armed forces may also weaken military confidence in civilian competence to govern effectively, which is, in turn, an important determinant of military role beliefs. Diminished military confidence in civilian leadership reinforces those officers who argue for maintaining the military's guardian role. The long-term task of changing military role beliefs and building military loyalty to the democratic regime thus involves a delicate balance between giving the military a voice and adequate incentives to work within the system[3] and, on the other hand, avoiding military prerogatives that make that system undemocratic. Civilian leaders are thus faced with complex and difficult choices in military policy, with serious tensions between the long-term goal of more democratic civil-military relations and the short-term goal of political survival. While the objective is clear, it is not at all certain how to get there from here, especially when different countries begin the journey from such divergent starting points.

Case Studies in Military Policy

Less than twenty years have passed since the installation of civilian governments in the Andean countries that led the democratic transition. In other cases, including Brazil and Guatemala, civilian presidents have been in office only since 1985. Chile is in only its second civilian administration. Still, the experiences to date of the new democracies illustrate the multiple difficulties facing civilians attempting to redefine existing relationships with the armed forces.[4] The analysis that follows compares cases *within* the basic types of civil-military relations described in chapter 2 in order to reduce some of the variance in the context of civilian choices about how to approach relationships with the armed forces. It is neither politically realistic nor analytically useful to compare President Cerezo's policies in Guatemala with those of President Alfonsín in Argentina. Existing patterns of civil-military relations provide the basic context in which military policy choices are made, setting constraints on what choices are politically feasible or opening possibilities for reform. Focusing on (roughly) comparable cases allows us to examine the similarities and differences in policy choices by governments facing similar constraints and similar agendas for reform.

Asserting Civilian Control: Argentina and Uruguay

By all accounts, Argentina enjoyed the most favorable initial conditions for major changes in civil-military relations.[5] The military's defeat in the Malvinas/Falklands war with Great Britain divided and demoralized the armed forces. The economic and political failures of the military regime convinced most officers that they were unprepared for the task of governing. Civilian repudiation of human rights violations by the military regime isolated the military from its traditional civilian allies. Under these circumstances, initially the armed forces had no alternative but to accept their subordination to the new regime.

During his first three years in office, President Alfonsín took advantage of the military's unusual weakness to impose a substantial degree of democratic control. The civilian Ministry of Defense was upgraded from a minor administrative office into an instrument for defense and military policy, with planning, interservice coordination, and oversight functions. A new system of financial management gave the government greater control over military budgets and disbursement of funds. Control over military enterprises was transferred from the individual services to the Ministry of Defense, with promises that non-defense firms would be privatized.[6] The traditionally autonomous commanders of the three services were replaced by chiefs of staff for each service.[7] Primary responsibility for internal security was assigned to the Ministry of the Interior and efforts were made to demilitarize the state intelligence agency. A number of generals, including several Army chiefs, were fired for speaking publicly on what the government considered to be political questions. The military budget was slashed from 3.8 percent of GDP to 1.9 percent.[8] Military salaries declined sharply. Budget restrictions limited the rate and duration of military conscription, substantially reducing the size of the armed forces.[9]

From the very beginning, Alfonsín's relations with the military were complicated by the problem of how to deal with the legacy of the past, particularly the question of accountability for thousands of "disappearances" during the military regime.[10] Amid widespread rumors that the Peronist candidate might accept the military's self-amnesty, Alfonsín's promise to punish human rights violators was an important factor in his unexpected victory in the 1983 elections.[11] Shortly after taking office, the government sent to Congress legislation that repealed the self-amnesty decreed by the military government and mandated automatic appeal of all decisions of the Supreme Military Tribunal to civilian courts. A national commission was appointed to investigate the fate of the disappeared persons. Its report documented the existence of a clandestine military-police network of more than 300 detention centers in which suspected subversives were tortured and, in most cases, summarily executed. The commission documented nearly nine thousand disappearances.[12] Criminal charges for murder, kidnapping, and falsification of documents were filed against the nine service commanders who constituted the first three military juntas. The government hoped that the military would "purify itself" by conducting its own trials of the worst offenders, but after repeated delays, the Supreme Military Tribunal finally ruled that there were no grounds for prosecution of the juntas. The case thus passed to the civilian court of appeals, which eventually sentenced two members of the first junta to life imprisonment, imposed varying prison terms on three others, and acquitted the rest. General Camps, one of the most outspoken defenders of the dirty war, was sentenced to twenty-five years in prison in a separate trial.[13] Charges were subsequently filed against a growing number of other officers.

Military reaction to the trials was overwhelmingly, bitterly negative. Despite Alfonsín's insistence that only individuals were on trial, not the military as an institution, in practice the trials became a highly emotional civilian condemnation of the military regime.[14] For a society whose normal ethical instincts had been intimidated by the *Proceso*'s intense culture of fear,[15] the trials triggered an outpouring of moral outrage at the daily stories of torture, rape, robbery, and extortion. For the armed forces, the trials could not be a judgment against individuals since the "campaign against subversion" involved all three forces and all levels of the military hierarchy. Moreover, in the military's view, the defeat of the Montonero and ERP guerrillas was virtually the only success of the military regime, a war they fought and won against a large and well-organized enemy.[16] Military reaction to the trials also reflected other discontents—declining salaries, budgetary restrictions, and constant criticism in the press and mass media—which were widely perceived as attempts to undermine or destroy the armed forces.[17] Still, the most deeply felt attack was the challenge to the military's self-image as an institution based on moral values. Defense of the military's conduct in the internal war thus became a moral defense of the institution.[18] The military's unrepentant stance was captured in a widely distributed flier:

> That we were cruel? So what! Meanwhile you have a fatherland that is not compromised for doing so. We saved it because we believed that we ought to save it. Were there other means? We did not see them, nor did we believe that with other means we would have been capable of doing what we did. Throw the blame in our face and enjoy the results. We will be the executioners, so you can be free men.[19]

Active duty officers conspicuously attended masses organized by families of victims of the guerrillas. Military intelligence units and former dirty war operatives conducted a clandestine campaign of propaganda bombings and death threats, which forced the government to declare a state of siege shortly before the 1985 elections.

Belatedly recognizing the depth of the military opposition to the trials, Alfonsín sent to Congress a new law, setting a date after which no new charges could be filed. However, the *Punto Final* law mobilized human rights groups to file charges against several hundred more officers, including many on active duty who had been lieutenants and captains during the dirty war. In April 1987,

Major Ernesto Barreiro refused to appear in court and declared a barracks revolt against the Army chief of staff for failing to defend the institution. Despite a massive mobilization of the civilian population to defend the democratic regime, other military units refused to suppress the rebellion in a carefully coordinated campaign of passive resistance. Donning combat gear and camouflage paint to emphasize their criticism of desk-bound generals, the *carapintadas* insisted "Operation Dignity" was not an attempted coup, but a necessary step to put an end to the trials.

After a dramatic last-minute meeting with rebel leaders, Alfonsín announced that he had obtained their surrender without concessions. Nevertheless, he quickly accepted the resignation of the Army chief and subsequently sent to Congress the "Law of Due Obedience," which effectively exonerated most active-duty officers from human rights charges, although some still faced trial.[20] Two new revolts in 1988 extended military demands to include dismissal of all disciplinary actions against rebel officers, release of all officers already convicted of human rights violations, and public vindication of military actions in the "war against subversion." The revolts resulted in minor concessions, but Alfonsín refused to accept the rebels' other demands. Equally important, he refused to appoint an Army chief of staff supported by the *carapintadas*.

The balance sheet for Alfonsín's military policies is a mixture of achievements and failures, which many analysts find disappointing relative to the unusual opportunity for reforms with which his administration began.[21] On the positive side, for the first time since 1928, a democratic government finished its term of office and transferred power to a democratically elected successor. The affirmation of the principles of civilian control and the rule of law set important precedents that have not been repudiated, despite concessions designed to reduce the level of civil-military tensions. Starting almost from scratch, the government and Congress forged a new institutional framework for defense and military policy, which gives civilian authorities a series of instruments taken for granted in established democracies. The commission on disappearances and the trial of the juntas deepened the military's loss of civilian support and strengthened civilian commitment to avoid a return to military rule. As shown in chapter 3, the political subordination of the armed forces to the democratic regime was widely accepted by the military, despite the more overtly political stance of some *carapintadas* in the 1988 elections.[22]

On the negative side, the intense conflict generated by the human rights trials and by the sharp loss of military prerogatives resulted in a substantial retreat from the strong civilian control of the early years of the Alfonsín administration. In practice, the military revolts were internal coups, which forced the resignation of army chiefs who supported administration policies against the wishes of the officer corps. The Semana Santa revolt forced the government to make a convoluted legal retreat on the trials, which seriously damaged its political credibility. The trials unified an otherwise divided military, although they deepened the split between junior and senior officers, with the former— particularly commando veterans of the Malvinas—assuming leadership of the movement to stop the trials and redress other institutional grievances. After the first revolt, Alfonsín was repeatedly trapped in a situation in which the liberal "professionalist" faction could argue that, unless concessions were made on the trials and military salaries, they would lose support in their contest with the *carapintadas* for control of the army. Whether or not these policy changes were warranted on their merit, they resulted in the perception that Alfonsín was making major concessions under military pressure.[23]

Removing the threat of criminal trials in civilian courts for junior officers was morally indefensible, but probably essential to overcoming the *carapintada* threat. As long as the trials continued, the rebels could claim to be defending the military institution, thus capturing broad support from other officers. Once the trials were ended, subsequent rebellions were increasingly perceived by other officers as the defense of particular leaders or ideological positions. Proponents of unrestricted trials argue that, in the Semana Santa revolt, the government should have mobilized the civilian population to surround military bases and to cut off water, electricity, and food supplies. However, the "passive resistance" argument overlooks the fact that military bases normally have their own power and stockpiled supplies, hence the confrontation could have continued for weeks or months, like the sieges of the Freemen and Branch Davidians in the United States. The critical question is whether military forces would have fired on those who "attacked their bases." In Iran and the Philippines, large military forces were neutralized by the massive mobilization of opposition until soldiers and officers refused to continue firing on the protestors. Short of such revolutionary situations, fomenting mass civilian-military confrontation seems likely to end in large-scale bloodshed. Tiananmen Square demonstrated both the power and the limitations of unarmed protestors facing tanks and machine guns. In reality, the rule of law in Argentina's new democracy was too weak to put on trial those who were responsible for the human rights abuses of the *Proceso*. Passage of the Due Obedience law can only be justified as a political decision to save the democratic regime from the threat of even greater dangers, including more debilitating concessions imposed by force and/or a complete loss of civilian control.

Although the concessions undercut military support for the rebels, the threat posed by the *carapintadas* was, in part, the result of the government's confrontational military policies and its inability to control the trials once the decision was made to deal with the human rights issue through the courts. Fearing a coup by hard-line officers, the government originally planned only limited trials, focusing on the juntas and other notorious cases to set an example, but exonerating the rest in order to limit the military backlash. Alfonsín and other key members of the government believed it was the gradual but cumulative erosion of the rule of law that was responsible for the revolutionary violence and counterrevolutionary state terrorism of the 1970s. Hence, the trials were seen as a critical symbolic reaffirmation of the rule of law as the foundation of the new regime.[24] However, national and international law provided no clear legal means for limiting the trials to some officers and not others. In international law, Nuremberg Principle IV holds that "following orders" is not a valid defense against criminal charges for actions committed pursuant to those orders, unless "a moral option was not possible in practice."[25] If, for example, a soldier would have been shot by a superior officer for not following an order to execute a prisoner, due obedience might be invoked in the soldier's defense. However, it was impossible to argue that a "moral option" did not exist in Argentina since some officers did oppose the dirty war, for which they were purged from the army in 1980.[26] In the euphoria of the repeal of the military's amnesty law, the public outcry over the findings of the CONADEP investigation and the immense popularity of the trial of the juntas, the Alfonsín government did not publicly acknowledge its intention to limit the trials. Hence, the government must bear substantial responsibility for the acute sense of public betrayal resulting from the Due Obedience Law.

Plans for military modernization made little or no progress in the face of declining military budgets, lack of civilian direction, and the military's reluctance to cut the size of the officer corps. Especially in the initial years of the new regime, neither the government nor the opposition displayed much interest in substantive issues of military reform or defense policy.[27] The military policy agenda was dominated by the trials and the military revolts; other issues received scant attention from the public or the political leadership. The administration and Congress took four years to replace the military's national security legislation with the new National Defense Law. In crisis situations, the major parties have worked closely to defend the democratic regime. On more mundane but fundamental issues of military policy, partisan differences and the absence of any sense of urgency repeatedly delayed key pieces of legislation.

On balance, the Alfonsín administration made major strides toward effective democratic control of the armed forces. Nevertheless, the gains were less

141

than they might have been. The convoluted retreat on the trials and the still-born military reforms were costly failures. Although the risk of a coup was small, the extraordinary civil-military conflicts of the period exposed the country to a substantial risk that control of the Army would be seized by the *carapintadas*. Although that outcome was ultimately avoided, the potential danger to Argentine democracy must also be counted as a cost of Alfonsín's policies.

For Alfonsín's successor, Carlos Menem, military policy was a distinctly secondary priority. During the last year of the Alfonsín administration, the government's heterodox economic policies collapsed. Production plummeted; inflation soared to more than 4,000 percent for 1989. With real wages in free fall, the presidential elections were a stunning repudiation of the Radical government. In a desperate attempt to avoid economic chaos, Congress hastily passed legislation allowing Alfonsín to hand over power six months ahead of time. The newly elected Peronist president stunned everyone when he decided to confront the economic crisis by allying with the neoconservative Unión de Centro Democrático and putting economic policy in the hands of economists linked to the country's financial elite.[28] Anxious to attract foreign capital and restore investor confidence, President Menem decreed an amnesty that ended the last of the human rights trials. A year later, despite widespread public opposition,[29] he issued a pardon for the convicted members of the juntas, two former police chiefs, civilian officials of the *Proceso,* and a former guerrilla leader. Military budgets were slashed another 23 percent in the first year of the government's harsh new austerity policies, although Menem later responded to military appeals for salary increases to offset the sharp rise in the cost of living resulting from the dollarization of the economy.[30]

Based on contacts with various intermediaries during the election campaign, *carapintada* leaders were initially hopeful of an alliance with Menem. After being forced into retirement following the Villa Martelli revolt, Colonel Seineldín was rumored to be under consideration for a position in the government.[31] The nationalism of the *carapintadas* was, however, fundamentally incompatible with the liberal internationalist policies to which Menem committed himself to solve the economic crisis. After Seineldín was jailed for a letter criticizing government treatment of the military, his followers staged another revolt in December 1990 on the eve of the arrival of U.S. President George Bush. Rebels seized the Army Command building and other installations near the capital. Menem ordered loyal military forces to crush the revolt. Angered by the death of a loyalist officer early in the revolt and fearful of the increasing role of noncommissioned officers in the *carapintada* movement, loyalist forces quickly and forcefully suppressed the revolt. In contrast to the first two rebellions, the 1990 clash left sixteen dead and fifty wounded.[32] Seineldín was subsequently court-martialed and sentenced to life in prison. Other rebel leaders received substantial prison terms rather than simply forced retirement.

In contrast to the frequent criticism by members of the Alfonsín government, Menem seldom misses an opportunity to praise the armed forces, whom he genuinely respects, despite his imprisonment during the military regime. The positive symbolic treatment of the armed forces compensates, at least in part, for the continuing cuts in the military budget, which by 1990 had fallen below the pre-military-regime level.

Menem's military policies achieved their limited purpose. The atmosphere of confrontation and crisis that characterized the Alfonsín years has been replaced by a sense of normalcy in civil-military relations, despite periodic tensions over military budgets and limits on the use of the military for internal security. Menem's 1990 decree authorizing the use of army troops in food riots or civil disturbances provoked acrimonious debates over whether this violated the National Defense Law. Congress finally passed the Internal Security Law, which permits the use of regular military forces under exceptional circumstances, but reaffirms that internal security is the responsibility of the police and security forces under the direction of the minister of the Interior.[33] Under heavy pressure from the United States, Menem and Brazil's President Collor agreed to cancel medium-range missile and nuclear weapons programs, despite strong nationalist opposition.[34] Military complaints about inadequate budgets have mostly been met with civilian indifference. Restructuring of the armed forces to fit lower budgets and diminished threats remains stalled. Despite the need to further downsize the military to allow it to operate effectively under the current budget limitations, no civilian constituency has any real vested interest in whether or not the armed forces have any effective military capability. Increased regional cooperation and the improbability of any military confrontation with Great Britain have virtually eliminated any plausible conventional conflict scenarios. Despite grudging reductions in the numbers of officers, interservice rivalries and corporate self-interest make it difficult for the military to reform itself. Hence, costly duplication continues, in separate military hospitals for each service and multiple schools for pilot training and military intelligence. A few bases have been moved or closed, but the Army continues to maintain its traditional brigade structure and deployment. Critics charge the government has tacitly agreed not to push for reforms as long as the military does not cause any political problems.[35]

The most significant policy change of the Menem era came after the death of a conscript galvanized civilian opposition to the draft. With almost no advance planning, President Menem ordered the end of military conscription in favor of an all-volunteer force. Despite public support for the all-volunteer concept, military defenders of the armed forces' traditional "civilizing role" had successfully blocked any serious internal consideration of ending the draft, claiming that the budget would not allow salaries high enough to attract volunteers. But when the Carrasco affair spurred the government to act, the changeover was accomplished without major obstacles. Women were also allowed into military service for the first time. Given high civilian unemployment, the quality of volunteers has been equivalent to that of draftees; female volunteers have been, on average, substantially better qualified than conscripts. Abolition of the draft will probably reinforce the movement toward relatively small military forces. It may also increase the pressure on the military to maintain a favorable public image in order to maintain an adequate flow of qualified volunteers.

Under Menem, civil-military tensions have been lowered and the political subordination of the military to the democratic regime has been firmly established. Civilian leadership in defense and military policy is still lacking. Given the divisions within the military, civilian leadership is necessary to overcome internal resistance to change. But, as long as civilians care only about possible political threats from the military, military reform will remain a low priority. The scope of democratic control has not increased relative to the Alfonsín years; in some areas, military autonomy has increased as a result of the government's tacit bargain with the armed forces. Still, democratic civil-military relations have become increasingly routine and institutionalized.

The other case where civilian leaders managed to establish a substantial degree of democratic control is Uruguay.[36] Despite the expansion of the armed forces during the 1970s in response to the Tupamaro insurgency and the decay of the traditional political system, Uruguay had a long history of military subordination to constitutional authority. After assuming power in 1985, President Sanguinetti and Defense Minister Hugo Medina, the head of the Army during the transition, fashioned a negotiated return to the status quo ante. Provisions of the Naval Club pact providing for military prerogatives in the new regime were terminated after the first year of the new government. Except on the question of human rights violations, military leaders generally refrained from intervening in policy matters. Sanguinetti took a personal interest in defense policy, particularly external defense strategy. Congress, on the other hand, has displayed little interest in military policy, conceding substantial autonomy to the armed forces in matters such as military education and doctrine. Cuts in military budgets and declining salaries generated military complaints, but no major public protests.

As in Argentina, the legacy of human rights violations under the military regime was the principal source of civil-military tensions.[37] Individual court cases were filed in 1985 against a number of military, police, and prison personnel. The issue came to a head in 1986 when Minister Medina and other military leaders refused to order officers to appear in court. Faced with a constitutional crisis and strong pressure from Sanguinetti, legislators representing the two traditional parties approved a complex legal formula by which the state agreed to forego its right to prosecute crimes committed during the military government. The de facto amnesty generated bitter protests from the left, but opposition spanned the political spectrum. Human rights groups spearheaded a campaign to gather petition signatures equal to 25 percent of the electorate to force a national referendum on repeal of the nonprosecution law. More than 630,000 signatures were presented; after much delay, the Electoral Tribunal was ultimately forced to allow the referendum. Influenced in part by the *carapintada* revolts in Argentina, moderate and conservative groups rallied behind warnings from Sanguinetti and Medina that repeal would lead to a destabilizing civil-military confrontation. After a heated and divisive campaign, the repeal initiative failed by a vote of 53 percent opposed, 41 percent in favor.

On balance, Sanguinetti's military policy was moderately successful. Elements of the military favoring a tutelary role in the new regime were isolated. Military reaction to the loss of prerogatives acquired during the 1970s was less intense than in Argentina. Sanguinetti managed to work with Medina and other military leaders to subordinate the military to constitutional authority without giving rise to an alternative military leadership challenging that authority. On the negative side, the political leadership was forced to concede that military officers could not be tried for human rights violations. The amnesty law resulted in a loss of legitimacy for Sanguinetti and the new regime, but the damage was limited by the fact that the decision not to repeal the amnesty was made by popular vote in a freely contested election.

Sanguinetti's successor, Luis Alberto Lacalle, symbolically reaffirmed the military's traditionally subordinate role by naming a civilian minister of defense and choosing his own candidates for service commanders, instead of naming the most senior officer in each service. Both moves generated criticism from active-duty and retired officers, suggesting that conflict still exists over the extent of civilian authority over the armed forces, particularly the limits to the military's professional autonomy.[38] The minister of defense appears to have less real power than his Argentine counterpart. Key positions within the ministry are reserved by law for active-duty officers; service commanders still meet directly with the president, rather than working through the defense minister.

145

On the other hand, military budgets have continued to decline; salaries are now estimated to have fallen by 30 percent.[39] Retired officers have been vocal in their criticism of the return to politics of former guerrillas as a legal party within the Frente Amplio coalition.[40] Under Lacalle, relations with the military appeared to be cooler and more formal, but after Sanguinetti's reelection in 1995, he also appointed a civilian to the Defense Ministry. Despite signs of alienation from sectors of the military, the basic subordination of the armed forces to the constitutional regime seems firmly established.[41]

Conditional Subordination: Living with Military Guardians

Ecuador and Peru are examples of military policy in regimes where the military has not renounced its role as the ultimate guardian in times of crisis. In Peru,[42] the debt crisis and a bitter internal war combined to offset the relatively clean and unconditional transition to a civilian regime. The victor in the 1979 elections was Fernando Belaúnde, whose 1968 overthrow initiated the previous military regime. Belaúnde was determined to complete his term of office despite a deteriorating economy and a rapidly growing war with the Sendero Luminoso and Movimiento Tupac Amaru (MRTA) guerrillas. Belaúnde adopted a cautious policy toward the armed forces, ignoring allegations of corruption during the military regime, respecting the military's institutional autonomy, and according the three military ministers their traditional place within the cabinet.

In the most visible instance of civil-military conflict, Belaúnde relieved the political-military commander of Ayacucho in 1984 for his public criticism of the lack of government development programs to combat Sendero advances in the Peruvian highlands.[43] Although the government fulfilled few of its promises, neither military officers nor civilians wanted to return to military rule so soon after the transition, so both were content to let Belaúnde serve out his term.

Belaúnde's successor, APRA's Alán García, initially profited — economically and politically — from his decision to unilaterally limit Peru's repayment of its foreign debt to 10 percent of its export earnings. Three years later, the economy was in shambles, with negative growth rates, skyrocketing inflation, and free-falling currency markets. Meanwhile, the guerrilla war spread to Lima and its sprawling shantytowns, with a steadily rising death toll of combatants and innocent bystanders. Despite widespread military opposition — led by the Air Force — García created a new Ministry of Defense and abolished the traditional separate ministries for each service. With army backing, he fired the Air

Force minister after a series of unauthorized overflights of the capital in protest against the loss of the separate ministries. Nevertheless, the initial ministers were military officers, who functioned as intermediaries between the government and the armed forces rather than agents of civilian authority.[44]

The conduct of the war against the Sendero insurgency was a constant source of tension with the military. Military leaders repeatedly complained that the war could not be won by military means alone and that the government was not cooperating in the kind of coordinated counterinsurgency strategy deemed necessary by the armed forces. Extensive human rights violations by the police and security forces resulted in the firing of several high-ranking officers but only in one conviction by military courts, in which two officers were found guilty of homicide. In early 1989, rumors of a coup against García were widespread, with the Lima press actively speculating about possible dates. Nevertheless, largely because of strong international opposition and the fear that a coup would lead sectors of the left to join the armed opposition, military leaders decided to tough out García's last year in office and wait for the 1990 elections.

The accomplishments of Belaúnde and García in military policy were unimpressive. Notwithstanding national security laws providing for military participation in state planning, intelligence, and the National Defense Council, military complaints about the conduct of counterinsurgency efforts under Belaúnde suggest that military influence in national policymaking was limited. Under García, the powers of the Defense Council were reduced by shifting many of its functions to the Council of Ministers.[45] Although the creation of the new Defense Ministry was a partial, negotiated reform, it contrasts sharply with the successful military veto of a similar proposal in Brazil. Some constitutional changes were introduced limiting the military's political role and restricting jurisdiction of military courts, but these changes do not appear to have been accepted as authoritative by the military. The situational factors impeding a potential coup — internal military divisions, the desire not to return to military rule, lack of external support or civilian allies, and the fear of aggravating the internal security threat — gave Belaúnde and García a sufficient margin of security to resist the tutelary model and insist on formal military subordination to constitutional authority, even if in practice both generally followed a policy of accommodation to military interests. While the majority of the officer corps ultimately rejected the option of a coup against García,[46] there is no evidence that this decision was based on a rejection of the principle of military intervention, as opposed to a calculated decision that, in these particular circumstances, the costs outweighed the potential benefits.

147

The armed forces enjoyed near total autonomy in their internal affairs and in the conduct of the counterinsurgency war. In insurgent-contested "emergency zones," which included over half the nation's population, the military exercised de facto political and military authority. Belaúnde's attempts to limit military influence and García's efforts to exert more political control over the armed forces had the perverse effect of frustrating military efforts to develop a coordinated response to the Sendero insurgency, at the same time that it left them wide latitude to pursue a military solution to the conflict. As a result, human rights violations increased and the insurgency grew.[47] The virtual collapse of the economy in the last years of the García administration radically reduced military salaries and threatened to bring military operations to a halt. As production plummeted, the poverty rate in Lima rose from 14 percent to 54 percent; the number of persons with "adequate" employment dropped from 60 percent to less than 10 percent.[48] During the first decade of democracy in Peru, the real minimum wage declined by 77 percent, the worst record in the region. In 1990, inflation exceeded 7,000 percent.[49] Not surprisingly, García's personal popularity plummeted from over 70 percent in 1987 to less than 10 percent.[50] By the end of the decade, Peru's two most important parties were totally discredited, opening the door for a presidential contest between two outsiders with virtually no prior political experience.

With the Izquierda Unida split between its moderate and radical wings and famed Peruvian novelist Mario Vargas Llosa running on a neoliberal ticket, the unlikely victor of the 1990 elections was Alberto Fujimori, an evangelical Christian, son of a Japanese immigrant family, and leader of the Cambio 90 Party, created just months before the election. Fujimori campaigned against the free-market "shock treatment" advocated by Vargas Llosa, but soon found himself forced to adopt much of the program he had opposed. Despite the resulting recession, prices stabilized. Like President Menem in Argentina, Fujimori reaped enormous political credit for rescuing the country from economic chaos, with over 70 percent approval ratings in urban polls. In April of 1992, faced with growing congressional opposition to his economic measures and congressional investigation of human rights abuses, Fujimori unexpectedly staged a government coup (*autogolpe*), closing Congress, suspending the Constitution, and arresting opposition leaders, claiming that it was impossible to restructure the economy or prosecute the war against Sendero under the existing system. Public protest was minimal; Fujimori's popularity again soared in the polls.[51] The international community condemned the *autogolpe* and suspended economic aid programs. International banks postponed vitally needed loans. Chastened, Fujimori moved to legitimize his regime with Constituent Assembly elections and a new constitution.[52]

148

The armed forces were silent but necessary partners in the *autogolpe*. Military support for Fujimori was the result of a complex situational calculus. Unlike Belaúnde and García, Fujimori placed a high priority on defeating Sendero since foreign investment was critical to his economic program. A coherent counterinsurgency strategy was finally implemented, with tough new antiterrorist laws and a more efficient defense structure. Military officers controlled both the Ministry of Defense and the Ministry of Interior (police).[53] Fujimori pledged to use his emergency powers to purge the judiciary of judges who were "soft on subversives." Many officers thus supported the *autogolpe* because Fujimori was perceived as dedicated to defeating an enemy who seriously threatened their existence. Closing Congress also put an end to investigations of human rights violations. While military salaries remained abysmally low, Fujimori was unabashedly promilitary. Despite the violation of the Constitution, which some officers found troubling, public opinion clearly supported the government's action. Forced to choose between the executive and the legislature, the military backed the president. Fujimori successfully constructed his own military command, which immediately backed the *autogolpe,* thus placing the burden of disobeying orders on those who opposed the president's actions. In September, the capture of the Shining Path's "maximum leader," Abimael Guzmán, struck a critical blow against the guerrillas, further enhancing the government's image as a decisive, effective force for order and stability. Two months later, a group of officers opposed to Fujimori's violation of the Constitution and to his growing personal control of the military attempted a countercoup. Despite the backing of many prestigious former military leaders, the coup failed to gain support within the active-duty ranks.[54]

Human right violations continue, despite the decline in the Sendero threat. In 1995, the government majority in Congress approved a blanket amnesty for all security personnel accused or convicted of human rights abuses. Military insistence that military courts have jurisdiction over military personnel has effectively stymied attempts to prosecute violations occurring since the amnesty. Civilians accused of treason are tried in military courts; terrorism cases are heard by anonymous judges in special civilian courts. A third of the population still lives in "emergency zones" controlled by the military.[55]

Nevertheless, presidential control of the military also increased. By law, the president now appoints the commander, chief of staff, and inspector general of each service, who serve for the duration of the administration unless removed by the president. Under the new constitution, the president, rather than congress, grants promotions for generals and admirals.[56] In the short run, Fujimori has achieved a substantial degree of personal control of the military by coopting a loyal clique of senior officers. However, military support for Fujimori also

149

rests on a calculus of institutional self-interest. Although Fujimori won military praise for his tough line after the MRTA seizure of the Japanese embassy, the military partner in this alliance has no inherent loyalty to the current arrangements if Fujimori falters and has no reason to concede greater authority to the current legal norms than to those violated in the *autogolpe*. Fujimori's highly personalized form of civilian control is neither democratic nor is it likely to be very long lasting, given the inevitable fluctuations of presidential popularity in weakly institutionalized regimes.[57]

In Ecuador,[58] the armed forces worked with moderate members of the opposition to forge a negotiated transition to a constitutional regime. According to a member of the civilian commission that drafted the new constitution adopted by plebiscite, the article dealing with the armed forces was based on draft language presented by the military that the commission considered "not radically different" from the traditional constitutional phrasing. The socioeconomic mission of the armed forces, first introduced in the 1967 Constitution, was treated as a nonissue. The absence of any permanent committee on the armed forces in the Congress appears not to have been noticed. Military affairs were assumed to be the province of the president and the National Security Council. The elimination of the traditional power of Congress to approve military promotions was accepted, after some discussion, on the argument that it tended to politicize the promotion process and involve senior officers in political clientelism. Functional representation of the armed forces in Congress, traditionally by a retired officer, was turned down as an incompatible mixture of corporatism with liberal democracy.[59]

The first civilian government under Presidents Roldós and Hurtado was characterized by a policy of mutual accommodation. The military stuck to its constitutional role and the new government was careful not to antagonize the armed forces. The government accepted legislation decreed by the military government that restricted the president's ability to choose senior military commanders and reserved the Ministry of Defense for a military officer. In return, the military refrained from any active participation in policy matters except in the area of national defense. After labor unrest and several general strikes, a conservative general was accused of proposing a coup in conversations with U.S. embassy personnel. The embassy denounced "the plot" and reaffirmed its commitment to support the democratic regime.[60] The officer in question, General Piñeiros, remained on active duty, but Hurtado completed his term without further incident.

The second civilian administration, under León Febres Cordero, was marked by repeated government confrontations with the opposition and a re-

150

turn to a clientelistic strategy of co-optation of senior military commanders. Febres Cordero's minister of defense became embroiled in a personal conflict with the Air Force commander, Frank Vargas, over mutual accusations of corruption in a European aircraft purchase. Vargas launched a brief rebellion and moved Air Force planes to his home province. After negotiations with the government, Vargas surrendered, but then revolted again, calling for a "civil-military government." The army acted quickly to suppress the revolt, which collapsed with little or no support. Within the air force, some officers initially supported the revolt as a "air force versus army" conflict, but quickly abandoned the fight when it become a political challenge to the government. There was no support from the army or navy for what was universally perceived as a personal feud, not a situation warranting any action from the military.[61] Several months later, Air Force commandos loyal to Vargas seized President Febres Cordero as he arrived at the air force base outside of Guayaquil, demanding that Vargas be freed. Loyal forces surrounded the base, but Febres Cordero signed an amnesty for Vargas and was released. A major earthquake in 1987 disrupted the oil pipeline, causing serious economic problems for the remainder of Febres Cordero's term, but with strong backing from conservative officers in the High Command, the stability of the government was never in question. In the 1988 elections, the Army Council of Generals debated whether to intervene if populist Abdalá Bucarám won,[62] but he was defeated in the runoff by the center-left candidate, Rodrigo Borja.

The Izquierda Democrática government took a less pro-U.S. stance than Febres Cordero, but its economic policies were constrained by foreign debts and low oil prices. Like Hurtado, Borja found his plans for social reforms stymied by budget deficits and an opposition-controlled Congress. Borja negotiated a ceasefire with the radical Alfaro Vive ¡Carajo! (AVC) group that had been engaged in sporadic terrorist actions. His decision to grant amnesty to Vargas's commandos generated perhaps more military opposition than the amnesty for the AVC. Senior army officers protested vigorously, but the president refused to back down.[63] Despite claims from right-wing officers that "the government is part of the marxist terrorist subversion"[64] and mounting complaints about the erosion of military salaries,[65] most officers saw Borja as incompetent, but not a crisis situation warranting a coup. Although rising labor unrest made the government somewhat more dependent on military support, in practice the military had relatively little leverage when the president turned a deaf ear on their complaints.

Sixto Durán Ballén won the 1992 elections, campaigning as a moderate, independent, "nonparty" alternative to his opponent, a protégé of Febres Cordero. His attempt to bring down inflation by a stringent austerity policy worsened unemployment and cut social programs. The economy stagnated, with only slow improvements in inflation. Efforts to privatize portions of Ecuador's large and inefficient state sector ran into heated opposition from public employee unions and roadblocks in Congress. The armed forces made it clear—respectfully—that they opposed the inclusion of any strategic or military-owned enterprises in the privatization program. Faced with the inevitable headaches of governing in Ecuador, the aging president governed less and less, leaving day-to-day operations in the hands of his ministers and Vice President Dahik, a free-market economist and principal author of the government's economic policies. Support for the government surged briefly as Ecuadorians rallied around the flag during the 1995 border war with Peru, but evaporated when the vice president became embroiled in a corruption scandal resulting from a slush fund used to purchase support from various members of Congress. Dahik fled into exile in Costa Rica rather than face charges. As the power vacuum deepened, the armed forces took a more forceful role on policies considered important to national security, complaining publicly about pervasive corruption and the lack of political leadership.

The 1996 election of Guayaquil populist Abdalá Bucarám generated new rumors of a possible coup, but the armed forces chose to work within the constitutional system rather than risk internal divisions and international condemnation.[66] The new government soon dissipated into a torrent of corruption scandals and intemperate clashes with the media and political opponents. The military took a disciplined and moderate stance, in marked contrast to the president's erratic behavior and the opposition's partisan frenzy. When the opposition-controlled Congress declared the presidency vacant instead of impeaching Bucarám, the chief of the Joint Staff played a key role in mediating a solution to the resulting constitutional crisis.

The major accomplishment of military policy in Ecuador has been the survival of the democratic regime despite a generally weak economy and repeated political crises during the last four administrations. On the negative side, the armed forces have consolidated a higher degree of professional autonomy than they enjoyed in earlier civilian regimes. Largely as a result of the country's hyperfragmented party structure and weak civilian commitment to constitutional rules, the military's self-proclaimed role as political guardians has gained support among both military officers and civilian groups. Relative to the opportunities available, the Ecuadorian record is clearly disappointing. Although an overt coup has been avoided, Ecuador has lost ground in term of democratic civil-military relations, moving toward a semitutelary regime with increasing

152

military participation in major policy decisions.[67] In this case, civilian political leaders have no one to blame but themselves.

Combating Tutelary Regimes

Among tutelary regimes, progress toward more democratic civil-military relations has varied substantially. The Brazilian experience vividly demonstrates the importance of the political context — particularly the political strength or weakness of the president — as a force shaping military policy. The initial post-transition government was weakened by the fact that it came to power through indirect elections and the vice presidency. As noted in chapter 2, President Sarney treated the military "as a separate, fourth power" and actively sought military support for his own policy objectives.[68] Sarney not only failed to challenge the tutelary pattern of civil-military relations, he actively defended that system when military prerogatives were challenged by opposition groups in the Constituent Assembly.

Surprising many analysts, Brazil's first directly elected president, Fernando Collor, asserted his right to name his own military ministers instead of promoting the most senior officers or merely ratifying the military's choices. With both Congress and the president reluctant to fund military projects, the military share of central government spending declined by 25 percent.[69] Decisions to cancel development of the military's nuclear and missile programs and to sign nonproliferation accords were sustained over significant military opposition. Fueled in part by complaints about declining military salaries and budgets, military criticism of the government increased. Three generals were disciplined for publicly criticizing Collor's policies.[70] However, as the government's economic program begin to falter, Collor was hit by media and congressional revelations of a vast scheme to collect kickbacks from companies doing business with the government.[71] Collor made a belated bid to secure military support by salary increases and supplemental appropriations, but it was too late. Facing impeachment and trial, Collor resigned in December of 1992.

His successor, Itamar Franco, was beset from the beginning by budget deficits, high inflation, and the lack of a strong political base. Not surprisingly, Franco was reluctant to risk conflicts with the military.[72] Responding in part to budgetary pressures, Franco requested and received military support for an expanded civic action role, in which military units provide health services, construct roads and sanitary facilities, and use their logistical capabilities to deliver relief and food supplies to impoverished areas. Despite reservations among professionalist officers, the military's expanded development role has

153

been popular with the public and Congress, leading to new calls for military patrols to fight Brazil's worsening crime problems. With new revelations of corruption in Congress, public military criticism of civilian leadership reappeared. Franco's response was to exempt the military from across-the-board budget cuts affecting other sectors.[73]

Nevertheless, since the 1995 election of Fernando Enrique Cardoso, Brazil seems to be moving toward the conditional subordination model. Cardoso reversed Franco's practice of naming military officers to nonmilitary posts. For the first time, under Cardoso the government has taken an active role in defense policy, redefining Brazil's traditional conflict hypotheses and emphasizing external rather than internal security.[74] Like Menem, Cardoso's political fortunes are closely tied to the success of his anti-inflationary policies, so he has avoided confrontation with the military. Cardoso did officially acknowledge more than one hundred disappearances and the torture of thousands of political prisoners during the military regime. Despite military criticism, the government paid reparations to the families of the victims.[75] Still, the cornerstone of Cardoso's policy is acceptance of the 1979 Amnesty Law blocking prosecution for actions by the security forces or the armed opposition. Thus far, the outcome is still more favorable to the armed forces than that of Chile (amnesty plus official investigation) or Uruguay (nonprosecution plus unofficial investigation).

Despite the reduction in the military's tutelary powers, the armed forces retain significant political prerogatives. In 1997, active duty officers still held five cabinet positions and five of the twelve seats on the National Defense Council. Despite some modifications, national security laws give military courts wide jurisdiction over civilians charged with political crimes. The armed forces effectively control the police; the military role in domestic intelligence is unresolved.[76] Civilian attempts to assert greater control of the armed forces have been intermittent and highly dependent on the political standing of the president. Many undemocratic features persist. The "rules of the game" for Brazilian civil-military relations remain ambiguous.

In Chile, General Pinochet envisioned a slow transition to a regime in which the armed forces would play a tutelary role.[77] The 1980 Constitution gave the military an open-ended mandate as "guarantors of the institutional order" and created a military-dominated National Security Council charged with responding to any action or issue that "in its judgment gravely threatens the institutional order or compromises national security."[78] Following his unexpected defeat in the 1988 plebiscite, Pinochet and leaders of the opposition negotiated a series of constitutional reforms which added another civilian to the Security Council and changed its mission to advising the president, Congress, and the Constitutional Tribunal on matters of national security. Although civilians would now hold half of the seats on the Security Council, two of the civilians were Pinochet appointees.[79] Before handing over power, the government also changed electoral laws to favor parties of the right[80] and passed a series of organic laws that constructed new barriers to government control of the military, including a guaranteed minimum budget for the armed forces. An earlier law gives the armed forces 10 percent of the profits from copper, Chile's primary export product.[81] The ultimate challenge for the new government was the most unusual: the commander of the Army would be none other than the former dictator, who could only be replaced by a majority vote of the Security Council. Chile thus presented another potential "difficult case" for democratic civil-military relations. Economically and politically, this was arguably the region's most successful military government. Despite his defeat in the plebiscite, Pinochet got 43 percent of the vote and enjoyed strong support from the Chilean right. Military spokesmen rejected civilian proposals for changes in military education and in defense policy, arguing that the former was outside of the jurisdiction of civilian authority.[82] The organic laws require a four-sevenths supermajority to amend or repeal; procedures for amending the 1980 Constitution were likewise intentionally cumbersome. With the outgoing government appointing nine of the forty-seven members of the Senate, in the short term the "rules of the game" set by Pinochet were relatively immutable.[83]

Yet, the Chilean military's project for a tutelary regime was highly contested. The political parties of the center and left that allied to form the Concertación de Partidos por la Democracia rejected Pinochet's vision of the successor regime. Despite their differences on other issues, opposition leaders were committed to reestablishing constitutional democracy and some form of civilian control of the military. Like Argentina, the human rights abuses of the military regime created a significant backlash against the armed forces in large sectors of Chilean public opinion. The potential for civil-military confrontation *à la argentina* was also high, given the deep polarization of the Allende era and seventeen years of military dictatorship dedicated to stamping out all vestiges of marxism.

In eight years of civilian administration, Christian Democratic governments led by Presidents Aylwin and Frei have successfully blocked Pinochet's plans for "protected democracy." The political influence of the military on issues other than human rights has been sharply limited, although the military still enjoy a degree of institutional autonomy that is clearly anomalous for any Western democracy. Despite tense moments, democratic leaders in Chile have avoided the kind of civil-military confrontation which threatened to destabilize Argentine democracy. While much remains to be done, Chile is a hopeful story of carefully crafted military policy, which has resulted in progress toward more democratic civil-military relations, even under less-than-ideal circumstances. The Chilean case emphasizes again the importance of civilian institutions and the larger economic and political context of civil-military relations. Chilean leaders also had the advantage of learning from earlier transitions in Argentina and Uruguay.

The first democratic government under Patricio Aylwin was careful to maintain correct relations with Pinochet, offering him the respect due him as Army commander without conceding any special powers to him as the former head of the military regime. Symbolically reaffirming his commitment to democratic civil-military relations, President Aylwin appointed a civilian minister of defense, despite the restrictions on his ability to exercise real policy control of the armed forces. The government refused to schedule regular meetings of the National Security Council[84] and declined to consult with the military commanders except on matters within their professional sphere of competence. As it had done throughout the transition, the Concertación engaged in a series of meetings and dialogues with retired and active-duty officers, in which it signaled its insistence on restoring the traditional subordination of the military to constitutional authority, but also its willingness to live within the confines of the 1980 Constitution and to accept the military's special status as an autonomous state institution for the duration of Pinochet's term as commander-in-chief of the Army.

The problem of how to deal with the legacy of human rights violations was again the most prickly issue facing the government. The military government had passed a self-amnesty law in 1978 that covered the most intense years of the repression. The status of those responsible for a substantial number of deaths and disappearances after that date was more ambiguous, but Pinochet pledged that "the day they touch any of my men will be the end of the rule of law" in Chile.[85] After much debate and reflection on the experiences of other countries, the government decided not to try to overturn the amnesty law since the conservative bloc in Congress — including Pinochet's nine appointed senators — had the votes to block repeal. The government also consciously decided that, unlike Argentina, the government itself would not seek prosecution of human rights cases. However, it would not extend the amnesty to prevent victims or their families from seeking justice on their own. The Supreme Court — packed with Pinochet appointees — upheld the amnesty law and agreed with military courts that the amnesty precluded prosecution of pre-1978 cases.[86] Conservative judges upheld military claims that charges against military personnel for actions "in the line of duty" should be tried in military courts. Pre-1978 cases have been thrown out under the amnesty; post-1978 cases have generally been stalled by uncooperative military judges or dismissed "for lack of evidence."

Anxious to avoid a confrontation with Pinochet, but also under heavy pressure from human rights groups not to turn a blind eye to past abuses, the Aylwin government empaneled the Truth Commission to investigate politically motivated killings by military and police forces as well as those caused by the left. After nine months of public testimony and investigation, the Rettig Commission documented more than 2,100 dead and nearly 1,000 disappearances during the military government, compared to roughly 100 killed by antigovernment forces. As expected, Pinochet angrily denounced the commission's "biased report" and defended the armed forces for having saved Chile from communism.[87] In a curious twist, a loophole in the amnesty law did permit prosecution of General Manuel Contreras, former head of the state intelligence agency, as the intellectual author of the deaths of Orlando Letelier and Ronny Moffitt in Washington, D.C., from a car bomb planted by a secret police agent. Contreras and his second-in-command were convicted and sentenced to seven-year prison terms. The government also established the Commission on Reparation and Reconciliation and provided pensions and other assistance to victims of human rights abuses and their families.[88]

On other issues, Aylwin and Frei have been insistent on principle, but flexible in practice. Early in his term Aylwin insisted on the government's right to accept or reject promotion lists for senior officers, but then promoted most of those nominated by Pinochet and the commanders of the other forces.[89] On two occasions, when Pinochet ordered all army personnel confined to barracks to review the situation facing the country, Aylwin rebuked the general for unnecessary saber rattling, but carefully avoided escalating the conflict.

Still, perhaps the most important factors in the success of Chile's quest for more democratic civil-military relations have little to do with military policy per se. First, Chile has had by far the best economic performance of any of Latin America's new democracies. With only minor modifications, both Christian Democratic governments have maintained Pinochet's free market, proexport policies. With the return to democracy, Chile has become a favorite of foreign investors and a candidate to join an expanded North American Free Trade Association. In marked contrast to the deep economic crises that shook other Latin American democracies in the 1980s, Chile has averaged 6 to 7 percent economic growth since the transition. Instead of plummeting real wages, Chile has increased the standard of living and reduced the poverty rate. Despite its social inequalities, Chile may be the only Latin American country to deliver on the promise that democracy would bring a better life for ordinary citizens.[90]

Chile's political elite has also succeeded in political leadership, where many others have failed or disgraced themselves. Aylwin was a likable, but bland president, a reassuring elder statesman to oversee the first democratic government.[91] Though his government was cautious and uninspiring, it was also remarkably free of the unnecessary conflicts and corruption scandals that have plagued civilian leaders in Brazil, Peru, and Ecuador. The center-left coalition may end with the next elections, but for nearly a decade the Concertación has been remarkably effective in holding together an ideologically diverse alliance of parties capable of defending the democratic regime and working together to reduce the many authoritarian components of the post-Pinochet regime.[92] In part because of their moderation and skilled leadership—in contrast to the military's often crude attempts to pressure the government—civilian leaders have substantially increased support for the democratic regime from sectors of the right and economic elites who initially backed continuation of the military government. The public image of Pinochet and the armed forces has been tarnished by revelations of arms contracts benefiting Pinochet's son-in-law and a fraudulent secret investment scheme in the armed forces. Conservative parties were outraged when military intelligence agencies were caught taping the telephone conversations of the conservative Renovación Nacional leaders.[93]

The weak point in this still-evolving Chilean pattern of civil-military relations is the extraordinary autonomy accorded to the armed forces. While this autonomy has no doubt helped reassure the Chilean military that they will be protected from partisan interference or "subversion," it perpetuates the military's view of itself as the guardian of national security and ultimate defender of national interests,[94] even when that self-image is widely rejected by the Chilean public. High military autonomy could also be viewed as an guarantee for the political and economic right wing, whose defection doomed the democratic regime under Allende. Given the economic and political performance of civilian governments since 1990, such a guarantee hardly seems necessary. The inability of civilian governments to change the repressive provisions of the Internal Security Law, the Anti-Terrorism Law, and other antisubversion legislation must be counted as another negative consequence of working within Pinochet's institutional framework.[95] Under the current leadership, this legislation has little practical importance. In a crisis situation, other leaders could, however, resurrect these laws to impose their own policies.

Chile today is a curious semidemocracy. Reforms to the institutional structure created by the 1980 Constitution have thus far been stymied by the conservative bloc in Congress. The armed forces remain a defiant authoritarian enclave, capable of threatening the regime, but weakened over time by the erosion of political support from former civilian allies. Assuming that the regime continues its present course, the military will be forced to adapt to their diminished political role. As long as the armed forces remain outside of the democratic regime, the danger of a reversion will continue. As long as the civilian leadership successfully manages the socioeconomic and political conflicts facing Chilean society, such a reversion is unlikely.

Conditioning Factors

Explaining these variations in military policy and in the outcomes of those policies is a complex task, involving multiple levels of analysis and interactions over time. Analytically it is difficult to separate out the independent impacts of variables, such as the nature of the party system, which affect not only military policy, but also the political transitions and subsequent patterns of civil-military interaction. Given this complexity, the analysis that follows suggests a conceptual framework and initial hypotheses for understanding the varying outcomes of military policy in the new democracies.

The first and perhaps most important set of factors shaping the outcome of military policy is the institutional context. In his 1974 review of the literature on the Latin American military, Abraham Lowenthal argued persuasively that the relative organizational strengths of civilian and military institutions are a key determinant of differences in civil-military relations.[96] Most of the South American countries have relatively professionalized militaries, with extensive training, technical sophistication, and socialization systems for officers that engender strong loyalties to the institution. With some notable exceptions — Venezuela, Mexico, Colombia, Uruguay, and Chile before 1973 — civilian institutions in Latin America have been characterized by limited resources, personal and ideological factionalism, and weak organization, particularly at the grass-roots level. Presidentialist constitutions in combination with fragmented or polarized party systems produce presidents with extensive formal powers, but weak political support. Dual round presidential elections generate electoral majorities, but diminish incentives for formal coalitions, increasing the odds that the president will face an opposition-controlled congress.[97]

The imbalance between civilian and military institutions contributes to military perceptions that they are better organized, better trained, more cohesive, and more patriotic than civilian political leaders. These perceptions, in turn, legitimate military demands for a guardian or tutelary role within civilian regimes. Although these military self-perceptions are often contradicted by their actual experience in power, anticivilian stereotypes usually reassert themselves unless the performance of civilian institutions actually improves. In many cases, however, military rule weakened civilian institutions by prohibiting normal political activities, disrupting leadership recruitment and succession, and repressing mass organizations. Weak civilian governments are unlikely to have the will or the capacity to assert civilian leadership over the armed forces. The combination of weak civilian institutions and an increasingly professionalized military encourages military and civilian support for an active, autonomous military role in the new regime.

160

In some countries, the organizational imbalance between civilian and military institutions has been partly offset by interparty pacts to cooperate in governing and defending the democratic regime. In Chile, Uruguay, and to a lesser degree Argentina, the negative experience of military rule and multiparty alliances created during the transition have helped to moderate partisan divisions and avoid destabilizing political crises. As in the earlier cases of Venezuela and Colombia, these improvements in civilian capability for conflict management are an important component of civilian efforts to reduce the political role of the armed forces.[98]

As Felipe Aguero has stressed in his insightful comparison of the South American and Southern European cases, the institutional balance between the military and civilian political forces was both a cause and a result of important differences in the democratic transition process, which in turn shaped the initial conditions under which civilian governments came to power.[99] In all of the cases considered here, the previous authoritarian regime institutionally represented the armed forces; consequently, the military directly negotiated the terms of the transition back to civilian government. Except in Argentina, the military generally negotiated from a position of strength, fashioning an orderly retreat from direct military rule and imposing various conditions on the transition—for example, the veto of direct elections in Brazil and the exclusion of certain presidential candidates in Uruguay and Ecuador. The institutional and historical factors underlying the relative bargaining strengths of military and political leaders continue into the initial posttransition era. Civilian political groups and the armed forces enter the posttransition regime with varying degrees of (dis)unity, which directly affects their capacity to demand or resist changes in civil-military relations. This negotiated transition process encourages a civilian view of the military as an autonomous political force to be bargained with or at the very least carefully respected. These initial conditions — in most cases, favoring the military — also establish a reference point for subsequent policy debates, shifting the burden of proof for justifying change onto civilian reformers.[100]

In a new work, David Pion-Berlin stresses the institutional framework as the dominant determinant of military policy outcomes. He argues that presidential policies are most likely to succeed where (1) the power to decide is highly centralized and (2) isolated from external pressures.[101] Thus, Alfonsín's decision to seek punishment for human rights violations through the courts was predictably problematic because it involved the risk of autonomous actions by Congress and the courts, both of whom were subject to political pressure from the public and the media and bound by their own institutional norms. For example, the administration's original bill to repeal the military self-amnesty was unexpectedly amended by a senator from a minor provincial party to bar use of the "due obedience" defense by officers engaging in "aberrant or atrocious actions." The Sapag amendment effectively scuttled the government's plan to limit the number of trials by focusing on junta leaders and top commanders, excusing junior officers who were "just following orders." No one could publicly defend torture and disappearance of political prisoners as "normal" military activities, especially when the courts made the ultimate determination of what was "aberrant" and "atrocious" behavior. Pressure from human rights groups and the courts themselves likewise nullified the attempt to put an end to the trials through the *Punto Final* Law. Federal courts in key provinces responded to the new law by working straight through their normal January holiday in order to permit as many cases as possible to be filed before the deadline.[102] In contrast, particularly under Menem, control over budgetary policy was highly centralized in the Ministry of the Economy, which was consciously insulated from attempts by the military or other state agencies to lobby for additional funds. Hence military complaints about inadequate budgets and declining salaries had little or no effect, except when the president could be convinced to override the Economics Ministry.[103] The varying institutional contexts in which military policies are decided thus play an important role in explaining why policy outcomes vary, even within countries where the institutional balance and the legacy of the transition are constants.

The institutional context thus sets the basic framework for civil-military interaction after the return to a civilian regime. If we take the analogy of civil-military relations as a play — as drama — the institutional context sets the stage and establishes the basic characteristics of the main players: their organizational capabilities, cohesion, and basic political orientations. In some cases, the play features evenly matched protagonists; in others, one character is clearly dominant. In some cases, civilian and military leaders share congruent world views; in others, ideological asymmetries or historical antagonisms define the players as opponents, rather than possible allies. The institutional context thus sets some important constraints on the range of plausible scripts for the interaction that follows. In the real world, David will probably not choose to confront Goliath with just a slingshot; without divine help, he would probably fail. Nevertheless, a David-and-Goliath script or even David's victory, while not probable, are not impossible. As the Brazilian case illustrates, a strong military and a weak party system did not preclude some progress toward more democratic civil-military relations.

162

The second set of factors that affect the outcome of military policies in the new democracies comprise the *political context*. These include the agenda of military issues facing the government and its margin of security vis-à-vis the threat of a coup d'état. Following the drama metaphor, the political context stipulates the key elements — the major givens — of the script. In particular, the political context includes the conflictual issues to be dealt with and the initial impulses to agree or disagree on what is the "proper" role of the military in the new regime. It also specifies the relationships of civilian and military leaders to the rest of the characters in the play, thus enlarging or limiting the range of possible relations among the principals. Various scripts — and different endings — are still possible, but the scripts will vary significantly depending on the elements from which they are composed.

Broadly speaking, the more serious the threat of military intervention to overthrow the government, the more constrained that government will be to avoid adding to that threat by trying to curtail military prerogatives. Conversely, the more politically secure the civilian government is, the greater its potential margin to attempt reforms even at the cost of antagonizing the armed forces. Thus military policy is always conditioned by political factors outside the civil-military interaction itself. In the 1980s, the regional debt crisis, in particular, focused government attention on economic rather than military issues and simultaneously reduced civilian capacity to push for military reforms. Four-digit inflation rates, stagnant or declining GNP, and sharply falling real wages aggravated social conflict, diminished regime legitimacy, and destroyed public confidence in incumbent governments. Despite their initial popularity, both Alfonsín and García finished their presidential terms with very low levels of public support. Reflecting that political weakness, neither was as aggressive in attempting to control the military in their later years.[104] To the extent that strikes, food riots, and protests against government economic policies require the use of military forces to maintain public order, civilian governments become more dependent on military support to remain in office, and hence less able to risk offending the armed forces. The debt crisis also imposed budget restrictions, which made it difficult for civilian governments to provide material and professional compensation for reductions in the military's political prerogatives.[105]

Despite the negative effects of the debt crisis, other factors tended to reduce the immediate risk of direct military intervention during the 1980s. International support for democratic regimes and opposition to overt military intervention added to the legitimacy of democratic regimes and discouraged potential coups. Even more important, domestic support for military intervention clearly declined. While the military still enjoys substantial backing from its traditional allies in Chile and parts of Central America, in much of the region the last round of military regimes disarticulated the military's traditional bases of civilian support. In addition, the collapse of communist regimes in Eastern Europe and the changes in the Soviet Union have generally weakened voter support for marxist parties and aggravated the historically fractious relationships among leftist parties. Except for the long-standing insurgencies noted below, the "communist threat" has receded in most of the region, thereby removing one of the major motives for military intervention.

163

Although the short-term risk of a coup was generally low, there were important variations in that risk and in the agenda of conflicts facing civilian governments. Some countries faced inherently difficult issues in civil-military relations that others were spared. In Argentina, Uruguay, and Chile, new civilian regimes were confronted with the dilemma of how to deal with the political legacy of large-scale human rights violations by the military. Human rights groups formed during the military regime generally enjoyed high legitimacy, international support, and political backing from groups hit hard by the repression. Organizations of the families of the disappeared led the battle to repeal self-amnesties for human rights violations granted by outgoing military regimes. Failure to respond to civilian demands for accountability alienated the political left, which democratic leaders were trying hard to incorporate as a loyal opposition within the constitutional regime. On the other hand, military opinion was near unanimous in rejecting the moral arguments for human rights trials. Insisting on legal accountability risked a bitter civil-military confrontation and alienation of many officers from the new regime. Acceding to military pressures to "forget the past" diminished the legitimacy of the new regime in the eyes of the rest of society.

Human rights violations have also been a recurrent source of civil-military tension in El Salvador, Peru, Colombia, and Guatemala, where new civilian governments confronted long-term internal wars against entrenched guerrilla forces. Notwithstanding the difficulties of distinguishing between insurgents and sympathizers in guerrilla warfare, the toll of noncombatants killed by regular and paramilitary forces has been staggering. With only rare exceptions, civilian governments have been unwilling to risk antagonizing the military by punishing those responsible. The government's inability to prevent or punish human rights violations has diminished regime legitimacy by baring the limits of the rule of law and exposing the government's inability to protect its own citizens. Internal wars also pose difficult issues of civil-military coordination in policy areas—from economic development to foreign policy—that affect the war effort. Internal wars thus generate strong pressures toward the tutelary model of civil-military relations. These pressures are reinforced by the fact that internal wars generally inhibit overt military takeovers for fear that a military coup might trigger a defection of the nonviolent left and the loss of U.S. aid. The tutelary alternative is to take over greater power within the regime rather than taking power directly. Internal war and international opposition to direct military rule may thus impose a "marriage of necessity" between the armed forces and civilian governments; the key question is how democratic is the resulting partnership.

Finally, policy outcomes are also affected by factors internal to military policy itself, including policy design and implementation. Although the political and institutional context set limits on what military policies are politically feasible, nevertheless there have been significant differences in the extent to which civilian governments have exploited opportunities for reforming existing patterns of civil-military relations.[106] Given the relatively low *short-term* risk of a military coup, most governments appear to have erred on the side of excessive caution in dealing with the armed forces. Fujimori provides a striking counterexample. With the Peruvian military internally divided and rejected by important segments of civil society, Fujimori took advantage of the absence of a viable military alternative to increase his power and reduce the autonomy of the armed forces. In contrast, most civilian leaders have been content with the appearance of military subordination to constitutional authority. Most have chosen to avoid issues—like the assertion of a greater civilian role in defense policy or creation of civilian ministries of defense—that would antagonize military leaders, even when there was little likelihood that more aggressive policies would have threatened the stability of the regime. In part, this failure to exploit the available opportunities results from civilian preoccupation with more immediate crises—particularly the economy—but it also reflects the natural tendency of busy leaders to ignore long-term threats, a failing hardly unique to

Latin America. Still, it is striking that Argentina is the only case where a civilian government arguably pursued overly ambitious policies from which it was ultimately forced to retreat. If the Radical government in Argentina suffered from hubris in the mid-1980s — believing that there were few limits to the policies that could be imposed on the military — most of the other governments in question have been excessively timid, accepting the military's definition of the rules of civil-military relations and thus foreswearing movement toward more democratic norms.

In his analysis of five South American cases, Paul Zagorski argues that military policy outcomes are directly affected by the nature of the military interests at stake. The more fundamental the interests being threatened by government policies, the more intense the military reaction against those policies. Thus, the reaction was the most severe in Argentina, where Alfonsín's policies were perceived as threatening the destruction of the armed forces.[107] Within limits, military budget cuts or salary losses are not likely to generate military revolts or serious acts of indiscipline.[108] In contrast, Felipe Aguero argues that the problem was not so much the nature of Alfonsín's objectives, but rather the pace and timing of their implementation. In his view, the government tried to go too far on too many fronts at the same time. In doing so, its military policies generated an unexpectedly intense military opposition, which the government could not overcome. In the end, the government was forced to retreat, thereby damaging its credibility and losing the initiative in relations with the armed forces. In contrast, the successful military reforms in Spain after Franco were marked by a deliberate pace, careful calculation of the limits of military tolerance, and small initial steps that eventually led to major reforms.[109]

In defense of the Alfonsín government, it must be acknowledged that what it was attempting had never been done before in Latin America, thus increasing the likelihood of unanticipated consequences. In their analysis of Alfonsín's policies, Carlos Acuña and Catalina Smulovitz stress the dynamic and uncertain nature of that civil-military conflict. The National Commission on Disappeared Persons (CONADEP) went further in its investigation and aroused far more public anger than the government ever anticipated. Despite Alfonsín's intention to pursue limited trials, once initiated, the judicial process followed its own logic, culminating in hundreds of officers facing trial and hundreds more called to testify. Timing also affected outcomes in unexpected ways. Proposals to limit the trials by excluding those who were "following orders" had been discussed privately since 1984. But, when the government finally proposed and passed the Due Obedience law after the Semana Santa revolt, it was almost universally viewed as a concession forced by the military rebellion and hence a violation of civilian control and a retreat from the government's commitment to the rule of law.[110] The ambiguity of Alfonsín's policies regarding the trials was doubly costly, in that it inflamed the military opposition and at the same time raised civilian expectations that the government was unable to sustain.[111] Given the uncertain and interactive nature of the policy process, a prudent military policy would have built in margins of safety in anticipation of such contingencies.

In addition to policy objectives appropriate to the context, successful military policy requires effective strategies for employing the available political and material resources to achieve the government's policy goals. One common element of good strategy is the presence of positive incentives for military acceptance of greater degrees of democratic control. In Argentina, from the military's perspective Alfonsín's policies were relentlessly negative: deep cuts in the military budget, which progressively curtailed even routine professional activities; severe decreases in real salaries, which led to growing numbers of officers holding second jobs; the unprecedented trials of high-ranking officers; nearly two years during which the worst abuses of the military regime were highlighted day after day by the mass media; the exclusion of the military from internal security functions; and finally the intrusion of civilian authority into areas previously viewed as part of the military's professional sphere. Partially because of budget constraints, partially because of the unexpected intensity of the confrontation over the trials, the government's plans for military modernization never got off the ground.[112] The absence of positive programs combined with the multiple deprivations inherent in Alfonsín's policies lent credence to hard-line military critics, who claimed that the government's objective was not civilian control, but the destruction or deprofessionalization of the armed forces. Only the hard lessons of the *Proceso* and the absence of any military alternative acceptable to civilian society kept the Argentine military from turning against the democratic regime.

In Uruguay, despite some budget cuts and reductions in military salaries, Sanguinetti projected an image of support and respect for the military in their professional sphere. He also campaigned hard for the nonprosecution law, despite the cost to his own popularity. Likewise, in Venezuela and in Spain, democratic consolidation was accompanied by strong civilian support for military modernization and a new emphasis on the specific military missions of the armed forces. In both cases, the development of a stronger, better-trained military was explicitly linked to a democratic definition of military professionalism stressing subordination to civilian control.[113] If the most common error in military policy in Latin America has been excessive timidity toward the armed forces, the second error has been the tendency to think of military policy primarily or exclusively in terms of stripping the military of its current prerogatives. In its extreme form, this becomes little more than a disguised demand for political retribution against the military, rather than a serious program to create conditions under which democratic control becomes possible. Even if well-intentioned, a purely punitive approach to military policy is almost certain to alienate the military, instead of engendering loyalty to democratic norms and enhancing the legitimacy of the democratic regime.

Finally, military policy in the new democracies has been hampered by the severe deficit in civilian analytical capabilities and personnel experienced in military and defense policy.[114] The European and North American tradition of military sociology and political analysis of the armed forces has no real Latin American counterpart. Reflecting the predominantly neomarxist intellectual traditions of most universities, Latin American writings on the military have traditionally been dominated by interpretations of military behavior as driven by structurally derived class conflicts. Despite some attention to military ideology, empirical studies of military attitudes and institutions are lacking for most countries. Although a new generation of Latin American specialists in civil-military relations is emerging, most countries lack a critical mass of scholars producing policy-relevant empirical analyses.

The resulting intellectual and empirical gaps in understanding military institutions account for some of the errors in the design of military policy. In Argentina, the hope that the military would conduct its own trials for human rights violators as well as the failure to anticipate the intense military reaction to the trials indicate serious deficiencies in the government's understanding of military attitudes and behavior. Alfonsín's concept of three levels of responsibility for human rights violations — those who designed the system and gave the overall orders, those who committed excesses that went beyond their orders, and those who merely followed orders — presumed a hierarchical command structure that was often nonexistent in the antisubversive campaign. In principle, antisubversive operations were subject to a dual chain of command. The zone commanders, generally colonels or generals, had the principal responsibility for detention of suspects and defense against guerrilla attacks; the heads of the detention centers had primary responsibility for extracting intelligence information from the detained and reporting to their respective military intelligence services. In practice, zone commanders varied substantially in their willingness to involve themselves directly in the antisubversive campaign. Some limited themselves to providing cover operations and personnel for the task groups engaged in detention of suspected subversives, leaving the de facto command of operations to the intelligence services and lower-ranking personnel in the centers where most of the torture and executions took place. Decisions to execute prisoners, to confiscate the property of the disappeared, or to release prisoners were not infrequently made by captains and majors. Officers involved in the repression were not given specific orders on how to combat subversion in their zone. Especially in the beginning, tactics were improvised on the spot by the police-military groups that ran the centers. Where senior officers preferred not to get their hands dirty, the "following orders" defense was particularly inappropriate. In fact, junior officers argued in their defense that since the military hierarchy did *not* comply with its responsibility for command, they should not be held accountable for the omissions of their superiors.[115] Alfonsín's claim that only individuals were on trial also failed to recognize the institutional character of the antisubversive campaign. By design, all three services were given detention centers to run; temporary assignments to the detention groups were deliberately widespread in order to diffuse responsibility across ranks and specialities.

These failures are attributable, in part, to the lack of knowledge of the armed forces by Alfonsín and his inner circle who had few personal contacts among senior officers of the period. The government was initially both contemptuous of the military and fearful of a possible coup.[116] Hence the initial plans called for only limited trials and a chance for the military to purge itself of those responsible for the dirty war. As the CONADEP report and the trial of the juntas deepened public outrage against the military, the government dismissed reports of military unrest from the minister of defense and postponed action to limit the trials.[117] In a meeting with a senior administration official in December 1985, I attempted to warn the government about the intensity of the military reaction to the trials and other policics perceived as attacks on the institution. He responded that the administration was aware that the military was unhappy, but in effect those were its just deserts. In practice, the absence of informal contacts with the military meant that government leaders only heard what came through the official channels (for example, the Ministry of Defense and the service chiefs), and that was immediately suspect as self-serving lobbying by a discredited institution. Despite reasonably good relations between Defense Ministers Borrás and Juanarena and the military chiefs of staff, relations with the rest of the government were complicated by horrific images of the *Proceso* and the antimilitary traditions of the Radical Party. By the spring of 1987, the government was fully aware of the military reaction and desperately trying to avoid military defiance of court orders, but by then it was too late.

The deficit in experienced civilian personnel qualified to assume policymaking or advisory roles in military and defense policy is a direct result of the long exclusion of civilian authorities from "military issues," which have historically been reserved for uniformed officers. Few, if any, Latin American countries have legislators or legislative staff with the kind of long-term specialized expertise which characterizes senior legislators and staff on the armed services committees of the U.S. Congress. The extended delay in legislating a new Defense Law in Argentina was at least partly attributable to the lack of relevant expertise in either Congress or the administration. As a result, most of Alfonsín's term passed without the fundamental legislation necessary to proceed with the rewriting of military regulations. Likewise, when Alfonsín moved early in his term to assert civilian control over the state intelligence agency, he discovered that there were simply not enough qualified civilians to replace the military personnel who dominated the agency. Remedying the deficit in civilian capabilities to manage military and defense policy will be a long-term process.

169

Strategies for Change

If the analysis above is correct — that civilian governments have missed opportunities to move toward more democratic civil-military relations — then it is fair to pose the question, What should they be doing? Larry Diamond suggests a series of progressively more difficult measures, beginning with purging "disloyal" officers and curtailing military control over civilian functions (police, intelligence, mass media, economic development) and then extending civilian control over the armed forces, ultimately to include reform of military education. However, he also acknowledges the need for positive incentives (respect, adequate salaries and military budgets, and possibly amnesty) for the armed forces to accept reductions in military prerogatives.[118] Reflecting on the early experiences of Brazil and the Southern Cone countries, Alfred Stepan also counsels against purely punitive strategies and emphasizes the importance of empowering civilian institutions to contest and control the armed forces.[119] Both recommendations are consistent with the lessons learned above. Neither fully accounts for the different starting points for these reform efforts. Given national differences in the political and institutional context of military policy, there are no simple recipes or proven strategies for civilian governments seeking to redefine relationships with the military. The suggestions that follow are rather an invitation to debate and a challenge to other specialists in this area to ponder the policy implications of our knowledge about the Latin American militaries. In keeping with the argument thus far, the proposed strategies are dependent on the system of civil-military relations they are designed to change.

In countries with military dominant or institutionalized tutelary regimes like Guatemala, weak civilian governments typically confront relatively well-organized militaries with a history of political activism. Unless challenged, the military's veto power is likely to result in a restricted transition to a quasi-democratic regime, which lacks legitimacy in the eyes of the civilian population or the military. Here the dilemma is that a fully democratic regime is not likely to be acceptable to the armed forces; a limited democracy is likely to be too weak to avoid crises, which then "require" further military intervention.

In such circumstances, an effective civilian pact not to seek to influence policy decisions via the military is perhaps the most important step toward redefining civil-military relations. With such a pact, civilian leaders can begin to negotiate more democratic norms for power sharing within a mixed regime. Those norms might include, for example, insistence that expressions of military views on policy matters be done only through the respective service chiefs after consultation with other top officers, rather than public statements by any high-ranking officer with an opinion on those policies. Military regulations might allow policy statements in the cabinet or before Congress, but not in unauthorized press statements or private meetings. Insofar as possible, the objective should be to channel and formalize military participation, gradually reducing such participation in areas outside the military's sphere of expertise. If civilian institutions can be strengthened by enhancing their capacity for conflict management—instead of being weakened by their lack of autonomy from military pressures—the incorporation of the armed forces *within* tutelary regimes may become an asset for democracy instead of a liability.

However, the experiences of Brazil and Chile suggest that such a gradualist strategy may not be necessary. In relatively mobilized societies, the interests adversely affected by military intervention in nonmilitary policy debates are natural opponents of military tutelage. In the Brazilian case, for example, labor unions and prolabor politicians actively opposed military attempts to impose restrictive strike legislation in the name of national security. These countries also have large and relatively professionalized militaries, with diverse policy preferences on nonmilitary issues. Hence, opposition to military tutelage on professional grounds will find support within the military. Even where civilian parties are relatively weak, presidents with strong public support can move fairly quickly to restrict military participation in policy matters outside the military sphere. To date, attempts to legitimize military tutelage have not encountered much support in the rest of society. A prudent strategy might couple opposition to military tutelage with respect for other institutional interests, including internal autonomy. Still, this is not a strategy for weak presidents or countries with no significant civilian constituency favoring greater control of the armed forces. Such a strategy will also be more difficult where military tutelage favors populist or nationalist policies.

In countries with conditional military subordination to civilian authority, the challenge is more subtle. In principle, the armed forces accept constitutional democracy and civilian authority. Military officers are not openly engaged in politics, but reserve their "right" to intervene in times of crisis. Civilian groups may encourage the military to play this guardian role. For civilian leaders, there is a strong temptation to ignore the problem of the military's limited commitment to the democratic regime until a crisis occurs; however, once a crisis is in progress, it is often too late. Escaping from this dilemma requires agreements among civilian political leaders to use and strengthen constitutional mechanisms for crisis resolution. Political scientists and constitution writers in Latin America have directed most of their attention in recent years to the problem of creating strong governments capable of governing politically divided and economically vulnerable societies. The alternative strategy would be to create more opportunities to get rid of weak governments via more frequent elections or impeachment.

Where the military is only conditionally loyal to the democratic regime, the second element of civilian strategy must be to try to prevent opposition groups from defecting and calling on the military to intervene. Political pacts among the major parties to defend the democratic regime are a logical part of that strategy. Legal sanctions against "incitement to rebellion" should be applied to civilians and to retired officers, who are often the linkage between disloyal civilian sectors and disgruntled active-duty officers. The posttransition Peruvian constitution contained a number of measures designed to increase the "cost" of military intervention, including a provision that debts and contracts by unconstitutional governments shall not be binding on their successors.[120] Fujimori's *autogolpe* is, however, a vivid reminder that such provisions mean little unless there is a political will to use them.

In these regimes, the military typically enjoys a high degree of institutional autonomy from government control. Here again, the issue is one of leadership and foresight. In the short term, the easiest path is to accept whatever degree of institutional autonomy the military has historically been accustomed to. Unfortunately, in most cases the military appetite for autonomy expanded during recent periods of military rule. In countries still seeking to establish the basic principle of political subordination to democratic rule, granting a high degree of policy autonomy may be unavoidable. In countries with at least conditional military allegiance to democracy, it may be possible to insist on democratic control of defense policy and military budgets without intruding into sensitive areas like military education, promotion policies, or military doctrine. Naming retired military officers — rather than civilians — to the ministry of defense may be a useful transitional device, provided that these officers are selected for professional competence and democratic allegiance rather than simply personal loyalty to the president.

One strategy would be to gradually increase civilian participation in policy decisions traditionally reserved for the armed forces, for example, line items within the military budget or counterinsurgency strategy, taking care not to disregard military expertise and to avoid partisan politics. Over time, the policy areas subject to civilian oversight could be expanded as military confidence increases that democratic oversight is not a threat to military professionalism or good policy. Gradually, distinctions could be drawn between areas subject to democratic control, such as military appropriations, and areas subject to civilian oversight, such as military education.

In countries that have achieved a substantial degree of democratic control of the armed forces, the first challenge is to manage the conflicts generated by the loss of the military's traditional political prerogatives. In both Argentina and Uruguay, civilian governments have faced difficult decisions in dealing with the institutional complaints of the armed forces. Refusing to make concessions may alienate the military from the democratic regime. Giving in to those complaints may encourage the reemergence of the military as an autonomous interest group. Demands from the left for institutional punishment of the military complicate these decisions. Here again, there are no easy answers. Nevertheless, the long-term strategy must provide the armed forces with sufficient resources to perform their assigned missions and accord them the social respect and material rewards appropriate for technically trained professionals. Integrating the military in a democratic regime requires more than simply controlling the armed forces; it also means defining a role for the armed forces in that regime.

The second challenge for these countries is a military policy to institutionalize democratic control. This will require civilian leadership for reforms in military education and patterns of interaction with civil society. Over the long term, these reforms are necessary to reduce civil-military asymmetries, promote mutual tolerance, and strengthen military loyalty to democratic rule. At this level, military policy requires civilian involvement in areas that have traditionally been tightly controlled by the armed forces. A process of confidence building may be necessary to reassure military leaders that changes in the curricula of military schools do not entail ideological indoctrination or attempts to civilianize the officer corps. Without a comprehensive military policy and effective implementation, the opportunity to institutionalize democratic control of the armed forces will likely be lost.

Policy Recommendations

Consolidation of fully democratic regimes in Latin America will require a long-term effort to develop and institutionalize more democratic systems of civil-military relations. Leadership of this effort is first and foremost a civilian responsibility. Democratic leaders must assess current patterns of civil-military relations and devise realistic strategies appropriate to the particular context in **173** which they must operate. Civilians must be willing to challenge the military's current prerogatives and to risk antagonizing some sectors of the armed forces; they must also be willing to make difficult judgments about when the risk is excessive and when compromises are necessary.

The first task facing civilian leaders is to reshape the institutional context by strengthening democratic institutions and practicing democratic politics. The military cannot be held responsible for crises that result from fragmented party systems, factionalized parties, or stalemates between the president and Congress. The existing institutional imbalance between civilian and military institutions must be redressed by empowering democratic institutions, building grass-roots organizations, and expanding opportunities for political participation. If civilian leaders cannot agree on constitutional norms and behave according to those norms, there is little likelihood that the military will respect democratic rules or submit to democratic control. In established democracies, institutionalized systems of civilian control can withstand weak governments. In unconsolidated democracies, weak governments are unlikely to attempt democratic reforms in civil-military relations or to overcome military resistance to those reforms. Strong political institutions are needed to create a political context in which democratic control of the armed forces becomes possible.

The second task is to clearly define the missions for which the armed forces exist. Integration of the armed forces as a component of the democratic regime will almost certainly fail if civilian leaders cannot specify a constructive role for the military within that regime. It is not sufficient for civilian leaders merely to specify what they do not want—political guardians, military repression, or "disappearances." At a minimum, civilian leaders must be able to articulate a coherent vision of the military in a democratic society and to identify the steps necessary to implement that vision over time.

Third, the developed democracies could help alleviate the deficit in civilian capabilities by sharing their expertise and experience in civilian oversight and control of the armed forces. The U.S. and Western European governments should initiate technical assistance programs providing training, short-term exchanges, and internships for civilian personnel involved in defense and military policy, for example, congressional staffs, presidential advisors, and Defense Ministry officials.[121] This is not to suggest that the U.S., German, or Spanish models of civil-military relations can be exported to Latin America. Still, exposure to different patterns of civil-military interaction can contribute to development of democratic models adapted to the special circumstances of Latin American societies. Institutes like the new U.S. Center for Hemispheric Defense Studies could contribute to greater civilian expertise in defense policy. Strengthening civilian skills in areas that have traditionally been monopolized by the military enhances civilian ability to incrementally assert greater democratic control and to earn military respect by doing so competently.

Stating what needs to be done is far easier than doing it. Each of these recommendations involves major, long-term civilian initiatives and sustained efforts to create the conditions that would make it possible to consolidate democratic patterns of civil-military relations. Despite hopeful signs in some difficult cases, the overall record of military policy in the new Latin American democracies is not particularly encouraging. The general weakening of military influence over the last decade has been more a product of societal changes and political dynamics than of conscious policy by civilian leaders. Analysts concerned with the future of democracy in the region must therefore redouble their efforts to understand both successful and unsuccessful policies and to provide more concrete short-term and long-term strategies for varying national contexts.

Democratic Professionalist Alternatives

Democratic consolidation in Latin America will require modification of politicized conceptions of military professionalism and changes in the institutional self-image of the military as political guardians. This chapter defines an alternative conception compatible with the requirements of democratic civil-military relations. Acknowledging differences in context between Latin America and U.S./European democracies, it prescribes mechanisms of democratic control for both conventional and developmentalist variants of democratic professionalism. The chapter concludes with a discussion of future prospects for civil-military relations in the region and recommendations for U.S. policymakers.

Democratic professionalism draws both on classical professionalism and professional norms in established democracies. However, this view of the armed forces and democracy also attempts to take into account the higher degree of ideological dissensus and social conflict characteristic of most Latin American societies. Unlike classical professionalism, it posits an ultimate allegiance to the nation, rather than the state. Unlike traditional Latin American variants of professionalism, it acknowledges democratic regimes as the only authentic expression of the shared interests and majority preferences of the nation, which the armed forces are sworn to defend.

The traditional training of Latin American officers focuses on the *patria*. Historically, the "fatherland" symbolizes not just the national territory, but also national resources, each country's unique sense of national identity, and particular values—such as Catholicism—seen as integral to that identity. For military officers, the *patria* signifies that which would be lost if the country were conquered by a foreign nation. This is as it should be. The profession of arms is unique in its willingness to die to defend the land and the people whom they serve. In Latin America, however, this devotion to the fatherland has historically been used to justify the political autonomy of the armed forces. In this view, the military does not serve particular governments or regimes. The armed forces are responsible for the survival of the fatherland. In the face of external and internal threats, the armed forces defend that which is permanent, the essence of the nation.[1] When crises erupt, when civilian incompetence threatens national interests, the armed forces have a duty to respond.

From the viewpoint of modern political theory, this transformation of military patriotism into a justification for military intervention in politics is untenable. National identities are complex and constantly evolving. Catholicism, for example, is an important part of Latin American history and culture, but Latin societies today are increasingly secular. If Catholicism is deemed part of the national identity, who decides which is the authentic Catholicism—the progressive Church of the 1960s and 1970s, conservative priests and bishops, or the (foreign) pope? Who represents "Western Christian values"—the military chaplains who gave communion to torturers or the Church that condemned human rights abuses and protected "subversives"? Who decides if divorce is contrary to "national values"? Given conflicting views of national identity in ideologically pluralistic societies, who then is empowered to define national values and national interests? In democratic societies, the answer is clear: only the duly elected representatives of the nation.

The key premise of democratic professionalism is thus the rejection of any military claim to a suprapolitical role as national guardians. Democratic theory denies the claim of any individual or group to represent the "national will" or define "national interests." Only a fully enfranchised electorate can speak for the nation as a whole.

Democratic professionalism accepts not only the political subordination of the armed forces, but also their subordination to the policy decisions of constitutionally designated state authorities. Defining security threats, determining the allocation of resources to defense relative to other national needs, and specifying the missions of the armed forces are fundamental policy choices in any society. Hence, these choices cannot be removed from the sphere of popular sovereignty and arrogated to the military. The professional expertise of the military is essential to informed policy choices, but those choices must be subject to democratic control. In this view, the armed forces are *instruments* of the nation for its self-defense and protection of its right to self-government, not the saviors of the nation nor the only repository of national values.

The political and policy subordination of the armed forces to democratic control are fundamental to any democratic conception of military professionalism. Nevertheless, as chapter 1 argued, the norms of professional behavior and the institutional mechanisms for exercising democratic control must be adapted to the Latin American context. Contemporary Latin American democracies share much of the philosophical tradition and many constitutional features of the Western democracies, but the societal context is substantially different. Latin American societies are distinguished by high levels of political and ideological conflict. Although capitalism in the broadest sense is generally accepted, that acceptance is more contested than in the United States. Deep divisions exist over what *kind* of capitalism should be encouraged and over the role of the state in economic development. In many countries, socialist parties rejecting capitalism command significant numbers of votes. Politically, there is widespread support for democracy, but considerable disagreement about the ultimate meaning of that term, ranging from oligarchical republics and "delegative democracy" to Sandinista-style "revolutionary democracy."

177

The economic structure of Latin American societies includes far greater inequality between the poorest and richest classes. Higher proportions of the population suffer from absolute poverty without benefit of government assistance. Government corruption is commonplace, sharpening the contrast between those who suffer from government policies and those who profit. These inequalities and social conflicts create a significant potential for political polarization and sustained domestic violence; internal security is necessarily a greater concern than in established Western democracies.

The pace of modernization and social change is also more rapid. The isolated peasant village living outside the money economy has virtually disappeared. Television and the consumer culture are now nearly universal, despite the limited purchasing power of most of the population. The dependence of Latin American economies on trade and investment from the United States, Europe, and Japan makes them vulnerable to the vagaries of the international economy. The movement toward an even more global economy accentuates the limited policy autonomy of Latin American governments on issues like exchange rates and fiscal policy. As a result, economic and political crises are to some degree inevitable.

The challenge is, therefore, to devise professional norms and institutional mechanisms that are consistent with the principles of democratic control, but also acknowledge the greater frequency and intensity of societal and civil-military conflicts in Latin America. There are no simple answers to the question of how to do this, but the following examples illustrate the kinds of adaptations that are needed.

Institutional Adaptations

Given the political diversity of Latin American democracies, professional norms need to provide for military dissent on matters of national defense within a framework of subordination to civilian authority. In any society, the most difficult moments in civil-military relations occur when military officers believe that civilian authorities are acting in ways that endanger national security. In most Latin American countries, the ideological asymmetries between political and military elites guarantee that such situations will occur, creating conflicts between the norm of obedience to democratic authority and the officer's sense of professional responsibility for national security. In these situations, the duty of the officer to his professional conscience requires that channels exist for objections to government policies to be expressed to the Ministry of Defense or to the president as commander-in-chief. If these appeals fail, military regulations should provide for direct access to the defense committees of the legislature. If these appeals also fail, the professional duty of the dissenting officer should be to resign and seek the appropriate democratic means to put the issues before the nation. Democratic mechanisms for resolving civil-military conflicts must be available *within* constitutional regimes in order to prevent recourse to nondemocratic means to resolve those conflicts. Democratically constituted national security councils, where military officers *advise* civilian decision makers, could provide an arena for policy debate and conflict resolution consistent with the principle of democratic control. Appropriately staffed legislative defense committees also contribute to this function.[2]

Given past practices, military officers fear that democratic control means that promotions will become politicized, particularly where Congress retains its traditional right to approve promotions of senior officers. The new democracies have, in fact, used their power to control military promotions sparingly, primarily to deny promotions to officers accused of human rights violations. Nevertheless, the danger of partisan bias remains. Hence, it may be desirable to provide legal or judicial mechanisms to prevent the president or Congress from violating merit-based criteria for military promotions and assignments. As noted below, military regulations should stipulate which military officials serve at the discretion of the commander-in-chief, for example, the High Command or presidential staff, and which officers should be subject to removal from office only for cause. The military court system could be used to appeal personnel decisions that violate professional norms or merit-based criteria for promotion. Where promotions have been denied for human rights violations, the accused should be allowed to defend themselves in a civilian court of appeals.

Professional norms must also specify appropriate military behavior in situations of political instability and internal war. The norm of obedience to higher authority is fundamental to any military organization. In order to carry out their military functions, the armed forces require a degree of hierarchy and discipline not found in civilian organizations. Nevertheless, democratic professionalism requires that the armed forces exist within the rule of law. In civilized nations, both international and internal wars are subject to laws and regulations. Officers must recognize their duty not to obey orders that contravene the law. An order to participate in an unconstitutional rebellion has no military or moral authority. Military officers are not robots blindly executing higher orders. An order to torture a prisoner to gain intelligence information must be no more professionally acceptable than an order to rob a bank or to assassinate a child at random just because a superior officer said so. Respect for human rights is both a key test of the performance of any democracy and a significant political advantage in combating terrorist or revolutionary groups. Therefore, instruction in the basic international law of war and human rights should be incorporated into all levels of military training. If not, the use of the military for internal security is likely to be outside the law and, therefore, antithetical to democracy and its long-term survival.

179

Civilian Institutions

Changes are also needed in civilian institutions in recognition of the special difficulties of the Latin American context. Weak civilian institutions invite military intervention in politics, encouraging antidemocratic role beliefs and undermining attempts to encourage military acceptance of civilian authority. Strengthening civilian institutions is thus an essential step toward creating a context in which democratic control of the armed forces becomes a real possibility, not just a distant ideal. Neither the deep social conflicts nor the ideological divisions of Latin American societies are likely to diminish in the short term. Economic growth is likely to be slow, unequal, and variable. Hence the key to successful civilian performance is to create institutional structures which make good leadership possible, instead of an exercise in frustration.

Institutional reform must begin with changes in party structures. Although the underlying political cleavages often have deep historical roots, the proliferation of political parties in recent decades is a major impediment to effective governance.[3] Hyperfragmented party systems make it difficult to hold any party accountable for specific policy outcomes or for the poor performance of the system as a whole, leading discontented citizens to blame the democratic regime. Governments find it impossible to construct working majorities in the legislature, reinforcing the authoritarian temptation to centralize power in the executive and rule by decree. Especially where small parties are transitory and political careers are short, short-term objectives take priority, enhancing the incentives for corruption and personal aggrandizement at the expense of public service. For this reason, laws governing political parties should set higher thresholds for the creation of new parties and eliminate parties that fail to maintain at least 5 percent of the national vote. In order to avoid simply creating monopolies for existing party elites, electoral tribunals should establish minimum norms for internal party democracy, including rules for primary elections and party conventions. These tribunals should be given broad authority to investigate complaints and to regulate internal party elections, in addition to their mandate to guarantee free and honest electoral competition between parties.[4]

Given the wide variations in past histories and institutional legacies, there is no single formula for institutional reform in Latin America.[5] Despite strong academic interest in parliamentary alternatives,[6] it seems likely that presidentialist regimes will predominate. Hence, the general strategy for reformers should be to facilitate strong presidential leadership without foregoing the checks on executive authority necessary to a democracy. Limited presidential powers to rule by decree on critical economic measures may be necessary. However, effective democracy will require strong legislatures as well as strong executives. Executive decrees should be subject to repeal by Congress, perhaps by supermajorities. Longer congressional terms, better staffing, and simpler procedures would enhance legislative performance. When impasses occur between the president and Congress, either should be able to initiate a resolution via a national referendum. Institutional mechanisms to counter corruption—for instance, an independent inspector general reporting to the Supreme Court—are critical to maintain the legitimacy of the democratic system.[7] Since political crises "inviting" military intervention often occur after civilian presidents have lost their base of civilian support, shorter presidential terms and more frequent elections would provide constitutional mechanisms for replacing ineffective and unpopular governments. Constitutional changes to facilitate presidential impeachment in times of crisis might likewise reduce the temptation to use the armed forces to perform the impeachment function.

Another important adaptation to the Latin American context could be greater use of political pacts and alliances. In principle, political pacts enhance the stability of democratic regimes by inhibiting polarization and reducing uncertainty for key political actors. In Venezuela, for example, after the failed

1945–48 democratic regime, the major parties agreed to a basic set of posttransition policies and at the same time excluded policy options that threatened the interests of the armed forces or the Catholic Church. The National Front that followed the 1957 restoration of constitutional democracy in Colombia provided for a formal power sharing between the Liberal and Conservative parties. Informal power sharing could be helpful in ameliorating partisan antagonisms, particularly the fear of exclusion by the governing party. As in Argentina, a political pact may simply express a shared sense of loyalty to the democratic regime and a commitment to cooperative action when that regime is challenged by disloyal groups. In times of crisis, such as the attempted *autogolpe* in Guatemala or the *carapintada* revolts in Argentina, concerted civilian action in defense of democracy can be critical. Pacts can be dangerous to the health of democratic regimes if power sharing creates an unresponsive governing elite or if the exclusion of potentially destabilizing policy options means that key issues cannot be raised within the regime.[8] But neither of these outcomes is preordained. Chile's Concertación de Partidos por la Democracia has provided an institutional framework for cooperation between the Christian Democrats and parties of the left without excluding heated debate on questions like prosecution of human rights abuses or inequalities within the current economic model.

As noted above, the structural features of Latin American societies create a greater likelihood that some conflicts will not be resolved within a democratic framework and that dissident groups will try to overthrow existing regimes by force. The peace accords that ended long-term civil wars in Nicaragua, El Salvador, and Guatemala demonstrate that peace is possible in Latin America. But persistent violence in Colombia and Peru cautions against any false optimism that political democracy will, by itself, be sufficient to end revolutionary insurgencies. Thus, democratic regimes must be prepared to defend themselves without sacrificing democracy in the process. Resort to extralegal means— assassinations, torture, disappearances—to repress antiregime forces destroys a key distinction between democratic regimes and their opponents, undermining their legitimacy in the struggle for the "hearts and minds" of the population. Hence, for their own survival, Latin American democracies must develop new institutions for internal security.

Revolutionary wars are fundamentally political rather than military; therefore, primary responsibility for internal security should be given to specialized paramilitary forces, trained in antiterrorist operations. The rule of law is an essential arm for the defense of democracy, hence these forces should operate under the jurisdiction of the Ministry of Interior or the Ministry of Justice. Nevertheless, in most cases, total exclusion of the armed forces from internal

security is not feasible. When guerrillas begin to undertake military operations, regular military forces will be needed, so these forces must be trained
in the conduct of counterinsurgency operations that respect the rights of bel-
ligerents as well as bystanders in order to politically isolate the insurgents. In
practice, civilian governments in Latin America have not been able to control
abuses by police, paramilitary, or military personnel. Hence domestic institutions for the protection of human rights in civil wars must be supplemented
by strengthened international institutions to provide monitoring of violations,
countervailing pressures for enforcement of human rights norms, and alternative judicial venues for pursuing sanctions against violators when local courts
are unable to protect victims or provide justice. Nongovernmental organizations, the Human Rights Commission of the Organization of American States
(OAS), and the United Nations should be legally empowered to assume a
greater role in the collective defense of human rights when domestic institutions are inadequate.[9]

182

Role and Missions: The Military Model

Since the fall of the Berlin Wall, the roles and missions of the armed forces have
been debated extensively within Latin America.[10] In most countries, the end
of the cold war has significantly reduced — but not eliminated — the perceived
threat to internal security. Notwithstanding the 1995 border war between Ecuador and Peru, democratic governments have worked hard to settle outstanding
territorial disputes, particularly in the Southern Cone. Tensions and potential flash points remain — Colombia and Venezuela, Honduras and El Salvador,
among others — but few citizens in Latin America today fear military attacks
from neighboring countries. If Latin American countries face neither external
nor internal threats, what is the role of the armed forces? Why do Latin American countries need a military? If the armed forces have to exist, what are their
missions? Are there missions that are not compatible with the goal of democratic consolidation?

One response to these questions is the "military option." In this view, the
mission of the armed forces is not to govern or to promote economic development, but to defend the nation. The primary activity of the armed forces
is neither nation building nor peacekeeping; it is preparation for war making.
Armies exist to defend against other armies. The principal, everyday function
of the armed forces is military deterrence. In the best of all possible worlds,
the armed forces never engage in war. The deterrent effect of probable defeat
and high costs imposed on potential aggressors is a vital guarantee for national

security and, if diplomacy fails, the best hope that the call to arms will never come. Successful deterrence requires that the military be prepared to fight—and to prevail—if war does come. There is, therefore, nothing paradoxical in a military that constantly practices for war that never happens.

For North Americans, the military rationale for the Latin American armed forces is puzzling, if not incomprehensible. From Washington (or Kansas), the differences between Latin American countries seem minor; the territorial disputes between them trivial. For Colombians and Venezuelans, Ecuadorians and Peruvians, the conflicts are no more trivial than the territorial disputes that led to various European wars. Despite the end of the cold war and high uncertainty about future threats to national security, the United States has not substantially reduced its military spending. It maintains a large nuclear arsenal to counter the nuclear weapons of the former Soviet states. Why is the logic of deterrence not equally valid south of the Rio Grande? Costa Rica offers proof that it is possible to maintain territorial integrity without regular military forces,[11] but other cases of unilateral disarmament are less reassuring. In 1941, Ecuador had only a small, minimally professionalized, and poorly equipped military, which mostly served as a political prop for the government. Larger, better-trained, and better-equipped Peruvian forces invaded the disputed frontier territory and southern provinces. Only international intervention prevented Peru from occupying Ecuador's major population centers. From the Ecuadorian perspective, the Rio Protocol ending the 1941 war resulted in the loss of half its claimed territory.

The deterrence argument also applies to internal security. In 1980, Sendero Luminoso unleashed a vicious campaign of bombings, assassinations, and guerrilla attacks designed to overthrow Peru's newly reestablished democracy in favor of a Maoist "peasant republic." After police forces were driven from many contested villages, President Belaúnde reluctantly called in the armed forces. Although government errors and human rights violations contributed to Sendero's support, this was a major guerrilla war aimed at establishing a nondemocratic regime. Military force was not the only factor in that war, perhaps not even the most important factor,[12] but there can be no doubt that Peru faced—and still confronts—a major threat to its internal security. Faced with that threat, it seems ingenuous to believe that Sendero could have been defeated without the armed forces. In Ecuador, the indigenous movement has been generally nonviolent, yet the potential for a Sendero-style movement remains. The military capacity of the armed forces to respond to that potential logically plays the same deterrent role as conventional military deterrence. In either internal or external security, potential aggressors may choose not to be deterred, par-

183

ticularly if they believe the odds favor their eventual victory. In that case, the armed forces must be capable of militarily preventing that victory.

In the military option, the armed forces are military forces, trained primarily for conventional external defense, but prepared if necessary to provide troops for internal security operations. All other functions are secondary. The military may use its logistical capabilities to aid victims, provide supplies, and maintain order during hurricanes, floods, or earthquakes, but these events are relatively rare and transitory. Depending on the foreign policy objectives of the government, the armed forces may supply forces for peacekeeping operations as part of OAS or U.N. collective security agreements, but the training and equipment of a peacekeeping force are different from those of war making, so this, too, is a secondary mission.

In most Latin American countries, such a model would probably entail relatively small military forces. However, these would have to be highly mobile and flexible enough to respond with high fire power or a high degree of fire control, depending on the situation. In contrast to past practices, joint operations and joint command will be necessary to maximize efficiency and economy of force. Because of the requirements for air and land transport, as well as more sophisticated technology and better training, smaller forces do not necessarily mean smaller military budgets.[13] Given high uncertainty about the nature of future security threats, officer training would include a mix of skills rather than narrow specializations. Rigid distinctions between services and branches would be deemphasized. Because of their small size and technical nature, such forces would most likely be volunteer forces with a professional core of noncommissioned officers and soldiers. But an essential component of such a strategy would be a military reserve system and the capacity to quickly mobilize a larger force around the professional nucleus if future conflict hypotheses should require expansion.[14]

This classical military view of the role of the armed forces lends itself naturally to democratic control. The professional disadvantages of military intervention in politics provide a powerful rationale for acceptance of civilian authority. Although the arts and science of war are no longer limited to combat strategy and leadership, professionalist officers recognize the limits of their expertise and acknowledge the different skills necessary for successful political leadership.[15] But as shown in chapter 1, professionalism alone is not sufficient to insure the political subordination of the military in Latin America. Democratic professionalism requires a commitment to defend democracy, not the state or some ideological conception of the fatherland. Hence military training, in military academies and war colleges in particular, must include instruction in democratic theories of governance and democratic norms for civil-military relations. In this view, the armed forces are an integral part of any democratic regime, not a separate state apparatus nor a power unto themselves.

However, in the "military" version of democratic professionalism, the armed forces would receive relatively little training in nonmilitary subjects, except for the small cadre of senior officers who would staff the National Security Council and act as liaisons and advisors to executive and legislative officials. Reflecting their specialized expertise and the lack of civilian equivalents for many military skills, the military career would be extended, with senior officers retiring at fifty-five to sixty-five. (At present, colonels often retire with thirty **185** years service and full pay at age fifty or less.[16]) The armed forces would not be deliberately isolated from society, but officers would spend more of their time in frontier areas and tension zones and in specialized military training, thus lessening the frequency of interaction with civilian elites. Because of the high priority given to operational efficiency and military effectiveness, the military option implies special efforts to protect the armed forces from penetration by partisan groups—of whatever persuasion—in order to avoid internal factionalization. For example, given the politicization of Latin American universities, most officers would not attend civilian universities; training in subjects like management and accounting would be done in military institutions focusing on specific military applications. By its nature, the military option entails a higher degree of separation of the military from politics in order to maximize its war making potential, thus enhancing its effectiveness as a deterrent force.

In this model, democratic control is exercised through the traditional mechanisms common to most established democracies, with appropriate adaptations to the Latin American context:

1. The president, in consultation with the National Security Council, defines the principal threats to defend against, specifying the hypotheses of conflict that provide the basic parameters for defense planning. She or he may also specify hypotheses of cooperation, identifying allies and opportunities for collective responses to security threats. In Latin America, to insure that the National Security/Defense Council is not just an executive agency, majority and minority representatives of Congress should be included in the council to provide alternative perspectives on the underlying premises of defense planning.

2. A civilian minister of defense is responsible for approval and management of the military strategy for responding to those threats. Strategy is the principal responsibility of the Joint Staff; implementation is shared by

the individual services and joint commands. Civilians within the Defense Ministry exercise oversight of the individual services to insure maximum effectiveness and compliance with the government's defense policy.

3. Congress—not the Ministry of Finance—is responsible for determining the budgetary allocation of resources between defense and other national objectives. As such, the legislature should have permanent defense committees, appropriately trained staffs of civilians and retired officers, and permanent liaison with the Ministry of Defense. In order to facilitate full and informed debate, the president and defense minister should strive for the maximum transparency possible in budgetary data on defense spending. The need for secrecy on some defense issues should not exclude Congress from exercising its responsibilities for budgetary control. As noted above, the defense committees also have an important appeal function for individual officers or commanders who feel that government policies are endangering national security. While military expertise is important to evaluate such claims, only the constitutionally designated civilian authorities can make the ultimate determination of the appropriate policies, including the decisions about what level of risk from potential threats is acceptable and what costs the nation should pay to reduce those risks.

4. The president as commander-in-chief is responsible for naming the heads of the individual military forces and the chief of the Joint Staff. This High Command is responsible for formulation and execution of the government's defense policies, hence these officers serve at the pleasure of the president. The High Command, in turn, is responsible for designating subordinate commanders, but military merit and seniority should be the sole criteria for such appointments, which should rotate according to the exigencies of the post rather than political cycles. Whether or not Congress formally approves promotions of senior officers, their political sympathies (or lack thereof) should be irrelevant. The nominations of military promotion boards should be respected and ratified as long as these are consistent with democratic professionalist norms of military merit, including respect for human rights.

5. The military role in internal security must be subject to strict policy control by the Ministries of Interior and Defense and subject to judicial and legislative oversight. Domestic intelligence should be under an appropriate state intelligence agency; military intelligence agencies should be excluded from internal security except when military forces are engaged in combat or security operations requiring operational intelligence. In times of peace and times of war, democratic governments are responsible for the formula-

tion and implementation of coordinated internal security policies, including effective control over all police, paramilitary, and military forces and the necessary coordination with other state agencies.

The military model, with its focus on external defense and echoes of classical professionalism, fits nicely with the predispositions of the Southern Cone militaries, but the traditional concept of the armed forces as the defenders of the nation's territorial sovereignty is in tension with global and regional trends. National frontiers are, in fact, becoming more permeable as a result of trade, economic integration, and legal and illegal immigration. The role of the state is diminishing, with more areas left to the private sector; large corporations are predominately transnational. In the global economy, few states, if any, exercise fully sovereign powers; even the great powers are increasingly interdependent. Wars are rarely between states, as in the classical European model, but between states and a variety of subnational and transnational forces. Hence, militaries oriented toward conventional defense roles may be advantageous for promoting democratic professionalism, but not very well suited for the amorphous conflicts of the twenty-first century.[17]

The Developmentalist Model

At least in theory, the military option is a tested and familiar model. However, actual practice in Latin America rarely fit that model very well. Nonmilitary roles were commonplace long before the national security doctrines of the 1960s. Both the colonial and preprofessional militaries were actively involved in the colonization of remote areas and the maintenance of internal order. The mass armies of the early professionalization era gave the military an important "nation-building" role, teaching literacy and socializing peasant and immigrant conscripts to a national identity. After World War I, the larger Latin American militaries promoted strategic industries and technological modernization. World War II and counterinsurgency warfare provided doctrinal justifications linking nonmilitary vulnerabilities to national security.

In the last three decades, nonmilitary activities have proliferated. This trend is particularly noticeable in Central America, where military, paramilitary, and police functions have never been sharply differentiated and limited budgets have encouraged the military to develop their own economic resources. However, similar tendencies were at work, perhaps less visibly, in South America. Chapter 4 described the extensive involvement of the Ecuadorian military in nonmilitary activities. The army owns both military and nonmilitary indus-

187

tries. The navy has its own shipping firms; the air force its own airline. All three forces are heavily involved in civic action and community development projects. The armed forces also offer educational programs ranging from elementary schools to the Army's Technical University, in response to what it views as the deficiencies of civilian education.

The problem with the "developmentalist model" as it currently exists is that these nonmilitary missions have accumulated behind the wall of institutional autonomy traditionally exercised by Latin American militaries. Although nationalist governments were sometimes eager partners in expanding the military's role in the economy, most of these activities were developed as a result of military initiative, often with only tacit government approval.[18] Government oversight is usually limited to the president or the minister of defense, who is typically a military officer rather than a civilian. In the extreme case, the armed forces operate a miniature government of their own — receiving petitions from various civilian groups, making policy decisions, allocating resources to different programs, and implementing those programs as they see fit. This military "state within the state" is not subject to democratic control, nor is it accountable to the nation through any democratic mechanisms except for superficial oversight by the president.[19]

There is nothing intrinsically undemocratic about the military building roads or delivering the mail or providing medical care in remote regions. Assigning missions to the military is fundamentally a political decision. Hence the first requirement is that this decision be made by the appropriate democratic process. If the democratically determined preference of the nation is for a developmentalist military, so be it. In Ecuador, the military's constitutional mandate to contribute to socioeconomic development was not widely debated, but it was approved by plebiscite as part of the 1978 Constitution. Polls suggest strong public support for the military's development role. Adapting the developmentalist option to the requirements of democratic civil-military relations will, however, require fundamental modifications of current practice. In brief, because these nonmilitary missions are inherently more political and controversial, the developmentalist option requires substantially higher degrees of democratic control.

In the developmentalist option, the armed forces are a disciplined, organized, multifunction institution at the service of the nation as represented by the constitutionally designated civilian authorities. The military retains its primary responsibilities for external security. Depending on the constitution and defense laws, the armed forces may have primary or shared responsibility for internal security and maintenance of internal order. In addition to these pri-

188

mary roles, the military also accepts and executes other secondary missions as specified by Congress and the president. With the appropriate authorization and oversight, the armed forces may run literacy programs, build dams and potable water supplies, and own their own industries. In every case, these activities involve politically controversial issues — the content of those literacy programs, deciding which village gets the road or the water supply, the application of agrarian reform laws to military properties, the labor and tax laws applicable to military-owned factories, and so forth. Hence, the developmentalist option requires greater democratic control and closer integration of the armed forces with the rest of society.   **189**

1. The president, in consultation with the National Security Council, sets the basic parameters for external and internal security policy. Development and oversight of implementation of government policies is the responsibility of a civilian minister of defense, who is advised by the Joint Staff. Civilian secretaries of defense for external security, internal security, and development have primary responsibility for coordinating the activities of the Defense Ministry with other ministries and agencies in their respective spheres.

2. As in the military model, Congress has responsibility for determining the allocation of budgetary resources between defense and nondefense needs, but Congress should also make the ultimate determination of the resources that should be assigned to military and civilian providers of development services. For example, Congress should determine the appropriate funding for roads to be built by military engineers and construction battalions, relative to those to be built by private contractors or state agencies. The appropriate congressional committees, for example, a Transportation or Public Works Committee, should exercise oversight of military activities within their respective jurisdictions. Lodging these resource allocation and oversight functions in the legislature is intended to maximize public debate and informed choice in policy decisions governing the military's development activities. Transparency and open discussion also reduce the risk that the governing party will attempt to use those activities for partisan purposes.

3. Interagency task forces coordinate government programs, including their military and nonmilitary components. In recognition of the government's responsibility for policy decisions and its political accountability for their success or failure, those task forces should be headed by civilian officials. For the same reason, military representatives on those task forces

should be officials of the Ministry of Defense, not the delegates of their respective services. In this model, the military and civilian participants are
both members of the government team. The military services do not run
their own teams.

4. As in the military model, the president freely names his own High
Command, but in order for the armed forces to participate effectively in
nonmilitary programs, officers serving in nonmilitary posts in the Defense
Ministry — such as the military representative to a Transportation Task Force
— or equivalent positions within the services also serve at the pleasure of the
president or minister of defense. Officers assigned to such positions should
have the right to refuse those assignments without prejudice to their careers.
For example, a nationalist officer assigned to oversee the privatization of
state enterprises should be able to request a different assignment. Congress
should approve nominations of the president for promotion to colonel and
general. Promotion should be on the basis of merit, but should also reward
nonpartisanship and effectiveness in carrying out nonmilitary missions.

5. The developmentalist option logically entails greater interaction with
the rest of society and more overlap between the skills of military officers
and civilian professionals. In order for military officers to function effectively in nonmilitary roles, the ideological asymmetries between the officer
corps and civil society have to be reduced. University degrees in civilian institutions should be the norm. Wherever possible, nonmilitary training —
such as management or public policy — should be provided in civilian settings rather than war colleges, where the military controls the curriculum.
The developmentalist model entails greater risks of political factionalization within the military, but the political risks can be reduced by insuring
ample military exposure to competing viewpoints and strong socialization
to norms of nonpartisanship in the performance of these duties. The military model minimizes the effects of ideological differences within the military and asymmetries with civil society because these are largely irrelevant
to the purely military functions of the armed forces. However, ideology is
central to defining both the preferred goals and tools for nonmilitary programs. Hence, the developmentalist option requires counterbalanced viewpoints within the military and an officer corps that is broadly representative
of the larger society.

6. Because of the extensive involvement of the armed forces in internal
security and nonmilitary tasks, the developmentalist option requires greater
changes in the traditional military *fuero*. Military courts should have jurisdiction only for violations of military regulations; all other charges should

be tried in civilian courts. Civilians accused of violating national security laws should be tried in civilian courts, if necessary in special courts that balance the needs for security and justice. Civilian courts are no guarantee of justice, but trying civilians in military courts is almost certain to privilege conviction over the legal rights of the accused.

7. Because involvement in nonmilitary activities like transportation contracts and state enterprises involves a high risk of corruption, the Defense Ministry and each military service should have a high-level inspector general for control of corruption in order to prevent the damage to the legitimacy of military institutions that inevitably occurs when corruption goes unpunished.

191

Although no such regime currently exists, active military participation in nonmilitary missions under democratic control is certainly possible. The developmentalist option differs substantially from the conventional military model, but it may be appropriate for smaller, poorer countries where civilian agencies are weak or nonexistent, especially in outlying areas. It recognizes that in many countries the armed forces have achieved a degree of institutional coherence and discipline which is imperfect, but still greater than that of competing civilian institutions. Under those circumstances, it may make sense to make maximum use of those institutional resources.

The use of the military in the "war on drugs" is a special case illustrating the dangers of unlimited use of the armed forces for nonmilitary tasks. Despite the North American attraction to military metaphors, drug trafficking in Latin America is more accurately characterized as transnational organized crime, fed by the enormous profits from the production and export of illegal drugs to the United States. As such, it is primarily a police problem, requiring methods of investigation, arrest, and punishment similar to those used to control other large-scale criminal activities. The military is not trained in or organized for those tasks.[20] The Medellín cartel used various terrorist methods — bombings, assassinations, intimidation — in its campaign to force repeal of Colombia's extradition treaty with the United States. In some cases, guerrilla groups have made tactical alliances with drug producers or traffickers to finance their activities. In Peru and Colombia, drug traffickers have also allied with military and paramilitary groups *against* local guerrilla forces, particularly where these attempt to enter the trade themselves.[21] But these are the exceptions. The principal weapons of the drug cartels are economic rather than military or terrorist; their objectives are the accumulation of (illicit) wealth within the existing social order, not its overthrow. Their private "armies" are generally small and lightly armed. Tanks and machine guns are of little use against the drug cartels. Colombia's National Police Anti-Narcotics Directorate is a force of only 2,500 men; half of its tactical companies are undercover units.[22] Given the enormous profits involved, it is also unlikely that the "war on drugs" is a war in which victory is possible. When interdiction efforts are increased on one route, shipments are shifted to other routes. When one drug cartel is dismantled, others move in to take its place. None of the massive U.S. and Latin American efforts of the last two decades has resulted in more than a temporary drop in the supply of drugs to U.S. and European markets.[23] The armed forces are, however, highly vulnerable to the corruption that accompanies contact with the drug trade. Compared to the payoffs offered by the drug mafias, military salaries are minuscule. In 1986, Bolivian traffickers were paying $20,000 for a "seventy-two hour window of impunity" for drug shipments; the going rate in Peru was $12,000 per planeload.[24] Even the use of the military's technical and logistical capacity to support antidrug operations invites bribes to warn of impending operations, to falsify information on drug operations, or to arrive "just a little too late." To the extent that drug traffickers succeed in corrupting the officer corps, the armed forces cease to be subject to democratic control. Drug corruption severely damages the public image and institutional legitimacy of the armed forces, thereby diminishing their capacity to respond to other security threats. In the "war against drugs," the armed forces should be the weapon of last resort.[25]

Other nonmilitary missions pose similar problems of the lack of fit between military training and organization and the requirements of those missions. Bringing troops into high-crime areas may temporarily force illegal activities to go elsewhere, but it is unclear what the military could do to reduce crime without exposing itself to corruption and involving the military in domestic intelligence operations similar to the antisubversive campaigns.[26] Use of the military in anticrime missions will inevitably involve the armed forces in conflicts over human rights violations committed by the police.

In addition, reinforcing military capabilities in nonmilitary tasks increases the likelihood that neither civilian agencies nor the private sector will ever develop those capabilities. The process of military role expansion in the United States is well documented. When civilian organizations fail, well-organized, mission-oriented military forces provide a ready alternative for political leaders seeking a quick fix. The armed forces then demand additional funding to plan and train for the new missions, which makes them better prepared to deal with the next problem.[27] In societies with scarce resources, finding the funds and the political will to develop civilian institutions to replace the development functions of the armed forces will be difficult. Nonetheless, the political risks of the military's growing role as a societal problem solver are not trivial in unconsolidated democracies. Until and unless the armed forces are politically and professionally subordinate to democratic authority, adding nonmilitary roles means expanding the military "state within the state."

Perhaps the greatest danger is that various secondary missions will take precedence over the military's primary responsibilities for external and internal security. That risk is very real, given civilian disinterest in the military functions of the armed forces and strong political support for using the military to fight crime, provide government services, and aid poor communities. It is unlikely that a highly trained airborne commando will also be an effective neighborhood liaison officer or social worker. Hence some form of compartmentalization, separating the core military organizations from those engaged in development activities, will probably be necessary, with separate career tracks for officers primarily engaged in military and nonmilitary activities, similar to those that already exist for military doctors and lawyers.

Thus, even under the developmentalist option, indiscriminate use of the military for other purposes is likely to have political and professional costs. Louis Goodman proposes useful criteria for determining whether a given nonmilitary mission should be assigned to the armed forces:

1. Does military involvement in that function, for example, road building, impede the development of civilian capabilities to deal with the problem?

2. Does the mission create special privileges or vested interests at the expense of other groups?

3. Does the mission detract from the military's ability to fulfill its responsibilities for national defense?

4. Does the mission include provisions for phasing out military involvement in that function?[28]

Under democratic norms, the developmentalist option requires a rigorous and demanding set of policy controls. Because these are politically controversial and complex problems—crime, drugs, poverty, development, and education—nonmilitary missions inevitably involve the armed forces in the associated policy conflicts. Both the armed forces and the larger society are ideologically divided on many of these issues. The armed forces cannot simply implement a "national consensus" policy. Developmentalist militaries will therefore inevitably be more politicized. Hence, the key question is whether these missions are under effective democratic control or whether they repre-

193

sent the military's own policies. The armed forces cannot demand the relatively greater professional autonomy of the military model with the unlimited missions of the developmentalist option. High military autonomy in combination with military control over internal security and extensive nonmilitary missions is a recipe for a tutelary regime, not a democracy. Developmentalist militaries without strong civilian control are inherently antidemocratic.

Professional Advantages

194 Under either the military or developmentalist options, the political advantages of democratic professionalism are obvious. It is less clear, however, that the armed forces of the region will consider democratic professionalism an attractive alternative to existing beliefs. On the one hand, for those officers concerned with core professional values, a democratic model of civil-military relations offers significant benefits. To the extent that the military role in politics is eliminated, the incentive is reduced to introduce political or personal loyalty into promotion and assignment decisions. Promotions based on professional merit and the absence of political diversions from military tasks will maximize the military capability that can be realized from the human and economic resources available for national defense. Officers who spend their time and energies in political intrigues and policy debates necessarily have less time to spend mastering new military technologies, modernizing military organization and training, or preparing to meet future threats to national security. Reducing the level of politicization of the armed forces is also a prerequisite to effective enforcement of the norms of military discipline and hierarchy. Military organization is inevitably undermined by the nonhierarchical logic of political alliances and conflicts. Maintaining military cohesion in divided societies is impossible when the military is an autonomous political actor. Military factionalism and internal disunity are the inescapable price of military intervention in politics. The real lines of power and authority within military organizations will never correspond to the formal organizational chart as long as those organizations function as political arenas. The rule of law—internally and externally—is the essential instrument for the control of military factionalism.[29]

Removing the military from politics will also enhance the legitimacy of the armed forces in the eyes of the rest of society. Military governments that engaged in widespread repression and human rights violations in the "struggle against subversion" severely discredited the armed forces, creating a legacy of negative public opinion that will take years to overcome. Even where military rule was less harshly repressive, corruption and government failure to deliver promised reforms tarnished the public image of the armed forces. Like direct military rule, conditional or tutelary democracies require the military to make political choices that invariably favor certain interests at the expense of competing interests. To the extent that civilian attitudes toward the armed forces affect the ability of the nation to meet a security crisis requiring national mobilization, the loss of institutional legitimacy adversely affects the military's ability to defend the country. By enhancing military discipline and expertise and protecting the public reputation of the armed forces, democratic professionalism enhances national security.

On the other hand, from the military's perspective, democratic professionalism also implies certain disadvantages. Giving up the military's claim to ultimate political control involves considerable uncertainty. There are indeed no guarantees that democratic governments will govern wisely. Given the asymmetries in military and civilian world views in Latin America, civilian governments will inevitably adopt policies that conflict with the policy preferences of some military factions. Those governments can either be forced to respond to military preferences through formal or informal military tutelage or they can be held accountable to the nation in elections. Given the absence of consensus within the armed forces on substantive policy matters, only the latter is likely to lead to stronger political institutions and opportunities for civilian leaders to learn from their errors. If civilian governments are forced to be responsive to the policy demands of the armed forces, they diminish their ability to be responsive to the rest of society, thereby reducing their legitimacy and increasing the risk of instability. Uncertainty is intrinsic to democratic regimes. If election results and policy outcomes are not uncertain — if political choices do not matter — democracy will lose its meaning and its legitimacy.[30] Like most bureaucratic organizations, professionalized militaries dislike uncertainty. Acting as a political guardian does not, in fact, reduce political instability; in most cases, it has the opposite effect. Still, convincing the military to give up their guardian role will be difficult.

Many Latin American officers also object to the idea of the professional subordination of the armed forces in defense and military policy on the grounds that civilian governments cannot be trusted not to endanger national security by reducing defense expenditures, letting equipment become obsolete, or failing to keep up with neighboring countries. Because the military has virtually monopolized defense and military policy in Latin America, there is indeed a deficit of trained, experienced civilian personnel with the ability to exercise civilian oversight of the armed forces. Nevertheless, there is a curious illogic to this argument. If there are real threats to national security and military leaders have ample access to the president, the congress, and public opinion to explain those threats, why would civilian leaders or the public disregard their own security? The experience of the United States and other Western democracies demonstrates that a strong defense posture generally enjoys widespread political support, notwithstanding minor disarmament movements. For U.S. politicians, being "soft on defense" is a serious political liability. Having monopolized national security policy for decades, Latin American militaries may be reluctant to put themselves in a position where they have to convince others that strong defense policies are necessary. The political resentments created by the military's political interventions may indeed create a backlash against military expenditures. Apart from that factor, military fears about having to justify their policy recommendations to democratic authorities appear to be either an unjustified lack of military confidence in the power of their own arguments or a suspicion that the security threats perceived by the military are not considered real threats by a majority of the civilian population.

In addition, many officers fear that professional subordination to civilian authority will lead to partisan meddling in promotions and other internal military matters. As noted above, mechanisms should be established to allow for appeal of executive branch decisions which violate professional norms or merit-based criteria for promotion and assignment.

Finally, military officers may fear that if the armed forces give up their political autonomy they will lose their corporate privileges, salaries, and other prerogatives. In fact, military salaries are generally not disproportionate to those of other educated professionals. Because of the fiscal crisis, officers' salaries vary substantially. These variations are, however, partly offset by differences in the cost of living and the availability of nonsalary benefits — such as subsidized housing, low interest mortgages, the right to import a car when returning from attaché duty, and generous health benefits — which compensate for low cash salaries. Economically, most military officers are part of the middle class; senior officers usually enjoy an upper-middle-class lifestyle. Except for retired officers with second careers or those with illegal sources of income, few officers would be considered wealthy. Retirement and health benefits are greater than for comparable government employees, but few would argue that military benefits should be reduced, as opposed to improving benefits for other workers. Except in countries where the military has engaged in widespread human rights violations against its own population, even the traditional military right to be tried in military courts is usually not contested by the civilian population. To the extent that the military constitute an economically privileged elite not subject to the laws that apply to other professional groups, military officers are likely to be resented, rather than respected, by the rest of society. To the extent that their economic and legal status corresponds to their real professional expertise and their essential role in defending the nation, there is every reason to believe that military officers in Latin American democracies will be accorded both the material rewards and the societal respect and legitimacy enjoyed by the armed forces of other Western democracies.

Prospects for the Future

Nevertheless, the logic of this book is that choice between democratic pro- **197** fessionalism and more politically autonomous militaries will not be made on the basis of scholarly arguments for or against either alternative. The primary determinant of that choice will be the political context in which the debate takes place. Despite many structural continuities, several important changes have taken place in the context of civil-military interaction over the last twenty years.[31]

First and perhaps most importantly, the historic alliance of the armed forces and the economic elites was significantly weakened, if not broken, by the last round of military regimes. With the singular exception of Chile, the theoretical advantages of military rule for promoting capitalist development proved to be illusory. Even when the elites prospered, they often found their political voice reduced by military leaders more inclined to listen to experts than to "special interests."[32] Since 1980, changes in the international economy and policymaking have widened that rift. Largely as a result of the debt crisis, virtually every Latin American government has been forced to adopt market-oriented economic policies to control inflation, encourage exports, and reduce the role of the state in the economy. Regardless of their electoral promises or ideological orientation, civilian governments have been forced to limit government spending, to reduce tariffs on imports, and to adopt more realistic exchange rates. The state role in the economy has been reduced by budget cuts, lack of resources, and sharp declines in public sector salaries. These factors often combined to produce a nonfunctioning state apparatus with only limited power to regulate the private sector or to offer meaningful corporate subsidies. Deficit reduction also led to privatization of many state-owned corporations. The immediate result of structural adjustment and debt repayment was massive economic recession. The less visible result has been to lessen the importance of who controls the government.

Compared to earlier democratic regimes, which seemed to promise (or threaten) radical changes, Latin American democracies in the 1980s were decidedly unradical, if not conservative. In most countries, the political left had been decimated by military repression. Industrial unions, typically the backbone of leftist parties, were weakened by the dismantling of tariff barriers and the resulting loss of jobs in import-substitution industries. The fall of communist regimes in Eastern Europe and the Soviet Union demoralized and divided marxist parties. Faced with severe recession, voters have been remarkably cautious, unwilling to risk radical alternatives that might lead to even worse outcomes.

From the perspective of the economic elites, the return to democracy has thus been remarkably successful. Even though probusiness parties have not done particularly well in elections, moderate and center-left parties have adopted more or less the same market-oriented policies as their conservative counterparts. Opposition to economic austerity policies from unions and moderate-left parties has been consciously restrained to avoid destabilizing democratic governments. Lower inflation and higher profits since 1990 have strengthened the perception that democratic regimes are quite compatible with elite interests. Although this outcome rests in part on the particular economic circumstances of the last fifteen years, the increasing globalization of the transnational economy reinforces the tendency toward more or less universal rules of the economic game. The increasing mobility of domestic and international capital forces all governments to pay more attention to the investment climate for national and international investors.[33] Third world governments that violate IMF rules risk large-scale capital flight and international isolation. Under these structural conditions, economic elites have little reason to favor a politically autonomous military.[34]

Second, in most countries, the traditional legitimacy of the armed forces as political actors has been significantly diminished by large-scale human rights violations committed under military rule (Argentina, Uruguay, Chile, Brazil, and Guatemala) or civilian governments (Peru, Colombia, Guatemala, El Salvador, and Honduras) or by revelations of widespread corruption among senior officers (Paraguay, Bolivia, Peru, and Honduras). With or without official investigations, human rights abuses by the military received widespread publicity. Military attempts to intimidate the press and human rights groups have not prevented diffusion of graphic accounts of torture, discoveries of mass graves, and exposés of village massacres. The traditional image of the military officer as the patriotic defender of national interests now competes with the image of the military as torturer. In some countries, the latter image is dominant for not only the left but also important segments of the middle class. Peace settlements in El Salvador and Guatemala, and partial accords in Colombia, have incorporated into the political process leftist groups ideologically opposed to military intervention in politics. Although the survey evidence is incomplete, public support for military tutelage or the traditional role of the military as political arbiter seems far more limited than most analysts expected in the early stages of the transition process. In Argentina and Uruguay, only 10 percent saw authoritarian regimes as sometimes preferable to a democratic government; roughly 20 percent agreed in Brazil and Chile. Only in Brazil did a significant minority, 33 percent, want the military to have more power.[35] In a 1985 poll, only 12 percent of Uruguayans surveyed viewed the military "sympathetically" or "neutrally"; 78 percent viewed the armed forces critically.[36]

Two caveats should be underlined here. As argued in chapter 2, prior experiences with military governments varied. Hence, there are important differences in the extent to which the military intervention in politics has lost its legitimacy. For the Argentine public, opposition to any political role for the military is virtually unanimous. In most countries, however, the military is still valued for its defense functions; in Ecuador, the armed forces retain a substantial degree of societal legitimacy.[37] Moreover, in most cases, the legitimacy of civilian political institutions has also declined. Economic crisis, petty partisanship, and corruption scandals have all contributed to high levels of public distrust in government. Although the military may have less public support today, public confidence in civilian institutions is also low.

The third significant change in the context that traditionally encouraged military intervention in Latin America has been in the international environment. From the early days of Teddy Roosevelt's "big stick" policies through the heyday of the cold war era, the United States supported military intervention against governments it disliked. The support of the United States was neither a necessary nor a sufficient cause for the armed forces to act, but backing from the United States emboldened conspirators in divided militaries and reassured them of international approval if the coup succeeded. Beginning with the Carter administration, the United States reversed its policy of allying with anticommunist military regimes to give greater weight to democracy and protection of human rights. Despite its initial ambivalence, the Reagan administration eventually adopted most of Carter's policies. Bush and Clinton have made support for democracy a cornerstone of U.S. foreign policy. Obvious gaps remain between U.S. rhetoric and U.S. action in cases like Peru and Guatemala; still, the United States actively supported the opposition to Pinochet and lobbied hard to stop potential coups in the Dominican Republic and Ecuador. When economic pressures and covert actions failed to dislodge recalcitrant dictators, the United States invaded Panama and Haiti.

Western European and Scandinavian governments have been equally, if not more, outspoken in defense of democracy and human rights. Latin American governments have actively promoted the concept of an international commitment to uphold democratic regimes, a commitment now institutionalized in various regional agreements. The 1996 Inter-American Conference of Defense Ministers proclaimed that "representative democracy is the fundamental basis of hemispheric security."[38] The collapse of the Soviet Union and the end of the cold war reinforce the image of democracy as the only legitimate political alternative for developing countries. This shift in the international environment changes the coup calculus. As shown in the Ecuadorian interviews, the threat of economic sanctions is a significant deterrent to potential coups, particularly for small countries. International condemnation and symbolic sanctions are equally important to countries who want to be internationally respectable partners in regional and subregional economic and security agreements.

The globalization of democracy and market capitalism thus changes the domestic political context in ways which reinforce the lessons of recent military regimes. As one observer notes, "the significance of twenty years [almost] without a coup is more than just symbolic. There is now a well-established norm of civilian constitutional government in the hemisphere, buttressed by a more vigilant regional and international community."[39] Nevertheless, the absence of coups is not the same as the creation of democratic civil-military relations. Whether these favorable changes in the political context result in democratic consolidation or simply new forms of military power within civilian regimes depends in part on two factors that are still uncertain.

The first unknown is the long-term outcome of the current economic model. The immediate effect of the debt crisis and subsequent structural adjustment policies was increased poverty and greater inequality. In 1990, per capita income for the region was 15 percent less than it was in 1980. "By the early 1990's, wealth was even more concentrated than in the 1970's, with the richest 10 percent of households receiving 40 percent of the total income while the bottom 20 percent got less than 4 percent."[40] In contrast to the previous two decades, the poverty rate increased. The absolute number of people living in poverty increased by more than 60 percent from 1970 to 1990. Nearly 100 million people, over 20 percent of the region's total, have incomes insufficient to cover basic needs. Some countries were particularly hard hit. Gross domestic product fell by more than 20 percent in Argentina, Venezuela, Peru, Bolivia, and Nicaragua. Real wages in Peru fell by more than 50 percent.[41]

Faced with the worst economic crisis in the region since the 1930s, democratic regimes proved to be surprisingly resilient. The ability of the new democracies to withstand economic hardship is now well-documented.[42] In the early years of the crisis, democratic regimes often enjoyed a special legitimacy because they were democratic, not military. In countries that experienced severe human rights violations, key political actors were willing to make economic sacrifices in order to avoid a possible reversion to authoritarian rule. Governments that failed to control inflation or protect real wages from the regressive effects of neoconservative policies almost invariably suffered a sharp loss in public support and defeat in the next elections. Governments failed, but regime legitimacy was sustained by political competition and participation.

Still, even if democracies are better equipped to withstand economic adversity than their authoritarian counterparts, it does not follow that economic outcomes are unimportant to the survival of democratic regimes.[43] The key question is whether market-oriented economic policies will ultimately benefit the broader society or only the elites. The elimination of various consumer subsidies—for electricity, telephone service, and public transportation—has significantly increased the cost of living for the poor and the middle class. Reduction in government payrolls and the loss of jobs in consumer goods industries have produced high levels of unemployment and underemployment. Regional inflation has been reduced from over 1,000 percent in 1991 to 11 percent in 1997,[44] but in most countries real wages have recovered only slowly from the sharp cuts of the 1980s. Argentina's unemployment rate rose to more than 18 percent in July 1995; "in real terms, [Argentina's] average income is only 60 per cent of what it was in 1980."[45] For the region as a whole, per capita income is still 10 percent less than it was fifteen years ago.

In the short term, most of the public sees no desirable alternative to democracy; government leaders see no easy alternatives to current economic policies. Yet, it seems incredulous to suppose that democracy can survive indefinitely with a small portion of the population prospering while the rest experience continued or greater poverty. At a minimum, some significant fraction of the population must feel less poor over the long run. Unlike many of their historical predecessors, the current democracies in Latin America have virtually universal suffrage; urbanization and mass communications contribute to higher levels of political awareness. As a result, "exclusionary democracies" that benefit and protect elite interests at the expense of broader sectors of the lower middle and working classes will be more difficult to sustain.[46] High unemployment, declining real wages, crime, and personal insecurity all add to the growing public disillusionment with government institutions. In functioning democracies, dissatisfaction is a normal part of politics. Dissatisfaction with the status quo provides incentives for enterprising politicians to propose alternative policies or launch new political movements. Disillusionment with public institutions provides a constituency for reform. In unconsolidated democracies, disillusionment may only breed apathy, especially if participation in the system yields no real results. Frustration with the inability to resolve policy problems affecting the poor is likely to lead to popular support for bending or suspending constitutional procedures, for strong leaders who promise quick results, for action at the expense of accountability. In the long run, if democratic regimes are incapable of satisfying public demands for at least minimal economic improvements through some combination of economic growth and social policies, other regime alternatives — including military rule — are likely to resurface.[47]

The second major uncertainty about the future involves changes in the relation of the military to the rest of society, changes that are so far only dimly perceived and poorly understood by either policymakers or students of civil-military relations. Although the evidence is fragmentary, the social composition of the Latin American military appears to be shifting. Increasing numbers of the applicants to military academies are from lower-middle-class backgrounds or the upper strata of the working class. Cadets are more likely to be sons of sergeants and corporals than sons of generals or colonels.[48] Over the last decade, declining military salaries and the loss of the military's traditional prestige and political power have almost certainly reinforced that trend. The "middle-class" military of twentieth-century Latin America will likely be a lower-middle-class military in the first decade of the twenty-first century. Military wives will have to work; at times, junior officers and noncommissioned officers will have to take second jobs to make ends meet. Pressures to control personnel costs will result in lower promotion rates, less job security, and fewer benefits.

The political effects of shifts in the social composition of the armed forces are uncertain. Systematic research on the military's changing links to civil society has yet to be done. Nonetheless, I offer the following hypotheses:

1. Individual officers will continue to identify strongly with the military institution, in part because it still represents a positive opportunity for social mobility for bright and hardworking sons (and daughters) of families of modest means, in part because of the strong socialization processes employed in the academies. Nevertheless, increasing numbers of officers will share the same economic circumstances faced by the lower middle class, including limited economic reserves and strong fears of downward mobility.

2. The ideological makeup of the officer corps will be diverse since neither the lower middle class nor the upper levels of the working class are

politically homogeneous. Nevertheless, liberal internationalists are likely to decline in number, while supporters of populist or labor parties will increase their representation. Conservative nationalists will also increase proportionately, although most officers will be, as now, only weakly identified with a particular party or ideology. Representation of the ideological extremes may increase. Enforcing ideological conformity will be more difficult in the post–cold war military.

3. Internal tensions will rise between officers who view the military as a professional career and those who view the armed forces as an institution. American views of civil-military relations stress the military as profession. In contrast, Latin Americans have traditionally viewed the military as a fundamental state institution. Officers are professionals to be sure, but the stress is on the permanent and vital functions of the "armed institution." This self-image is increasingly in tension with the realities of military life in Latin America. Many sectors of the public have decidedly unheroic images of the armed forces. Increasing economic integration and regional cooperation have already diminished conventional threats. Even minor wars seem increasingly unlikely. Opportunities to fulfill the heroic military ideal of self-sacrifice in defense of the fatherland will be rare. Officers are more likely to spend their time in unglamourous missions, patrolling city streets or fighting drug wars. Budgetary pressures will reinforce the trend toward declining rewards relative to other professions to which the military likes to compare itself, like senior judges and diplomatic officials. Taken together, these forces create a less favorable climate for the traditional Latin American view of the armed forces as a cornerstone of the State, with responsibilities and prerogatives paralleling those of institutions like the legislature and the judiciary. Nevertheless, this view of the military as far more than "just a job"[49] is deeply ingrained in the institutional ethos of Latin American militaries, in the socialization of officers in military academies and war colleges, and in the military's version of national history. As the objective conditions for realization of the military's self-image as a heroic, suprapolitical institution diminish, internal pressures for reaffirmation of the symbolic ideal are likely to intensify. These pressures will be particularly strong among junior officers and nonestablishment factions.

Alternative Scenarios

Given positive changes in the political context but also major uncertainties about the decade ahead, two potential futures seem plausible. In the first scenario, political democracies in Latin America muddle through. Reversions to overtly authoritarian regimes are rare; outright deviations from constitutional norms are met with international sanctions and quick retreats. Aided in part by regional integration and lower trade barriers in the United States and Europe, Latin American economies regain the economic dynamism of the 1950s and 1960s, when GDP grew roughly 5 percent per year.[50] Growth rates fluctuate, depending on prices for major exports, but expanding economies stimulate modest increases in real wages in both the formal and informal sectors. Increasingly visible consumption taxes make poor and middle-class voters more conscious of the cost of government. Corruption becomes the political issue of the next decade, with voters punishing corrupt officials the way they punished incumbent governments for hyperinflation and austerity programs in the 1980s. At the same time, competition for working-class votes between social democratic and leftist parties leads to a renewed emphasis on spending for medical care, education, and basic infrastructure. Economic growth and modest increases in wealth taxes finance more active poverty alleviation programs.

As in recent years, progress toward more democratic civil-military relations is neither universal nor uniform. Most governments are more concerned with other priorities, but media exposés and electoral concerns force more attention to curbing human rights violations by the police and military. Sporadically and unevenly, some civilian governments take a more assertive role in defense and security policy. Tight military budgets and civilian intrusion into traditionally military issues provoke plenty of military grumbling, but little organized resistance. High turnover among incumbent parties provides a continuing circulation of political elites, encouraging civilian and military expectations that diverse policy preferences can be realized by working within the system. Tutelary regimes are the exception rather than the rule; most governments exercise at least some degree of democratic control. In regimes still characterized by conditional military subordination, the armed forces are treated as a *factor de poder*, but the implausibility of military coups limits military influence to the defense of immediate corporate interests. Despite civil-military tensions on a variety of issues, most conflicts are resolved behind the scenes through regular channels. Occasional public confrontations are resolved constitutionally. Compared to other Western regimes, Latin American democracies still allow a relatively high degree of military autonomy on institutional matters. Given civilian disinterest, most governments exercise only limited policy control on defense and security issues. Still, in contrast to previous cycles of civilian rule in Latin America, the armed forces present no real threat to overthrow democratic governments. Equally important, the military wields no veto power, even on policy issues that affect the armed forces. Military commitment to the practice of democratic professionalism is uneven; attitudes are often contradictory and ambivalent. For the region as a whole, civil-military relations still falls short of the democratic ideal. In many respects, Latin American democracies are also less than perfect, but democracy remains the preferred alternative, in practice as well as in theory.

The alternative scenario seems less likely, but cannot be discarded as long as democratic regimes remain unconsolidated and relatively uninstitutionalized. In the pessimistic view, the neoliberal economic model imposed by the IMF will keep elites happy, but exclude most of the rest of the population from the benefits of economic growth. Ruthless economic competition playing Third World countries against each other keeps wages low; privatization and reduced government regulation result in higher prices for basic goods and services. Declining economic prospects for millions of young people entering the labor force and the erosion of social norms in decaying cities lead to spiraling crime and personal insecurity. Attempts by leftist parties to capitalize on economic discontents result in renewed military pressure to crack down on "subversive groups." Political fragmentation and partisan divisions prevent any coherent response to the growing social crisis. Political violence and violent repression increase, with sporadic but inconclusive outbreaks of guerrilla warfare. Public disillusionment is reflected in declining participation in elections and increased political apathy. In the absence of effective mechanisms for accountability, governments favor those interests whose support is most critical and those who can do them the most good in the short term. Parties of all stripes campaign against corruption, but few are willing to forego the rewards of power when it comes their turn to govern. Disillusionment with democratic regimes is reinforced by a political culture more predisposed to strong leaders than to the slow pace and ambiguous outcomes of procedural democracy. Military confidence in civilian regimes is weakened by corruption scandals and lack of attention to security issues. Military leaders take a more assertive role in a wide range of policy areas. Human rights violations increase as military intelligence agencies and paramilitary groups act on their own to control groups that are perceived as antimilitary or outside the spectrum of acceptable political alternatives.

In this pessimistic scenario, the future of civil-military relations is conventionally seen as a military dominated or tutelary regime, like Guatemala. Or the military may ally with civilian leaders, à la Fujimori, in highly personalized regimes that are nominally democratic, but repressive and authoritarian in practice. Both these conventional scenarios are plausible. However, both are probably too rooted in the recent past to accurately portray the longer term future. If democratic regimes fail, particularly if they fail dramatically, the results will not be limited to the conservative "hybrid" regimes[51] of the 1980s. The logic of the ideological disaggregation of the armed forces described in chapter 3 suggests that the military leadership of the (negative) future will be dominated by those factions that have thus far been disenfranchised in post-transition regimes. It is illogical to expect that the current military leadership will direct future military regimes. Just as the failure of the last military governments weakened certain groups within the military and strengthened others, the failure of democratic regimes will shift the balance among competing military factions.

206

If the current pattern of limited military intervention within constitutional regimes breaks down, the next military regimes will almost certainly be dominated by an alliance of nationalist factions. By their very nature, armies are inherently nationalist institutions. From the first day of their careers to the day of their retirement, the daily life of military officers revolves around symbols of national identity. In Latin America, nationalist factions—radical, conservative, and a variety of positions in-between—have a long history and numerous adherents. Officers are also exposed to strong international influences—foreign doctrines, training and travel abroad, and dependence on more industrialized countries for weaponry and military technology. Hence, internationalism also has a long history in the Latin militaries, including loyalist factions in the Wars of Independence, Germanophiles and Francophiles at the turn of the century, and many pro-American officers since then. Tensions between nationalist and internationalist tendencies are endemic in Third World militaries. During the cold war, these tensions were muted by the common fear of communism and the practical advantages of close military relations with the United States.

However, with the end of the cold war, U.S. policies now imply significant deprivations for the Latin American military: the reduction of traditional political prerogatives, increased questioning of military budgets, demeaning and dangerous missions like the drug wars, plus heavy-handed attempts to prevent the acquisition of more modern military technology. Pressure by the United States to eliminate missile programs and nuclear weapons research is widely viewed as part of a U.S. policy of limiting Latin American militaries to internal security and police roles. At the same time that U.S. policies are far less favorable to Latin American military interests, U.S. military assistance budgets have virtually disappeared. Grant military aid to nineteen Latin American countries totaled less than $28 million for fiscal year 1995; half of that went to Colombia and Bolivia. Grants for U.S. military training averaged just $200,000

per country. From 1981 to 1991, Brazil, Argentina, Mexico, Chile, and Venezuela—representing 70 percent of the region's population—together received
less than one-third as much U.S. military aid as Costa Rica, which does not
have a formal army.[52]

One indication of the nationalist reaction to the new U.S. agenda is the wide
circulation among Latin officers of the anti-American manifesto, *The Conspiracy to Destroy the Armed Forces and Nations of Hispanic America.* In his
introduction, imprisoned *carapintada* leader Colonel Mohamed Seineldín de-
nounces all forms of imperialism.

Today the voice of the people (not that of their illegitimate leaders) clamors for a [Latin
American] identity hinted at through history. Iberoamerican military history is in every
case the spinal column of the life of each one of our peoples. For that reason, the current rulers of the world ("the new international order") have resolved to eliminate the
armed forces [who are] the last obstacle to the total submission of [our] nations.[53]

Attempts by the United States to limit development of weapons of mass destruction are blasted as "technological apartheid." Human rights trials and
truth commissions are portrayed as "psychological warfare," punishing officers
who defended their countries against communism. In this view, the "new world
order" is a coordinated effort to destroy traditional Catholic values grounded
in natural law, to reduce the sovereignty of Latin American states and subordinate them economically, and therefore to strip the armed forces of their natural
role as "guardians of the highest interests of the nation" and the "armed fist of
the *patria*." [54]

The complaints of nationalist officers are not limited to military issues.
Latin American militaries have historically favored a strong state (and an active
role for themselves within that state).[55] Neoliberal economic programs imposed by the IMF have dismantled many of the state-owned enterprises created by earlier generations of nationalist officers. While many were inefficient
and costly, state-owned strategic industries were an integral part of nationalist efforts to lessen the risk of embargos cutting off access to vital weapons in
times of conflict. (The NATO ban on the sale of Exocet missiles to Argentina
during the Malvinas/Falklands war is the most recent example of that vulnerability.) Opening natural resource industries to foreign investment reverses
another key tenet of the nationalist program. Nationalist officers are also dis-
mayed by the prospect of a global culture dominated by MTV, CNN, and
American consumerism. Conservative and religious officers in particular often
associate democracy with increased tolerance for drugs, pornography, and sac-
rilege masquerading as art. In a new global culture, nationalist officers fear the

loss of any unique sense of national identity and the subversion of traditional values.[56] If there is no *patria* and no sovereignty to defend in the "new world order," what is the role of the armed forces?

Future military regimes are likely to be populist or reformist, rather than neoliberal. As noted above, elite economic interests have been more than adequately served by the current regimes. If those regimes fail, successor governments will logically seek alternative policies. Under current conditions, it will be difficult to shelter military officers from economic outcomes affecting the rest of society. Prudent presidents will try to protect military salaries, particularly those of senior officers, but attempts to co-opt the entire officer corps will run afoul of external pressures to restrict military spending and cut central government deficits. Junior officers forced to share apartments and military families faced with declining socioeconomic status will be the logical constituency for attempts to create civil-military coalitions in opposition to the current regimes. The leader of Venezuela's *Movimiento Bolivariano,* Lieutenant Colonel Chávez, complained, "[The poor] cannot buy meat; they cook the banana peel . . . . The basic cost of a week's food in Venezuela is approaching 60,000 bolívares. The majority of those who work earn less than 20,000 bolívares . . . . Thus, there isn't democracy here." [57]

According to news reports, the younger generation of military analysts at the Brazilian Superior War College believes that "poverty and social inequality" are now the principal threats to internal security.[58] The radical/reformist military regimes of Peru and Ecuador are thus a better model for the future than the conservative regimes of the Southern Cone. Like their Andean predecessors, military opponents of the current economic model are handicapped by the lack of a clear economic alternative and by simplistic notions of class conflict that seldom transcend crude distinctions between the oligarchy and "the people." Organic metaphors of society and Catholic doctrines of class reconciliation still appeal to officers seeking "national unity" in place of the fractious debates and partisanship of existing democracies.[59] Thus, the most likely outcome is military populism, a vague preference for policies favoring the masses, rather than any coherent economic alternative. Peronist-style labor-military coalitions or alliances with radical parties like Brazil's Partido dos Trabalhadores are also possible.

Finally, if there is a real breakdown of current patterns of civil-military relations, future military regimes are likely to be profoundly antidemocratic and illiberal. After nearly two decades, moderate factions have accommodated themselves to living within more or less civilianized regimes. Leadership of the military opposition to those regimes will be assumed by officers who have re-jected democracy in principle as well as in practice. The best example to date is the closed, ultra-Catholic thinking of Seineldín's fundamentalist faction of the *carapintadas*. In this view, legitimacy—the right to rule—comes not from popular consent or a constitutional contract with society, but from the actions of a moral elite in accordance with divinely ordained values. Actions benefiting the poor or plebiscites approving presidential actions may enhance govern-ment legitimacy; still, the leader rules because he is pure in the midst of moral decay, because he has a vision in the midst of confusion. In the most benign versions, these regimes may resemble the authoritarian regimes of the 1930s, a new Vargas, a Perón, or perhaps a Carlos Luis Prestes. In the more extreme versions, fundamentalist ideologies might be combined with mobilizational politics and economic pump priming. The result may be little fascisms, scape-goating foreigners and Jews, rigidly enforcing "national" mores, and repressing "subversive" ideologies.

This brief excursion into the future suggests two important lessons for the present. First, the negative scenario represents a serious rupture with present trends. In the short term, such an outcome seems quite unlikely relative to minor departures from the status quo, for example, a temporary intervention behind the scenes or a quasi-coup without visibly taking power. Yet, if it occurs, the breakdown of current regimes is likely to come after a long period of ero-sion of public faith in democratic alternatives. In O'Donnell's terms, the even-tual "sudden death" of democracy is likely to be preceded by a long period of sickness, a slow death resulting from a thousand small failures rather than any one cataclysmic event. For democratic leaders in Latin America and abroad, the critical question is how to determine whether a given country is, in fact, on such a downward slide or just muddling through. The fatal temptation will be to ignore the warning signs and continue business as usual. Thus, a criti-cal question for scholars and policymakers is how to avoid the kind of surprise that confronted Venezuelan leaders in 1992.

The second lesson is that the fate of democracy in Latin America and the future of civil-military relations are inextricably intertwined. If a reversion to military rule occurs, it will be because democracy has failed. Economic crises and inequalities inherent in dependent economies or neoliberal policies may contribute to that failure, but these contrasting futures are not economically determined. As noted above, Latin American democracies have demonstrated their ability to overcome economic adversity. Declining real wages and eco-nomic insecurity have been punished, as they should be, with stinging defeats

209

at the ballot box. The Latin American experience demonstrates that a fairly wide range of economic outcomes are possible within the structural limitations of dependent capitalism. If the majority of the population is excluded from even modest improvement in economic conditions, it will be because the current regimes have been unable to respond to majority preferences, because they are incapable of devising policies to aid job creation and provide essential services to their poor constituents, because they are insufficiently democratic. If "exclusionary democracy" is the result, declining legitimacy and lack of public confidence in civilian institutions will inevitably encourage greater military intervention within these regimes. Weak civilian governments will be unable to resist military pressures for more autonomy and more influence over critical policy choices.

But the converse is also true. To the extent that government leaders have to worry about the military's conditional loyalty to democratic rules, their accountability to society is diminished. To the extent that tutelary pressures from the armed forces distort the policy process, the responsiveness of democratic regimes declines. However well-intentioned, military attempts to compensate for what they view as the failings of constitutional democracy, the existence of a military "ministate" within the state and the proliferation of parallel policy processes aggravate, rather than alleviate, the weaknesses of the current regimes. Democratic consolidation is thus a cause and effect of democratic control of the armed forces.

International Support for Democratic Civil-Military Relations

The challenges facing democratic leaders in Latin America are formidable. Structural conditions and historical patterns of civil-military relations in Latin America are less conducive to democratic control than in Western European democracies. As argued above, established democracies and Latin American leaders have partially offset this negative inheritance by forging an international context that discourages traditional patterns of military intervention in politics. Promoting democratic civil-military relations is a far more ambitious goal, one that will require a more long-term and sophisticated strategy to succeed under Latin American conditions.

First, this analysis suggests that U.S. policymakers and other international organizations should concentrate their attention on the underlying causes of conditional subordination and military tutelage. At the policy level, military intervention in politics is too often attributed to the ambitions of individual officers or the collective greed of the armed forces. Individual and institutional self-interest are important elements in the explanation of military behavior, but military attitudes and behavior are also rooted in the larger structures of the societies in which they live. Military actions are often responses to the civilian institutions with which they interact. Effective democracy is thus the most important long-term strategy for promoting more democratic civil-military relations. Strengthening civilian institutions — political parties, legislatures, and judiciaries — is primarily a task for Latin Americans, but foreign governments and international institutions can provide technical assistance, monetary support, and political pressure to offset internal resistance to reform. Strengthening democracy also means enhancing the capacity of civilian regimes to reduce poverty and meet the basic needs of their populations for food, education, and medical care. Although the foreign debt is no longer discussed in crisis terms, substantial portions of Latin America's export earnings still go to debt repayment.[60] Debt relief tied directly to poverty-alleviation programs could help restore public confidence in democratic regimes. Effective democracies, in turn, are more likely to be able to promote reforms in civil-military relations and to win military acceptance of those reforms over the long term.

Second, in its military training programs and military-to-military contacts in Latin America, the United States should be clear and consistent in its advocacy of democratic professionalism as the preferred model of civil-military relations. Both U.S. and Latin American officers should receive explicit instruction in democratic norms of civil-military relations and the rule of law for international and internal wars. Equally, if not more, important, the United States must practice what it preaches. If the military model is the preferred option, then the United States has to take seriously the Latin American military's role in external security and deterrence. That means accepting the need for military budgets and arms consistent with the defense policies of democratic governments, not externally generated budget standards or arms bans. It means respecting and encouraging the efforts of Latin American countries to develop their own regional and subregional agreements for military cooperation and collective security. Conversely, we should restrict our advocacy of "civic action" and "nation building" roles for Latin American militaries, roles that our own military clearly views as very peripheral to its central mission of preparation for fighting wars. If we take seriously the military role of the Latin American armed forces, then these are secondary missions better performed by civilian agencies. The most difficult issue of practice is likely to be the use of the Latin American armed forces in antidrug missions. Democratic control means that such missions should be approved, not just by the executive, but by Congress; that antidrug operations must be subject to the appropriate civilian oversight; and that such operations are subject to the rule of law. We may not give aid to governments that do not cooperate with U.S. antidrug policies, but we cannot deny the right of other countries to decide democratically for themselves whether their armed forces should be charged with such a mission.

Finally, the United States, other major powers, and regional institutions have an important role to play in the evolution and enforcement of democratic norms for civil-military relations. Egregious violations, such as military coups or attempts to reestablish military rule, must be meet with clear collective sanctions. Civilian *autogolpes* are equally undemocratic and should be sanctioned, regardless of the president's standing in the public opinion polls. To be effective, sanctions must include economic measures with serious consequences, for example, exclusion from most-favored-nation status, loss of membership in regional trade groups, and loss of loans from international financial organizations. On the other side of the coin, democratic countries should make special efforts to reward Latin American countries that do make significant progress toward more democratic civil-military relations. Symbolic rewards include special recognition in hemispheric military fora and more frequent professional interaction, such as joint exercises and exchange visits. Material rewards could include greater access to U.S. military training programs and preferential treatment in the foreign military sales program. Officers in democratically controlled militaries and those practicing military tutelage should be aware that they are received differently by the U.S. government and by our military representatives.

Still, these are complex distinctions, with notable variations in the extent of democratic control over the armed forces, sometimes even within a single presidential administration. Except at the extremes, external rewards and sanctions will be difficult to administer. As noted above, the leverage provided by military assistance and training programs is now quite limited. In crisis situations, diplomatic pressures on key officers may be helpful, but jawboning is not likely to make much difference if the officer corps is not predisposed to accept democratic norms. The critical efforts to strengthen civilian institutions and reshape the political context must, therefore, come from within. "Democracy is not an export commodity; it cannot simply be shipped from one setting to another. By its very nature, democracy must be achieved by each nation, largely on its own."[61] Constructing democratic systems of civil-military relations will require civilian and military leaders who have studied and learned from their past, leaders who are committed to establishing stronger institutions and setting higher standards of public service and democratic governance. The record of the past twenty years demonstrates that reforming civil-military relations will not be easy nor automatic.[62] But that history also demonstrates that progress is possible. Democratic control of the armed forces is still a central task for democratic consolidation in Latin America.

.

Interview List

I . A R G E N T I N A 1 9 8 5

*Military Interviews**

Gen. (r**) Mario Aguado Benítez
Gen. (r) Augusto Alemanzor
Rear Adm. (r) Oscar Allara
Anonymous, Lt. Col. on active duty
Anonymous, Col. on active duty
Anonymous, Air Force Brigadier (r)
Rear Adm. (r) Guillermo Arguedas
Gen. (r) Jorge Hugo Arguindegui
Col. (r) Horacio Ballester
Col. (r) Juan Jaime Cesio
Capt. (r) Guillermo Cogorno
Capt. (r) Ricardo Colombo
Lt. Col. (r) Eduardo D'Amico
Gen. (r) Américo Daher
Maj. Raúl de Cristóbal
Col. (r) Alfredo Díaz
Rear Adm. (r) Guillermo Dickson
Gen. (r) Julio Fernández Torres
Gen. (r) Isaias García Enciso
Col. (r) José Luis García
Gen. (r) José Teófilo Goyret
Gen. (r) Albano Harguindeguy
Brig. (r) José Insua
Gen. (r) Jorge Leal
Gen. (r) Horacio Liendo
Capt. Carlos López Meyer
Gen. (r) Ernesto López Meyer
Gen. (r) Miguel Alfredo Mallea Gil

Col. (r) Bernardo Menéndez
Gen. (r) Alberto Numa La Plane
Lt. (r) Alejandro Obán
Col. (r) Ramón Orieta
Lt. Col. (r) Mario Orsolini
Col. (r) Luis César Perlinger
Gen. (r) Ricardo Pianta
Gen. (r) Víctor Pino
Col. (r) Augusto B. Rattenbach
Gen. Héctor Rios Ereñú
Gen. (r) Héctor Rodríguez Espada
Capt. (r) Mario Rossi
Gen. (r) Tomás Sánchez y Bustamonte
Col. (r) Carlos Sánchez Toranzo
Ship Lt. (r) Carlos Schroeter
Gen. (r) Adolfo Sigwald
Brig. (r) Alberto Cristóbal Simari
Maj. (r) Luis Tibiletti
Marine Lt. (r) Julio César Urien
Gen. (r) José Antonio Vaquero
Gen. (r) Alberto Villareal

Other Interviews

Dr. Juan Alemán
Ship Capt. (r) Ricardo Anzorena
Dr. Rubén Blanco
Dr. Atilio Borón
Dr. Natalio Botana

Licenciada María Carvallo
Dr. Marcelo Cavarozzi
Guillermo Cherashny
Dr. Andrés Fontana
Dr. Dante Giadone
Guy Gugliota
Dr. Horacio Juanarena
Dr. Hugo Karplus
Licenciado Ernesto López
Dr. Emilio Mignone
Dr. José Enrique Miguens
Dr. Héctor Muzzopapa
Dr. Carlos Nino
Dr. Roberto Martínez Noguera
Dr. José Nun
Dr. Julio Raffo
Dr. María Susana Ricci
Dr. Roberto Russell
Manfred Schoenfeld
Dr. Jorge Schwartzer
Eduardo Stover
Licenciado Jorge Taiana

II. ECUADOR 1991

Military Interviews

Division Gen. (r) Carlos Aguirre Asanza
Brig. Gen. (r) Galo Almeida Nieto
Brig. Gen. (r) Jaime Andrade B.
Brig. Gen. Jorge Andrade Piedra
Anonymous, Major on active duty
Vice Adm. (r) Ramón Apolo Herrera
Brig. Gen. (r) Juan Araújo Proaño
Division Gen. (r) Jorge Arciniegas
Division Gen. (r) Miguel Arellano R.
Rear Adm. (r) Andrés Arrata Meneses
Div. Gen. (r) Jorge Asanza Acaiturri
Vice Adm. (r) Nelson Baildal Yépez
Division Gen. (r) Luis Berrazueta Pastor
Brig. Gen. (r) Jorge Borbua B.
Rear Adm. (r) Fernando Cabrera Toala
Adm. (r) Santiago Coral Terán
Col. Ramiro Correa
Division Gen. (r) Marcelo Delgado A.
Rear Adm. (r) LeGoff Gallegos Anda
Division Gen. (r) Marcos Gándara E.

Vice Adm. (r) Víctor Garcés Pozo
Lt. Gen. (r) Carlos Jaramillo A.
Vice Adm. (r) Mario Jaramillo del C.
Vice Adm. (r) Raúl Jaramillo del Castillo
Division Gen. (r) Carlos Jarrín Jarrín
Division Gen. (r) Richelieu Levoyer A.
Division Gen. (r) Joffre Lima Iglesias
Rear Adm. (r) Aurelio Maldonado Mino
Brig. Gen. (r) Héctor Miranda G.
Brig. Gen. Paco Moncayo Gallegos
Col. Galo Monteverde
Brig. Gen. (r) Cristóbal Navas A.
Division Gen. (r) Rodrigo Orbe Recalde
Gen. of the Army (r) Luis Piñeiros Rivera
Division Gen. (r) Germán Ruiz Zurita
Division Gen. (r) Medardo Salazar Navas
Brig. Gen. (r) Fausto Sevilla Aguilar
Division Gen. (r) Eduardo Silva Bucheli
Vice Adm. (r) Raúl Sorraza Encalada
Brig. Gen. (r) Luis Toscano Gallegos
Vice Adm. Hugo Unda Aguirre
Division Gen. (r) René Vargas Pazzos
Brig. Gen. (r) Frank Vargas Pazzos
Brig. Gen. (r) Edmundo Vivero B.

Other Interviews

Dr. Walter Spurrier Baquerizo
Dr. Leonardo Carrión
Engineer León Febres Cordero
Economist Mauricio Dávalos
Licenciado Jaime Durán
Dr. Galo García Feraud
Dr. Osvaldo Hurtado
Dr. Simón Pachano
Dr. Gonzalo Salgado Rivas
Licenciada Alejandra Vela

III. ARGENTINA 1992

Military Interviews

Gen. (r) Augusto J. B. Alemanzor (85)
Anonymous, Maj. on active duty
Anonymous, Navy Capts. on active duty
Anonymous, Navy Lts. on active duty
Rear Adm. (r) Guillermo Arguedas (85)

Gen. (r) Jorge Hugo Arguindegui (85)
Ship Capt. Martín Arrillaga
Brig. Gen. (r) Heriberto Auel
Frigate Capt. (r) Eduardo Balbi
Col. (r) Horacio Ballester (85)
Maj. (r) Ernesto Barreiro
Col. (r) Enrique Basso
Capt. Bermúdez
Maj. Bertolini
Ship Capt. (r) Miguel Boix
Col. Ricardo Brinzoni
Capt. Brown
Maj. Carlos Candia
Col. Hugo Luis Cargnelutti
Vice Commo. Jorge Carnevalini
Lt. Col. (r) Julio Víctor Carretto
Lt. Col. Héctor Cerrato
Lt. Col. (r) Dr. Alberto Cerúsico
Ship Capt. Jorge Colombo
Lt. Col. Raúl de Cristóbal (85)
Brig. Maj. (r) Héctor Luis Destri
Lt. Col. Díaz
Rear Adm. (r) Guillermo Dickson (85)
Brig. Gen. (r) Julio Fernández (85)
Lt. Col. (r) Ernesto Fernández Maguer
Vice Adm. (r) Argimiro Luis Fernández
Gen. (r) Fausto González
Gen. (r) José Teófilo Goyret (85)
Ship Capt. Julio Grosso
Rear Adm. José Heredia
Commo. Kettle
Gen. Aníbal Laíño
Col. (r) Miguel Angel Li Puma
Col. (r) José Lobaiza
Maj. Carlos López Meyer (85)
Gen. (r) Ernesto López Meyer (85)
Gen. (r) Miguel Alfredo Mallea Gil (85)
Gen. (r) Jorge Alberto Marque
Adm. Enrique Molino Pico
Commo. Noguera
Col. (r) Ramón Orieta (85)
Adm. Emilio José Ossés
Brig. Juan Manuel Paulik
Col. Maj. Víctor Peralta
Ship Capt. Basilio Pertiné
Gen. (r) Ricardo Pianta (85)

Gen. (r) Víctor Pino (85)
Col. (r) Héctor Aníbal Pipet
Lt. Col. (r) Luis Nicolás Polo
Corvette Capt. (r) Dr. Luis Alberto Pons
Col. Raúl Oscar Racana
Ship Capt. (r) Dr. Carlos Raimondi
Col. (r) Augusto Rattenbach (85)
Lt. Col. Daniel Reimundes
Gen. (r) Héctor Rios Ereñú (85)
Ship Capt. Daniel Robelo
Gen. (r) Héctor Rodríguez Espada (85)
Rear Adm. Alvar Carlos Rodríguez
Col. Maj. Romero
Capt. (r) Mario Rossi (85)
Col. (r) Carlos Sánchez Toranzo (85)
Capt. (r) Martín Eduardo Sánchez Zinny
Capt. (r) Licenciado Luis Tibiletti
Commo. Walter Félix Videla
Ship Capt. Carlos Zevalla

Other Interviews

Licenciado Carlos Acuña
Maj. (r) Dr. Virgilio Beltrán
Guillermo Cherashny
Dr. Andrés D'Alessio
Licenciada Rut Clara Diamint
Col. Alan Fenty
Dr. Juan Ferreira Pinho
Col. John Fesmire
Dr. Andrés Fontana
Dr. Rosendo Fraga
Dr. Dante Giadone
Licenciado Félix González Bonarino
Dr. Horacio Juanarena
Engineer Carlos Lacerca
Licenciado Ernesto López
Economist Thomas Scheetz
Catalina Smulovich
Dr. Dámaso Uriburu

I V .   A R G E N T I N A   1 9 9 6

Military Interviews

Lt. Col. (r) Santiago Roque Alonso
Division Gen. (r) Ramón Díaz Bessone
Lt. Col. (r) Carlos Doglioli

217

Col. (r) Luis Lagos
Division Gen. Aníbal Laíño

Other Interviews

Dr. Raúl Alfonsín
Maj. (r) Dr. Virgilio Beltrán
Dr. Oscar Camilión
Dr. Andrés Fontana
Dr. Rosendo Fraga
Lic. Ernesto López
Dr. Juan Ferreira Pinho
Commander Gen. (r) Juan M. Zorzenón

V . E C U A D O R   1 9 9 6

Military Interviews

Gen. (r) Carlos Aguirre Asanza
Gen. (r) Jorge Andrade Piedra
Col. Gustavo Lalama

Gen. Paco Moncayo
Lt. Col. Jorge Peña
Gen. César Villacís
Gen. (r) Héctor Villamil

Other Interviews

Dr. Alberto Acosta
Dr. Fernando Bustamante
Dr. Osvaldo Dávila
Dr. Berta García
Dr. Osvaldo Hurtado
Dr. Simon Pachano
Edgar Ponce
Dr. Alejandra Vela
Economist César Verduga

*Rank at time of interview.
**Officer retired (r) at time of interview.

Notes

Introduction: The Armed Forces and Democracy

1. Lt. Col. Francisco Arias, quoted in "Venezuela Crushes Army Coup Attempt," *New York Times,* 5 February 1992, A10. See also Richard Hillman, *Democracy for the Privileged: Crisis and Transition in Venezuela* (Boulder, Colo.: Lynne Rienner Publishers, 1994), 137; Felipe Aguero, "Crisis and Decay of Democracy in Venezuela: The Civil-Military Dimension," in Jennifer McCoy et al. (eds.), *Venezuela: Democracy Under Stress* (New Brunswick, N.J.: Transaction Publishers, 1995), 215–235; "Debilitating Democracy: Political Elites and Military Rebels," in Louis Goodman et al. (eds.), *Lessons of the Venezuelan Experience* (Baltimore: Johns Hopkins University Press, 1995), 136–162; and Deborah Norden, "Democracy and Military Control in Venezuela: From Subordination to Insurrection," unpublished ms., 9–17.

2. "Venezuela Crushes Army Coup Attempt," A10; James Brooke, "Venezuela Recounts How Coup Failed," *New York Times,* 6 February 1992, A3.

3. "2nd Venezuelan Coup Attempt Fails," *Denver Post,* 28 November 1992, 2A; "Venezuela Faces 2d Day of Violence," *New York Times,* 29 November 1992, I7; James Brooke, "Venezuela Chief Rules Out Resigning as 2d Coup Fails," *New York Times,* 30 November 1992, A4.

4. Quoted in Hugo Chumbita, *Los carapintada: Historia de un malentendido argentino* (Buenos Aires: Editorial Planeta, 1990), 29.

5. James Gerstenzang and William Long, "Argentina's Fragile Democracy Praised by Bush," *Los Angeles Times,* 6 December 1990, A4; and Dan Balz and Eugene Robinson, " 'Day of Dictator Past' Bush Tells Argentines," *Washington Post,* 6 December 1990, A33.

6. José Ulloa Vernimmen, *Paquisha: Un hito de la gloria* (Guayaquil, Ecuador: Editorial Cultura y Democracia, 1981), 234–353. In 1995, Ecuadorian and Peruvian forces again clashed in the Cordillera del Condor, leaving twenty-seven Ecuadorians and forty-six Peruvians dead and several hundred wounded.

7. Interviews EC800391, EC952191, and EC557091. Unless otherwise noted, all translations are by the author.

8. Interview EC445591.

9. Interviews EC059391 and EC952391.

10. Robert Dix, "Military Coups and Military Rule in Latin America," *Armed Forces and Society* 20, 3 (Spring 1994): 443–445.

11. Alfred C. Stepan, *Rethinking Military Politics: Brazil and the Southern Cone* (Princeton, N.J.: Princeton University Press, 1988), 104–105.

Chapter 1: The Military and Politics in Latin America

1. Samuel Huntington, *The Soldier and the State* (New York: Random House, 1957), 79. See also "Civilian Control of the Military: A Theoretical Statement," in Heinz Eulau, Samuel Eldersveld, and Morris Janowitz (eds.), *Political Behavior: A Reader in Theory and Research* (New York: Free Press, 1956), 380–384; and "The Soldier and the State in the 1970's," in Andrew Goodpaster and Samuel Huntington (eds.), *Civil-Military Relations* (Washington, D.C.: American Enterprise Institute, 1977), 5–27.

2. Cf. Morris Janowitz, *The Professional Soldier: A Social and Political Portrait* (Glencoe, Ill.: Free Press, 1960), 5–6; and Arthur Larson, "Military Professionalism and Civil Control: A Comparative Analysis of Two Approaches," *Journal of Political and Military Sociology* 2, 1 (1974): 57–72.

3. R. D. McKinlay, "Professionalization, Politicization, and Civil-Military Relations," in M. R. Van Gils, *The Perceived Role of the Military* (Rotterdam: Rotterdam University Press, 1971), 245–264; and Bengt Abrahamsson, *Military Professionalization and Political Power* (n.p.: Akademisk avhandling, 1971), 151–163.

4. Abrahamsson, *Military Professionalization,* 159; and S. E. Finer, *The Man on Horseback: The Military in Politics,* 2d ed. (London: Penguin Books, 1975), 20–26.

5. Russell Weigley, "The American Military and the Principle of Civilian Control: From McClellan to Powell," *Journal of Military History* 57 (October 1993): 34.

6. Brian Loveman, *For La Patria: Politics and the Armed Forces in Latin America* (in press: Scholarly Resources), chap. 2.

7. Frederick Nunn, "The South American Military Tradition: Preprofessional Armies in Argentina, Chile, Peru, and Brazil," in Linda Rodríguez (ed.), *Rank and Privilege: The Military and Society in Latin America* (Wilmington, Del.: Scholarly Resources, 1994), 74, 77, 81.

8. Alain Rouquié, *The Military and the State in Latin America* (Berkeley: University of California Press, 1987), 41, 49–71.

9. This analysis draws in part on an earlier paper, "Hacia un modelo democrático en las relaciones civiles-militares para América Latina," in *Democracia y Fuerzas Armadas* (Quito: CORDES, 1988), 277–320.

10. The definitive work on the European military missions is Frederick Nunn, *Yesterday's Soldiers: European Military Professionalism in South America, 1890–1940* (Lincoln: University of Nebraska Press, 1983).

11. Loveman, *For La Patria,* chap. 2.

12. Liisa North, *Civil-Military Relations in Argentina, Chile, and Peru* (Berkeley: Institute of International Studies, University of California, Berkeley, 1966), 14.

13. Genaro Arriagada, *El pensamiento político de los militares* (Santiago: Editorial Aconcagua, 1986), 109–168.

14. Nunn, *Yesterday's Soldiers,* 37.

15. Guillermo O'Donnell, "Comparative Historical Formations of the State Apparatus and Socio-economic Change in the Third World," *International Social Science Journal* 32, 4 (1980): 725.

16. Rouquié, *The Military and the State*, 98–99.

17. Arriagada, *El pensamiento político*, 84–107; Nunn, *Yesterday's Soldiers*, 145, 170, 176, 266–267, 274; and Donald Hodges, *Argentina's Dirty War: An Intellectual Biography* (Austin: University of Texas Press, 1991), 23–31.

18. Robert Hayes, *The Armed Nation: The Brazilian Corporate Mystique* (Tempe: Center for Latin American Studies, Arizona State University, 1989), 119–121, 129, 143–144; Marvin Goldwert, "The Rise of Modern Militarism in Argentina"; Ronald Schneider, "The Military and Brazilian Politics to World War II"; and Victor Villanueva, "Military Professionalization in Peru"; in Brian Loveman and Thomas Davies (eds.), *Politics of Antipolitics: The Military in Latin America*, rev. ed. (Lincoln: University of Nebraska Press, 1989), 43–45, 75–81, and 110–125 respectively.

19. See Richard Millett, "The Central American Militaries," in Abraham Lowenthal and J. Samuel Fitch (eds.), *Armies and Politics in Latin America*, rev. ed. (New York: Holmes & Meier, 1986), 204–223.

20. Jose Nun, "The Middle-Class Military Coup Revisited," in Lowenthal and Fitch, *Armies and Politics*, 59–95. See also Rut Diamint, "The Militarization of Argentine Political Culture: The Worship of San Martin," unpublished ms., Centro de Estudios Europeo-Latinoamericanos (EURAL), Buenos Aires, 1990.

21. Frederick Nunn, "An Overview of the European Military Missions in Latin America," in Loveman and Davies, *Antipolitics*, 38. See also in the same volume "Emil Korner and the Prussianization of the Chilean Army," 67–74; and Stanley Hilton, "The Armed Forces and Industrialists in Modern Brazil: The Drive for Military Autonomy," in Rodríguez, *Rank and Privilege*, 95–142.

22. See Alm. (r) Mario César Flores, *Bases para una política militar* (Provincia de Buenos Aires: Universidad de Quilmes, 1996), 53–54.

23. Linda Rodríguez, "Introduction," in Rodríguez, *Rank and Privilege*, xiii.

24. Rouquié, *The Military and the State*, 101–104.

25. Flores, *Bases para una política militar*, 36.

26. Frederick Nunn, *The Military in Chilean History* (Albuquerque: University of New Mexico Press, 1976), 20–43.

27. Dietrich Rueschemeyer, Evelyne Huber Stephens, and John Stephens, *Capitalist Development and Democracy* (Chicago: University of Chicago Press, 1992), 176.

28. Nunn, *The Military in Chilean History*, 183–188, 195–217, 224; North, *Civil-Military Relations*, 11–13, 17–20, 27–29, 34–37; and Nun, "The Middle-Class Military Coup Revisited," 68–69, 83.

29. Anthony Maingot, "Colombia," in Lyle McAlister, Anthony Maingot, and Robert Potash, *The Military in Latin American Sociopolitical Evolution* (Washington, D.C.: Center for Research in Social Systems, 1970), 137.

30. Maingot, "Colombia," 140–145, 166.

31. Jonathan Hartlyn, "Military Governments and the Transition to Civilian Rule," in Lowenthal and Fitch, *Armies and Politics*, 417–427; Jorge Pablo Osterling, *Democracy in Colombia: Clientelistic Politics and Guerrilla Warfare* (New Brunswick, N.J.: Transaction Publishers, 1989), 45–103; Daniel Premo, "Coping With Insurgency: The Politics

of Pacification in Colombia and Venezuela," in Donald Herman, *Democracy in Latin America: Colombia and Venezuela* (New York: Praeger Publishers, 1988), 227–240; and Robert Dix, *Colombia: The Political Dimensions of Change* (New Haven, Conn.: Yale University Press, 1967), 99–147, 294–305.

32. Rouquié, *The Military and the State,* 60.

33. Rueschemeyer, Stephens, and Stephens, *Capitalist Development,* 179. See also Ruth Berins Collier and David Collier, *Shaping the Political Arena* (Princeton, N.J.: Princeton University Press, 1991), 273–288, 438–456.

34. Juan Rial, *Estructura legal de las fuerzas armadas del Uruguay: Un análisis político* (Montevideo, Uruguay: CIESU/PEITHO, 1992), 3–6.

35. John Booth and Thomas Walker, *Understanding Central America,* 2d ed. (Boulder, Colo.: Westview Press, 1993), 30–31; and John Peeler, "Early Democratization in Latin America: Costa Rica in the Context of Chile and Uruguay," paper presented to the Latin American Studies Association (henceforth LASA), Washington, D.C., September 1995, 8–15.

36. Ronald McDonald and J. Mark Ruhl, *Party Politics and Elections in Latin America* (Boulder, Colo.: Westview Press, 1989), 170–171.

37. N. Patrick Peritore, "Costa Rica: The Crisis of Demilitarization," in Constantine Danopoulos (ed.), *From Military to Civilian Rule* (London: Routledge, 1992), 81, 91–93; and Burt English, *Liberación Nacional in Costa Rica: The Development of a Political Party in a Transitional Society* (Gainesville: University of Florida Press, 1971), 42–43.

38. Thomas Skidmore and Peter Smith, *Modern Latin America,* 3d ed. (New York: Oxford University Press, 1992), 223–224.

39. Roderic Ai Camp, *Generals in the Palacio: The Military in Modern Mexico* (New York: Oxford University Press, 1992), 17–25; Edwin Lieuwen, *Arms and Politics in Latin America* (New York: Council on Foreign Relations, 1960), 106–118; and Lyle McAlister, "Mexico," in McAlister, Maingot, and Potash, *The Military in Latin American Sociopolitical Evolution,* 200–207.

40. Camp, *Generals in the Palacio,* 67–68; and Peter Smith, *Labyrinths of Power: Political Recruitment in Twentieth Century Mexico* (Princeton, N.J.: Princeton University Press, 1979), 94–96.

41. Camp, *Generals in the Palacio,* 81; and Stephen Wager, "The Mexican Military: The Dilemma of Functioning in a One-Party System," in Richard Millett and Michael Gold-Bliss (eds.), *Beyond Praetorianism: The Latin American Military in Transition* (Miami: North-South Center Press, 1996), 103–115. See also David Ronfeldt, "The Modern Mexican Military," in Lowenthal and Fitch, *Armies and Politics,* 230–235; William Ackroyd, "Military Professionalism and Non-Intervention in Mexico," in Rodríguez, *Rank and Privilege,* 219–234; and Franklin Margiotta, "Civilian Control and the Mexican Military," in Claude Welch (ed.), *Civilian Control of the Military: Theory and Cases from Developing Countries* (Albany: State University of New York Press, 1976), 213–253.

42. This analysis draws heavily on the pioneering work of Alfred Stepan, "The New Professionalism of Internal Warfare and Military Role Expansion," in Lowenthal and Fitch, *Armies and Politics,* 134–150, and *The Military in Politics: Changing Patterns in Brazil* (Princeton, N.J.: Princeton University Press, 1971), 172–187. See also John Markoff and Silvio Duncan Baretta, "Professional Ideology and Military Activism in Brazil: Critique of a Thesis of Alfred Stepan," *Comparative Politics* 17, 2 (1985): 175–191; and Frank

McCann, "Origins of the 'New Professionalism' of the Brazilian Military," in Loveman and Davies, *Antipolitics,* 57–66.

43. Crnl. Alfonso Littuma Arízaga, *Doctrina de Seguridad Nacional* (Caracas: Ministerio de Defensa, 1967), is a representative Latin American work on national security. See also Ernesto López, *Seguridad nacional y sedición militar* (Buenos Aires: Editorial Legasa, 1987); and Margaret Crahan, "National Security Ideology and Human Rights," in Margaret Crahan (ed.), *Human Rights and Basic Needs in the Americas* (Washington, D.C.: Georgetown University Press, 1982), 100–127.

44. Carina Perelli, "The Military's Perception of Threat in the Southern Cone of South America," in Louis Goodman, Johanna Mendelson, and Juan Rial (eds.), *The Military and Democracy: The Future of Civil-Military Relations in Latin America* (Lexington, Mass.: Lexington Books, 1990), 100–101.

45. Rueschemeyer, Stephens, and Stephens, *Capitalist Development,* 169–171, 192–193.

46. For a description of training and career patterns in nine Latin American countries, see Robert Wesson (ed.), *The Latin American Military Institution* (New York: Praeger Publishers, 1986), 19–69.

47. See Richard Millett, "The Central American Militaries," in Lowenthal and Fitch, *Armies and Politics,* 204–223.

48. Stepan, "The New Professionalism," 142; and Frederick Nunn, *The Time of the Generals: Latin American Professional Militarism in Comparative Perspective* (Lincoln: University of Nebraska Press, 1992), 206–225.

49. Cf. David Pion-Berlin, "Latin American National Security Doctrines: Hard- and Softline Themes," *Armed Forces and Society* 15, 3 (1989): 411–428.

50. López, *Seguridad nacional y sedición militar,* 171–173.

51. See n.a., *Filosofía y plan de acción del gobierno revolucionario y nacionalista del Ecuador,* and *Bases ideológicas de la revolución peruana* (Lima: Oficina Central de Información, 1975). On the development of security and development doctrine in Peru, see North, *Civil-Military Relations,* 52–57; and Luigi Einaudi and Alfred Stepan, *Latin American Institutional Development: Changing Military Perspectives in Peru and Brazil* (Santa Monica, Calif.: Rand Corporation R-586-DOS, 1971).

52. Crnl. Raúl Meneses Arata, "Lineamientos de la política del gobierno revolucionario y sus principales realizaciones," Centro de Altos Estudios Militares conferencias sustenadas con motivo de la visita del Colegio Nacional de Guerra de los EE.UU. de N.A., April 1970, II.

53. Perelli, "Perception of Threat," 100–101.

54. Horacio Verbitsky, *La última batalla de la Tercera Guerra Mundial* (Buenos Aires: Editorial Legasa, 1985), 17–22.

55. Interviews AR965192 and AR267592.

56. The influence of French military advisors and the introduction of the French doctrine of revolutionary war in Argentina's Superior War College are documented in Interviews AR200985, AR346785, AR453085, AR559885, and AR081892, although one intelligence officer directly involved in the antisubversive campaign claims that French doctrine had relatively little influence at the operational level. Interview 764992. The most comprehensive analyses of the French doctrinal influence are Carina Perelli, "From Counterrevolutionary Warfare to Political Awakening: The Uruguayan and

Argentine Armed Forces in the Seventies," *Armed Forces and Society* 20, 1 (1993): 25–49 ; and López, *Seguridad nacional y sedición militar,* 137–160. Especially in the urban context, U.S. counterinsurgency doctrine was not particularly relevant. Interview AR168185.

57. Stepan, *Military in Politics,* 65–66, 75–76.

58. Ibid., 116–118.

59. On the 1945–64 period, see Peter Flynn, *Brazil: A Political Analysis* (Boulder, Colo.: Westview Press, 1978), 132–307; and Thomas Skidmore, *Politics in Brazil, 1930–1964: An Experiment in Democracy* (New York: Oxford University Press, 1967), 62–302.

60. Stepan, *Military in Politics,* 62–84. Cf. Guillermo O'Donnell, *Modernization and Bureaucratic-Authoritarianism: Studies in South American Politics* (Berkeley: Institute of International Studies, University of California, Berkeley), 145.

61. O'Donnell, *Modernization,* 136–145.

62. Ibid., 166–193.

63. Robert Potash, *The Army and Politics in Argentina, 1945–1962: Perón to Frondizi* (Stanford, Calif.: Stanford University Press, 1980), 181–376. See also Edwin Lieuwen, "Factionalism and Attitudes toward *Peronismo,*" and Philip Springer, "Some Differences Between *Legalistas* and the *Gorilas,*" in Richard Fagen and Wayne Cornelius (eds.), *Political Power in Latin America: Seven Confrontations* (Englewood Cliffs, N.J.: Prentice-Hall, 1970), 116–119.

64. Guillermo O'Donnell, "Modernization and Military Coups: Theory, Comparisons, and the Argentine Case," in Lowenthal and Fitch, *Armies and Politics,* 102–106; and O'Donnell, *Modernization,* 158–160.

65. O'Donnell, *Modernization,* 157.

66. See Karen Remmer, "The Sustainability of Political Democracy: Lessons from South America," *Comparative Political Studies* 29, 6 (1996): 624.

67. Cf. Reuschemeyer, Stephens, and Stephens, *Capitalist Development and Democracy,* 196–207.

68. See O'Donnell, *Modernization; 1966–1973, El estado burocrático autoritario: Triunfos, derrotas, y crisis* (Buenos Aires: Editorial Belgrano, 1982); and the critical analysis of O'Donnell's work in David Collier (ed.), *The New Authoritarianism in Latin America* (Princeton, N.J.: Princeton University Press, 1979). See also Hector Schamis, "Reconceptualizing Latin American Authoritarianism in the 1970's: From Bureaucratic Authoritarianism to Neoconservatism," *Comparative Politics* 23 (1991): 201–220. For an incisive and delightfully well-written account of the Chilean regime, see Pamela Constable and Arturo Valenzuela, *A Nation of Enemies: Chile Under Pinochet* (New York: W.W. Norton, 1991).

69. In most cases, these economic policies reflected the particular choice of civilian economists, international trends in economic doctrine, and the ideological balance within the officer corps rather than any fine-grained politicoeconomic rationale. In Chile and Argentina, military leaders initially had little or no understanding of the economic doctrines they adopted. Constable and Valenzuela, *A Nation of Enemies,* 169, 190–191; Gary Wynia, *Argentina: Illusions and Realities,* 2d ed. (New York: Holmes & Meier, 1992), 89; and interview with a member of the economic team of the *Proceso,* Buenos Aires, 13 November 1985. Cf. Paul Cammack, *Generals in Retreat: The Crisis of Military Rule in Latin America* (Manchester: University of Manchester Press, 1985).

70. See Dirk Kruijt, *Revolution by Decree: Peru 1968–1975* (Amsterdam: Thela Publishers, 1994); Cynthia McClintock and Abraham Lowenthal (eds.), *The Peruvian Experiment Reconsidered* (Princeton, N.J.: Princeton University Press, 1983); George Philip, *The Rise and Fall of the Peruvian Military Radicals 1968–1976* (London: University of London, 1978); Anita Isaacs, *Military Rule and Transition in Ecuador, 1972–92* (Pittsburgh: University of Pittsburgh Press, 1993); Catharine Conaghan, *Restructuring Domination: Industrialists and the State in Ecuador* (Pittsburgh: University of Pittsburgh Press, 1988); and John Martz, *Politics and Petroleum in Ecuador* (New Brunswick, N.J.: Transaction, 1987).

71. Julio Cotler, "Democracy and National Integration in Peru," in McClintock and Lowenthal, *The Peruvian Experiment Reconsidered,* 33.

72. See José María Maravall, "The Myth of the Authoritarian Advantage," in Larry Diamond and Marc Plattner (eds.), *Economic Reform and Democracy* (Baltimore: Johns Hopkins University Press, 1995), 15–17; Stephan Haggard and Robert Kaufman, *The Political Economy of Democratic Transitions* (Princeton, N.J.: Princeton University Press, 1995), 11–12, 29–42, 45–74; and Karen Remmer, *Military Rule in Latin America* (Boulder, Colo.: Westview Press, 1991), 77–106.

73. For a more detailed exposition of this argument, see María Susana Ricci and J. Samuel Fitch, "Ending Military Regimes in Argentina: 1966–1973 and 1976–1983," in Goodman, Mendelson, and Rial, *The Military and Democracy,* 55–74. See also Christopher Clapham and George Philip (eds.), *The Political Dilemmas of Military Regimes* (Totowa, N.J.: Barnes & Noble Books, 1985), 1–26.

74. Stepan, *Military in Politics,* 253–266; and Alfred Stepan, "Paths Toward Redemocratization: Theoretical and Comparative Considerations," in Guillermo O'Donnell, Philippe Schmitter, and Laurence Whitehead (eds.), *Transitions from Authoritarian Rule: Comparative Perspectives* (Baltimore: Johns Hopkins University Press, 1986), 72–78.

75. Robert Potash, *The Army and Politics in Argentina 1962–1973: From Frondizi's Fall to the Peronist Restoration* (Stanford, Calif.: Stanford University Press, 1996), 254–307.

76. Thomas Skidmore, *The Politics of Military Rule in Brazil, 1964–1985* (New York: Oxford University Press, 1988), 95–101, 150–152, 164–178, and 197–200.

77. On the structure of the Pinochet regime, see Genaro Arriagada, "The Legal and Institutional Framework of the Armed Forces in Chile," in Samuel Valenzuela and Arturo Valenzuela (eds.), *Military Rule in Chile: Dictatorship and Oppositions* (Baltimore: Johns Hopkins University Press, 1986), 117–143; and *Pinochet: The Politics of Power* (Boston: Unwin Hymin, 1988), 102–169; Remmer, *Military Rule in Latin America,* 113–145; and Karen Remmer, "Neopatrimonialism: The Politics of Military Rule in Latin America, 1973–1987," *Comparative Politics* 21, 2 (1987): 152–165.

78. Peter Cleaves and Henry Pease García, "State Autonomy and Military Policy Making," in Lowenthal and Fitch, *Armies and Politics,* 358–364; James Malloy, "The Politics of Transition in Latin America," in James Malloy and Mitchell Seligson (eds.), *Authoritarians and Democrats: Regime Transition in Latin America* (Pittsburgh: University of Pittsburgh Press, 1987), 246–248; Alfred Stepan, *The State and Society: Peru in Comparative Perspective* (Princeton, N.J.: Princeton University Press, 1978), 301–316; Conaghan, *Restructuring Domination,* 76–119.

79. Augusto Varas, "The Crisis of Legitimacy of Military Rule in the 1980s," in Paul Drake and Iván Jaksi (eds.), *The Struggle for Democracy in Chile*, rev. ed. (Lincoln: University of Nebraska Press, 1995), 74–90; and Alan Angell, "The Soldier as Politician: Military Authoritarianism in Latin America," in Dennis Kavanaugh and Gillian Peele (eds.), *Comparative Government and Politics: Essays in Honour of S. E. Finer* (Boulder, Colo.: Westview Press, 1984), ·130.

80. See Wilfred Bacchus, "Long-Term Military Rulership in Brazil: Ideologic Consensus and Dissensus, 1963–1983," *Journal of Political and Military Sociology* 13 (Spring 1985): 99–123; and Stepan, *Military in Politics*, 216–266.

81. Military councils of senior officers in Uruguay and Honduras provided a forum for policy debates, but the majoritarian logic of such assemblies conflicted with the command hierarchy.

82. Merilee Grindle, "Civil-Military Relations and Budgetary Politics in Latin America," *Armed Forces and Society* 13, 2 (1987): 255–272.

83. Claude Welch, *No Farewell to Arms: Military Disengagement from Politics in Africa and Latin America* (Boulder, Colo.: Westview Press, 1987), 196–197, 204.

84. Samuel Huntington, "Reforming Civil-Military Relations," *Journal of Democracy* 6, 4 (1995): 13.

85. Interviews AR279585, AR349985, and AR595485. The quotations in this section are responses to the question "What does it mean in the Argentine/Ecuadorian army/navy/air force to be a professional officer? When someone says that General Fulano has a reputation as being very professional, of what personal qualities are we speaking?"

86. Interviews AR186792 and AR360492.

87. Interviews EC208691 and EC454291.

88. Later I argue that a significant percentage of the Argentine and Ecuadorian interviewees could be classified as "democratic professionalists" in terms of their beliefs about the role of the military in politics. Nevertheless, even among many of these officers, professional behavior was not explicitly linked to support for a democratic regime or democratic norms of civil-military relations.

89. Interviews AR305385 and AR608292.

90. See Patricia Estupiñán, "Los militares quieren votar," *Vistazo* s.n. (1991): 76–81. The constitutional disenfranchisement of military personnel was originally intended to prevent military *caudillos* from controlling elections through the votes of their soldiers.

91. Interviews AR335685 and AR597485. See López, *Seguridad nacional y sedición militar*, 83–90.

92. Interview AR021492.

93. Interviews AR852592 and EC829391.

Chapter 2: Contemporary Patterns of Civil-Military Relations

1. Philippe Schmitter and Terry Karl, "What Democracy Is . . . And Is Not," *Journal of Democracy* 2, 3 (1991): 76. See also Terry Lynn Karl, "Dilemmas of Democratization in Latin America," *Comparative Politics* 23 (1990): 2.

2. J. Samuel Valenzuela, "Democratic Consolidation in Post-Transitional Settings: Notion, Process, and Facilitating Conditions," in Scott Mainwaring, Guillermo O'Donnell, and J. Samuel Valenzuela (eds.), *Issues in Democratic Consolidation: The New South*

American Democracies in Comparative Perspective (Notre Dame, Ind.: University of Notre Dame Press, 1992), 62–64, 67–68; Schmitter and Karl, "What Democracy Is," 81; and Kenneth Kemp and Charles Hudlin, "Civil Supremacy over the Military: Its Nature and Limits," *Armed Forces and Society* 19, 1 (1992): 9.

3. Valenzuela, "Democratic Consolidation," 64–66. Cf. Augusto Varas, "Autonomización castrense y democracia en América Latina," in Augusto Varas (coordinador), *La Autonomía Militar en América Latina* (Caracas: Editorial Nueva Sociedad, 1988), 20–29; and David Pion-Berlin, "Military Autonomy and Emerging Democracies in South America," *Comparative Politics* 25 (October 1992): 83–102.

4. See Gerardo Munck, "Disaggregating Political Regime: Conceptual Issues in the Study of Democratization," Kellogg Institute Working Paper, no. 228, University of Notre Dame, August 1996, 5–6.

5. *Constitución Política de la República de Chile* (Santiago: n.p., n.d.); and Mark Ensalco, "Military Prerogatives and the Stalemate of Chilean Civil-Military Relations," *Armed Forces and Society* 21, 2 (1995): 258–262.

6. Stepan, *Rethinking Military Politics*, 93–114; and Eliézar Rizzo de Oliveira, "O aparelho militar: Papel tutelar na Nova República," in J. Quartim de Moraes, Wilma Peres Costa, and Eliézar Rizzo de Oliveira, *A Tutela Militar* (n.p.: Vértice, 1987), 54–81. Cf. Luis Humberto Guzmán, "Nicaragua's Armed Forces: An Assessment of Their Political Power," in Millett and Gold-Bliss, *Beyond Praetorianism*, 162–165, 173–174.

7. Interviews EC290191, EC952191, EC210591, and EC194591.

8. Interview EC880591.

9. J. Mark Ruhl, "Redefining Civil-Military Relations in Honduras," *Journal of Interamerican Studies and World Affairs* 38, 1 (1996): 38.

10. Juan Linz and Alfred Stepan, *Problems of Democratic Transition and Consolidation: Southern Europe, South America, and Post-Communist Europe* (Baltimore: Johns Hopkins University Press, 1996), 5–6; and Phillipe Schmitter, "The Consolidation of Political Democracies: Processes, Rhythms, Sequences, and Types," in Geoffrey Pridham (ed.), *Transitions to Democracy: Comparative Perspectives from Southern Europe, Latin America, and Eastern Europe* (Aldershot, U.K.: Dartmouth Publishing, 1995), 544.

11. Jennifer Schirmer, "Rule of Law or Law of Rule: Guatemalan Military Attitudes Toward Law, National Security, and Human Rights," paper presented to the Northeast Council on Latin American Studies, Wellesley College, October 1988, 3–6; and "The Guatemalan Military: Theories of National Stability, Democracy, and Political Practice," unpublished ms., Program in Human Rights Policies, Harvard University.

12. Stepan, *Rethinking Military Politics*, 93–102; and Felipe Aguero, "The Military and the Limits to Democratization in South America," in Mainwaring, O'Donnell, and Valenzuela, *Issues in Democratic Consolidation*, 155, 164–166. The degree of acceptance or contestation of the existing norms of civil-military relations is treated here as one component of the institutionalization of different patterns of military-state-society relations.

13. Aguero, "Limits to Democratization," 168–172; and *Soldiers, Civilians, and Democracy: Post-Franco Spain in Comparative Perspective* (Baltimore: Johns Hopkins University Press, 1995), 29–30, 44–58, 219–245; Linz and Stepan, *Problems of Democratic Transition*, 66–68; and n.a., "Ejército expresa su malestar," *El Mercurio*, 11 April 1989, A1, A12.

14. Douglas Chalmers and Craig Robinson, "Why Power Contenders Choose Liberalization: Perspectives from South America," in Lowenthal and Fitch, *Armies and Politics*, 399–405.

15. Guillermo O'Donnell and Philippe Schmitter, *Transitions from Authoritarian Rule: Tentative Conclusions about Uncertain Democracies* (Baltimore: Johns Hopkins University Press, 1986), 23–25, 65–72.

16. Carlos Acuña and Catalina Smulovitz, "Adjusting the Armed Forces to Democracy: Successes, Failures, and Ambiguities in the Southern Cone," in Elizabeth Jelin and Eric Hershberg, *Constructing Democracy: Human Rights, Citizenship, and Society in Latin America* (Boulder, Colo.: Westview Press, 1996), 16; Haggard and Kaufman, *The Political Economy of Democratic Transitions*, 109–139; and O'Donnell and Schmitter, *Transitions from Authoritarian Rule*, 31–32.

17. Aguero, *Soldiers, Civilians, and Democracy*, 241–242; Aguero defines military unity as "the extent to which definitions of institutions, mission, and role are shared by the officer corps and particularly by the top hierarchy," 30.

18. Comisión Nacional sobre la Desaparición de Personas (CONADEP), *Nunca mas: Informe de la Comisión Nacional sobre la Desaparición de Personas* (Buenos Aires: Editorial Universitaria de Buenos Aires, 1985), 296, 375–387; and Paul Buchanan, "State Terror as a Complement to Economic Policy, 1976–1981," in George Lopez and Michael Stohl (eds.), *Dependence, Development, and State Repression* (New York: Greenwood Press, 1989), 48–49.

19. Stepan, *Rethinking Military Politics*, 68–92.

20. David Pion-Berlin, *The Ideology of State Terror: Economic Doctrine and Political Repression in Argentina and Peru* (Boulder, Colo.: Lynne Rienner Publishers, 1989), 179.

21. Francisco Rojas Aravena, "Transición y relaciones civil-militares en Chile en el nuevo marco internacional," Nueva serie Flacso, Santiago, 1996, 22–23.

22. Felipe Aguero, "The Military in the Processes of Democratization in South America and Southern Europe: Outcomes and Initial Conditions," paper presented to LASA, San Juan, Puerto Rico, September 1989, 36–38; and Karl, "Dilemmas of Democratization in Latin America," 8–15.

23. Peter Hakim and Abraham Lowenthal, "Latin America's Fragile Democracies," in Pridham, *Transitions to Democracy: Comparative Perspectives*, 301; and Ian Roxborough, "Organized Labor: A Major Victim of the Debt Crisis," in Barbara Stallings and Robert Kaufman (eds.), *Debt and Democracy in Latin America* (Boulder, Colo.: Westview Press, 1989), 91–92.

24. Thomas Skidmore and Peter Smith, *Modern Latin America*, 3d ed. (New York: Oxford University Press, 1992), 331–332; and Ruhl, "Redefining Civil-Military Relations in Honduras," 35.

25. John Booth and Thomas Walker, *Understanding Central America*, 2d ed. (Boulder, Colo.: Westview Press, 1993), 47–51.

26. Ruhl, "Redefining Civil-Military Relations in Honduras," 37–38. This section draws heavily from Ruhl's detailed and insightful analysis of the Honduran case.

27. J. Samuel Fitch, "The Decline of U.S. Military Influence in Latin America," *Journal of Interamerican Studies and World Affairs* 35, 2 (1993): 9.

28. Thomas Anderson, "Honduras in Transition," *Current History* 84, 500 (1985): 115–116; and Ruhl, "Redefining Civil-Military Relations in Honduras," 38–39. A 1993

report by the human rights commissioner documented 184 disappearances during the 1980s, far fewer than Guatemala or El Salvador.

29. Anderson, "Honduras in Transition," 132.

30. Anderson, "Honduras in Transition," 132; and "Politics and the Military in Honduras," *Current History* 87, 533 (1988): 426; Timothy Ashby, "Honduras' Role in U.S. Policy for Central America," *Heritage Foundation Reports*, no. 412, February 1985, 3; and Inter-American Development Bank, *Latin America in Graphs: Two Decades of Economic Trends 1971–1991* (Baltimore: Johns Hopkins University Press for the Inter-American Development Bank, 1992), 21, 117.

31. Ruhl, "Redefining Civil-Military Relations in Honduras," 40–41; Anderson, "Politics and the Military in Honduras," 425.

32. "Honduras: U.S. Announces Drastic Cuts in Military Aid," Inter Press Service, 9 March 1994, 1.

33. Ruhl, "Redefining Civil-Military Relations in Honduras," 44–47.

34. U.S. Department of State, "Honduras Human Rights Practices, 1994," Department of State Dispatch, March 1995, 16.

35. Ruhl, "Redefining Civil-Military Relations in Honduras," 48–50; and "Spotlight on the Honduran Military," *Latin America Regional Reports: Mexico and Central America* RM-91-08, 31 October 1991, 4.

36. By 1996, military forces in El Salvador had also been reduced from 57,000 to 21,000 men; Nicaraguan military personnel dropped from 100,000 to less than 15,000. Douglas Farah, "Central American Armies Get Down to Business," *Washington Post*, 4 June 1996, A11.

37. Ruhl, "Redefining Civil-Military Relations in Honduras," 48, 43, 51–52; Mark Rosenberg and J. Mark Ruhl, "Honduras: Democratization and the Role of the Armed Forces," in Jorge Dominguez and Abraham Lowenthal (eds.), *Constructing Democratic Governance: Latin America and the Caribbean in the 1990s* (Baltimore: Johns Hopkins University Press, 1996), 73; and "Army Resistance Backfires," *Latin American Weekly Report* (hereafter cited as *LAWR*) (15 August 1996): 371.

38. Rizzo de Oliveira, "O aparelho militar," 54–81; and Joâo Martins Filho and Daniel Zirker, "The Metamorphosis of Military Tutelage in Brazil," paper presented to LASA, Washington, D.C., 1995, 1–2.

39. Stepan, *Rethinking Military Politics*, 104–105.

40. Wendy Hunter, "Politicians Against Soldiers: Contesting the Military in Post-authoritarian Brazil," *Comparative Politics* 27, 4 (1995): 431–436.

41. Hunter, "Politicians Against Soldiers," 436–439; and Paulo Wrobel, "Gastos militares en Brasil: actores claves y el proceso del presupuesto," in Francisco Rojas Aravena, *Gasto Militar en América Latina: Procesos de decisiones y actores claves* (Santiago: CINDE and FLACSO-Chile, 1994), 192.

42. Eliézer Rizzo de Oliveira, "A adaptaçâo dos militares á democracia no Brasil," paper presented to the Inter-University Seminar on Armed Forces and Society, Baltimore, 1995, 16–17.

43. Bonnie Tenneriello with Geoff Thale and Richard Millett, "Unfinished Business: Military Reform and Peace Processes in El Salvador and Guatemala," in Millett and Gold-Bliss, *Beyond Praetorianism*, 181–205; and Tricia Juhn, "Life After Wartime: Civil-Military Relations in the Salvadoran Reconstruction," in the same volume, 207–222.

44. Franklin Patterson, "The Guatemalan Military and the Escuela Politécnica," *Armed Forces and Society* 14, 3 (1988): 359; Richard Adams, *Crucifixion by Power: Essays on Guatemalan National Social Structure, 1944–1966* (Austin: University of Texas Press, 1970), 263; and George Black, "Military Rule in Guatemala," in Loveman and Davies, *Antipolitics,* 501–513.

45. See Jennifer Schirmer, "The Looting of Democratic Discourse by the Guatemalan Military: Implications for Human Rights," in Elizabeth Jelin and Eric Hershberg (eds.), *Constructing Democracy: Human Rights, Citizenship, and Society* (Boulder, Colo.: Westview Press, 1996), 84–96; Jim Handy, "Resurgent Democracy and the Guatemalan Military," *Journal of Latin American Studies* 18 (November 1986): 383–408; Susanne Jonas, "Contradictions of Guatemala's Political Opening," in Susanne Jonas and Nancy Stein (eds.), *Democracy in Latin America: Visions and Realities* (New York: Bergin & Garvey Publishers, 1990), 65–84; and Gabriel Aguilera, "The Armed Forces, Democracy, and Transition in Central America," in Goodman, Mendelson, and Rial, *The Military and Democracy,* 23–38.

46. Estado Major de la Defensa Nacional, Ejército de Guatemala, "27 años de lucha por la libertad," conferencia dictada al Consejo Empresarial, Guatemala, August 1987, 30.

47. Article 244, quoted in Dirección de Asuntos Civiles, Ejército de Guatemala, "Conceptos doctrinarios de asuntos civiles," Guatemala, May 1988, 28.

48. N.a., "Estabilidad nacional," *Revista Militar* (Guatemala) (May–August 1986): 74–79.

49. Alfonso Yurrita, "Guatemala and the Transition," paper presented to American University-PEITHO conference, "Civil-Military Relations and the Challenge of Democracy in Latin America," Washington, D.C., May 1988, A10.

50. Estado Mayor, "27 años de lucha," 42; Dirección de Asuntos Civiles, "Conceptos Doctrinarios," 14–18; and Schirmer, "Rule of Law," 5.

51. Susanne Jonas, *The Battle for Guatemala* (Boulder, Colo.: Westview Press, 1991), 161–175.

52. Gral. Héctor Gramajo, Lección inaugural, 10th promoción, Curso de Comando y Estado Mayor, Centro de Estudios Militares, 30 April 1987, 11 (emphasis added).

53. Patterson, "The Guatemalan Military," 384–385; Stephen Kinzer, "Guatemalan Stays in Step with Army," *New York Times,* 11 May 1986, sec. 1, 4; and "Walking the Tightrope in Guatemala," *New York Times,* 9 November 1986, sec. 1, 32.

54. Jennifer Schirmer, "Oficiales de la Montaña," *Human Rights Internet Reporter* 13, 1 (1989): 13–16; and "The Guatemalan Military Project and Democracy: An Interview with General Hector Gramajo," *Harvard International Review* 13, 3 (1991): 10–13.

55. "Guatemala: Killings," *LAWR* WR-91-06 (14 February 1991): 12; and Robert Trudeau, *Guatemalan Politics: The Popular Struggle for Democracy* (Boulder, Colo.: Lynne Rienner Publishers, 1993), 116–128.

56. Edelberto Torres-Rivas, "Guatemala: Democratic Governability," in Domínguez and Lowenthal, *Constructing Democratic Governance,* 52–53.

57. "Last Round of Peace Talks in Sight," *LAWR* WR-91-10 (14 March 1991): 8.

58. "Arzú Wants To Get Rid of Mónica Pinto," *LAWR* WR-96-12 (28 March 1996): 143; and Raúl Molina Mejía, "Demilitarization of Guatemalan State and Society," paper presented to LASA, Washington, D.C., September 1995, 12–16.

59. Susanne Jonas, "Dangerous Liaisons: The U.S. in Guatemala," *Foreign Policy* 103 (Summer 1996): 158; and Francisco Villagrán de León, "Thwarting the Guatemalan Coup," *Journal of Democracy* 4, 4 (1993): 120–124.

60. Torres-Rivas, "Guatemala: Democratic Governance," 58–60; "De León Reshuffles the High Command," *LAWR* WR-94-08 (3 March 1994): 92; and "More About Coups and Unrest in the Army," *LAWR* WR-94-09 (10 March 1994): 105.

61. John Anderson, "Guatemala Military Returns to Barracks as Power Shifts to Civilians," *Denver Post,* 4 December 1996, 21A.

62. Molina Mejía, "Demilitarization of Guatemalan State and Society," 22.

63. Gobierno de la República de Guatemala et al., *Acuerdo Sobre el Fortalecimiento del Poder Civil y Función del Ejército en una Sociedad Democrática* (Guatemala City: Fundación Friedrich Ebert, n.d.); and "Agreement on Military Marks Last Stage of Guatemala's Peace Negotiations," *LAWR* WR-96-38 (3 October 1996): 445.

64. "Guatemala Set To OK Amnesty," *Denver Post,* 18 December 1996, 17A; and Anita Snow, "Rights Groups Threaten Suit Over Guatemalan Amnesty," *Denver Post,* 20 December 1996, 14A.

65. Personal communication from Jennifer Schirmer, 17 October 1996; Rachel McCleary, "Guatemala's Postwar Prospects," *Journal of Democracy* 8, 2 (1997): 138–142; and Tenneriello, "Unfinished Business: Military Reform and Peace Processes," in Millett and Gold-Bliss, *Beyond Praetorianism,* 190–198.

66. See Geraldo Lesbat Cavagnari Filho, "Autonomía militar y construcción de la potencia," in *Democracia y Fuerzas Armadas* (Quito: CORDES, 1988), 47–89.

67. Aguero, *Soldiers, Civilians, and Democracy,* 33–34, 243–244; and Linz and Stepan, *Problems of Democratic Transition,* 219–220.

68. Domingo Acevedo and Claudio Grossman, "The Organization of American States and the Protection of Democracy," in Tom Farer (ed.), *Beyond Sovereignty: Collectively Defending Democracy in the Americas* (Baltimore: Johns Hopkins University Press, 1996), 137; and n.a., "OAS Charter Amendments Take Effect Seeking to Bolster Democracy," 25 September 1997, http://www.oas.org/EN/PINFO/WEEK/092597ce.htm.

69. Kathryn Sikkink, "Nongovernmental Organizations, Democracy, and Human Rights in Latin America," in Farer, *Beyond Sovereignty,* 165.

70. Arturo Valenzuela, "Paraguay: The Coup That Didn't Happen," *Journal of Democracy* 8, 1 (1997): 44–45, 52–54.

71. Deborah Norden, *Military Rebellion in Argentina: Between Coups and Consolidation* (Lincoln: University of Nebraska Press, 1996), 125–130.

72. Acuña and Smulovitz, "Adjusting the Armed Forces to Democracy," 27.

73. "Honduras," *LAWR* WR-96-50 (27 December 1996): 597.

74. Felipe Aguero, "Las Fuerzas Armadas en una Época de Transición: Perspectivas para el Afianzamiento de la Democracia en América Latina," paper prepared for the project "La Cuestión Militar en las Nuevas Democracias de América Latina," November 1996, 2.

Chapter 3: Military Role Beliefs

1. Claude Welch, "Military Disengagement from Politics: Paradigms, Processes, or Random Events," *Armed Forces and Society* 18, 3 (1992): 338.

2. On the importance of role beliefs in coup decisions, see J. Samuel Fitch, *The Military Coup d'Etat as a Political Process: Ecuador 1948–1966* (Baltimore: Johns Hopkins University Press, 1977), 129–145; and Stepan, *Military in Politics*, 72–79, 168–187.

3. Brian Loveman, "'Protected Democracies' and Military Guardianship: Political Transitions in Latin America, 1978–1993," *Journal of Interamerican Studies and World Affairs* 36, 2 (Summer 1994): 105–189; and Patrice McSherry, "Military Power, Impunity and State-Society Change in Latin America," *Canadian Review of Political Science* 25, 3 (1992): 473–478.

4. Frederick Nunn, "The South American Military and (Re)Democratization: Professional Thought and Self-Perception," *Journal of Interamerican Studies and World Affairs* 37, 2 (1995): 2–3.

5. Brian Loveman, *The Constitution of Tyranny: Regimes of Exception in Spanish America* (Pittsburgh: University of Pittsburgh Press, 1993), 181.

6. See Catharine Conaghan, "Loose Parties, 'Floating' Politicians, and Institutional Stress: Presidentialism in Ecuador, 1979–1988," in Juan Linz and Arturo Valenzuela, (eds.), *The Failure of Presidential Democracy* (Baltimore: Johns Hopkins University Press, 1994), 329–333; "Party Politics and Democratization in Ecuador," in James Malloy and Mitchell Seligson, eds., *Authoritarians and Democrats: Regime Transition in Latin America* (Pittsburgh: University of Pittsburgh Press, 1987), 153–159; Osvaldo Hurtado, *Political Power in Ecuador* (Albuquerque: University of New Mexico Press, 1980), 128–166, 192–233; Howard Handelman, "Prospects for Ecuadorian Democracy," paper presented to LASA, Atlanta, 1994, 12–13; Amparo Menéndez-Carrión, "Partidos Políticos, Representación, y Ciudadanía en el Ecuador Contemporáneo: Dilemas y Perspectivas," paper presented to the Seminar for Ecuadorian Legislators, Instituto Latinoamericana de Investigaciones Sociales (ILDIS), Quito, 1990; and Ronald McDonald and J. Mark Ruhl, *Party Politics and Elections in Latin America*, 305–320.

7. See Cynthia McClintock, "The Prospects for Democratic Consolidation in a 'Least Likely' Case: Peru," *Comparative Politics* (January 1989): 127–148.

8. See Silvio Waisbord, "Politics and Identity in the Argentine Military: Cleavages and the Generational Factor," *Latin American Research Review* (henceforth *LARR*) 26, 2 (1991): 162, 168, and J. Patrice McSherry, *Incomplete Transition: Military Power and Democracy in Argentina* (New York: St. Martin's Press, 1997), 269–291.

9. Robert Lane, *Political Ideology* (New York: Free Press, 1962), 9; and William McGuire, "Attitudes and Attitude Change," *Handbook of Social Psychology*, vol. 2 (New York: Random House, 1985), 241–250.

10. Interviews AR030792, EC445591, and AR335685, respectively.

11. Samuel Huntington, "Civilian Control: A Theoretical Statement," in Heinz Eulau et al. (eds.), *Political Behavior: Reader in Theory and Research* (Glencoe, Ill.: Free Press, 1956), 380–384.

12. Interviews EC445791, AR389692, and AR175485, respectively.

13. Interviews AR942092 and AR577192, respectively.

14. Quoted in Andrés Fontana, "Percepciones militares del rol de las fuerzas armadas en Argentina," Fundación Simón Rodríguez Serie Cuadernos, no. 27, Buenos Aires, August 1993, 5. In an interview with Mayor (r) Lic. Luis Tibiletti shortly after the Argentine transition, one officer said candidly, "Since my graduation from the National Military College, I learned and was taught that [the mission was safeguarding the national

interests,] which I took an oath [to do] on four or five occasions; now I *don't know*" (emphasis added).

15. Interviews EC445792 and EC226991, respectively.

16. Fitch, *Coup d'Etat as a Political Process,* 133, 136.

17. Interviews AR267192, AR039985, and AR583185.

18. Interviews AR154785 and EC454291.

19. McGuire, "Attitudes and Attitude Change," 251–253.

20. Cf. Andrés Fontana, "Mas entendimiento entre civiles y militares," *El Cronista,* 18 June 1992, 17; and Rosendo Fraga, "El debate sobre la cuestión militar," *La Nación,* 20 July 1992, 9. In Fontana's 1991–92 survey, when Argentine officers were asked about the possibility of a coup, the responses were consistently negative. Fontana, "Percepciones," 10.

21. Interview AR732196 and interviews with Lic. Ernesto López (6 August 1996), Dr. Rosendo Fraga (7 August 1996), and Dr. Oscar Camilión (13 August 1996), Buenos Aires.

22. For a comprehensive and balanced account, see Lawrence Freedman and Virginia Gamba-Stonehouse, *Signals of War: The Falklands Conflict of 1982* (Princeton, N.J.: Princeton University Press, 1991).

23. James McGuire, "Interim Government and Democratic Consolidation: Argentina in Comparative Perspective," in Yossi Shain and Juan Linz (eds.), *Between States: Interim Governments and Democratic Transitions* (New York: Cambridge University Press, 1995), 189–190, disputes the standard characterization of Argentina as a transition by collapse of the preceding regime, but even if the Peronist candidate had won in 1983, military defeat, internal divisions, and high levels of societal rejection would have produced fewer military conditions on the political transition than any other Latin American case.

24. See Anita Isaacs, *Military Rule and Transition in Ecuador* (Pittsburgh: University of Pittsburgh Press, 1993); Rafael Quintero y Erika Silva, *Ecuador: Una nación en ciernes* Tomo III (Quito: FLACSO, ABYA-YALA, 1991), 225–268; Conaghan, *Restructuring Domination;* John Martz, *Politics and Petroleum in Ecuador* (New Brunswick, N.J.: Transaction Books, 1987); and David Schodt, *Ecuador: An Andean Enigma* (Boulder, Colo.: Westview Press, 1987).

25. Interviews AR401592 and AR334392.

26. Interviews AR168185 and AR939692, respectively.

27. Interviews AR443785, AR485085, AR401592, and AR264792, respectively. The idea of the armed forces as guardians or saviors was explicitly rejected in ten of the Argentine interviews, compared to only one such statement from an Ecuadorian officer.

28. Interview EC154191. On the tendency to maintain existing beliefs, see Harold Lasswell, *Power and Society* (New Haven, Conn.: Yale University Press, 1950), 113–14, and Robert Abelson, "Beliefs Are Like Possessions," *Journal for the Theory of Social Behavior* 16, 3 (October 1986): 223–250.

29. Robert Abelson, "Conviction," *American Psychologist* 43, 4 (1988): 270, 273; and "Conjunctive Explanations: When Two Arguments Are Better Than One," *Journal of Personal and Social Psychology* 47, 5 (1984): 935.

30. On the inoculation effect of prior debate, see William McGuire and Demetrios Papageorgis, "Effectiveness of Forewarning in Developing Resistance to Persuasion,"

Public Opinion Quarterly 26, 1 (1962): 24–34; and Abelson, "Beliefs Are Like Possessions," 233–235.

31. "The establishment of a belief as commonsensically, necessarily true privileges it—by protecting it from reevaluation in the face of events or pressures that might otherwise affect it." Ian Lustic, *Unsettled States, Disputed Lands: Britain and Ireland, France and Algeria, Israel and the West Bank-Gaza* (Ithaca, N.Y.: Cornell University Press, 1993), 43.

32. A number of officers made this comparison spontaneously, which supports the hypothesis that the history of previous military regimes is reevaluated over time in comparison to subsequent civilian performance. Dirk Kruijt, "Peru: The State Under Siege," in Millett and Gold-Bliss, *Beyond Praetorianism*, 269, reports the same kind of comparison among Peruvian officers.

33. See, e.g., Guillermo O'Donnell, "Transitions, Continuities, and Paradoxes," in Mainwaring, O'Donnell, and Valenzuela, *Issues in Democratic Consolidation*, 33; Catherine Conaghan and Rosario Espinal, "Unlikely Transitions to Uncertain Regimes? Democracy Without Compromise in the Dominican Republic and Ecuador," Helen Kellogg Institute for International Studies Working Paper, no. 139, University of Notre Dame, May 1990, 3; and Claude Welch and Arthur Smith, *Military Role and Rule* (North Scituate, Mass.: Duxbury Press, 1974), 248–249.

34. Interviews AR583185, AR875385, AR200985, and AR186185.

35. "Un año después del levantamiento," *Hoy*, 4 June 1991, 5A. See also Leon Zamosc, "Agrarian Protest and the Indian Movement in the Ecuadorian Highlands," *LARR* 29, 3 (1994): 37–68.

36. In constant currency. Thomas Scheetz, "The Evolution of Public Sector Expenditures: Changing Political Priorities in Argentina, Chile, Paraguay, and Peru," *Journal of Peace Research* 29, 2 (1992): 186; and "Military Expenditures in South America," U.N. Disarmament Center, Lima, forthcoming, 21.

37. Ernesto López, *Ni la ceniza ni la gloria: Sistema político y cuestión militar en los años de Alfonsín* (Buenos Aires: Universidad Nacional de Quilmes, 1994), 76.

38. Capt. de Navío (r) Dr. Carlos Raimundi, "Los gastos para la defensa nacional," *La Nación*, 13 November 1986, n.p.; and Scheetz, "Military Expenditures," table 5.

39. Luis Torres, cited in Frank Zagorski, *Democracy vs. National Security: Civil-Military Relations in Latin America* (Boulder, Colo.: Lynne Rienner Publishers, 1992), 156.

40. See chap. 5 and Deborah Norden, *Military Rebellion in Argentina: Between Coups and Consolidation* (Lincoln: University of Nebraska Press, 1996); David Pion-Berlin and Ernesto López, "A House Divided: Crisis, Cleavage, and Conflict in the Argentine Army," in Edward Epstein (ed.), *The New Argentine Democracy: The Search for a Successful Formula* (Westport, Conn.: Praeger Publishers, 1992), 63–96; Ernesto López, *El último levantamiento* (Buenos Aires: Editorial Legasa, 1988); and Hugo Chumbita, *Los carapintada* (Buenos Aires: Editorial Planeta Argentina, 1990).

41. World Bank, *Argentina: From Insolvency to Growth* (Washington, D.C.: World Bank Country Study, 1993), 250. Expenditure data are from U.S. Arms Control and Disarmanent Agency data cited in n.a., "Gasto militar latinoamericano," *Informe*, Area de Relaciones Internacionales y Militares, FLACSO-Chile, August 1994, 4. See also Rosendo Fraga, *Menem y la Cuestión Militar* (Buenos Aires: Editorial Centro de Estudios Unión para la Nueva Mayoría, 1991).

42. "Es tema de debate interno, dice canciller sobre presupuesto de las FFAA," *Hoy,* 8 January 1991, n.p.; "Presupuesto de FFAA se justifica, según PSC," *Hoy,* 9 January 1991, n.p.

43. Gaitán Villavicencio, "Crisis económica y desmovilización social. La década de los ochenta: Actores y desmovilización social," *Síntesis: Revista documental de ciencias sociales iberoamericanas* 16 (January–April 1992): 222.

44. Inter-American Development Bank, *Latin America in Graphs: Two Decades of Economic Trends* (Baltimore: Johns Hopkins University Press, 1992), 7, 39, 103; for Ecuador, 16, 48, 112. Ecuador's debt repayment level was substantially lower after 1985, suggesting that the milder recession was achieved in part by deferring the economic and political costs of repayment onto subsequent governments.

45. Edgardo Catterberg, *Argentina Confronts Politics: Political Culture and Public Opinion in the Argentine Transition to Democracy* (Boulder, Colo.: Lynne Rienner Publishers, 1991), 91.

46. Centro de Estudios Unión para la Nueva Mayoría, "Se mantuvieron estables los conflictos laborales durante el mes de agosto," Buenos Aires, September 1992, 24–27.

47. For insightful analyses, see Catharine Conaghan, "Politicians Against Parties: Discord and Disconnection in Ecuador's Party System," in Scott Mainwaring and Timothy Scully (eds.), *Building Democratic Institutions: Party Systems in Latin America* (Stanford, Calif.: Stanford University Press, 1995), 434–458; Anita Isaacs, "Ecuador: Democracy Standing the Test of Time?" in Jorge Dominguez and Abraham Lowenthal (eds.), *Constructing Democratic Governance: Latin America and the Caribbean in the 1990s,* Part III (Baltimore: Johns Hopkins University Press, 1996), 43–47; Simón Pachano, *Democracia sin sociedad* (Quito: ILDIS, 1996), 30–110; and *Los diputados: Una élite política* (Quito: Corporación Editora Nacional, 1991), 91–92, 128–130, 147.

48. Fernando Bustamante, "Fuerzas Armadas en el Ecuador: ¿Puede institucionalizarse la subordinación al poder civil?" *Síntesis: Revista documental de las ciencias sociales iberoamericanas* 16 (January–April 1992): 186–187.

49. "President Walks Out of Congress," *LAWR* WR-95-32 (24 August 1995): 377; *LAWR* WR-94-12 (31 March 1994): 154; and n.a., "Ecuador: Una Peligrosa Crisis de Liderazgo," *Peace and Security in the Americas* (October 1993): 3. See also Conaghan, "Loose Parties, 'Floating' Politicians, and Institutional Stress," 328–359; and Nick Mills, *Crisis, Conflicto, y Consenso: Ecuador 1979–1984* (Quito: Corporación Editora Nacional, 1984).

50. See Carlos Acuña, "Business Interests, Dictatorship, and Democracy in Argentina," in Ernest Bartell and Leigh Payne (eds.), *Business and Democracy in Latin America* (Pittsburgh: University of Pittsburgh Press, 1995), 7–9; and "Politics and Economics in Argentina of the Nineties," in William Smith, Carlos Acuña, and Eduardo Gamarra (eds.), *Democracy, Markets, and Structural Reform in Latin America* (New Brunswick, N.J.: Transaction Publishers, 1993), 59–60.

51. Interview AR902585.

52. Catterberg, *Argentina Confronts Politics,* 56.

53. From survey data provided by Jaime Durán Barba, director of the *Informe Confidencial* and the Instituto de Estudios de la Opinión Pública (IESOP), who also provided space in IESOP's regular poll for questions regarding public perceptions of different types of military intervention in politics. Both surveys are based on stratified random samples of 400 persons each in Quito and Guayaquil, with an estimated error margin of

5 percent. For the sake of brevity, the Quito and Guayaquil results are averaged, rather than reported separately. See also Forrest Colburn, "El abismo entre los ecuatorianos y sus partidos políticos," *Cuadernos de Economía* 6 (February 1996): 137.

54. "Ecuatorianos se declaran defensores de la democracia," *Hoy* (ECNET), bulletin 31, October 1996, n.p. See also Marta Lagos, "Latin America's Smiling Mask," *Journal of Democracy* 8, 3 (1997): 133.

55. Interview AR764992.

56. Interview AR669992.

57. Interview AR485085.

58. Interviews AR651892 and AR939692.

59. Interview EC137691.

60. Interview EC800391.

61. Interviews EC880591 and EC154491.

62. Interviews EC890591 (*"no es conveniente"*) and EC056391, respectively.

63. Gen. José Villamil de la Cadena, inaugural lecture of the seminar "Armed Forces, Development, and Democracy," in Hernán Andrade Tobar et al., *Fuerzas Armadas, Desarrollo y Democracia* (Quito: ILDIS, EDLA, Academia de Guerra de la Fuerza Terrestre, Ediciones ABYA-YALA, 1996), 8.

64. See Gabriel Marcella, "War and Peace in the Amazon: Implications for the United States and Latin America of the Ecuador-Peru Conflict," Strategic Studies Institute, U.S. Army War College, Carlisle Barracks, Penn., November 1995, 1, 10–11, 14–16.

65. "Arteaga Rules in Ecuador, But for How Long Is Anybody's Guess," *LAWR* WR-97-07 (11 Februrary 1997): 73; Diana Jean Schemo, "Ecuador's Military Code: Democracy Is Better," *New York Times,* 11 February 1997, A3; and "Ecuadorean Crisis Over, Presidency Ends Peacefully," 10 February 1997, A1, A6.

66. Stepan, *Rethinking Military Politics,* 30–31.

67. O'Donnell and Schmitter, *Transitions from Authoritarian Rule,* 15–36. See also Andrés Fontana, *Fuerzas Armadas, Partidos Políticos, and Transición a la Democracia en Argentina* (Buenos Aires: Estudios CEDES, 1984).

68. Martin Needler, *Political Development in Latin America: Instability, Violence, and Evolutionary Change* (New York: Random House, 1968), 66. See Deborah Norden's insightful analysis of the differences between branches of the Argentine army, *Military Rebellion in Argentina,* 113–119, 169–178.

69. Interview AR595485.

70. The problems of defining the ideological spectrum and classifying officers in terms of their positions on that spectrum are too extensive for full discussion here. The operational measures used in this analysis include responses to the question "Which party best represents your political ideals?" Often officers said "None," but then went on to identify themselves as liberals, conservatives, etc. With retired officers, I also often asked for whom they voted in recent elections. Taking all of this information and their responses to a series of questions about U.S. policy in Latin America, I then attempted to classify each officer in terms of ideological position and party preference. The first measure suffers from the variable meaning of terms like "center" or "center right"; the second suffers from the wide range of ideological positions represented within the more broad-based parties, particularly the Peronists, who span the spectrum from nationalist conservatives to Montonero sympathizers. Donald Hodges, *Argentina's Dirty War: An Intellectual Biography* (Austin: University of Texas Press, 1991), 44–46, and Deborah

Norden, *Military Rebellion in Argentina,* 119–125, also distinguish liberal, Peronist, and Catholic nationalist factions in the Argentine military. Among students of civil-military relations, Alain Rouquié has most consistently recognized the ideological differences among Latin American officers. See "The Military in Latin American Politics Since 1930," in Leslie Bethell (ed.), *The Cambridge History of Latin America,* vol. 6, *Latin America Since 1930: Economy, Society and Politics* (Cambridge: Cambridge University Press, 1994), 246–247, 263–270.

71. Examples of the nationalist, reformist perspective include Gen. Paco Moncayo Gallegos, *Fuerzas Armadas y Sociedad* (Quito: Corporación Editora Nacional, 1995); Crnl. de E. M. Alberto Molina Flores, *Las Fuerzas Armadas Ecuatorianas: Paz y Desarrollo,* 2d ed. (Quito: ALDHU, 1994); and selections by Gen. José Villamil de la Cadena y General Paco Moncayo in *Fuerzas Armadas, Desarrollo y Democracia* (Quito: ILDIS, CELA, Academia de Guerra Terrestre, Ediciones Abya-Yala, 1996), 7–16 and 71–85, respectively.

72. "Liberal" is used here in its Latin American sense to denote those who support free market and free trade policies.

73. See Ernesto López, "Doctrinas militares en Argentina: 1932–1980," in Carlos Moneta, Ernesto López, and Aníbal Romero, *La Reforma Militar* (Buenos Aires: Editorial Legasa, 1985), 116–124.

74. Interviews AR305385 and AR608292, respectively.

75. Interview AR133992.

76. Interviews AR326485 and AR922192.

77. Interview AR081892. Reactions to Carlos Escudé's argument for dependency on the United States, arguably the blueprint for Menem's foreign policy, constitute a simple litmus test for identifying nationalists and internationalists. *Realismo periférico: Fundamentos para la nueva política argentina* (Buenos Aires: Editorial Planeta Argentina, 1992).

78. Interviews AR762992 and EC210591, respectively.

79. Carlos Acuña and Catalina Smulovitz, "¿Ni olvido ni perdón? Derechos humanos y tensiones cívico-militares en la transición argentina," Centro de Estudios de Estado y Sociedad (CEDES), Documento 69, Buenos Aires, July 1991, 39. The original Semana Santa revolt was code named Operation Dignity. The revolts that occurred under Seineldín's leadership were named "Virgin of Luján" and "Virgin of the Valley." Deborah Norden, "The Rise of the Lieutenant Colonels," *Latin American Perspectives* 23, 3 (1996): 81.

80. Interviews AR942092 and AR401592. See also Interviews 924292, AR325092, AR572292, and AR726092.

81. Interviews EC579191, EC154491, and EC229391.

82. Cf. Peter Haas, "Introduction: Epistemic Communities and International Policy Coordination," *International Organization* 46, 1 (Winter 1992): 2–3; and Maarten Hajer, "Discourse Coalitions and the Institutionalization of Practice: The Case of Acid Rain in Britain," in Frank Fischer and John Forester (eds.), *The Argumentative Turn in Policy Analysis and Planning* (Durham, N.C.: Duke University Press, 1993), 45.

83. See Nancy Pennington and Reid Hastie, "A Cognitive Theory of Juror Decision Making: The Story Model," *Cardozo Law Review* 13, 2–3 (November 1991): 527–528; and Abelson "Beliefs Are Like Possessions," 235–239.

84. A 1985 survey focusing on trust in thirteen public institutions found the armed

forces ranked dead last in Argentina and Uruguay. In contrast, the military ranked third highest in Brazil, above Congress and the presidency. Cited in Howard Wiarda, *Latin American Politics: A New World of Possibility* (Belmont, Calif.: Wadsworth Publishing, 1995), 98.

85. Interviews AR050492, AR474192, AR726092, AR568292, and AR529292, respectively.

86. Interviews EC229391, EC287691, and EC435691, respectively.

87. Interview EC162891.

88. Conaghan, *Restructuring Domination*, 138–141; Isaacs, *Military Rule and Transition*, 69–84; and Martz, *Politics and Petroleum in Ecuador*, 117–123.

89. Interviews EC287691 and EC473991.

90. Margarita Vallejo, "Los roles de las fuerzas armadas ecuatorianas en el postretorno: Un acercamiento a su análisis," master's thesis, Facultad Latinoamericano de Ciencias Sociales (FLACSO), Sede Quito, Ecuador, March 1992, 30–70.

91. Cf. "Brizola Issues Coup 'Invitation,'" *LAWR* WR-95-20 (1 June 1995): 236.

92. Stepan, *Rethinking Military Politics*, 128–145; Welch, *No Farewell to Arms*, 199.

93. Interview AR595885.

94. World Bank, *Argentina*, 313. See also Rosendo Fraga, *La cuestión militar en los Noventa* (Buenos Aires: Editorial Centro de Estudios Unión para la Nueva Mayoría, 1993), 220.

95. Francisco Rojas Aravena, "El proceso de asignación de gasto militar en América Latina," in Francisco Rojas Aravena (ed.), *Gasto militar en América Latina: Procesos de decisiones y actores claves* (Santiago: CINDE y FLACSO-Chile, 1994), 57–58.

96. See, e.g., the comparisons in Fraga, *La Cuestión Militar*, 127–172; and Wendy Hunter, "Contradictions of Civilian Control: Argentina, Brazil, and Chile in the 1990's," *Third World Quarterly* 15, 4 (1994): 633–653.

Chapter 4: National Security

1. See, e.g., Stepan, "The New Professionalism," in Lowenthal and Fitch, *Armies and Politics*, 134–150.

2. *A Ideologia da Segurança Nacional: O Poder Militar na América Latina,* A. Veiga Fialho, trans. (Rio de Janeiro: Editora Civilização S.A., 1978), 13, 30, 47, and 50.

3. Comblin, *A Ideologia da Segurança Nacional,* 56–59, 70–88, and 218–224. Cf. Margaret Crahan, "National Security Ideology and Human Rights," in Margaret Crahan (ed.), *Human Rights and Basic Needs in the Americas* (Washington, D.C.: Georgetown University Press, 1982), 100–127.

4. Claude Welch, "Military Disengagement from Politics: Paradigms, Processes, or Random Events," *Armed Forces and Society* 18, 3 (1992): 323–342. See J. Patrice McSherry, *Incomplete Transition: Military Power and Democracy in Argentina* (New York: St. Martin's Press, 1997), 117–147, for a similar argument but a different conclusion about Argentina.

5. See Robert Lane, *Political Ideology* (New York: Free Press, 1962), 14–15.

6. Cf. Comblin, *A Ideologia da Segurança Nacional,* 13–16.

7. Geopolitics is another common component of military writing on national security. See Pion-Berlin, "Latin American National Security Doctrines," 413; Jack Child,

"Geopolitical Thinking in Latin America," *LARR* 14, 2 (1979): 89–111, and "Geopolitical Thinking," in Goodman, Mendelson, and Rial, *The Military and Democracy,* 143–163.

8. See Crnl. Alfonso Littuma Arízaga, *Doctrina de Seguridad Nacional* (Caracas: Ministerio de Defensa, 1967). Cf. General Golbery do Couto e Silva, quoted in María Helena Moreira Alves, *State and Opposition in Military Brazil* (Austin: University of Texas Press, 1985), 20–21.

9. In the "Officer's Library" published by the Argentine army officers' club, readings on communism and guerrilla warfare increase markedly after 1961. Books on subversion appear in 1967 and 1970. The term "national security" first appears as a title in 1969.

10. See Gral. Juan Gugliamelli, "Fuerzas Armadas para la Liberación Nacional," *Estratégia* (Buenos Aires) 5, 23 (1973): 7–30.

11. Skidmore, *The Politics of Military Rule in Brazil,* 43, 97–99.

12. N.a., "La realidad de la situación del hombre y de la sociedad en los principales países con gobiernos marxistas," *Revista de Educación del Ejército* 31 (1977): 51–53.

13. N.a., "Subversión en el ámbito educativo (Conozcamos a nuestro enemigo)," *Boletín de Educación del Ejército* 30 (1977): 79, 83 (emphasis added).

14. N.a., "Forma de orientar el desarrollo de temas sugeridas por la DEE, contribuyentes al logro de objetivos en lo ético-espiritual," *Boletín de Educación del Ejército* 29 (1977): 66.

15. Perelli, "From Counterrevolutionary Warfare to Political Awakening," 27. Cf. George Lopez, "National Security Ideology as an Impetus to State Violence and State Terror," in Michael Stohl and George Lopez (eds.), *Government Violence and Repression* (New York: Greenwood Press, 1986), 73–95.

16. Interviews AR780385, AR037885, AR168185, AR346785, AR595485, and AR682585.

17. Interviews AR764992, AR200985, AR346785, AR595485, and AR897792.

18. Interview AR004585.

19. Stepan, *The State and Society,* 26 fn. 58, 26–45. See also Howard Wiarda, *Latin American Politics: A New World of Possibility* (Belmont, Calif.: Wadsworth Publishing, 1995), 85–94.

20. Interview with a member of Ecuador's 1963–66 military junta, Quito, Ecuador, 1971.

21. Interviews AR719392, EC137791, and EC137691.

22. Loveman and Davies, *Antipolitics,* 3–14, and passim.

23. Cf. Guillermo O'Donnell, "Delegative Democracy," *Journal of Democracy* 5, 1 (1994): 59–62.

24. Interviews AR039985, AR346785, AR326692, and EC229391.

25. Tnte. Crnl. Julio Carretto, *La ideología y la nueva guerra* (Buenos Aires: Circulo Militar, 1987), 18, 20, 21.

26. Interviews AR595485, AR793785, and EC952191.

27. Interviews EC445591, EC056391, and an anonymous interview conducted by Margarita Vallejo, Quito, 1991.

28. Fernando Bustamante, "Fuerzas Armadas en el Ecuador: ¿Puede institucionalizarse la subordinación al poder civil?" *Síntesis: Revista documental de las ciencias sociales iberoamericanas* 16 (January–April 1992): 190–191.

29. Interview 302487.

30. Interviews AR443785 and AR875385, respectively.

31. As noted previously, these are nonrandom samples, with some significant differences in the composition of each sample. Accordingly, small differences in responses should be disregarded.

32. The chief military advisor to Brazil's president concurred. "Argentina presents hardly any military threat." Gen. Alberto Cardoso, quoted in "Brazil: Bringing Defence Thinking Up to Date," *LAWR* WR-96-45 (21 November 1996): 532. See also Mario Pastore, "Democracia, defensa, integración y desarrollo en América Latina," *Fuerzas Armadas y Sociedad* 12, 1 (1997): 36–41; and Deborah Norden, "The Transformation of Argentine Security," in Millett and Gold-Bliss, *Beyond Praetorianism*, 251–255.

33. Interview AR325092.

34. Crahan, "National Security Ideology," 111–112.

35. Rosendo Fraga, *La cuestión militar 1987–1989* (Buenos Aires: Editorial Centro de Estudios Unión para la Nueva Mayoría, 1989), 97–103; López, *Ni la ceniza ni la gloria*, 85–86.

36. World Bank, *Argentina: From Insolvency to Growth* (Washington, D.C.: World Bank, 1993), annex 7.1, table 4.5.

37. Congreso de la Nación Argentina, *Ley de Seguridad Internal* (Buenos Aires, n.p., 1992); and Ministerio de Defensa, "Defensa Nacional Decreto 1116/96," Buenos Aires, 2 October 1996, Base de Datos SER en el 2000.

38. N.a., *Verde Olive* 2 (June 1992): 2.

39. This section draws from Margarita Vallejo, "Los roles de las fuerzas armadas." See also Gen. de Brigada Miguel Iturralde, "Las fuerzas armadas del Ecuador en el desarrollo nacional" (Cuenca, Ecuador: Ministerio de Defensa Nacional, 1991), n.p., which cites more than a dozen mixed enterprises with an estimated 15,000 employees.

40. "Ley de Seguridad Nacional" (Quito: Ediciones Jurídicas, n.d.). The 1991 parade celebrating the independence of Guayaquil, for example, included 10,000 high school students participating in volunteer military training, half of them women. Personal communication from Margarita Vallejo, November 26, 1991, 1.

41. Interview EC166491.

42. Interviews EC287691, EC056391, EC445591, and EC445791.

43. *LAWR* WR-94-16 (5 May 1994): 190.

44. Vallejo, "Los roles de las fuerzas armadas," 67.

45. Ibid., 4.

46. The complexity of the issue stems in part from the difficulty of access to the official manuals of the military intelligence schools. Articles on revolutionary war and subversion appear in various military journals, but these are relatively few in number and often varied in content. Hence it is not easy to infer which, if any, of these represents the prevailing "doctrine" of revolutionary war in a particular military institution.

47. Carretto, *La ideología y la nueva guerra*, 1–15, 39–47. Carretto is a prominent member of Rico's faction of the *carapintadas*.

48. Ibid., 64, 75–79.

49. Ibid., 115.

50. Interviews AR200985 and AR349985. See also interview AR875385 quoted above.

51. N.a., "Los hombres del Presidente," typescript, n.d., n.p.

52. Capt. de Corbeta (r) Luis Pons, *La Violencia Antidemocrática* (Buenos Aires: Colección Biblioteca de Camarote, 1990).

53. Cf. n.a., "Las características y fines de la concepción democrática," *Revista de Educación del Ejército* 31 (1979): 34–36.

54. Pons, *La Violencia Antidemocrática*, 88–99.

55. Ibid., 21, 23, 106, 123–125.

56. José Manuel Ugarte, *Seguridad Interior* (Buenos Aires: Fundación Arturo Illia para la Democracia y la Paz, 1990). The applicability of the European experience with terrorist movements such as the Red Brigades to the Argentine context is a major point of contention, particularly in relation to the 1970s.

57. Ibid., 240, 239.

58. Interviews AR808685, AR346785, and Tnte. Crnl. (r) Mario Orsolini, "Organización Armada Clandestina (OAC) Montoneros: Sus Proyectos y Planes 1966–1983," unpublished ms., Buenos Aires, n.d., 35. See also the "Final Document of the Military Junta Regarding the War Against Subversion and Terrorism: Fundamental Concepts, 1983," in Loveman and Davies, *Antipolitics*, 163–170.

59. Some critics preferred execution after a summary court martial—in effect, a formal legality—rather than substantive protection for human rights under the rule of law. Interviews AR924992, AR897792, and AR453085.

60. Interviews AR598592 and AR951492.

61. "Half-buried 'Dirty War' Is Exhumed," *LAWR* WR-95-17 (11 May 1995): 194–195; "Argentina: Balza Replies," *LAWR* WR-95-31 (17 August 1995): 372.

62. Interview 389692.

63. Gral. Martín Balza, "Conceptos expresados por el Gral. Balza a los egresados de los institutos de formación del Ejército," typescript, Buenos Aires, n.d.

64. Interview EC287691.

65. Interviews EC435691, EC056391, and EC952191, respectively.

66. Interview EC445591. See Berta García Gallegos, "El concepto de 'Seguridad Interna' en el Marco de las Relaciones Sociedad-Fuerzas Armadas en el Ecuador," in n.a., *Diálogo Civil-Militar* (Quito: Programa de Estudios Interamericanos, Pontificia Universidad Católica del Ecuador, 1997), 103–109.

67. Fitch, *Coup d'Etat as a Political Process*, 136.

68. See, e.g., the military speeches in Loveman and Davies, *Antipolitics*, 193–303.

69. Interview AR200885.

70. N.a., "Ecuador: Una peligrosa crisis," 3–4.

71. E.g., the works of Herbert Simon, *Models of Man* (New York: John Wiley & Sons, 1957), 196–206, and *Reason in Human Affairs* (Stanford, Calif.: Stanford University Press, 1983), 11–29, 66–97; James March, "Theories of Choice and Making Decisions," *Knowledge, Information, and Decisions* (1992): 29–39; and John Holland, "Complex Adaptive Systems," *Daedulus* 121, 1 (1992): 17–30.

72. See, e.g., the journals *Seguridad Estratégica Regional* (Buenos Aires), *Fuerzas Armadas y Sociedad* (Santiago), the working papers of the Comisión Sudamericana de Paz (Santiago) and the Fundación Simón Rodríguez (Buenos Aires), and Juan Somavía and José Miguel Insulza (eds.), *Seguridad Democrática Regional: Una concepción alternativa* (Caracas, Venezuela: Editorial Nueva Sociedad, 1990).

73. Hernán Patiño Mayer, "The Future of Cooperative Hemispheric Security in the Americas," in Millett and Gold-Bliss, *Beyond Praetorianism,* 7–8.

Chapter 5: *Military Policy and Democratic Consolidation*

1. Guillermo O'Donnell, "Challenges to Democratization in Brazil," *World Policy Journal* 5 (Spring 1988): 281. See also Adam Przeworski, "The Games of Transition," in Mainwaring, O'Donnell, and Valenzuela, *Issues in Democratic Consolidation,* 131–134.

2. Andrés Fontana, "La política militar en un contexto de transición: Argentina 1983–1989," paper presented to the CEDES-Schell Center for Human Rights conference, "Transición a la Democracia en Argentina," Yale University, March 1990, 2.

3. David Pion-Berlin, "Between Confrontation and Accommodation: Military and Government Policy in Democratic Argentina," *Journal of Latin American Studies* 23 (1991): 546. See also Albert Hirschman, *Exit, Voice, and Loyalty: Responses to Decline in Firms, Organizations, and States* (Cambridge, Mass.: Harvard University Press, 1970); and Adam Przeworski, *Democracy and the Market: Political and Economic Reforms in Eastern Europe and Latin America* (Cambridge: Cambridge University Press, 1991), 29–32.

4. For general overviews, see Felipe Aguero, "The Military and the Limits to Democratization in South America," in Mainwaring, O'Donnell, and Valenzuela, *Issues in Democratic Consolidation,* 153–198; Pion-Berlin, "Military Autonomy and Emerging Democracies," 83–102; and Zagorski, *Democracy vs. National Security.* For comparative analysis of selected countries, see also Stepan, *Rethinking Military Politics;* Acuña and Smulovitz, "Adjusting the Armed Forces to Democracy," 13–38; Linz and Stepan, *Problems of Democratic Transition;* Wendy Hunter, *Politicians on the Advance: Eroding Military Influence in Brazil* (Chapel Hill: University of North Carolina Press, 1997); and David Pion-Berlin, *Through Corridors of Power: Institutions and Civil-Military Relations in Latin America* (University Park: Pennsylvania State University Press, 1997).

5. In addition to the works cited in the previous note, see Ernesto López, *Ni la ceniza ni la gloria: Actores, sistema político y cuestión militar en los años de Alfonsín* (Buenos Aires: Universidad Nacional de Quilmes, 1994); *El último levantamiento* (Buenos Aires: Editorial Legasa, 1988); Ernesto López and David Pion-Berlin, *Democracia y cuestión militar* (Buenos Aires: Universidad Nacional de Quilmes, 1996); Deborah Norden, *Military Rebellion in Argentina: Between Coups and Consolidation* (Lincoln: University of Nebraska Press, 1996); Fraga, *La Cuestión Militar 1987–1989;* and Prudencio García, *El drama de la autonomía militar: Argentina bajo las Juntas Militares* (Madrid: Alianza Editorial, 1995).

6. Carlos Acuña and William Smith, "The Politics of Arms Production and the Arms Race Among the New Democracies of Argentina, Brazil, and Chile," in Lars Schoultz, William Smith, and Augusto Varas (eds.), *Security, Democracy, and Development in U.S.-Latin American Relations* (New Brunswick, N.J.: Transaction Publishers, 1994), 208–213.

7. In practice, the chiefs of staff for each service have maintained most of their traditional place in the chain of command. Personal communications from Dr. Virgilio Beltrán, former Subsecretary for Policy and Strategy, Ministry of Defense, Buenos Aires, 29 August and 5 September 1997.

8. López, *Ni la ceniza ni la gloria*, 123; and Robert Potash, "Alfonsín and the Argentine Military," paper presented to LASA, Miami, December 1989, 5.

9. Ernesto López, "Argentina: Desarme de hecho y cooperación para la paz," paper presented to the Twelfth Meeting of RIAL (International Relations of Latin America), Santiago, Chile, 21–25 October 1990, 6.

10. On Alfonsín's human rights policies, see Alison Brysk, *The Politics of Human Rights in Argentina: Protest, Change, and Democratization* (Stanford, Calif.: Stanford University Press, 1994); Carlos Acuña and Catalina Smulovitz, "¿Ni olvido, ni perdón? Derechos humanos y tensiones cívico-militares en la transición argentina," CEDES, Documento 69, Buenos Aires, July 1991; Kathryn Crawford, "Due Obedience and the Rights of Victims: Argentina's Transition to Democracy," *Human Rights Quarterly* 12 (February 1990): 17–52; and Jaime Malamud Goti, *Game Without End: State Terror and the Politics of Justice* (Norman: University of Oklahoma Press, 1996).

11. Carina Perelli, "Settling Accounts with Blood Memory: The Case of Argentina," *Social Research* 59, 2 (1992): 430; and James McGuire, "Interim Government and Democratic Consolidation," in Juan Linz and Yossi Shain (eds.), *Between States: The Role of Interim Governments in Transitions to Democracy* (New York: Cambridge University Press, 1995), 189–190. However, even before the elections several courts had declared the self-amnesty to be unconstitutional. Brysk, *The Politics of Human Rights*, 61.

12. CONADEP, *Nunca Mas: Informe de la Comisión Nacional sobre la Desparición de Personas* (Buenos Aires: Editorial Universitaria de Buenos Aires, 1985), 54, 293. See also Alison Brysk, "The Politics of Measurement: The Contested Count of the Disappeared in Argentina," *Human Rights Quarterly* 16, 4 (1994): 676–692.

13. Brysk, *The Politics of Human Rights*, 80. See also Sergio Ciancaglini y Martín Granovsky, *Nada más que la verdad: El juicio a las Juntas* (Buenos Aires: Grupo Editorial Planeta, 1995).

14. Perelli, "Settling Accounts," 435–436.

15. Patricia Weiss Fagen, "Repression and State Security," and Juan Rial, "Makers and Guardians of Fear: Controlled Terror in Uruguay," in Juan Corradi, Patricia Weiss Fagen, and Manuel Antonio Garretón (eds.), *Fear at the Edge: State Terror and Resistance in Latin America* (Berkeley: University of California Press, 1992), 39–71 and 90–103, respectively; and Guillermo O'Donnell, "Democracia en la Argentina: *micro y macro*," Kellogg Institute Working Paper, no. 2, University of Notre Dame, December 1983, 2–14.

16. Critics dispute the characterization of the antisubversive campaign as an internal war. Daniel Frontalini and María Cristina Caiati claim that the ERP had only 120 men in the rural *foco* in Tucumán and that the Montoneros never numbered more than 400 armed insurgents. *El mito de la guerra sucia* (Buenos Aires: CELS, 1984), 63. According to more recent evidence, the ERP and Montoneros together had roughly 5,000 active participants in the mid-1970s. María Moyano, *Argentina's Lost Patrol: Armed Struggle, 1969–1979* (New Haven, Conn.: Yale University Press, 1995), 102–105.

17. Interview AR485085.

18. Fontana, "La política militar: 1983–1989," 12; and Norden, *Military Rebellion in Argentina*, 105.

19. Author's translation.

20. Zagorski, *Democracy vs. National Security*, 105.

21. For other appraisals, see the works cited above by Stepan, Linz and Stepan, Fontana, Aguero, López, Pion-Berlin, Potash, Norden, and Zagorski.

22. Norden, *Military Rebellion*, 136–138. Cf. Major Ernesto Barreiro, "If Menem Falters in Argentina," *New York Times*, March 23, 1990, A35.

23. Perelli, "Settling Accounts," 443.

24. Raúl Alfonsín, "The Transition toward Democracy in a Developing Country: The Case of Argentina," in Daniel Nelson (ed.), *After Authoritarianism: Democracy or Disorder* (Westport, Conn.: Greenwood Press, 1995), 18–20; and Carlos Nino, *Un país al margen de la ley: Estudio de la anomía como componente del subdesarrollo argentino* (Buenos Aires: Emecé Editores, 1992).

25. José Zalaquett, "Confronting Human Rights Violations Committed by Former Governments," in Apen Institute, *State Crimes: Punishment or Pardon* (Queenstown, Md.: Aspen Institute, 1989), 43.

26. Interviews AR559885, AR595885, AR780385, and AR793785. After the transition, Congress granted retroactive promotions to the "33 orientales" but, bowing to military opposition, did not reincorporate them to active duty.

27. López, *Ni la ceniza ni la gloria*, 73–86.

28. See Carlos Acuña, "Politics and Economics in Argentina of the Nineties," in William Smith, Carlos Acuña, and Eduardo Gamarra (eds.), *Democracy, Markets, and Structural Reform in Latin America* (Brunswick, N.J.: Transaction Publishers, 1993), 38–51; and Gary Wynia, *Argentina: Illusions and Realities*, 2d ed. (New York: Holmes & Meier, 1992), 194–213.

29. Acuña and Smulovitz, "¿Ni olvido ni perdón?" 26.

30. Military expenditures in 1993 were still 12 percent below the 1989 level. Data compiled by Thomas Scheetz, quoted in Pion-Berlin, *Through Corridors of Power*, 125.

31. Acuña and Smulovitz, "Adjusting the Armed Forces to Democracy," 18–19.

32. Acuña y Smulovitz, "¿Ni olvido ni perdón?" 40.

33. "Siempre listos: Los planes del Ejército ante el aumento de la tensión social," *Pagina/12* (Buenos Aires), 22 February 1990, 1–4; and Congreso de la Nación Argentina, *Ley de Seguridad Interior* (Buenos Aires: n.p., 1992).

34. Paul Zagorski, "Civil-Military Relations and Argentine Democracy: The Armed Forces Under the Menem Government," *Armed Forces and Society* 20, 3 (1994): 429–431; and Eduardo Barcelona y Julio Villalonga, *Relaciones Carnales: La verdadera historia de la construcción y destrucción del misil Condor II* (Buenos Aires: Editorial Planeta, 1992).

35. Interviews AR863896 and AR298896; and Thomas Scheetz, "La necesaria reforma militar argentina," *Nueva Sociedad* 138 (July–August 1995): 132–138.

36. Juan Rial, "Uruguay: From Restoration to the Crisis of Governability," in Jorge Dominguez and Abraham Lowenthal (eds.), *Constructing Democratic Governance: Latin America and the Caribbean in the 1990s* (Baltimore: Johns Hopkins University Press, 1996), 134–140; Charles Gillespie, *Negotiating Democracy: Politicians and Generals in Uruguay* (Cambridge: Cambridge University Press, 1991); Stepan, *Rethinking Military Politics*, 116–118; Linz and Stepan, *Problems of Democratic Transition*, 151–165; and Carina Perelli, "The Legacies of the Transitions to Democracy in Argentina and Uruguay," in Goodman, Mendelson, and Rial, *The Military and Democracy*, 39–54.

37. Carina Perelli, "Amnistía sí, amnistía no, amnistía puede ser," PEITHO, Monte-

video, n.d. See also Lawrence Weschler, *A Miracle, A Universe: Settling Accounts with Torturers* (New York: Pantheon Books, 1990).

38. "Lacalle Runs Into His First Problem," *LAWR* WR-90-07 (22 February 1990): 11.

39. Pion-Berlin, *Through Corridors of Power*, 184–194.

40. "General Sounds 'Red Alert' on Left," *LAWR* WR-91-16 (2 May 1991): 3; and "Military and Politics: Vindicating the Dirty War Toll," *LAWR* WR-96-38 (3 October 1996): 454.

41. Linz and Stepan, *Problems of Democratic Transition*, 159; Rial, "Uruguay," 139–140.

42. Philip Mauceri, "Military Politics and Counter-Insurgency in Peru," *Journal of Interamerican Studies and World Affairs* 33, 4 (1991): 83–109; Marcial Rubio Correa, "The Military in Peruvian Politics," in Varas, *Democracy Under Siege*, 40–44; and Cynthia McClintock, "The Prospects for Democratic Consolidation in a 'Least Likely' Case: Peru," *Comparative Politics* 21 (January 1989): 127–148.

43. Luis Abugattas, "Populism and After: The Peruvian Experience," in James Malloy and Mitchell Seligson, *Authoritarians and Democrats: Regime Transition in Latin America* (Pittsburgh: University of Pittsburgh Press, 1987), 139; Mauceri, "Military Politics and Counter-Insurgency in Peru," 93–94.

44. Aguero, "Limits to Democratization," 8–9.

45. Ibid., 8.

46. Enrique Obando, "The Power of Peru's Armed Forces," in Joseph Tulchin and Gary Bland (eds.), *Peru in Crisis: Dictatorship or Democracy* (Boulder, Colo.: Lynne Rienner Publishers, 1994), 112; and Dirk Kruijt, "Peru: The State Under Siege," in Millett and Gold-Bliss, *Beyond Praetorianism*, 283.

47. Mauceri, "Military Politics and Counter-Insurgency in Peru," 90–102.

48. Carol Graham, "Democracy in Crisis and the International Response," in Tuchin and Bland, *Peru in Crisis*, 2.

49. Cynthia McClintock, "The Breakdown of Constitutional Democracy in Peru," paper presented to LASA, Atlanta, 1994, 4, 14.

50. Aguero, *Soldiers, Civilians and Democracy*, 237.

51. McClintock, "The Breakdown of Constitutional Democracy in Peru," 12. See also Catharine Conaghan, "Polls, Political Discourse, and the Public Sphere: The Spin on Peru's Fuji-golpe," in Peter Smith (ed.), *Latin America in Comparative Perspective: New Approaches to Methods and Analysis* (Boulder, Colo.: Westview Press, 1995), 227–255.

52. David Scott Palmer, "Peru: Collectively Defending Democracy in the Western Hemisphere," in Farer, *Beyond Sovereignty*, 267–268, 273–275.

53. Susan Stokes, "Peru: The Rupture of Military Rule," in Dominguez and Lowenthal, *Constructing Democratic Governance*, 63, 67–68; Henry Pease García, "La democracia colapsada: Peru 1990–1992," unpublished ms., Lima, 1992, 19–25; Obando, "The Power of Peru's Armed Forces," 113–114; n.a., "Peruvian Cabinet," *LAWR* WR-92-15 (16 April 1992): 12; and Kruijt, "Peru: The State Under Siege," 284.

54. Obando, "The Power of Peru's Armed Forces," 115; McClintock, "The Breakdown of Constitutional Democracy in Peru," 18–19; and Phillip Mauceri, "State Reform, Coalitions, and the Neoliberal *Autogolpe* in Peru," *LARR* 30, 1 (1995): 20, 24–25, 30.

55. Coletta Youngers, "Update on Human Rights and Democracy Related Issues in Peru," *WOLA Brief,* Washington Office on Latin America, 25 November 1996, 2–10.

56. Obando, "The Power of Peru's Armed Forces," 114.

57. Larry Diamond, "Democracy in Latin America: Degrees, Illusions, and Directions for Consolidation," in Farer, *Beyond Sovereignty,* 64; Pease García, "La democracia colapsada," table 1.

58. See Catherine Conaghan, "Ecuador: The Politics of Locos," *Hemisphere* 1, 2 (Winter 1989): 13–15, and "Politicians Against Parties: Electoralism and the New Economic Fatalism in Ecuador," *Dialogues,* Occasional Paper Series, Florida International University, Miami, 1988; Fernando Bustamante, "Fuerzas Armadas en Ecuador: ¿Puede institucionalizarse la subordinación al poder civil?" in *Democracia y Fuerzas Armadas,* 129–160; and "The Armed Forces of Colombia and Ecuador in Comparative Perspective," in Varas, *Democracy Under Siege,* 17–34.

59. Interview EC445691.

60. Interviews EC226991, EC454291, and EC676091.

61. Interviews EC154191, EC290191, EC401991, EC393491, EC557091, and EC628091.

62. Interviews EC290191, EC952191, EC210591, and EC194591.

63. Interview EC952191.

64. Interview EC287691.

65. Interview EC383591.

66. See "Anti-corruption Net Cast Ever Wider," *LAWR* WR-95-37 (28 September 1995): 443; and "Congress Accepts President's Choice," *LAWR* WR-95-42 (2 November 1995): 502–503.

67. "FFAA Confirman Posición," *Hoy* (ECNET), bulletin, 25 September 1996.

68. Aguero, "Limits to Democratization," 13; and Jorge Zaverucha, "The 1988 Brazilian Constitution and Its Authoritarian Legacy: Formalizing Democracy while Gutting its Essence," paper presented to LASA, Guadalajara, April 1997, 8–9. See also Wendy Hunter, *Eroding Military Influence in Brazil: Politicians Against Soldiers* (Chapel Hill: University of North Carolina Press, 1997), 43–60; Stepan, *Rethinking Military Politics,* 69–127; Linz and Stepan, *Problems of Democratic Transition,* 166–189; Paul Zagorski, "The Brazilian Military Under the 'New Republic,'" *Review of Latin American Studies* 1, 2 (1988): 45–64; and Geraldo Lesbat Cavagnari Filho, "Autonomía militar y construcción del poder," in *Democracia y Fuerzas Armadas,* 47–89.

69. Wendy Hunter, "Contradictions of Civilian Control: Argentina, Brazil, and Chile in the 1990s," *Third World Quarterly* 15, 4 (1994): 643.

70. *LAWR* WR-90-19 (24 May 1990): 8–9. See also Daniel Zirker and Marvin Henberg, "Amazonia: Democracy, Ecology, and Brazilian Military Prerogatives in the 1990s," *Armed Forces and Society* 20, 2 (1994): 270, 274.

71. Ben Ross Schneider, "Brazil Under Collor: Anatomy of a Crisis," in Roderic Ai Camp (ed.), *Democracy in Latin America: Patterns and Cycles* (Wilmington, Del.: Scholarly Resources, 1996), 232–236; and Ken Serbin, "Collor's Impeachment and the Struggle for Change," *North-South Focus: Brazil* 2, 2 (1993): 1–4.

72. "Franco Rides the Military Tiger," *LAWR* WR-94-13 (7 April 1994): 152.

73. Hunter, "Contradictions of Civilian Control," 644–646.

74. Presidéncia da República, "Política de Defesa Nacional," Brasilia 1996, Base de Datos SER en el 2000.

75. Rizzo de Oliveira, "A adaptação dos militares á democracia no Brasil," 23–28;

and Scott Tollefson, "Civil-Military Relations: The Myth of Tutelary Democracy," paper presented to LASA, Washington, D.C., 1995, 9–10.

76. Jorge Zaverucha, "The 1988 Brazilian Constitution," 17–22.

77. David Pion-Berlin and Craig Arceneaux, "Tipping the Civil-Military Balance: Human Rights Policy and Institutions in Democratic Argentina and Chile," paper presented to LASA, Washington, D.C., 1995, 11. See also Robert Barros, "Consolidation Before Transition: The *Tribunal Constitucional* and Regime Change in Chile (1981–1988)," paper presented to the American Political Science Association, San Francisco, 1996, 3.

78. Brian Loveman, "*¿Misión Cumplida?* Civil-Military Relations and the Chilean Political Transition," *Journal of Interamerican Studies and World Affairs* 33, 3 (1991): 46–47.

79. Mark Ensalaco, "Military Prerogatives and the Stalemate of Chilean Civil-Military Relations," *Armed Forces and Society* 21, 2 (1995): 265; and Linz and Stepan, *Problems of Democratic Transition,* 208, fn. 11.

80. Peter Siavelis and Arturo Valenzuela, "Electoral Engineering and Democratic Stability: The Legacy of Authoritarian Rule in Chile," in Arend Lijphart and Carlos Waisman (eds.), *Institutional Design in New Democracies: Eastern Europe and Latin America* (Boulder, Colo.: Westview Press, 1996), 79–85.

81. Hunter, "Contradictions of Civilian Control," 647. See also Acuña and Smith, "The Politics of Arms Production," 214–218.

82. Gen. (r) Alejandro Medina Lois, statement to the International Seminar on "Estados Unidos y América Latina," FLACSO-Chile, Santiago, 21 June 1989. "General Zincke dio la voz del Ejército en materias candentes," *Crónica del hoy* (Santiago), 18 May 1989, 3; "Inquietudes en la trinchera," *Qué Pasa* (Santiago), n.p.; and "El programa militar de la oposición," *Apsi* (Santiago) 300 (17–23 April 1989), 14–19.

83. Pion-Berlin and Arcenaux, "Tipping the Balance," 14–16.

84. Ibid., 28; and Rhoda Rabkin, "The Aylwin Government and 'Tutelary' Democracy: A Concept in Search of a Case," *Journal of Interamerican Studies and World Affairs* 34, 4 (1992–93): 155.

85. "Don't Touch 'My' Men, Says Pinochet," *LAWR* WR-89-2 (26 October 1989): 3. As in Uruguay, military commanders could have ordered their subordinates not to appear in court, thus provoking a constitutional crisis.

86. Pion-Berlin and Arceneaux, "Tipping the Balance," 31, 25; and Rabkin, "The Aylwin Government and 'Tutelary' Democracy," 148–149.

87. Brian Loveman, "The Transition to Civilian Government in Chile," in Paul Drake and Iván Jasi (eds.), *The Struggle for Democracy in Chile,* rev. ed. (Lincoln: University of Nebraska Press, 1995), 312–314.

88. Jim Landers, "Chile's Army Still a Force," *Denver Post,* 26 July 1996, 22A; "Officers Stage a Massive Prison Demo," *LAWR* WR-95-29 (3 August 1995): 339; and Felipe Aguero, "Chile: South America's Success Story," *Current History* (March 1993): 132. For a thoughtful critique of the limitations of these policies, see Manuel Antonio Garretón, "Human Rights in Democratization Processes," in Elizabeth Jelin and Eric Hershberg (eds.), *Constructing Democracy: Human Rights, Citizenship, and Society in Latin America* (Boulder, Colo.: Westview Press, 1996), 42–52.

89. Loveman, "*¿Misión Cumplida?*" 66 fn. 17; and Loveman, "The Transition to Civilian Government in Chile," 316–320.

90. Kurt Weyland, "'Growth With Equity' in Chile's New Democracy?" *LARR* 32, 1 (1997): 47–48. Costa Rica also survived the debt crisis (1980–95) without an increase in the poverty rate. Osvaldo Hurtado, "Gobernabilidad, Democracia y Pobreza," Programa de las Naciones Unidas para el Desarrollo, Documento de Trabajo no. 7, November 1996, 28.

91. José Zalaquett Daher, "The Ethics of Responsibility: Human Rights: Truth and Reconciliation in Chile," *Issues in Human Rights*, paper no. 2, Washington Office on Latin America, 1991, 1; and Loveman, "*¿Misión Cumplida?*" 54–63.

92. See Francisco Rojas Aravena, "Transición y relaciones civil-militares en Chile en el nuevo marco internacional," Nueva Serie Flacso, Santiago, 1996, 11–14.

93. Rabkin, "The Aylwin Government and 'Tutelary' Democracy," 160–161.

94. "Chilean Military Slams Reforms and Claims Its Role as Institutional 'Counterweight,'" *LAWR* WR-92-30 (6 August 1992): 1.

95. Loveman, "*¿Misión Cumplida?*" 48–52.

96. "Armies and Politics in Latin America: Introduction to the First Edition," in Lowenthal and Fitch, *Armies and Politics*, 18–21. Arturo Valenzuela, "A Note on the Military and Social Science Theory," *Third World Quarterly* 7, 1 (1985): 138–140, argues that, without careful specification and operationalization, the relative institutionalization hypothesis can easily become a post hoc rationalization, rather than meaningful explanatory theory. Particularly on the civilian side of the equation, averaging across different kinds of political institutions involves complex, multidimensional judgments. Nevertheless, the measures of institutionalization suggested by Huntington — adaptability, autonomy, coherence, and organizational complexity — could be applied to both the military and political parties. See Scott Mainwaring and Timothy Scully (eds.), *Building Democratic Institutions: Party Systems in Latin America* (Stanford, Calif.: Stanford University Press, 1995), for useful measures of institutionalization, volatility, and fragmentation of party systems for twelve countries. On the military side, high professionalization is marked by meritocratic promotion patterns, extensive military schooling, and use of sophisticated technology.

97. Arturo Valenzuela, "Latin America: Presidentialism in Crisis," *Journal of Democracy* 4, 4 (1993): 8–11; and Scott Mainwaring, "Presidentialism, Multiparty Systems, and Democracy: The Difficult Equation," Kellogg Institute Working Paper, no. 144, University of Notre Dame, September 1990, 5–22.

98. Welch, *No Farewell to Arms*, 202.

99. Aguero, "The Military in the Processes of Political Democratization in South America and Southern Europe: Outcomes and Initial Conditions," paper presented to LASA, 1989; and "The Limits to Democratization," 18–25.

100. Aguero, "Democratic Consolidation," 13.

101. Pion-Berlin, *Through Corridors of Power*, 36–41.

102. Acuña and Smulovitz, "*¿Ni olvido ni perdón?*" 18.

103. Pion-Berlin, *Through Corridors of Power*, 122–133.

104. Interview AR863896.

105. Aguero, *Soldiers, Civilians, and Democracy*, 235–236. Cf. Rita Giacalone and Rexene Hanes de Acevedo, "The Military in a Subsidized Democracy: Venezuela," in

Constantine Danopoulos (ed.), *From Military to Civilian Rule* (London: Routledge, 1992), 146–147.

106. For a similar argument in a different policy area, see William Ascher, *Scheming for the Poor: The Politics of Redistribution in Latin America* (Cambridge, Mass.: Harvard University Press, 1984), 17–19, 25–47.

107. Interviews AR302485, AR039985, AR200985, AR349985, AR993885, and AR485085.

108. Zagorski, *Democracy vs. National Security,* 64–66, 200–201. The problem is, however, determining what is a "core" military interest. Large budget cuts or declining salaries may in fact be perceived as threatening the existence of the armed forces. See Gral. (r) Luciano Benjamín Menéndez, "La destrucción de nuestras Fuerzas Armadas," *La Nación,* 18 June 1992, 9.

109. Aguero, "Democratic Consolidation," 24–28.

110. Carlos Acuña and Catalina Smulovitz, "How to Guard the Guardians: Feasibility, Risks, and Benefits of Judicial Punishment of Past Human Rights Violations in New Democracies," paper presented to LASA, Washington, D.C., September 1995, 26.

111. Marcelo Cavarozzi and Oscar Landi, "Political Parties Under Alfonsín and Menem," in Edward Epstein (ed.), *The New Argentine Democracy: The Search for a Successful Formula* (Westport, Conn.: Praeger, 1992), 211–212. Cf. Ascher, *Scheming for the Poor,* 314–316.

112. Interview AR997396.

113. See Felipe Aguero, "The Military and Democracy in Venezuela," in Goodman, Mendelson, and Rial, *The Military and Democracy,* 257–276; and Rafael Bañon, "Democratizing the Spanish Military: Strategy of Reform, Organizational Format, and Democratic Consolidation," paper presented to the Inter-University Seminar on Armed Forces and Society, Baltimore, October 1989.

114. Virgilio Beltrán, "Precondiciones para las relaciones cívico-militares en la democracia: Algunas lecciones de América Latina," unpublished ms., Buenos Aires, 1996, 4.

115. Interview AR764992 and Pion-Berlin, *Through Corridors of Power,* 84–85.

116. Interview AR997396 and personal conversations with members of the Alfonsín administration.

117. See Pion-Berlin, *Through Corridors of Power,* 92–96.

118. Diamond, "Democracy in Latin America," 89–91.

119. Stepan, *Rethinking Military Politics,* 128–145. Claude Welch, "Two Strategies of Civilian Control," in Claude Welch (ed.), *Civilian Control of the Military: Theory and Cases from Developing Countries* (Albany: State University of New York Press, 1976), 318–326, argues for a combination of both strategies, encouraging military disengagement from politics and simultaneously strengthening civilian institutions and enhancing the legitimacy of the civilian regime.

120. Aguero, "Limits to Democratization," 8.

121. Louis Goodman, "Military Roles: Past and Present," in Larry Diamond and Marc Plattner (eds.), *Civil-Military Relations and Democracy* (Baltimore: Johns Hopkins University Press, 1996), 41–42.

Chapter 6: Democratic Professionalist Alternatives

1. See Loveman, *For La Patria*, passim.

2. See Capt. (r) Luis Eduardo Tibiletti and José Manuel Ugarte, "El rol de las comisiones de defensa parlamentarias como ámbito de interacción cívico-militar: Ideas para incrementar y fortalecer dicho rol," in National Democratic Institute for International Affairs, *Hacia una nueva relación: El papel de las Fuerzas Armadas en un gobierno democrático* (Washington, D.C.: National Democratic Institute, 1990), 147–167.

3. Scott Mainwaring and Timothy Scully, "Introduction: Party Systems in Latin America," in Mainwaring and Scully (eds.), *Building Democratic Institutions: Party Systems in Latin America* (Stanford, Calif.: Stanford University Press, 1995), 2–5, 21–28; and Dieter Nohlen, "Electoral Systems and Electoral Reform in Latin America," in Arend Lijphart and Carlos Waisman (eds.), *Institutional Design in New Democracies: Eastern Europe and Latin America* (Boulder, Colo.: Westview Press, 1996), 46–55.

4. Forrest Colburn, "La problemática democracia de Ecuador: ¿Que hacer?" *Cuadernos de Economía* 5 (December 1994): 6–13, and "El abismo entre los ecuatorianos y sus partidos políticos," *Cuadernos de Economía* 6 (February 1996): 137–146, provide useful suggestions for institutional reforms in Ecuador. See also Osvaldo Hurtado Larrea, *Gobernabilidad y reforma constitucional* (Quito: Corporación Editora Nacional, 1993).

5. See Diamond, "Democracy in Latin America," in Farer, *Beyond Sovereignty*, 78–86, for a detailed discussion of institutional changes to promote democratic consolidation.

6. Linz and Arturo Valenzuela, *The Failure of Presidential Democracy*; Arturo Valenzuela, "Latin America: Presidentialism in Crisis," *Journal of Democracy* 4, 4 (1993): 4–16; Juan Linz, Arend Lijphart, Arturo Valenzuela, and Oscar Godoy (eds.), *Hacia una democracia moderna: La opción parlamentaria* (Santiago: Ediciones Universidad Católica de Chile, 1990); Donald Horowitz, "Comparing Democratic Systems," *Journal of Democracy* 1, 4 (1990): 73–79; and Alfred Stepan and Cindy Skach, "Constitutional Frameworks and Democratic Consolidation: Parliamentarianism versus Presidentialism," *World Politics* 46, 1 (1993): 1–22.

7. See Robert Klitgaard, "Political Corruption: Strategies for Reform," *Journal of Democracy* 2, 4 (1991): 86–100, for other recommendations.

8. Terry Lynn Karl, "Petroleum and Political Pacts: The Transition to Democracy in Venezuela," *LARR* 22, 1 (1988): 63–94; Richard Hillman, *Democracy for the Privileged: Crisis and Transition in Venezuela* (Boulder, Colo.: Lynne Rienner Publishers, 1994), 51–69; and Jennifer McCoy, William Smith, Andrés Serbin, and Andrés Stambouli (eds.), *Venezuelan Democracy Under Stress* (Boulder, Colo.: Lynne Rienner Publishers, 1995).

9. Kathyrn Sikkink, "Nongovernmental Organizations, Democracy, and Human Rights in Latin America," in Farer, *Beyond Sovereignty*, 150–168. See also the chapters by Acevedo and Grossman, Nelson and Eglinton, Isaacs, and Remmer in the same volume, and Michael Shifter and Sean Neill, "Implementing the Summit of the Americas: Guaranteeing Democracy and Human Rights," North-South Center Working Paper, University of Miami, November 1996.

10. Carina Perelli and Juan Rial, "Changing Military World Views: The Armed Forces of South America in the 1990s," in Millett and Gold-Bliss, *Beyond Praetorianism*, 65–75.

11. See Laura Chinchilla Miranda, "La experiencia costarricense en el ámbito de la desmilitarización," *Paz y Seguridad en las Américas* 12 (July 1997): 7–10.

12. Cynthia McClintock, "The Breakdown of Constitutional Democracy in Peru," paper presented to LASA, Atlanta, 1994, 15; David Scott Palmer, "Conclusion: The View from the Windows," in David Scott Palmer, *Shining Path of Peru* (New York: St. Martin's Press, 1992), 243–247; and Carlos Iván Degregori, "Shining Path and Counterinsurgency Strategy Since of the Arrest of Abimael Guzmán," in Joseph Tulchin and Gary Bland, *Peru in Crisis: Dictatorship or Democracy* (Boulder, Colo.: Lynne Rienner Publishers, 1994), 82–97.

13. Cf. Thomas Scheetz, "Un ensayo sobre misiones, despliegue y costos militares para países medianos: el caso argentino," *Revista de Ciencias Sociales* 5 (December 1996): 85–102.

14. Crnl. (r) Gustavo Cáceres y Thomas Scheetz, *La Defensa No Provocativa: Una propuesta de reforma militar para Argentina* (Buenos Aires: Editora Buenos Aires, 1995), provides one detailed proposal for what such a military might look like.

15. Samuel Huntington, "Civilian Control of the Military: A Theoretical Statement," in Heinz Eulau, Samuel Eldersveld, and Morris Janowitz (eds.), *Political Behavior: A Reader in Theory and Research* (New York: Free Press, 1956), 380–384.

16. In 1990, pension and retirement benefits constituted more than a quarter of Argentina's military budget. Carlos Kulikowski, "Reforma del Sistema Previsional Military," in Cáceres y Scheetz, *Defensa No Provocativa*, 410–411.

17. I am indebted to Ernesto López for this suggestion. See also, Fernando Bustamante, "La seguridad hemiférica en los años 90," *Neuva Sociedad* 138 (July–August 1995): 113–119.

18. Felipe Aguero, "The Latin American Military: Development, Reform, and "Nation-Building," in Lars Schoultz, William Smith, and Augusto Varas (eds.), *Security, Democracy, and Development in U.S.-Latin American Relations* (New Brunswick, N.J.: Transaction Publishers, 1994), 246–247.

19. Felipe Aguero, "Limits to Democratization," in Mainwaring, O'Donnell, and Valenzuela, *Issues in Democratic Consolidation*, 155. See also Gabriel Aguilera Peralta, "El camino desconocido: Las nuevas funciones de los ejércitos centroamericanos," *Nueva Sociedad* 138 (July–August 1995): 125–131.

20. Donald Mabry, "The U.S. Military and the War on Drugs," in Bruce Bagley and William Walker (eds.), *Drug Trafficking in the Americas* (New Brunswick, N.J.: Transaction Publishers, 1994), 53–54.

21. Peter Lupsha, "Toward an Etiology of Drug Trafficking and Insurgent Relations," *International Journal of Comparative and Applied Criminal Justice* 13, 2 (1989): 63–64; Grant Wardlaw, "Linkages Between the Illegal Drugs Traffic and Terrorism," *Conflict Quarterly* 8, 3 (1988): 16–17; and Cynthia McClintock, "The War on Drugs: The Peruvian Case," *Journal of Interamerican Studies and World Affairs* 30, 2–3 (1988): 137.

22. Bruce Bagley, "Colombia and the War on Drugs," *Foreign Affairs* 67 (Fall 1988): 77. U.S. House of Representatives, Committee on Operations, "Stopping the Flood of Cocaine with Operation Snowcap: Is It Working?" (Washington, D.C.: U.S. Government Printing Office, 1990), 9; and Alejandro Reyes, "Drug Trafficking and the Guerrilla Movement in Colombia," in Bagley and Walker, *Drug Trafficking in the Americas*, 123–124.

23. Rafael Perl, "U.S.-Andean Drug Policy," in Bagley and Walker (eds.), *Drug Trafficking in the Americas,* 29; and in the same volume, Eduardo Gamarra, "U.S.-Bolivia Counter-Narcotics Efforts During the Paz Zamora Administration: 1989–1992," 220–247.

24. Bruce Bagley, "The New Hundred Year's War: U.S. National Security and the War on Drugs in Latin America," in Donald Mabry, *The Latin American Narcotics Trade and U.S. National Security* (New York: Greenwood Press, 1988), 43.

25. Louis Goodman and Johanna Mendelson, "The Threat of New Missions: Latin American Militaries and the Drug War," in Goodman, Mendelson, and Rial, *The Military and Democracy,* 194.

26. Wendy Hunter, "State and Soldier in Latin America: Redefining the Military's Role in Argentina, Brazil, and Chile," *Peaceworks* No. 10, United States Institute of Peace, October 1996, 25–26; and Richard Millett, "The Future of Latin America's Armed Forces," in Millett and Gold-Bliss, *Beyond Praetorianism,* 294–295.

27. James Dickey, "A Personal Statement," in Bruce Russett and Alfred Stepan (eds.), *Military Force in American Society* (New York: Harper & Row, 1973), 17–33.

28. Louis Goodman, "Military Roles: Past and Present," in Larry Diamond and Marc Plattner (eds.), *Civil-Military Relations and Democracy* (Baltimore: Johns Hopkins University Press, 1996), 37–38, 40.

29. See Linz and Stepan, *Problems of Democratic Transition,* 122–123.

30. Adam Przeworski, "Some Problems in the Study of the Transition to Democracy," in O'Donnell, Schmitter, and Whitehead, *Transitions: Comparative Perspectives,* 57–58.

31. On the importance of structural factors in democratic consolidation, see Felipe Aguero Piwonka and Mariano Torcal Loriente, "Elites, factores estructurales y democratización (Una discusión de aportes recientes en la literatura)," *Revista de Estudios Políticos* (Nueva Epoca) 80 (April–June, 1993): 329–350; Karen Remmer, "New Wine or Old Bottlenecks: The Study of Latin American Democracy," *Comparative Politics* 23, 4 (1991): 491; and Karl, "Dilemmas of Democratization in Latin America," 6–8.

32. David Pion-Berlin, *The Ideology of State Terror: Economic Doctrine and Political Repression in Argentina and Peru* (Boulder, Colo.: Lynne Rienner Publishers, 1989), 188–197; and Constable and Valenzuela, *A Nation of Enemies,* 200–217.

33. Karen Remmer, "Democratization in Latin America," in Robert Slater, Barry Schutz, and Steven Dorr (eds.), *Global Transformation and the Third World* (Boulder, Colo.: Lynne Reinner Publishers, 1993), 105–106; Carlos Acuña, "Business Interests, Dictatorship, and Democracy in Argentina," in Ernest Bartell and Leigh Payne (eds.), *Business and Democracy in Latin America* (Pittsburgh: University of Pittsburgh Press, 1995), 9–46; and William Roberts Clark, "Democratization and the Loss of National Policy Autonomy: The Domestic Political Implications of Global and Regional Financial Integration," paper presented to LASA, Washington, D.C., 28–30 September 1995, 9–13.

34. Leigh Payne and Ernest Bartell, "Bringing Business Back In: Business-State Relations and Democratic Stability in Latin America," in Bartell and Payne (eds.), *Business and Democracy in Latin America,* 260–271; and Guillermo O'Donnell, "Substantive or Procedural Consensus? Notes on the Latin American Bourgeoisie," in Douglas Chalmers, Maria do Carmo Campello de Souza, and Atilio Boron, *The Right and Democracy in Latin America* (New York: Praeger, 1992), 43–45. Cf. Atilio Boron, "Becoming Demo-

crats? Some Skeptical Considerations on the Right in Latin America," in Chalmers, Campello de Souza, and Boron, *The Right and Democracy in Latin America,* 75–93.

35. Linz and Stepan, *Problems of Democratic Transition,* 222, 224.

36. Ibid., 158.

37. See Carina Perelli and Juan Rial, "Percepción de la situación de las FFAA en los países andinos, 1994," unpublished ms., Montevideo, 1994.

38. N.a., "Declaración de San Carlos de Bariloche," 6 November 1996, Base de Datos SER en el 2000.

39. Michael Schifter, "Tensions and Tradeoffs in Latin America," *Journal of Democracy* 8, 2 (1997): 116.

40. Moisés Naím, "Latin America the Morning After," *World Politics* 74, 4 (1995): 55; and Samuel Morley, *Poverty and Inequality in Latin America: The Impact of Adjustment and Recovery in the 1980s* (Baltimore: Johns Hopkins University Press, 1995), 1. Morley estimates the regional decline in per capita income at 11 percent.

41. Morley, *Poverty and Inequality in Latin America,* 80; Guillermo O'Donnell, "Poverty and Inequality in Latin America: Some Political Reflections," Kellogg Institute Working Paper, no. 225, University of Notre Dame, July 1996, 1; and Albert Berry, "The Income Distribution Threat in Latin America," *LARR* 32, 2 (1997): 5, 30–36.

42. Karen Remmer, "The Sustainability of Political Democracy," 611–633; and "Democracy and Economic Crisis: The Latin American Experience," *World Politics* 42, (1990): 315–335.

43. See Adam Przeworski et al., *Sustainable Democracy* (New York: Cambridge University Press, 1995), 11; Haggard and Kaufman, *The Political Economy of Democratic Transitions,* 310, 325–334; Larry Diamond, "Economic Development and Democracy Reconsidered," in *Reexamining Democracy: Essays in Honor of Seymour Martin Lipset* (Newbury Park, Calif.: Sage Publications, 1992), 93–139; and Linz and Stepan, *Problems of Democratic Transition,* 79–81. See also Linz and Stepan's discussion of the complex relation between regime legitimacy and efficacy, 223–230.

44. "Economy: Best Year for a Quarter-Century," *LAWR* WR-98-09 (6 January 1998): 4.

45. Luigi Manzetti, "Argentina: Market Reforms and Old-Style Politics," *North-South Focus on Argentina* 4, 3 (1995): 4; and Carlos Vilas, "Economic Restructuring, Neoliberal Reforms, and the Working Class in Latin America," in Sandor Halebsky and Richard Harris, *Capital, Power, and Inequality in Latin America* (Boulder, Colo.: Westview Press, 1995), 144–146, 154–155.

46. See Karen Remmer, "Exclusionary Democracy," *Studies in Comparative International Development* 20 (1985–86): 64–85.

47. See Przeworski, *Sustainable Democracy,* 80–90, 109–112; and Haggard and Kaufman, *The Political Economy of Democratic Transitions,* 316–325.

48. Frank McCann, "The Military," in Michael Conniff and Frank McCann (eds.), *Modern Brazil: Elites and Masses in Historical Perspective* (Lincoln: University of Nebraska Press, 1989), 66–74.

49. The prominent American military sociologist Charles Moskos has argued that the U.S. and other Western militaries are becoming more like civilian organizations. With increasing technical specialization and only limited fighting, many parts of the military are staffed with mechanics, computer programmers, personnel managers, and

public relations experts, for whom working for the military is not very different from working for a civilian employer. Charles Moskos, "Institutional and Occupational Trends in the Armed Forces," *The Military: More Than Just a Job?* (New York: Pergamon Press, 1988), 15–25. In my experience, Latin American officers emphatically reject even the possibility of the occupational model, despite evident signs that some of the same trends are also occurring there. See Perelli and Rial, "Changing Military World Views," 71–79.

50. Przeworski, *Sustainable Democracy,* 1.

51. Terry Lynn Karl, "The Hybrid Regimes of Central America," *Journal of Democracy* 6, 3 (1995): 73–76.

254 52. Fitch, "The Decline of U.S. Military Influence in Latin America," 9; and Defense Security Assistance Agency, Department of Defense, *Foreign Military Sales, Foreign Military Construction Sales and Military Assistance Facts* (Washington, D.C.: Directorate for Information Operations and Reports, 1996).

53. "Presentación," in Gretchen Small and Dennis Small (eds.), *El complot para aniquilar a las Fuerzas Armadas y a las naciones of Iberoamérica* (Washington, D.C.: Executive Intelligence Review, 1993), xiv. This work was written and distributed by followers of Lyndon LaRouche. See also Norberto Ceresole, *Argentina y el ocaso de los poderes hegemónicos de la política mundial* (Buenos Aires: ILCTRI, 1992).

54. Mohamed Seineldín, "Síntesis del proyecto mundialista 'nuevo orden,'" in Small and Small, *El complot para aniquilar a las Fuerzas Armadas,* 365–380.

55. Alain Rouquié, "The Military in Latin American Politics Since 1930," in Leslie Bethell (ed.), *The Cambridge History of Latin America,* vol. 6, *Latin America Since 1930: Economy, Society and Politics* (Cambridge: Cambridge University Press, 1994), 241–243. See also Bustamante, "La seguridad hemisférica en los años 90," 118–119.

56. Nationalist officers agree with Samuel Huntington, who categorizes Latin America as its own civilization, distinct from Western Europe. "Clash of Civilizations," *Foreign Affairs* 72, 3 (Summer 1993): 25.

57. Quoted in Deborah Norden, "Democracy and Military Control in Venezuela: From Subordination to Insurrection," *Latin American Research Review* 33 (Spring 1998): 143–165. Norden notes that the military "appear to have developed a high level of identification with civilians," 15–16. See also Deborah Norden, "The Rise of the Lieutenant Colonels: Rebellion in Argentina and Venezuela," *Latin American Perspectives* 23, 3 (1996): 74–86.

58. "Brazil: Bringing Defence Thinking Up to Date," *LAWR* WR-96-45 (21 November 1996): 532; and Max Manwaring, "Brazilian Security in the New World Disorder," in Millett and Gold-Bliss, *Beyond Praetorianism,* 232–233.

59. See Alfred Stepan on the organic-statist tradition of political thought and its application in the 1968–75 military regime in Peru. *The State and Society,* 26–66, 117–316.

60. Jorge Nef, "Demilitarization and Democratic Transition in Latin America," in Halebsky and Harris, *Capital, Power, and Inequality,* 91.

61. Abraham Lowenthal, "Learning from History," in Abraham Lowenthal (ed.), *Exporting Democracy: The United States and Latin America: Themes and Issues* (Baltimore: Johns Hopkins University Press, 1991), 262. See also his suggestions for what the United States can do to support democracy in Latin America, 262–264.

62. For an optimistic view, see Samuel Huntington, "Reforming Civil-Military Relations," *Journal of Democracy* 6, 4 (1995): 9–17.

Index

257

Index

Library of Congress Cataloging-in-Publication Data

Fitch, John Samuel.
  The armed forces and democracy in Latin America / J. Samuel Fitch.
  p. cm.
  Includes bibliographical references and index.
  ISBN 0-8018-5917-4 (alk. paper). — ISBN 0-8018-5918-2 (pbk. : alk. paper)
    1. Civil-military relations — Latin America.   2. Armed Forces — Latin
America — Political activity.   I. Title.
JL956.C58F57   1998
322'.5'098 — dc21   98-16210   CIP